THE PSYCHOLOGY OF ORGANIZATIONAL CHANGE

This volume brings together recent insights about the psychology of organizational change. The authors are leading scholars in the study of organizational change, taking on a micro-perspective for understanding the processes through which responses to change emerge and impact work-related outcomes. Each chapter approaches the topic from a different perspective, highlighting a different aspect of the phenomenon. The book includes review chapters, chapters with new theoretical developments, and descriptions of empirical studies and their findings. It is intended for both academics and practitioners who wish to keep up to date about the mechanisms that explain how recipients of organizational change respond to and cope with change.

SHAUL OREG is Professor of Organizational Behavior at the Hebrew University Business School, Israel. He studies interactions between personal and situational factors and their role in shaping behavior, with a particular interest in people's responses to organizational change. He is a former associate editor of the *Journal of Organizational Behavior* and of *Personnel Psychology*.

ALEXANDRA MICHEL is Scientific Director and Professor at the Federal Institute for Occupational Safety and Health, Germany, and Associate Professor for Work and Organizational Psychology at Heidelberg University, Germany. She is also an experienced Human Resources and Change Manager, as well as a Coach. Her research interests refer to organizational change, resource-oriented interventions at work, occupational health, and coaching.

RUNE TODNEM BY is Professor of Leadership at University of Stavanger, Norway. He is also chairholder of the UNESCO Chair on Leadership, Innovation and Anticipation and editor-in-chief of *Journal of Change Management: Reframing Leadership and Organizational Practice*. In the 2021 article 'Leadership: In Pursuit of Purpose' he introduced the Telos Leadership Lens (TLL), and further developed Drath et al.'s (2008) DAC leadership ontology into the PAC ontology with a focus on facilitating for Purpose, Alignment, and Commitment. In his 2019 TEDx talk 'Let's go EPICally MAD' Rune shares some thoughts around the leadership responsibility of making a difference, www.youtube.com/watch?v=Nno1faLhoWk.

THE PSYCHOLOGY OF ORGANIZATIONAL CHANGE

New Insights on the Antecedents and Consequences of Individuals' Responses to Change

EDITED BY

SHAUL OREG

The Hebrew University of Jerusalem

ALEXANDRA MICHEL

Heidelberg University and Federal Institute for Occupational Safety and Health

RUNE TODNEM BY

University of Stavanger

CAMBRIDGE
UNIVERSITY PRESS

CAMBRIDGE
UNIVERSITY PRESS

Shaftesbury Road, Cambridge CB2 8EA, United Kingdom

One Liberty Plaza, 20th Floor, New York, NY 10006, USA

477 Williamstown Road, Port Melbourne, VIC 3207, Australia

314–321, 3rd Floor, Plot 3, Splendor Forum, Jasola District Centre, New Delhi – 110025, India

103 Penang Road, #05–06/07, Visioncrest Commercial, Singapore 238467

Cambridge University Press is part of Cambridge University Press & Assessment,
a department of the University of Cambridge.

We share the University's mission to contribute to society through the pursuit of
education, learning and research at the highest international levels of excellence.

www.cambridge.org
Information on this title: www.cambridge.org/9781316514313

DOI: 10.1017/9781009086721

© Cambridge University Press & Assessment 2023

First published 2023

A catalogue record for this publication is available from the British Library.

Library of Congress Cataloging-in-Publication Data
NAMES: Oreg, Shaul, 1970- editor. | Michel, Alexandra, 1967- ditor. | By, Rune Todnem editor.
TITLE: The psychology of organizational change : new insights on the antecedents and consequences
on the individual's perspective / editors, Shaul Oreg, Alexandra Michel and Rune Todnem By.
DESCRIPTION: Second Edition. | New York : Cambridge University Press, [2023] | Revised edition of
The psychology of organizational change, 2013.
IDENTIFIERS: LCCN 2022060742 (print) | LCCN 2022060743 (ebook) | ISBN 9781316514313
(hardback) | ISBN 9781009078078 (paperback) | ISBN 9781009086721 (epub)
SUBJECTS: LCSH: Organizational change–Psychological aspects. | Employees–Psychology.
CLASSIFICATION: LCC HD58.8 .P79 2023 (print) | LCC HD58.8 (ebook) |
DDC 302.34–dc23/eng/20221219
LC record available at https://lccn.loc.gov/2022060742
LC ebook record available at https://lccn.loc.gov/2022060743

ISBN 978-1-316-51431-3 Hardback
ISBN 978-1-009-07807-8 Paperback

Contents

v

Contributors

JOHAN SIMONSEN ABILDGAARD, Copenhagen Business School, Denmark and The National Research Centre for the Working Environment, Copenhagen, Denmark

JEAN M. BARTUNEK, Boston College, USA

LEONID V. BELETSKI, The University of Western Ontario, Canada

FRANK BELSCHAK, University of Amsterdam, The Netherlands

DAVE BOUCKENOOGHE, Brock University, Canada

RUNE TODNEM BY, University of Stavanger Business School, Norway

KAREN VAN DAM, Open University, The Netherlands

HANS DE WITTE, Research Group Work, Organisational & Personnel Psychology, KU Leuven, Belgium

ROLF VAN DICK, Goethe University Frankfurt, Germany

STEFFEN R. GIESSNER, Erasmus University, The Netherlands

KATERINA GONZALEZ, Suffolk University, USA

BRADLEY HASTINGS, UNSW Business School, Australia

KATE E. HORTON, Federal University of Pernambuco, Brazil and Erasmus University, The Netherlands

GABRIELE JACOBS, Erasmus University Rotterdam, The Netherlands

PETER J. JORDAN, Griffith University, Australia

ROUVEN KANITZ, Erasmus University, The Netherlands

ESBEN LANGAGER OLSEN, National Research Centre for the Working Environment, Denmark

SHUANG LIANG, ClickPaaS, China

ANNA LUPINA-WEGENER, School of Management and Law, ZHAW, Switzerland

JOHN P. MEYER, The University of Western Ontario, Canada

ALEXANDRA MICHEL, Federal Institute for Occupational Safety and Health and University of Heidelberg, Germany

PEDRO NEVES, Nova School of Business and Economics, Portugal

KARINA NIELSEN, Institute of Work Psychology, University of Sheffield, UK

IRINA NIKOLOVA, Maastricht University School of Business and Economics, The Netherlands

SHAUL OREG, The Hebrew University of Jerusalem, Israel

ALANNAH E. RAFFERTY, Griffith University, Australia

GAVIN M. SCHWARZ, UNSW Business School, Australia

ASHLEA C. TROTH, Griffith University, Australia

JOHANNES ULLRICH, University of Zurich, Switzerland

JORIS VAN RUYSSEVELDT, Open University, The Netherlands

PART I

Introduction

CHAPTER I

Introduction

Alexandra Michel, Shaul Oreg, and Rune Todnem By

1.1 About This Second Edition

In 2013 we published the first edition of *The Psychology of Organizational Change* – a collection of manuscripts describing theoretical developments and empirical research about organization members' reactions to organizational change. In contrast to most books at the time, which relied heavily on a macro, strategic perspective of organizational change, we took on in our book a micro approach, focusing on change recipients' perspectives. By "organizational change" we referred to any adjustment or alteration in an organization that has the potential to influence the stakeholders' physical or psychological experience. Such alterations include, but are not limited to, changes to the organizational structure and culture, the implementation of new organizational practices, changes in employees' conditions and job descriptions, and geographical relocation of the organization or its branches (Oreg et al., 2013).

In the decade that has passed since the first edition, the world has faced radical, overwhelming, changes that have drastically challenged how organizations and their members' functioning. Although the chapters in this second edition were commissioned prior to the COVID-19 pandemic, the latest IPCC reports (Intergovernmental Panel on Climate Change), and the war in Ukraine, and does not focus on specific events such as Brexit or those leading up to the 2021 attack on the United States Capitol, the types of changes covered in the book's chapters and the mechanisms studied for explaining the responses to them, are fundamental and relevant for understanding the basic tenets of changes at large. The specific changes studied herein include technological changes (Chapter 6); innovation, downsizing, restructuring, and personal development (Chapter 5); cross-cultural mergers and acquisitions (Chapters 7 and 8); and leader development (Chapter 10). Drawing on these examples, we acknowledge that organizational change extends beyond specific organizational conditions, and often involves challenges to the status quo in the broader and more complex organizational environment. Dealing with change – whether proactively or reactively – is likely to remain an essential agenda item for both organizations and their members to address.

Accordingly, change in general, and in organizations in particular, remains a key phenomenon of interest among practitioners and scholars alike. Of particular interest is the amount of attention that recipients' views of change have been receiving, in line with growing acknowledgment of recipients' roles in the success of change. Although the number of studies per year focusing on organizational change is plateauing, a much more significant portion of this research is now focused on recipients' perspectives of change. We compare these two trends in Figure 1.1. The white bars represent the number of entries in Google Scholar with the term "organizational change" in the title, per decade. As a rough means of capturing organizational change research that focuses on recipients' perspectives, we included the term "reactions to change" in our search. The black bars in Figure 1.1 thus represent the number of Google Scholar

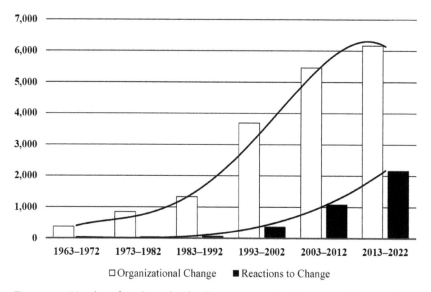

Figure 1.1   Number of articles with titles about organizational change and about reactions to change over the past sixty years
White bars represent the number of publications listed in Google Scholar with a title including the term "organizational change." Black bars represent the number of publications with the terms "organizational change" AND "reactions to change," anywhere in the manuscript (data extracted July 21, 2022).

entries with the terms "organizational change" and "reactions to change" anywhere in the manuscript. As can be seen, researchers have only recently, over the past two to three decades, begun to consider recipients' reactions to change, and this interest has doubled over the past decade (increased from 4,760 until 2012 to 8,860 by 2022). We join in this edition this trend and, like the previous edition, aim to update academics' and practitioners' knowledge about the state of the art of research on individuals' responses to organizational change, and the antecedents and outcomes of these responses.

As in previous years, organizational change continues to be studied from a variety of disciplinary perspectives, including ongoing research from a strategic view, focusing on organizational actions in the process of managing change. The growing body of research focusing on change recipients' perspective considers recipients' cognitive, emotional, and behavioral reactions, the factors that drive them, and their consequences. Despite the significant progress in knowledge about organizational change, and the numerous books on the topic, there are still very few books that address the psychological underpinnings of organizational change, and none that we know of with an explicit focus on organization members' responses. In this volume, we thus bring together thirty leading scholars from thirteen countries who provide integrative reviews, descriptions of theoretical developments, and new empirical findings about recipients' responses to organizational change. Chapter authors, several of whom also contributed to the first edition, are well established within this line of research, and have conducted impactful research on the topic of organizational change in general and on reactions to change in particular. Although practical implications can be drawn from each of the individual chapters, and in some cases are explicitly highlighted, our main aim is to provide scientific, empirically based, insights about how members of the organization experience and respond to organizational change, and about the factors that drive these experiences and responses.

1.2 Structure of the Book

This second edition consists of thirteen chapters classified within six parts: I. Introduction (Chapter 1), II. The Evolution of Change and Its Responses (Chapters 2–4), III. Change in Context: Exploring Types and Contexts of Change (Chapters 5–8), IV. The Development of Change Leadership (Chapters 9 and 10), V. The Process of Change Leadership (Chapters 11 and 12), and VI. Conclusions and Commentary

(Chapter 13). The chapters introduce a variety of approaches to conceptualizing organization members' reactions to change, predicting these reactions, and understanding their potential consequences. Contributions consist of both conceptual and empirical chapters, focusing on both change leaders and followers, using data and insights from a large variety of cultural settings. Several of the chapters provide extensive and integrative reviews of the literature accumulated in a given subfield within the topic of responses to change. We hope to follow up on the first edition's success in providing an updated benchmark for (a) integrating and classifying extant research in this field; (b) theory building and (c) how research on organization members' responses to change could be conducted. The book should be of great relevance to researchers, students, and practitioners with an interest in organizational change, its leadership and management in general, and its psychological underpinnings in particular.

Following this introduction, Part II of the book focuses on the evolution of change and the responses to it. The first two chapters bring to focus the notion of time. In Chapter 2, Pedro Neves proposes the concept of *intentions to resist future change* and develops a framework that incorporates individual- and context-level factors that contribute to such intentions. In line with established frameworks about the predictors of reactions to change (e.g., Armenakis & Bedeian, 1999), the predictors on which Neves focuses include organization members' personal attributes, such as dispositional resistance to change, alongside attributes of members' ties with the organization, attributes of the change leader, and aspects of the change history. These factors together bring about members' intentions to resist future changes, which, in turn, drive members' present behaviors in the organization. Moreover, Neves highlights other factors, such as attributes of the specific change at hand and broader factors in the organization's environment, such as the COVID-19 pandemic, that serve to attenuate or exacerbate the impact of the various individual and contextual factors on the intentions to resist future changes and on present workplace behaviors.

The focus on the temporal aspects of change is even more salient in Chapter 3, in which Gabriele Jacobs and Frank Belschak explicitly discuss the role of time. Addressing recurring calls to better acknowledge and study the dynamic nature of change (e.g., Kunisch et al., 2017; Berson et al., 2021), Jacobs and Belschak propose trajectories of responses to such change and highlight the various factors shaping these trajectories. After reviewing existing knowledge about the role of time in organizational change, and *phase models of organizational change* (e.g., Stouten et al.,

2018), they describe a series of possible trajectories in change recipients' responses to change. They first describe the *classic change curve*, characterized by initial positive (cognitive, emotional, behavioral) responses to change, which transition into negative responses as recipients realize the complexities, costs, and losses involved in the change, and then back to positive once recipients adapt to the new situation and come to appreciate the change's potential benefits and rewards. They then explain how characteristics of change recipients and of the change project, and actions on the part of those managing the change, can impact the change curve in ways that can deepen, attenuate, or even prevent altogether the dip in change response favorability.

The focus in Chapter 4, by Alannah Rafferty, Ashlea Troth, and Peter Jordan, is on recipients' emotional responses to change. The authors discuss the nature of such responses and the processes through which they develop. Time is highlighted in their discussions of how emotional responses diffuse in the organization and how they evolve over time. After describing the nature and structure of the emotional response to change, Rafferty, Troth, and Jordan describe the antecedents and consequences of these reactions. In the integrative framework developed, they address the roles of the change process, context, and content, along with that of cognitive appraisals in forming the emotional response to change, and the outcomes of this response as manifested in recipients' coping with the change and its longer-term consequences at the individual and team levels. They also discuss the moderating roles of change recipients' and leaders' emotional intelligence and of leaders' interpersonal emotion regulation strategies.

In Part III we include a set of chapters addressing specific types and contexts of organizational change. The section begins with Chapter 5, in which Joris van Ruysseveldt, Karen van Dam, Hans De Witte, and Irina Nikolova provide a long called-for investigation of the role that the *change content* has in determining the consequences of change. Specifically, they develop a classification of organizational change types on the basis of two dimensions. The first, which they describe as "qualitative," has to do with the degree to which the change involves innovation. The second, termed "quantitative," focuses on whether the change at hand involves growth or decline, in which case the authors distinguish between whether or not the change also involves restructuring. Using these dimensions and distinctions, they collected data from 1,010 Dutch private sector employees about their experiences of change in their organizations. A cluster analysis of these data pointed to six types of change: Expansion, Shrinkage, Lean restructuring, Thriving, Innovative restructuring, and Innovation expansion. They then tested the effects of the six types on employees' emotional exhaustion, newly acquired KSAOs, workload, and learning opportunities. They found that *innovative restructuring*, which combines decline, restructuring, and innovation, yielded the highest levels of emotional exhaustion and only moderate levels of active learning. This is in contrast to the *thriving* type – combining product innovation and growth – which yielded the lowest levels of emotional exhaustion and high levels of active learning. The authors end the chapter with a discussion of their findings' theoretical implications and suggestions for future research.

Chapters 6–8 focus on specific types of organizational change. In Chapter 6, Katerina Gonzalez and Rouven Kanitz provide a review of research on employees' responses to technological change. They begin by conducting a review of the literature on technological change, which resulted in a list of sixty-seven empirical studies of employees' reactions to technological change. They then use two dimensions of change characteristics for distinguishing among four categories of technological change – *Broad and Radical, Broad and Incremental, Narrow and Radical, Narrow and Incremental* – providing examples of each category. The authors then adapt earlier frameworks about the antecedents and consequences of the reaction to organizational change (e.g., Oreg et al., 2011) to the specific context of technological change. Similar to the antecedents highlighted in Chapters 2 (Neves) and 4 (Rafferty et al.), Gonzalez and Kanitz refer to recipient characteristics and the internal context, adding attributes of the technology introduced as well as time-related attributes, such as the rate at which the technological change is introduced and changes in recipients' perceptions over time. They link these antecedents with change recipients' decisions to accept or resist the technology, and with the longer-term consequences of the change on recipients' personal and work-related outcomes.

The two following chapters of this part focus specifically on the context of organizational mergers and acquisitions (M&As). Chapter 7, by Anna Lupina-Wegener, Rolf van Dick, and Shuang Liang, looks at how organization members' identity changes following M&As. They focus on Chinese acquisitions and argue for their unique nature, given their cultural context. Specifically, they argue that the cultural collectivism and power distance that characterize China may predispose Chinese organization members to be more tolerant than their Western counterparts to the conflicts that typically emerge in M&As. In the framework they develop, the authors discuss how organizational leaders influence change recipients' sense of continuity and congruence between the pre-merger and post-merger condition, and the particularly strong impact they are likely to have in the Chinese context. They then demonstrate their framework through the case of EuroMall's acquisition by ChinaCorp.

In Chapter 8, the same team of scholars, together with Johannes Ullrich (Liang, Lupina-Wegener, Ullrich, and van Dick), describe three studies in which they investigate the processes through which Eastern and Western managers make sense of M&As. They begin in Study 1 with a set of online experiments for testing the effects of different motives for the M&A on participants' responses to ingroup and outgroup criticisms following the M&A. They found that participants were more sensitive to ingroup versus outgroup criticisms, regardless of the motive for the M&A. In Study 2 they used interviews with managers in a European company acquired by a multidivisional Chinese firm, to learn about how managers in the acquired firm construct their multiple identities following the M&A. They found that the initial response to the acquisition was that of ambivalence, which decreased over time, whereas collaboration and knowledge sharing with members of the Chinese firm increased. In Study 3, interviews with the Chinese managers of the acquiring company and analyses of archival data showed that an *agile organizational identity* helped members of the Chinese company cope with the challenges involved in the M&A.

Part IV includes two chapters about the development of change leadership. In Chapter 9, Johan Abildgaard, Karina Nielsen, and Esben Olsen focus on managers acting as change agents of the daily implementation of change processes, while simultaneously managing daily operations. This double role puts them under pressure, suggesting a need for tools and techniques to improve managers' change competencies. The authors address this issue by describing a case study of a four-day change management competency intervention. Intervention participants had to deal with change dilemmas related to different challenges: change phases, change resistance/readiness, and balancing change and stability. Intervention effectiveness was evaluated using interviews with managers participating in the training. Thereby, the authors analyze the key role of sensemaking processes to describe the complexity of change competency development.

In Chapter 10, Bradley Hastings, Dave Bouckenooghe, and Gavin Schwarz discuss *mindset activation* as a process through which change leaders can develop themselves and learn to switch between the different behaviors that are required for dealing with a variety of responsibilities presented when managing change. They begin by describing mindset theory and the notions of fixed and growth mindsets, and link these with top-down and bottom-up change processes, respectively. In their *mindset activation theory*, they explain the roles of situational cues in driving mindsets and the roles of mindsets in driving desired top-down and bottom-up leader behaviors. The differences between top-down and bottom-up processes are highlighted using the dimensions of *goals, temporal frames, activities*, and *leaders' interactions with their followers*. By linking the four dimensions with the desired leader behaviors, the authors demonstrate the value of mindsets for leading change. Whereas fixed mindsets may be useful for promoting top-down behaviors, such as setting performance goals, a growth mindset may be more useful for promoting bottom-up behaviors, such as setting learning goals. Given the role of situational cues in driving mindsets, the authors propose that change leaders can activate the mindset most appropriate for the change activity with which they are currently dealing.

In Part V the focus shifts from the processes that help develop change leaders to those that change leaders engage in to effectively implement change. In Chapter 11, John Meyer and Leonid Beletski explore the concept of change commitment and leaders' role in developing it. They begin by defining the concepts of commitment and commitment to change, and the concepts of leadership and change leadership. They then review the literature on leadership and commitment to change and highlight the types of leader behaviors that have been most frequently and consistently linked with change commitment, the mechanisms that mediate the effects of these leader behaviors, and the conditions that moderate them. In line with the literature on leadership and change in general, the largest portion of studies linking leadership with commitment to change focused on transformational leaders. The authors also found that affective commitment to change is the most frequently studied type of change commitment. As their review demonstrates, using a variety of methodological approaches, studies find positive relationships between direct managers' transformational leadership behaviors and their followers' affective commitment to the organizational change. Among the mechanisms through which transformational leadership is said to achieve its effect is through the development of trust between leader and follower. In their suggestions for future research, Meyer and Beletski elaborate on several promising directions, including research that could determine the unique value of the different types of leader behaviors, more research on commitment dimensions beyond affective commitment, and research about the role of national culture in moderating the effects of leadership on change commitment.

In Chapter 12, Steffen Giessner and Kate Horton focus on change leadership from a social identity perspective. Such an approach sheds light on why organization members resist or support change and on how managers may facilitate positive change behaviors. The authors begin by describing the types of leader behaviors that have been linked with followers' support for change, and the conditions that maximize the effect of these behaviors. They then describe social identity theory and its extensions, and develop a multi-identity pathway model, describing how leaders can support their subordinates during change. They discuss leaders' role in promoting perceptions of identity continuity and enhancing a sense of identity gain during the organizational change. They conclude by discussing the notion of *leadership in the plural*, concerning the combined influence of multiple leaders, and its role in the process of organization members' identity management.

The book ends with a commentary by Jean Bartunek, who integrates and critically discusses the book's chapters. Bartunek classifies the chapters into seven themes that offer a somewhat different classification than that offered in the book's current structure: types of organizational changes, the importance of change leaders, the development of change leaders, the importance of affective processes in change, the importance of sensemaking and cognitive processes in change, the importance of identity processes in change, and the importance of temporal processes in change. She then highlights the contributions of each chapter, draws links between them and other findings in the field, and points to directions for further extending them. Bartunek also compares and contrasts the chapters in this edition to those in the previous one, and summarizes the developments included in this edition. She concludes by proposing possible directions for management to follow given the insights provided in this volume, and several open questions to be addressed in future investigations.

As emphasized in each of the book's chapters, understanding the backdrop and causes of organizational change, as well as the alternatives available to us, is becoming increasingly important. As a field of practice and study, organizational change has arguably been rather static, with an imprinted but perhaps fictional and constructed divide between "us and them" as in the distinctions between "managers and employees" and "change agents and change resistors." Each member of the organization, across levels and hierarchies, can simultaneously initiate one change, support a second, and oppose/resist a third (often with good reason). This highlights the fact that change recipients can also be change initiators and agents, and vice versa. Hence, it is becoming increasingly important to further enable a deeper and more complex understanding of the psychology of organizational change. This second edition of *The Psychology of Organizational Change* compiles a broad range of efforts to provide such deeper and more complex understandings of organization members' experience of, and response to change, as well as of the factors preceding and resulting from these experiences and responses.

REFERENCES

Armenakis, A. A., & Bedeian, A. G. (1999). Organizational change: A review of theory and research in the 1990s. *Journal of Management, 25*(3), 293–315.

Berson, Y., Oreg, S., & Wiesenfeld, B. (2021). A construal level analysis of organizational change processes. *Research in Organizational Behavior, 41,* 100148.

Kunisch, S., Bartunek, J. M., Mueller, J., & Huy, Q. N. (2017). Time in strategic change research. *Academy of Management Annals, 11*(2), 1005–1064.

Oreg, S., Michel, A., & By, R. T. (eds.) (2013). *The psychology of organizational change: Viewing change from the employee's perspective.* Cambridge: Cambridge University Press.

Oreg, S., Vakola, M., & Armenakis, A. (2011). Change recipients' reactions to organizational change: A 60-year review of quantitative studies. *Journal of Applied Behavioral Science, 47*(4), 461–524.

Stouten, J., Rousseau, D. M., & De Cremer, D. (2018). Successful organizational change: Integrating the management practice and scholarly literatures. *Academy of Management Annals, 12,* 752–788.

PART II

The Evolution of Change and Its Responses

CHAPTER 2

Preparing for Change Starts Now
Intentions to Resist Future Changes

Pedro Neves

Multiple frameworks have been offered to describe change processes, from Lewin's seminal unfreeze–change–freeze model (Lewin, 1948) to Kotter's widely used eight-step model (Kotter, 1995, 1996; for a comparison of prescriptive models of planned change, see Stouten et al., 2018). Despite their differences, all these models mention the importance of accounting for employees' reactions to change. As Oreg et al. (2011) framed it, "at the heart of events [...] is how change recipients react to organizational change" (p. 462). There is a myriad of concepts associated with employees' reactions to change (see Oreg et al., 2011 for a review), including affective (e.g., change-related stress; Bordia et al., 2006), cognitive (e.g., cynicism about change; Wanous et al., 2000), and behavioral components (e.g., coping with change; Cunningham et al., 2002). Related constructs and models such as readiness for change (Armenakis et al., 1993), commitment to change (Herscovitch & Meyer, 2002), or openness to change (Wanberg & Banas, 2000) also garnered significant attention in the change management literature. Although conceptually distinct (for a review see Choi, 2011), they all reflect the overall appraisal, positive or negative, of a specific change initiative. Moreover, they share one important characteristic: their ability to predict resistance to a specific change (Choi, 2011). This is why I focus on resistance to change rather than other change attitudes as, ultimately, (a) their *raison d'être* is precisely their predictive role in the resistance to change process and (b) understanding resistance provides a key opportunity to help organizations identify weaknesses in the execution of change strategies (Ford & Ford, 2010).

The empirical evidence highlights the centrality of examining resistance to change (e.g., Oreg, 2006; Jones & Van de Ven, 2016), although there is much less research on the consequences of, than on the antecedents of resistance to change. A few exceptions can be found in the literature. For example, Jones and Van de Ven (2016) found that resistance to change reduced organizational commitment and perceived organizational effectiveness, particularly as time passed during a three-year period of significant organizational changes. Resistance to change has also been associated with turnover intentions (Srivastava & Agrawal, 2020), insomnia, and lowered psychological well-being (Rafferty & Jimmieson, 2017). Thus, either for effectiveness or health and well-being reasons, overcoming – or dealing with – resistance to change appears to be at the core of the change management literature, whether tackled directly or indirectly.

With this chapter, I aim to review the empirical evidence on predictors of resistance to change across four dimensions (change-specific, individual-related, leadership, and organizational factors) and develop a framework of intentions to resist future changes. I argue that this provides useful insights for the discussion of resistance given that (a) individuals form general intentions to resist future, unspecified, change initiatives (e.g., Neves et al., 2018, 2021) and (b) addressing such intentions requires managers to set up the right conditions in times of stability (and not just be concerned with the merits of a specific change effort when it is decided upon). In the final section of the chapter, based on Uncertainty Reduction Theory (Berger & Calabrese, 1975) and on the argument that individuals engage in a sensemaking process to forecast and anticipate potential futures (Weick & Quinn, 1999), I provide a framework that highlights the importance of examining the interactive effects among the various dimensions that antecede responses to change (change-specific, individual-related, leadership, and organization) in order to predict intentions to resist future changes. The framework I propose also integrates these dimensions with the characteristics of the ongoing change efforts and the overarching environment within which the change takes place.

2.1   Where Does Resistance to Change Come From?

The first description of resistance to change seems to have emerged in the early nineteenth century by the Luddite movement, members of which opposed the implementation of new machines in Nottinghamshire (Bruckman, 2008). Resistance to change quickly became at the core of change interventions, with the goal of reducing "the resistance of production workers to the necessary changes in methods and jobs" (p. 512). The issue quickly gathered the attention of researchers and practitioners alike, but eventually fell prey to simplistic judgments of blame that can be summed up in one expression: people (i.e., employees) resist change (Dent & Goldberg, 1999). Resistance has been equated with inertia and defined as mere persistence to avoid change, with the purpose of hindering the process of change (del Val & Fuentes, 2003). It is systemic in nature, as it reflects the dynamics among various forces for and against change anywhere within a system of roles, attitudes, norms, and other factors (Lewin, 1947). The difficulties in capturing the true nature of the phenomenon have already been described in the early writings of Kurt Lewin: "the mere constancy of group conduct does not prove stability in the sense of resistance to change, nor does much change prove little resistance" (pp. 13–14).

A significant amount of research suggests that the processes underlying resistance to change are complex and involve both forces for and against change. I group the predictors of resistance in four dimensions: change-specific factors (i.e., pertaining to the specific change process under examination), individual-related factors (i.e., employees' personal characteristics), leadership factors (i.e., actions by those in leadership positions), and, finally, organizational factors (i.e., perceptions of and attitudes toward the organization as a whole). Although the first dimension may overlap with the other three, I classified articles based on the factor on which the article tended to focus. In the following paragraphs, I present several sample studies that represent the research conducted with respect to each dimension.

The change-specific dimension includes several important contributing factors. For example, the type of change strategy (rational–empirical, i.e., relying on reasoning as a tactic for change, versus normative–re-educative, i.e., assuming individuals should participate in the design, development, and implementation of change, versus power–coercive, i.e., built around the formal power position of the leader) contributes to the type of response enacted by employees (Szabla, 2007). When individuals perceive the benefits of change and are involved in the change process, their attitudes toward change are more positive, which translates into lower resistance to change (Peccei et al., 2011). Similarly, communication about the change is important for reducing change-specific cynicism, which increases intentions to resist the change (Stanley et al., 2005). Overall, the provision of information and participation in the change decision-making process emerge as central facets in the reduction of resistance to change (van Dam et al., 2008).

With respect to the dimension of individual-related factors, the most representative work has been on dispositional resistance to change, which reflects an individual's tendency "to resist or avoid making changes, to devalue change generally, and to find change aversive across diverse contexts and types of change" (Oreg, 2003, p. 680). The disposition has been associated with a significant number of outcomes, including lower career planning, less networking (Turgut & Neuhaus, 2020), and negative reactions to voluntary change (Oreg, 2003), as well as higher resistance to change (Oreg, 2006) and innovation (Oreg & Goldenberg, 2015). There is also research supporting its association with emotional exhaustion, particularly for individuals with low perceived organizational support and a high informational team climate (Turgut et al., 2016), and with the level of uncertainty felt during change and with perceptions of change fairness (Xu et al., 2016).

Other individual differences factors have also been examined in the context of resistance to change, including employee adaptability, which constitutes a set of characteristics that allows individuals to maintain effectiveness under uncertain and novel situations (van Dam & Meulders, 2020). The role of organization-based self-esteem (OBSE), which reflects the degree to which individuals believe their participation in organizational roles satisfies their personal needs (Pierce et al., 1989), has also been examined. OBSE not only reduces resistance to change but it models the positive effects of participation in change, as they seem to be dependent on high levels of OBSE (Garcia-Cabrera & Hernández, 2014). The role of unconscious defense mechanisms, particularly projection, acting out, and isolation, on resistance responses have also been demonstrated (Bovey & Hede, 2001). Mindfulness can also serve as a coping mechanism and can, therefore, help reduce resistance to change, at least during the post-integration period of a merger (Charoensukmongkol, 2016).

With respect to the leadership dimension, although there is extensive research on the leadership of change, there is still much to be explored, especially in terms of the interplay between strategic and behavioral factors (Oreg & Berson, 2019). The most widely studied model in the context of organizational change is that of transformational leadership. The elements of inspiration and enthusiasm created through the articulation of a vision and by inviting participation, while stimulating the intellect of organizational members, explains why transformational leadership is negatively related to resistance to change (Bommer et al., 2005). Meta-analytic evidence further supports this assertion and demonstrates a negative moderate effect of transformational leadership on employee resistance to change (Peng et al., 2021). In the three-year study of health clinics undergoing change, Jones and Van de Ven (2016) also found that supportive leadership became increasingly important for the reduction of employee resistance as time passed.

Similarly, leader–member exchange (LMX) has also been associated with lower levels of resistance to change (van Dam et al., 2008).

Interestingly, several manager tactics (sanctions, legitimization, and ingratiation) were associated with higher levels of resistance to change, but only when LMX was low (Furst & Cable, 2008). When LMX was high, sanctions and legitimization did not affect resistance, whereas ingratiation reduced it. These findings show that employees' interpretation of the tactics used by leaders relies heavily on the nature – or quality – of the relationship developed with that leader. Consultation was the only tactic examined by Furst and Cable that reduced resistance to change regardless of the LMX. Building on moral agency theory, Moutousi and May (2018) proposed that unethical change-related leader behaviors contributed to employee resistance. Such a proposition was confirmed in an empirical study conducted by Rahaman et al. (2021). In other research, trust in management (Oreg, 2006; van Dam et al., 2008) also emerged as an important predictor of resistance. This is not surprising given that trust is one of the pillars of social exchanges and is, therefore, central for understanding interpersonal dynamics, particularly in uncertainty charged moments such as in major organizational changes (Neves & Caetano, 2006).

Regarding the organizational dimension, fewer studies have been conducted, but evidence nevertheless exists for the important role of the organizational context in shaping resistance to change. Organizational fairness is one factor shown to reduce resistance to change, particularly in the early stages of change (Jones & Van de Ven, 2016). When considering organizational justice and dispositional resistance to change in predicting commitment to change, Foster (2010) found that only justice was significantly related to the three dimensions of commitment to change, supporting the claim that the traditional view of individual resistance to change provides a limited account of the phenomenon.

A significant set of studies has taken an integrative approach to exploring how the various dimensions of predictors interact with one another, demonstrating the interplay among change-specific, individual-related, leadership, and organizational factors. Most of these studies attempted to interpret employee dispositions (e.g., dispositional resistance to change) in light of other surrounding factors. For example, Battistelli et al. (2013) examined an administrative division that had undergone organizational restructuring and found that dispositional resistance to change reduced innovative work behaviors, but only when employee decision-making autonomy was low. They also found that dispositional resistance became beneficial for innovative behaviors when feedback from the job was high, demonstrating how dispositional resistance may function in conjunction with other factors. Along similar lines, Oreg (2018) found that dispositional resistance to change can be beneficial for the performance of routine tasks (whereas harmful for creative ones). Drawing from a sense-making perspective, Hon et al. (2014) found that dispositional resistance to change yielded negative effects on employee creative performance, but only when organizational modernity, coworker support, and empowering leadership were low. Fugate and Soenen (2018) found that change management support is more helpful in driving a challenge appraisal of the change, which in turn predicts compliance and championing of change, particularly among individuals with high dispositional resistance to change. Additional studies demonstrated how the negative impact of dispositional resistance to change may be conditional on several moderators, including transformational leadership (Oreg & Berson, 2011), trust in management, trust in the change agent, and organizational identification (Oreg & Sverdlik, 2011).

Less common are studies that examine the interplay between supervisor-related and organizational constructs. One exception is a study by De Ruiter et al. (2017) that focused on the anticipatory stage of change. They found evidence that high supervisory informational justice was associated with a reduction in the strength of the relationship between perceptions of psychological contract breach and resistance to change. One qualitative study provided an interesting interpretation to the effect of charismatic leadership on resistance to change, as it proposed that charismatic leadership can work either to increase or decrease employee resistance, depending on the organization's structure and on other factors, such as perceived threat from the change (Levay, 2010).

It is interesting to note the difference in the number of studies conducted on individual and supervisor-focused predictors of resistance, relative to those on organizational forces, despite the rooting of change research in a systemic approach, which should attempt to include forces at all intervening levels (Dent & Goldberg, 1999). I believe that such an emphasis on individual and leadership factors is a natural outcome of how resistance to change is typically understood: it is a negative employee reaction that leaders need to address. However, such a traditional view of resistance fails to consider the positive intentions that often underlie resistance (Piderit, 2000) and the potential role of organizational factors in shaping resistance, such as inconsistencies between the required demands and the overall purpose of the change (Kotter, 1995).

I also recognize that there is an inherent appeal to becoming *the* transformational leader that "changes people," as can be seen in the number of self-help books designed to help "change someone's mind" and "deal with difficult people." In fact, transformational leadership has been associated with grandiose narcissism, characterized by entitlement, self-confidence risk taking, manipulation, and hostility (O'Reilly & Chatman, 2020). Sometimes managers fall into this trap (i.e., higher entitlement and willingness to engage in deceitful and hostile tactics) and become more focused on their mere (expected or potential) impact on others rather than their success in creating the organizational conditions that promote readiness for change.

A practical reflection of this is the significant number of interventions aimed at tackling resistance to change focused on improved communication, highlighting purpose, demonstrating integrity, and building trust, namely by improving managerial negotiation skills (Bruckman, 2008). This is, of course, not in itself a limitation, as visible in the research previously presented on leadership behaviors and resistance to change. However, it is a one-sided, incomplete approach to a phenomenon that goes way beyond the role of the leader. Research shows that improving leadership practices indeed contributes to lower levels of resistance to change, and, accordingly, executive education programs often include discussions with managers about the importance of applying these practices. However, these discussions also highlight the insufficient attention to the company's culture and to the degree of alignment between the actions required by the change and the overarching organizational context. The importance of considering the history of change in the organization has also been indicated. Carucci (2019) even argues that, given the track record of failure in most organizations, "it's better to start with the assumption that people don't trust your intentions or approach and are expecting you to fail as well" (p. 2). Thus, building on a systemic approach to change (Lewin, 1947), I argue that, to understand resistance to change, one needs to account for change-specific factors, individual characteristics, leadership behaviors, and the organizational context.

2.2 Foe or Friend: Different Views of Resistance to Change

The concept of resistance to change still sparks debate, specifically about what constitutes resistance and whether it should be seen as a negative reaction in and of itself (By, 2020). Part of the answer seems to lie in who is being asked, as individuals working in different functions within the organization may have rather distinct views of what constitutes resistance and on how to deal with it. A study of change agents and recipients found that not only do leaders perceive more resistance than employees, but they favor different strategies for dealing with it; employees expect leaders to engage in *framing* behavior (i.e., being realistic, showing confidence and building trust, not running away from difficulties), whereas leaders emphasize engaging in creating behaviors (i.e., organizing discussions, creating room to think differently, spending time with employees to create innovative solutions; Vos & Rupert, 2018).

Regardless of whom you ask, excessive weight seems to be placed on the shoulders of change recipients. Terms often used by managers such as "push-back," "not buying into," or "foot dragging" reflect such a perspective (Ford & Ford, 2010). This "almost unconscious pull for managers" is the product of a range of factors, including cognitive biases, social dynamics, and managerial missteps (Ford & Ford, 2010, p. 25). Cognitive biases shape how managers interpret their own actions and those of their subordinates, specifically by relying on erroneous judgments, as driven by the fundamental attributional error (e.g., Ross, 1977). This includes overstating their own role in the achievement of objectives and diminishing the hurdles felt by others (and attributing it to their personality). Social dynamics include themes such as a fear of failure and a loss of status or reputation, which severely influence managers' own behavior toward the team as openly assuming difficulties and mistakes is often not an easy task. Such dynamics make them become protective of their position and find alternative explanations to the challenges faced during change. As Ford and Ford (2010, p. 26) argue, "blaming resistance is a socially acceptable explanation among managers because 'everyone knows' that people resist change." Finally, managerial missteps include not keeping promises and not restoring trust after a significant breach occurs, overselling or misrepresenting change, not acting consistently, or even taking shortcuts and signaling that some promises are implicitly meant to be broken. All of these have lingering consequences for recipients' perceptions of agents' trustworthiness (Ford & Ford, 2010).

One important step toward a deeper understanding of resistance was provided by a series of articles that called for the reexamination of resistance as a valuable resource for change initiatives (Ford et al., 2008; Ford & Ford, 2009, 2010). This view relies on the systemics approach put forth by Lewin (1947), according to which resistance is the outcome of a series of forces, for and against change, that might emerge in any part of the system. Dent and Goldberg (1999) built on Lewin's work to argue that, as the concept developed over time, the role of the change context in the enactment of these forces has become lost and the view of employees and managers has become dichotomous, such that employees are seen as creating forces against change, and management as driving forces for change. These authors reach the point of calling for the abandonment of the term "resistance to change" in favor of another that better encompasses the dynamics of change (Dent & Goldberg, 1999).

The basic argument of these authors (Dent & Goldberg, 1999; Ford et al., 2008; Ford & Ford, 2009, 2010) is that resistance is thoughtful, rather than "irrational," and that ignoring it or merely trying to silence it will impair the organization's ability to improve the change (Ford et al., 2008). Change agents can learn from resistance and resistors through a sensemaking process that involves information gathering, interpreting the information, and taking action. This implies scanning both the internal and external environments to identify relevant events or factors that might carry consequences for the future, interpreting the information collected during the scanning process, and taking action relying on the outputs of the scanning and subsequent interpretation of strategic information (Thomas et al., 1993). If each individual or group of individuals is actively involved in its own process of sensemaking, then standard management strategies (e.g., increased information) may not suffice for tackling perceived problems or difficulties, as the integrative approach demonstrates (e.g., Battistelli et al., 2013; Hon et al., 2014; De Ruiter et al., 2017). For example, if change recipients fear losing status, then that fear needs to be dealt with; if the organization's culture is misaligned with the goals of change, then this misalignment needs to be addressed. If change agents perceive resistance merely as a threat, the operational logic becomes protective, defensive, and often competitive (Ford & Ford, 2009), whereby, in order to "win" (i.e., move forward with the change), the other party (i.e., "the resistors") has to lose. This view is based on the assumption that, without resistance, change can progress smoothly. However, the reality is that "if you learn to embrace resistance you can use it as a resource and find your way to a better solution" (Ford & Ford, 2009, p. 100).

Ford and Ford (2009) highlight five strategies to help managers better deal with, and take advantage of, resistance to change. Four of these focus on the preparation for and the ongoing change process: (a) boosting awareness to the implications of change for individuals, not just the benefits for the organization; (b) highlighting the purpose of the change by discussing the "why" underlying the change effort; (c) changing the change, which signals the recognition of potential pitfalls and the willingness to learn from and improve the change process; and (d) building participation and engagement, showing that all members are heard and can speak freely. The fifth strategy does not focus on the current change, but rather on how the change connects to the history of the organization, namely previous change experiences or, as the authors framed it: completing the past. This final strategy suggests that resistance to change is not merely a reaction to the specifics of a particular change process. It is rather the pinnacle of a process that extends over time and begins long before the change is initiated and in which organization members make sense of and integrate the change's past, present, and future. I agree that this fifth factor is fundamental when preparing for the future by anticipating resistance to change. However, I would argue that not only do we need to take the organization's change history into account, but also the full history of the individual's experience within the organization.

2.3 A Change of Perspective: From Resistance to "This" Change to Intentions to Resist Future Changes

Ford and Ford (2009) were not the first to argue that the history of the organization is an important piece of the change management puzzle. Such claims have been made since the 1980s, during which Pettigrew (1985) highlighted the fact that research of organizational change was largely a-contextual, a-historical, and a-processual. Since then, we have seen tremendous advances in the inclusion of context and process in change research; however, such advances did not reach the study of history and time. As Pettigrew et al. (2001, p. 700) later argued, "this emphasis on continuity and change in organizations is underrepresented in the change literature." Twenty years later, I argue that the lack of attention to organizational continuity in the study of change remains a key limitation that constrains our understanding of why individuals resist change efforts.

One example of this lack of attention can be found in the readiness for change literature. The need to assess and address the organization's level of readiness for change, often as an indicator of the amount of resistance to be expected, has captured the attention of academics and practitioners alike (Rafferty et al., 2013; Stouten et al., 2018). However, and aligned with my previous point, the focus on this assessment of readiness for change is aimed at identifying organization members' awareness of the need for change at the beginning of the change implementation process (Stouten et al., 2018). Awareness of the readiness of those who will be impacted by the change may be used as a short-term strategy to increase employee engagement in the change process. This is what Stouten et al. (2018) call "mobilizing energy for change" (identified in most change models), where the focus is on planning the current change implementation. By focusing on the current change process, such a perspective largely ignores the fact that change does not occur in a vacuum (van Dam et al., 2008). Namely, how previous organizational events, the general organizational climate, and the nature of the relationships within the work context, particularly with the leader, influence individuals' sensemaking processes and ultimately influence individuals' expectations about change efforts.

Uncertainty Reduction Theory (URT; Berger & Calabrese, 1975) provides a useful lens, which highlights the importance of integrating the change antecedent dimensions discussed in the previous sections. The main tenet of the theory is that individuals strive to reduce uncertainty and increase predictability about others' behavior because it facilitates continued interactions (Berger & Calabrese, 1975). This framework has been presented as a unifying perspective for understanding how individuals select and maintain a network of potential supporters (i.e., individuals who can help them cope with difficulties), understanding these individuals' roles (i.e., are they peers, friends, managers?), and the nature of such relationships (i.e., do these relationships provide resource assistance, information, support?; Albrecht & Adelman, 1984). Based on these three elements (i.e., who can help me, what is their role, and what is the nature of our relationship), individuals develop forecasts about others' potential intentions and behavior even before these others had the opportunity to act. Such forecasts stem from an attempt to interpret cues from the environment (Maitlis, 2005) and rely heavily on prior interactions with those individuals whose behavior they are trying to predict (Berger & Calabrese, 1975). As Suddaby and Foster (2017, p. 27). framed it, "the cognitive frames that we use to experience the reality of the present are based on retrospective and collective interpretations of past events." Such anticipation is important, as it allows the individual to maintain a sense of continuity (Giessner, 2011), a key aspect of sensemaking.

Indeed, sensemaking is critical for organizational activity (Weick, 1995), as it explains how individuals scan and interpret environmental cues which ultimately influence their decisions and actions. It is a social process construed across multiple interactions with others (Maitlis, 2005). It becomes especially important in fast-changing environments that require more flexibility or when the situation is particularly surprising or confusing because it helps reduce discontinuity and preserve direction (Weick & Quinn, 1999). Additionally, it is most effective in the interaction with others who share the stressful context (e.g., other organizational members). They will likely share their view and understanding of the situation, thus providing resource assistance and information (Albrecht & Adelman,

1984). From a URT and sensemaking lens, it becomes clear that the act of resistance, or intention to resist, involves a rather thoughtful process, which can contribute to improving the change by helping to complete the past (i.e., discussing past events, with both positive and negative take-aways, and explaining how the lessons learned will be integrated in future actions). Individuals use resistance to call attention to past issues and current inefficiencies that need to be addressed in order to build momentum for change (Ford & Ford, 2010).

Building on these arguments, I claim that an important extension of the research on resistance to change involves the examination of individuals' intentions to resist future changes, that have yet to be defined. In the current pace of change (as reflected, for example, in the response to the recent COVID-19 pandemic), organizations spend a significant amount of time adapting processes as the circumstances quickly change. In such a context, it seems fundamental to move away from a viewpoint that examines change as a one-off phenomenon and rather to interpret it as grounded in the broader organizational life. For example, how can we detach an individual's heightened resistance to a given change process from the preceding pattern of abusive supervision or the consistent lack of empowerment experienced in his/her relationship with the supervisor (or from the poor attention given to the HR practices)? I propose to integrate past, present, and future in our view of change as embedded in organizational life, and move from the question "how will the individual cope with *this* change?" to "how does the individual intend to behave in the case that further change will be required?"

The empirical evidence supporting the need for such a transition is still scarce, but it nevertheless provides relevant insights. If we consider the four sets of factors identified earlier in the resistance to change literature – change-specific, individual-related, leadership, and organizational – evidence suggests not only the need to take all levels of analysis into account but, most importantly, the need to understand how these sets of factors interact with one another in reducing uncertainty about potential futures, not just about the current situation. Of the four dimensions, only the first involves change-specific factors, whereas the other categories focus on factors that extend beyond a given change. Because I am interested in how individuals anticipate future potential changes, I broadened the change-specific dimension to include the impact of prior changes on the development of individual intentions to resist future changes (Ford & Ford, 2009). I, therefore, henceforth refer to this category as *history of change*. Evidence suggests that assessments concerning prior changes and general knowledge about the theme underlying the change effort influence individuals' approaches toward current attempts to change as well as potential future changes (e.g., Bordia et al., 2011; Neves et al., 2018; Zeng et al., 2019). This stream of research adopts a phenomenological view of the change history. It assumes that human interpretation of history should be privileged, as we all continuously engage in a retrospective interpretation of past events. More importantly, it argues for the powerful influence of past events in determining future behaviors, as the passage of time promotes a "sedimentary accumulation of past events and experiences" (Suddaby & Foster, 2017, p. 21). For example, Neves et al. (2018) found that affective commitment to the most recent change enacted by the organization emerged as a key sensemaking mechanism for future changes because it reflects a belief in the inherent benefits of change (Herscovitch & Meyer, 2002) and ultimately signals the organization's ability to change "in the right direction." This affective commitment predicted intentions to resist future changes, due to launch four weeks later.

Although focused on resistance to a specific change (rather than on intentions to resist future changes), Rafferty and Jimmieson (2017) found that subjective perceptions regarding the frequency with which change occurred in their workplace were positively associated with cognitive, affective, and behavioral resistance to change. Such findings are in line with those of two additional studies. One study showed that poor change management history beliefs predicted voluntary turnover two years later (Bordia et al., 2011). The second study, conducted by Rafferty and Restubog (2017), showed that a poor change history influenced how individuals evaluate a specific change effort. Namely, it reduced challenge appraisal and increased threat and harm appraisals, with consequences for voluntary turnover two and a half years later. Feeling stuck in constant change is burdensome to employees and affects how they approach additional change efforts.

In a study focused on how medical specialists interpret the use of electronic medical records, Samhan (2020) found that assessments concerning the value and threat of using such records were associated with intentions to resist the personal use of electronic medical records in the future. Along similar lines, Zeng et al. (2019) examined residents' future behavioral intentions to resist the installation of nuclear power plants in the vicinity of their community and found, against their expectations, that information acquisition, and, in particular, knowledge about nuclear power technology was associated with higher intentions to resist the building of nuclear plants in the neighborhood. This shows that the effect of prior information is not necessarily positive and may backfire and contribute to assessments of increased risks.

With respect to individual-related factors, research found that organization-based self-esteem (OBSE; Pierce et al., 1989) contributes to the development of intentions to resist future changes. It reflects "the degree to which organizational members believe that they can satisfy their needs by participating in roles within the context of an organization" (Pierce et al., 1989, p. 625). Although it was not directly related to intentions to resist future changes, it did affect how empowerment was interpreted and translated into the context of potential future changes (Neves et al., 2021).

Regarding the leadership dimension, there is also evidence suggesting that leader behaviors, namely ethical (Neves et al., 2018) and empowering (Neves et al., 2021) leadership, are important drivers of intentions to resist future changes, at least indirectly. Ethical leadership refers to "the demonstration of normatively appropriate conduct through personal actions and interpersonal relationships, and the promotion of such conduct to followers through two-way communication, reinforcement, and decision-making" (Brown et al., 2005, p. 120). Similarly, empowering leadership emphasizes participative decision-making and the provision of autonomy and delegation (Ahearne et al., 2005). Both ethical and empowering leaders contribute to the uncertainty reduction process of their subordinates by highlighting a long-term investment on their team members and signaling their core underlying beliefs: ethical leaders show that actions are taken in accordance with the moral philosophy of the organization. Empowering leaders indicate the importance of developing employees and the belief that they can succeed if given enough leeway in determining how to approach work challenges.

With respect to the organizational dimension, the evidence points to the central role played by human resource (HR) practices, particularly commitment-based HR. These are practices designed to motivate employees to contribute with high levels of discretionary behaviors through the alignment of individual and organizational interests and goals (Collins & Smith, 2006). These practices help build long-term relationships between the employing organization and the individual by emphasizing the organization's orientation toward selection (e.g., privileging internal promotions and organization fit), incentives (e.g., highlighting the importance of the business unit performance on top of individual performance), and training and development (e.g., providing relevant training opportunities) policies (Collins & Smith, 2006). Neves et al.

(2018) found support for an indirect negative relationship between commitment-based HR practices (via affective commitment to the most recently enacted change) and intentions to resist future changes. These findings also draw attention to the need to examine how these sets of factors (i.e., history of change, individual-related, leadership, and organizational) interact with each other, as their effects are likely to be largely dependent on one another. The beneficial effect of commitment-based HR practices on the reaction to the most recent change (operationalized as affective commitment to change) and, indirectly, on behavioral intentions to resist future changes, was only significant when accompanied by high ethical leadership (Neves et al., 2018). As Neves et al. argue, this suggests that leaders' ethical actions and role-modeling are among the factors that determine how the sensemaking process about the organization's intentions, as reflected in its HR practices, unfolds. Similarly, the effects of empowering leadership on affective and cognitive intentions to resist future changes were contingent on employees' level of OBSE: the negative effect of empowering leadership on affective and cognitive resistance intentions, via structural empowerment, was significant only when OBSE was high (Neves et al., 2021). Curiously, Neves et al. also found that psychological empowerment increases cognitive intentions to resist future changes, but only when OBSE is high. Such an unexpected finding suggests that empowerment might also carry potential burdens (Cheong et al., 2016) whereby, as a side-effect, psychological empowerment might lead high OBSE individuals to protect the status quo in the face on uncertainty.

2.4   A Prospective Model of Intentions to Resist Future Changes

In this section, I build on Uncertainty Reduction Theory (Berger & Calabrese, 1975) to put forth a framework of intentions to resist future changes, encompassing antecedents that contribute to individuals' sensemaking processes. To do so, I rely on the four sets of factors previously identified: history of change, individual characteristics, leadership behaviors, and the organizational context. I also propose two conditions that (a) influence how these factors drive intentions to resist future changes (i.e., potential moderating factors) and (b) model employee behavior, be that directed at a specific change process or at the organization (and its agents) as a whole. It is important to note that this is not an exhaustive list of predictors, but rather an illustration of potential constructs to consider in future research and to spark discussion on the topic. Figure 2.1 depicts the proposed framework.

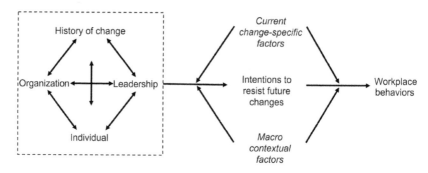

Figure 2.1   Intentions to resist future changes framework

2.4.1   History of Change

The first component of the model focuses on the interpretation of past organizational change events. The recent history of change, including successes, failures, and lessons learned, should be taken into account when trying to determine intentions to resist future change efforts. History as sensemaking provides a view of history that relies on the weight of human interpretation of events to propose that past interpretations strongly influence future behavior as meaning is translated into action (Suddaby & Foster, 2017). The process involves retrospective enactment, selection, and identity to provide a sense of order, clarity, and rationality (Weick, 1995). Individuals create a coherent reconstitution of history to interpret potential futures. Namely, whether such futures are construed as a continuation or discontinuation of past practices. A poor track record of change management (Rafferty & Restubog, 2017) should heighten uncertainty about the organization's ability to tackle future challenges.

The frequency of change should also be taken into consideration. We know that a climate of recurrent changes is a source of stress and contributes to affective, cognitive, and behavioral resistance (Rafferty & Jimmieson, 2017). The dynamism inherent to the current macroeconomic context calls for (almost) continuous adjustments. The need for change increases dramatically and has its costs. How individuals make sense of such frequency, specifically whether they become accustomed to or exhausted by the rhythm of change (Rafferty & Restubog, 2017), has yet to be examined. Its role in setting up a climate of uncertainty should also be further examined, in particular how it interacts with the other dimensions described in the following sections.

2.4.2   *Individual Characteristics*

The second category is dedicated to individual differences. I start by focusing on dispositional resistance to change, given its centrality in change research. As previously mentioned, dispositional resistance to change involves a general aversion to change, often reflected in avoidance or resistance behaviors (Oreg, 2003). There is evidence that it should not always be viewed in a negative light (Oreg, 2018) and that its effect depends on other conditions (e.g., Oreg & Sverdlik, 2011; Battistelli et al., 2013). Dispositional resistance to change contributes to the sense-making of change as it provides a lens through which individuals interpret surrounding events, namely situational cues (Oreg & Berson, 2011). For example, the greater the dispositional resistance, the more likely the individual will perceive potential harm and the less likely they will perceive potential benefit (Oreg & Goldenberg, 2015).

Vakola et al. (2013) reviewed the literature on individual differences as predictors of recipients' responses to change and found that characteristics such as need for control, self-efficacy, and openness to experience were among the most studied dispositional antecedents of change reactions. Because parallels can be drawn between the challenges faced by entrepreneurs and those elicited by change efforts (as can be seen in the centrality of self-efficacy in both contexts), I would also like to highlight the findings of Rauch and Frese's (2007) meta-analysis about personality and entrepreneurial behavior, to identify other traits that contribute to the intentions to resist future changes. Constructs such as proactive personality, stress tolerance, and need for autonomy should be examined as they contribute to decision-making under conditions of uncertainty and resource constraint (Rauch & Frese, 2007).

2.4.3   *Leadership*

The third dimension focuses on leadership-related factors. I expand existing frameworks on the roles of ethical and empowering leadership on intentions to resist future changes (Neves et al., 2018, 2021) and incorporate two recent conceptualizations of leadership into the realm of organizational change. The first, instrumental leadership, is an extension of the transformational leadership concept and focuses on "the application of leader expert knowledge on monitoring of the environment and of performance, and the implementation of strategic and tactical solutions" (Antonakis & House, 2014, p. 749). This form of leadership highlights strategic leadership and follower work facilitation as necessary conditions for organizational adaptation and change, particularly in the presence of economic turbulence and technological advances (Antonakis & House, 2014). Identifying key strategies and goals while providing day-to-day direction and resources without putting employees' welfare at risk should contribute to a positive assessment of the intentions and ability of the organization to further monitor the environment and adjust accordingly.

The second conceptualization zooms in on the collective self and identity components of leadership. Such a social identity approach sees leadership as "a recursive, multi-dimensional process that centers on leaders' capacities to represent, advance, create, and embed a shared sense of social identity for group members" (Steffens et al., 2014, p. 1002). The identity leadership approach attempts to answer questions such as "who are we?" and "what do we stand for?" and focuses on how the self is defined in terms of shared group membership. It involves elements of identity prototypicality (being one of us), advancement (doing it for us), entrepreneurship (crafting a sense of us), and impresarioship (making us matter) (Steffens et al., 2014). These facets influence the leaders' ability to engage with their team and constitute dimensions of a critical construct for the understanding of dynamic processes that unfold over time. Identity connects past, present, and future (Ibarra & Barbulescu, 2010). Through sensemaking, a central feature of uncertainty reduction, individuals develop their identity and the understanding of how this identity relates to the work context (Lord et al., 2016).

2.4.4 *Organization*

In terms of the employee–organization relationship, I would like to highlight the roles of psychological contracts and psychological safety. Psychological contracts refer to "an individual's beliefs regarding the terms of conditions of a reciprocal exchange agreement between that focal person and another party" (Rousseau 1989, p. 123). It focuses on explicit, that is, verbal and written agreements, and implicit, that is, interpretations of patterns of behavior, promise making (Coyle-Shapiro et al., 2018), which create expectations about the future behavior of those who communicated the (perceived) promise, thus helping individuals in the prediction of the intentions and actions of organizational agents. Psychological contract violation has been linked with a poor change history (i.e., whether past changes were poorly managed; Rafferty & Restubog, 2017) and cognitive resistance to change in the anticipatory stages of change (De Ruiter et al.,

2017) and, therefore, should be an important determinant of how individuals anticipate future change events.

Similarly, psychological safety, the extent to which individuals perceive the (work) environment as safe for interpersonal risk-taking (e.g., admitting an error or asking for help; Edmondson, 1999) should also contribute to intentions to resist future change. Psychological safety, by signaling that the organization is a safe place to take risks and that individuals will not be punished for trying new solutions, facilitates the willingness to contribute with ideas and actions to the organization, including making suggestions, sharing information, and taking initiative, while enabling team and organizational learning (Edmondson & Lei, 2014). Recent research shows that interventions aimed at creating a psychosocially safe climate help individuals cope with the COVID-19 pandemic (Dollard & Bailey, 2021), suggesting that psychological safety is a relevant condition to consider in the context of change.

2.4.5 Boundary Conditions of the Development and Impact of Intentions to Resist Future Changes

Our understanding of intentions to resist future changes (i.e., how the interpretation of past events and behaviors shapes how individuals make sense of potential futures) would not be complete without taking the present into account. I argue that at least two contextual factors within the organization's present need to be considered for predicting intentions to resist future changes and their impact on workplace behaviors: one related to the enactment of change efforts (because the specificities of a given change process influence how individuals appraise and react to it); and one related to the macro socio-economic context (because organizational life and external events, such as crisis, international conflicts, and market fluctuations, are inseparable).

The change-specific factors surrounding the actual implementation of change processes could potentially moderate (while also presenting a direct effect on) how individuals develop their intentions to resist future changes and the degree to which these intentions translate into actual behavior. Prior research on the type of change strategy (Szabla, 2007), the perceived benefits of change (Peccei et al., 2011), and change communication (Stanley et al., 2005) provide strong support for such an assertion. For example, one might work for an organization with a positive history of change and a strong record of providing resources to employees but nevertheless have significant doubts about a specific change initiative, which might result in increased intentions to resist future changes, compared with individuals with fewer concerns about the change. Similarly, an organization's track record may not be positive or the team leader may behave in a manner that reduces trust, but individuals may overcome such barriers (in terms of intentions to resist change and the consequences of these intentions) if they perceive an ongoing change as important for the success or sustainability of the organization. This should reduce intentions to resist future changes, compared with individuals who do not perceive the change as meaningful.

Macro-contextual factors also likely play an important role in determining the strength of the reactions to the four antecedent dimensions. Shocks such as the COVID-19 pandemic have important consequences for the sensemaking processes of individuals, as they upend routines, disrupt relationships, and force individuals to reassess risks continuously (Christianson & Barton, 2021). In such contexts, the track record of the organization, its practices, or its leaders' behavior may become of lesser importance given the need to quickly adjust to the surrounding conditions. Additionally, individual attitudes toward change are grounded in broader societal values and understandings (Danisman, 2010), and there is evidence of differences between cultural clusters in their change orientation dimensions (Oreg & Sverdlik, 2018). This suggests the cultural values and norms in which the individual and the organization are embedded need to be taken into account if we want to develop a comprehensive view of intentions to resist future change. For example, working with an empowering leader in a culture characterized by high levels of routine seeking (i.e., the degree to which a society prefers stable and routine environments; Oreg & Sverdlik, 2018) may not yield the negative effect on intentions to resist future changes we would expect when empowerment is enacted in a low routine-seeking environment.

2.5 Conclusion

In this chapter, I provided a review of the research on the antecedents of resistance to change as a starting point toward identifying a systemic, future-oriented, approach to the phenomenon of intentions to resist future changes. Building on Uncertainty Reduction Theory (Berger & Calabrese, 1975), I adopted a systemic approach (as initially proposed by Lewin, 1947, 1948), and examined the existing research on resistance to change, under the premise that it is the result of a thoughtful individual process where individuals engage in sensemaking, rather than arising spontaneously as a reaction to change (i.e., Ford et al., 2008). Based on these arguments, coupled with recent research on the topic (Neves et al., 2018, 2021), I claim that individuals foresee whether they will be willing to support or intend to resist future change efforts. If organizations want to learn from resistance and improve their ability to enact change, anticipating intentions to resist future changes is an important step forward. I hope my framework stimulates research on the development and consequences of intentions to resist future changes and contributes to a shift in how we, academics and practitioners, view resistance.

REFERENCES

Ahearne, M., Mathieu, J., & Rapp, A. (2005). To empower or not to empower your sales force? An empirical examination of the influence of leadership empowerment behavior on customer satisfaction and performance. *Journal of Applied Psychology, 90*(5), 945–955.

Albrecht, T. L., & Adelman, M. B. (1984). Social support and life stress: New directions for communication research. *Human Communication Research, 11*, 3–32.

Antonakis, J., & House R. J. (2014). Instrumental leadership: Measurement and extension of transformational–transactional leadership theory. *The Leadership Quarterly, 25*, 746–771.

Armenakis, A. A., Harris, S. G., & Mossholder, K. W. (1993). Creating readiness for organizational change. *Human Relations, 46*, 681–703.

Battistelli, A., Montani, F., & Odoardi, C. (2013). The impact of feedback from job and task autonomy in the relationship between dispositional resistance to change and innovative work behaviour. *European Journal of Work and Organizational Psychology, 22*(1), 26–41.

Berger, C. R., & Calabrese, R. J. (1975). Some explorations in initial interaction and beyond: Toward a developmental theory of interpersonal communication. *Human Communication Research, 1*, 99–112.

Bommer, W. H., Rich, G. A., & Rubin, R. S. (2005). Changing attitudes about change: Longitudinal effects of transformational leader behavior on employee cynicism about organizational change. *Journal of Organizational Behavior, 26*, 733–753.

Bordia, P., Jones, E., Gallois, C., Callan, V. J., & DiFonzo, N. (2006). Management are aliens! Rumors and stress during organizational change. *Group & Organization Management, 31*(5), 601–621.

Bordia, P., Restubog, S. L. D., Jimmieson, N. L., & Irmer, B. E. (2011). Haunted by the past: Effects of poor change management history on employee attitudes and turnover. *Group & Organizational Management, 36*, 191–222.

Bovey, W. H., & Hede, A. (2001). Resistance to organizational change: The role of defense mechanisms. *Journal of Managerial Psychology, 16*(7), 534–548.

Brown, M. E., Treviño, L. K., & Harrison, D. A. (2005). Ethical leadership: A social learning perspective for construct development and testing. *Organizational Behavior and Human Decision Processes, 97*, 117–134.

Bruckman, J. C. (2008). Overcoming resistance to change: Causal factors, interventions, and critical values. *The Psychologist-Manager Journal, 11*, 211–219.

By, R. (2020). Organizational change and leadership: Out of the quagmire. *Journal of Change Management, 20*(1), 1–6.

Carucci, R. (2019). Leading change in a company that's historically bad at it. *Harvard Business Review*, August 6.

Charoensukmongkol, P. (2016). Contributions of mindfulness during post-merger integration, *Journal of Managerial Psychology, 32*(1), 104–118.

Cheong, M., Spain, S. M., Yammarino, F. J., & Yun, S. (2016). Two faces of empowering leadership: Enabling and burdening. *The Leadership Quarterly, 27*, 602–616.

Christianson, M. K., & Barton, M. A. (2021). Sensemaking in the time of COVID-19. *Journal of Management Studies, 58*, 572–576.

Choi, M. (2011). Employees' attitudes toward organizational change: A literature review. *Human Resource Management, 50*, 479–500.

Collins, C. J., & Smith, K. G. (2006). Knowledge exchange and combination: The role of human resource practices in the performance of high-technology firms. *Academy of Management Journal, 49*, 544–560.

Coyle-Shapiro, J., Costa, S. P., Doden, W., & Chang, C. (2018). Psychological contracts: Past, present, and future. *Annual Review of Organizational Psychology and Organizational Behavior, 6*, 145–169.

Cunningham, C. E., Woodward, C. A., Shannon, H. S., MacIntosh, J., Lendrum, B., Rosenbloom, D., & Brown, J. (2002). Readiness for organizational change: A longitudinal study of workplace, psychological and behavioral correlates. *Journal of Occupational and Organizational Psychology, 75*, 377–392.

van Dam, K., & Meulders, M. (2020). The adaptability scale: Development, internal consistency, and initial validity evidence. *European Journal of Psychological Assessment, 37*(2), 123–134.

van Dam, K., Oreg, S., & Schyns, B. (2008). Daily work contexts and resistance to organizational change: The role of leader-member exchange, perceived development climate, and change process quality. *Applied Psychology: An International Review, 57*(2), 313–334.

Danisman, A. (2010). Good intentions and failed implementations: Understanding culture-based resistance to organizational change. *European Journal of Work and Organizational Psychology, 19*(2), 200–220.

De Ruiter, M., Schalk, R., Schaveling, J., & van Gelder, D. (2017). Psychological contract breach in the anticipatory stage of change: Employee responses and the moderating role of supervisory informational justice. *The Journal of Applied Behavioral Science, 53*(1), 66–88.

Dent, E. B., & Goldberg, S. G. (1999). Challenging "resistance to change". *The Journal of Applied Behavioral Science, 35*(1), 25–41.

Dollard, M. F., & Bailey, T. (2021). Building psychosocial safety climate in turbulent times: The case of COVID-19. *Journal of Applied Psychology, 106*(7), 951–964.

Edmondson, A. C. (1999). Psychological safety and learning behavior in work teams. *Administrative Science Quarterly, 44*(2), 350–383.

Edmondson, A. C., & Lei, Z. (2014). Psychological safety: The history, renaissance, and future of an interpersonal construct. *Annual Review of Organizational Psychology and Organizational Behavior, 1*, 23–43.

Ford, J. D., & Ford, L. W. (2009). Decoding resistance to change. *Harvard Business Review*, April, 99–103.

(2010). Stop blaming resistance to change and start using it. *Organizational Dynamics, 39*, 24–36.

Ford, J. D., Ford, L. W., & D'Amelio, A. (2008). Resistance to change: The rest of the story. *Academy of Management Journal, 33*, 362–377.

Foster, R. D. (2010). Resistance, justice, and commitment to change. *Human Resource Development Quarterly, 21*(1), 3–39.

Fugate, M., & Soenen, G. (2018). Predictors and processes related to employees' change-related compliance and championing. *Personnel Psychology, 71*, 109–132.

Furst, S. A., & Cable, D. M. (2008). Employee resistance to organizational change: Managerial influence tactics and leader–member exchange. *Journal of Applied Psychology, 93*(2), 453–462.

Garcia-Cabrera, A. M., & Hernández, F. G. (2014). Differentiating the three components of resistance to change: The moderating effect of organization-based self-esteem on the employee involvement-resistance relation. *Human Resource Development Quarterly, 25*(4), 441–469.

Giessner, S. R. (2011). Is the merger necessary? The interactive effect of perceived necessity and sense of continuity on post-merger identification. *Human Relations, 64*, 1079–1098.

Herscovitch, L., & Meyer, J. P. (2002). Commitment to organizational change: Extension of a three-component model. *Journal of Applied Psychology, 87*(3), 474–487.

Hon, A., Bloom, M., & Crant, J. M. (2014). Overcoming resistance to change and enhancing creative performance. *Journal of Management, 40*(3), 919–941.

Ibarra, H., & Barbulescu, R. (2010). Identity as narrative: Prevalence, effectiveness, and consequences of narrative identity work in macro work role transitions. *Academy of Management Review, 35*(1), 135–154.

Jones, S., & Van de Ven, A. (2016). The changing nature of change resistance: An examination of the moderating impact of time. *The Journal of Applied Behavioral Science, 52*(4), 482–506.

Kotter, J. P. (1995, 2007). Leading change: Why transformation efforts fail. *Harvard Business Review*, March–April, 59–67.

(1996). *Leading change*. Cambridge, MA: Harvard Business Press.

Levay, C. (2010). Charismatic leadership in resistance to change. *The Leadership Quarterly, 21*, 127–143.

Lewin, K. (1947). Frontiers in group dynamics: Concept, method and reality in social science; social equilibria and social change. *Human Relations, 1,* 5–41.
(1948). *Resolving social conflicts: Selected papers on group dynamics.* New York: Harper.

Lord, R. G., Gatti, P., & Chui, S. L. M. (2016). Social-cognitive, relational, and identity-based approaches to leadership. *Organizational Behavior and Human Decision Processes, 136,* 119–134.

Maitlis, S. (2005). The social processes of organizational sensemaking. *Academy of Management Journal, 48,* 21–49.

Moutousi, O., & May, D. (2018). How change-related unethical leadership triggers follower resistance to change: A theoretical account and conceptual model. *Journal of Change Management, 18*(2), 142–161.

Neves, P., Almeida, P., & Velez, M. J. (2018). Reducing intentions to resist future change: Combined effects of commitment-based HR practices and ethical leadership. *Human Resource Management, 57,* 249–261.

Neves, P., & Caetano, A. (2006). Social Exchange processes in organizational change: The roles of trust and control. *Journal of Change Management, 6*(4), 351–364.

Neves, P., Pires, D., & Costa, S. (2021). Empowering to reduce intentions to resist future change: Organization-based self-esteem as a boundary condition. *British Journal of Management, 32,* 872–891.

O'Reilly, C. A., & Chatman, J. A. (2020). Transformational leader or narcissist? How grandiose narcissists can create and destroy organizations and institutions. *California Management Review, 62*(3), 5–27.

Oreg, S. (2003). Resistance to change: Developing and individual differences measure. *Journal of Applied Psychology, 88*(4), 680–693.
(2006). Personality, context, and resistance to organizational change. *European Journal of Work and Organizational Psychology, 15,* 73–101.
(2018). Resistance to change and performance: Toward a more even-handed view of dispositional resistance. *Journal of Applied Behavioral Science, 54*(1), 88–107.

Oreg, S., & Berson, Y. (2011). Leadership and employees' reactions to change: The role of leaders' personal attributes and transformational leadership style. *Personnel Psychology, 64,* 627–659.
(2019). Leaders' impact on organizational change: Bridging theoretical and methodological chasms. *Academy of Management Annals, 13,* 272–307.

Oreg, S., & Goldenberg, J. (2015). *Resistance to innovation.* Chicago: University of Chicago Press.

Oreg, S., & Sverdlik, N. (2011). Ambivalence toward imposed change: The conflict between dispositional resistance to change and the orientation toward the change agent. *Journal of Applied Psychology, 96*(2), 337–349.
(2018). Translating dispositional resistance to change to the culture level: Developing a cultural framework of change orientations. *European Journal of Personality, 32,* 327–352.

Oreg, S., Vakola, M., & Armenakis, A. (2011). Change recipients' reactions to organizational change: A 60-year review of quantitative studies. *The Journal of Applied Behavioral Science, 47*, 461–524.

Peccei, R., Giangreco, A., & Sebastiano, A. (2011). The role of organizational commitment in the analysis of resistance to change: Co-predictor and moderator effects. *Personnel Review, 40*(2), 185–204.

Peng, J., Li, M., Wang, Z., & Lin, Y. (2021). Transformational leadership and employees' reactions to organizational change: Evidence from a meta-analysis. *The Journal of Applied Behavioral Science, 57*(3), 369–397.

Pettigrew, A. M. (1985). *The awakening giant: Continuity and change in ICL.* Oxford: Blackwell.

Pettigrew, A., Woodman, R. W., & Cameron, K. S. (2001). Studying organizational change and development: Challenges for future research. *Academy of Management Journal, 44*, 697–713.

Piderit, S. K. (2000). Rethinking resistance and recognizing ambivalence: A multidimensional view of attitudes toward an organizational change. *Academy of Management Review, 25*(4), 783–794.

Pierce, J., Gardner, D. G., Cummings, L. L., & Dunham, R. B. (1989). Organization-based self-esteem: Construct definition, measurement, and validation. *Academy of Management Journal, 32*(3), 622–648.

Rafferty, A. E., & Jimmieson, N. L. (2017). Subjective perceptions of organizational change and employee resistance to change: Direct and mediated relationships with employee well-being. *British Journal of Management, 28*, 248–264.

Rafferty, A. E., Jimmieson, N. L., & Armenakis, A. A. (2013). Change readiness: A multilevel review. *Journal of Management, 39*(1), 110–135.

Rafferty, A. E., & Restubog, S. L. D. (2017). Why do employees' perceptions of their organization's change history matter? The role of change appraisals. *Human Resource Management, 56*(3), 533–550.

Rahaman, H. M., Camps, J., Decoster, S., & Stouten, J. (2021). Ethical leadership in times of change: The role of change commitment and change information for employees' dysfunctional resistance. *Personnel Review, 50* (2), 630–647.

Rauch, A., & Frese, M. (2007). Let's put the person back into entrepreneurship research: A meta-analysis on the relationship between business owners' personality traits, business creation, and success. *European Journal of Work and Organizational Psychology, 16*(4), 353–385.

Ross, L. (1977). The intuitive psychologist and his shortcomings: Distortions in the attribution process. In L. Berkowitz (ed.), *Advances in experimental social psychology*, vol. 10 (pp. 173–220). New York: Academic Press.

Rousseau, D. M. (1989). Psychological and implied contracts in organizations. *Employee Responsibility and Rights Journal, 2*, 121–139.

Samhan, B. (2020). Can cyber risk management insurance mitigate healthcare providers' intentions to resist electronic medical records? *International Journal of Healthcare Management, 13*, 12–21.

Srivastava, S., & Agrawal, S. (2020). Resistance to change and turnover intention: A moderated mediation model of burnout and perceived organizational support. *Journal of Organizational Change Management, 33*(7), 1431–2020.

Stanley, D. J., Meyer, J. P., & Topolnytsky, L. (2005). Employee cynicism and resistance to organizational change. *Journal of Business and Psychology, 19*(4), 429–459.

Steffens, N. K., Haslam, S. A., Reicher, S. D., Platow, M. J., Fransen, K., Yang, J., Ryan, M. K., Jetten, J., Peters, K., & Boen, F. (2014). Leadership as social identity management: Introducing the Identity Leadership Inventory (ILI) to assess and validate a four-dimensional model. *The Leadership Quarterly, 25*, 1001–1024.

Stouten, J., Rousseau, D., & de Cremer, D. (2018). Successful organizational change: Integrating the management practice and scholarly literatures. *Academy of Management Annals, 12*(2), 752–788.

Suddaby, R., & Foster, W. M. (2017). History and organizational change. *Journal of Management, 43*(1), 19–38.

Szabla, D. B. (2007). A multidimensional view of resistance to organizational change: Exploring cognitive, motional, and intentional responses to planned change across perceived change leadership strategies. *Human Resource Development Quarterly, 18*(4), 525–558.

Thomas, J. B., Clark, S. M., & Gioia, D. A. (1993). Strategic sensemaking and organizational performance: Linkages among scanning, interpretation, action, and outcomes. *Academy of Management Journal, 36*, 239–270.

Turgut, S., Michel, A., Rothenhöfer, L. M., & Sonntag, K. (2016). Dispositional resistance to change and emotional exhaustion: Moderating effects at the work-unit level. *European Journal of Work and Organizational Psychology, 25* (5), 735–750.

Turgut, S., & Neuhaus, A. E. (2020). The relationship between dispositional resistance to change and individual career management: A matter of occupational self-efficacy and organizational identification? *Journal of Change Management, 20*(2), 171–188,

Vakola, M., Armenakis, A., & Oreg, S. (2013). Reactions to organizational change from an individual differences perspective: A review of empirical research. In S. Oreg, A. Michel, & R. T. By (eds.), *The psychology of organizational change: Viewing change from the employee's perspective* (pp. 95–122). Cambridge: Cambridge University Press.

del Val, M. P., & Fuentes, C. M. (2003). Resistance to change: A literature review and empirical study. *Management Decision, 41*(2), 148–155.

Vos, J., & Rupert, J. (2018). Change agent's contribution to recipients' resistance to change: A two-sided story. *European Management Journal, 36*, 453–462.

Wanberg, C. R., & Banas, J. T. (2000). Predictors and outcomes of openness to changes in a reorganizing workplace. *Journal of Applied Psychology, 85*, 132–142.

Wanous, J. P., Reichers, A. E., & Austin, J. T. (2000). Cynicism about organizational change: Measurement, antecedents and correlates. *Group & Organization Management, 25*(2), 132–153.

Weick, K. E. (1995). *Organizational sensemaking*. Thousand Oaks, CA: Sage.

Weick, K. E., & Quinn, R. E. (1999). Organizational change and development. *Annual Review of Psychology, 50*, 361–386.

Xu, X., Payne, S. C., Horner, M. T., & Alexander, A. L. (2016). Individual difference predictors of perceived organizational change fairness. *Journal of Managerial Psychology, 31*(2), 420–433.

Zeng, J., Wei, J., Zhu, W., Zhao, D., & Lin, X. (2019). Residents' behavioural intentions to resist the nuclear power plants in the vicinity: An application of the protective action decision model. *Journal of Risk Research, 22*(3), 382–400.

CHAPTER 3

The Role of Time in Organizational Change

Frank Belschak and Gabriele Jacobs

Most organizations undergo moderate to major changes every four to five years (e.g., Gordon et al., 2000; Uhlaner & West, 2011). As the label of a change *process* suggests, organizational change is an inherently temporal phenomenon that unfolds over time and, therefore, deserves a temporal perspective (Pettigrew et al., 2001). For instance, change processes are difficult to predict, often take unforeseen turns, and are often implemented sequentially. This typically causes uncertainty and ambiguity for participants (Fugate et al., 2012) and affects the appraisal of a change project and the related beliefs, expectations, emotions, and behavioral reactions (Jansen et al., 2016; Oreg et al., 2018). Such processes over time are reflected, for instance, in models like the "change curve" (Elrod & Tippett, 2002) and have been the foundation of theoretical conceptualizations of organizational change (see Lewin 1947a, 1947b, 1947c; Bartunek & Woodman, 2015) as well as practitioner models (e.g., Kotter, 1995). Despite the high relevance of a temporal perspective on organizational change, the role of time as an important characteristic of change initiatives has been under-researched and only recently attracted more attention (e.g., Bartunek & Woodman, 2015; Kunisch et al., 2017). This lacuna was noted by several scholars in the field, who identified the largely atemporal approach of organizational research as a weakness in the field of organizational psychology in general (George & Jones, 2000) and in the field of organizational change in particular (Pettigrew et al., 2001). The core argument of this criticism is that organizational change phenomena are inherently temporal, and thus theory building and empirical studies should systematically include time as a variable (Heracleous & Bartunek, 2021).

Ignoring a temporal perspective on change might lead, for instance, to a misevaluation of the outcome of change endeavors. The change literature broadly suggest that the majority of change projects usually fail to fully achieve their goals. For instance, Lovallo and Kahneman (2003) note that about three out of four mergers and acquisitions never pay off, and Balogun and Hope Hailey (2004) similarly argue that about 70 percent of all change initiatives fail. Yet, these overall rates do not systematically include or even neglect the temporal nature of change outcomes (Hughes, 2011). The complexity and ambiguity of change processes (Jacobs et al., 2013) imply that change outcomes vary in their qualitative and quantitative nature over time. For instance, turnover rates right after the implementation of an organizational change may be low, then go up a year later, only to drop again after two years. Thus, the categorization of a change as success or failure depends on the time perspective chosen (Hughes, 2011; cf. temporal depth, Heracleus & Bartunek, 2021). At the antecedent side, explaining success and failure of a change project may be more fruitful when investigating *shifts* in change recipients' responses to change over time rather than assuming a static perspective and focusing only on variables at any one moment in time (Piderit, 2000). In this respect, Jansen et al. (2016) note that change experiences are inherently situated in time and shifts in change perceptions are able to provide additional insights into the momentum and success of a change project over and above "snapshots" of perceptions.

In this chapter we explore the time-related psychological aspects of change, that is, how change processes can be theoretically modeled to include a temporal perspective, how change recipients' cognitive and emotional experiences and reactions to organizational change evolve over time, and how individual and organizational factors influence these experiences and reactions to change. We start the chapter by providing an overview of different theoretical conceptualizations of the role of time in organizational change, followed by an overview of process models of organizational change that aim at modeling change as a process that unfolds over time. We conclude the chapter by proposing a phases model of change, in which we describe the development of change recipients' reactions to organizational change over the course of a change project. Here, we draw equally on literature in the fields of organizational psychology and behavior, as well as change management and sensemaking. We hope that a more systematic acknowledgment of the temporal aspects of change stimulates additional research in this area but also helps change practitioners to better plan and target their interventions before and during the change process.

3.1   Temporal Aspects of Change

3.1.1   The Role of Time in Theorizing on Change

In their seminal work on the role of time in theory and theory building, George and Jones (2000) have offered a general framework for analyzing how time affects Organizational Behavior theorizing that also helps to show the importance of time for theorizing in the area of organizational change. Drawing on Whetten (1989), they distinguish six elements which a theory should include: the creation and/or definition of the core constructs of the theory ("what"), the specification of the relationships between these constructs ("how"), the explanation of the causality in these relationships ("why"), and specifications about the targets ("who"), space ("where"), and time ("when") the theory covers. While Whetten (1989) sees the latter specifications ("who," "where," "when") as boundary conditions of the first three elements, George and Jones (2000, p. 658) point out that, in particular, the role of time goes much further than acting as a boundary condition. Rather, time directly impacts the "what," "how," and "why" of a theory and affects the conceptualization of the constructs as well as their relationships with each other. For instance, seeing change as a process over time suggests that change-related constructs like change readiness, resistance, or commitment are variable and change over time rather than being stable, and different factors might be the main drivers of these variables at different stages of a change project. In what follows we provide some illustrations for the effects of time on theorizing in the area of change.

The "What" of Change: The "what" of change refers to how core constructs of change theories may change during a change process. Many studies treat change as an atemporal event (Pettigrew et al., 2001). Commitment to change, for instance, is often not investigated over time but rather measured in a snapshot-like fashion or as an aggregate over an unspecified period of time (e.g., Herscovitch & Meyer, 2002). Such a static perspective ignores the fact that commitment can vary over time. It usually takes time for change processes to unfold, and changes are often implemented sequentially, leading to cumulative effects (Pettigrew et al., 2001; Herold et al., 2007; Jacobs et al., 2013). In line with this, change-related variables like change recipients' perceptions, attitudes, or reactions are also likely to unfold and change over time. Indeed, studies have provided support for the variability of change-related variables like change beliefs (Belschak et al., 2020) or change appraisals (Kaltiainen et al., 2020).

Showing change-supportive behavior can trigger sensemaking activities in individuals who may interpret their change-supportive behaviors as caring about and being committed to the change project, resulting in increases in their commitment to change over time. In line with this, work on prosocial sensemaking (Grant et al., 2008) found that employees who gave back to their organization interpreted their own behavior as caring and showed increased organizational commitment. Theorizing on organizational change should, therefore, include dynamics in the conceptualization of constructs.

The "How" of Change: The "how" of change, that is, the relationships between change-related constructs, may also vary over time. First, the role of antecedents of change outcomes may differ during different stages of a change process. For instance, Kotter (1995) has emphasized the importance of establishing a sense of urgency at the start of a change initiative, but not much is known as to whether this variable is of equal importance at later stages of a change process. Second, given the dynamic nature of organizational change constructs, it may be that changes in antecedents may explain more or additional variance in change outcomes than static measures of the antecedent. In support of this, Chen et al. (2011) found that *variations over time* in job satisfaction explained variance in turnover intentions over and above absolute or average levels of satisfaction. More recent longitudinal research on organizational change indeed showed that variations in terms of increases or decreases in change commitment during a change project were related to a corresponding change in change momentum (Jansen et al., 2016), and changes in change-related beliefs explained employees' changes in work engagement (Belschak et al., 2020). Third, it is important to consider that antecedents of change may not have immediate consequences and the time frames in which outcomes of change manifest themselves need to be considered and conceptualized, as the impact of a large-scale change process on change recipients' direct working environment may only become clear over time. To illustrate, Rafferty and Restubog (2010) found that recipients' perceptions of the history of past changes of an organization and formal organizational information efforts before a change project affected change recipients' commitment to change before the start of the change, their job satisfaction and turnover intentions seven months later, and their actual turnover behavior up to two years after the announcement of the change project. Finally, recipients' reactions to change are likely compared to and conditioned by the past, for example, through past experiences or comparison standards. A successful change history of an organization comes with learning experiences for change recipients and, hence, leads to more openness to change (Devos et al., 2007). The above-mentioned points illustrate the need and usefulness of including temporal aspects in theorizing about the relationships between constructs in the area of organizational change.

The "Why" of Change: The "why" of change addresses how causal relationships between change variables are affected by and can vary over time. Causal relationships are inherently related to time, as they argue for a temporal ordering of variables, that is, antecedents precede consequences. Existing change theories mostly ignore temporal aspects that go further than such ordering, even though authors have emphasized that these relationships are dynamic. For instance, change recipients try to interpret and give meaning to a change initiative, and such sensemaking affects their reactions to change and hereby ultimately also the change initiative and its success or failure (e.g., Weick, 1995). Organizational change activities hence lead to sensemaking activities of change recipients' who, in turn, react to the sense and meaning they ascribe to the change, hereby influencing the change situation and activities. Sensemaking is, therefore, a dynamic process with retrospective and prospective elements that is affected by and affects the change process at the same time (e.g., Konlechner et al., 2019). Also, in their sensemaking efforts, individuals compare their expectations based on past experiences to their current change experiences, and these comparisons can lead to ambiguities that affect their reactions to change in case of a misfit between expectations and experiences (Konlechner et al., 2019). Change initiators act in the shadow of the change history of their organizations and their employees (Bordia et al., 2011). Regardless of whether they conducted the former changes themselves or whether change recipients witnessed another change initiator implementing these changes, aspects of former change processes influence change recipients' perceptions of current change. Investigating individuals' expectations can, therefore, help in understanding why a relationship in the present is affected by the past. Another recent example of a study that shows the complexity of causal relationships when including the time component into the analysis is the research by Kaltiainen et al. (2020). These authors found reciprocal relationships over time between change recipients' threat appraisals and their work engagement. As George and Jones (2000, p. 673) note, "A complete understanding of causal relationships necessitates consideration of the manner in which causes have their effects over time and why." Theorizing in organizational change should, therefore, include the effects of time in conceptualizations of the causal relationships between constructs.

3.1.2 Temporal Dimensions

To complement the picture, different (individual and situational) temporal characteristics have been distinguished that affect the success or failure of a change process and change recipients' reactions to change (see Bartunek & Woodman, 2015; Kunisch et al., 2017; Heracleus & Bartunek, 2021).

Individual Characteristics: As scholars have noted (e.g., see Ancona et al., 2001; Kunisch et al., 2017), individuals differ in their perception and experience of time. Some important temporal dimensions at the individual side are urgency, temporal focus, temporal depth, and polychronicity. A person (e.g., change initiator) high on time *urgency* feels generally hurried and may, thus, tend to take faster change actions and set shorter deadlines. Individuals can also vary in terms of their *temporal focus* (e.g., on the past or on the future; Zimbardo & Boyd, 1999), which influences the weight that they give to different antecedents of their change reactions. For instance, a focus on the past may lead to an increased importance of the change history of the organization (Rafferty & Restubog, 2010), while a focus on the future may rather strengthen the importance of an attractive change vision. Somewhat related to the temporal focus, people not only differ in terms of the quality of their temporal focus (future, present, past) but also in the quantity of their focus, that is, how far their focus reaches into the past or future (*temporal depth*). While some people may focus more on the short-term adaptation to or success of change initiatives, others may put more emphasis on the long-term adaptation and effects of a change project. Depending on their temporal depth, change initiators may, thus, plan change processes differently (e.g., slow implementation with change recipients' participation versus fast top-down implementation), and change recipients may react differently to these changes (e.g., quick adoption/resistance versus carefully trying out resulting in slower change acceptance/resistance). Finally, individuals differ in their preferences for working on multiple tasks at the same time (*polychronicity*) versus working only on one task (*monochronicity*) (Ancona et al., 2001; Kunisch et al., 2017). This may, for example, lead to problems for monochronic change recipients who need to learn new skills while performing their standard tasks at the same time, which is a typical situation in organizational change.

Situational Characteristics: Scholars have noted that time should not always be considered as a continuous linear stream of divisible, quantifiable units (*clock time*; McGrath, 1988). In particular organizational change is often a reaction to a specific internal or external event, and time thus resides in these events (*event time*), not the events in clock time (e.g., Kunisch et al., 2017). This has implications, for example, for determining the success or failure of a change process that might be affected by certain events (e.g., installing a new CEO; see Kunisch et al., 2017) and hence depends on event time, not clock time. Researchers have also emphasized that events do not always happen sequentially in a predetermined order (e.g., Amis et al., 2004). Rather, different events can happen simultaneously, overlap, and even interact with each other (*polyphony*; see Bartunek & Woodman, 2015). For instance, a new software system may be implemented as future users receive training on how to use this system, and the successful implementation of the system may depend on the success of the training, that is, the success of one event influences the success of the other. Finally, the *frequency*, *pace*, and *duration* of a change are also temporal aspects of a change initiative that have been shown to affect its outcomes (e.g., Amis et al., 2004; see Bartunek & Woodman, 2015). For example, frequent changes or change projects of a long duration create uncertainty in change recipients that leads to negative outcomes (Rafferty & Griffin, 2006).

3.2　Phase Models of Organizational Change

In what follows we will investigate change models which explicitly incorporate the temporal aspect and its effects on the "what," "how," and/or "why" of change. These models conceptualize change as a process that covers several different phases that unfold over time (e.g., Kotter, 1995; Chung & Choi, 2018; Stouten et al., 2018; Belschak et al., 2020). Even though the models seem to suggest a linear temporal sequence of these phases it should be noted that this is not necessarily the case, and the sequence of phases may vary (e.g., skipping phases, moving backwards again to earlier phases, or parallel phases; see also polyphony, e.g., Kunisch et al., 2017).

3.2.1　"Changing as Three Steps": Lewin's Model of Change

A first phase model of change was introduced by Kurt Lewin (1947a, 1947b, 1947c). In this model he describes three steps of a change project:

unfreezing, change, (re)freezing. Albeit simple, Lewin conceptualizes change as an event over time. He further theorizes that change success is contingent on different antecedents in each of the three steps and that the three steps usually naturally occur in this sequence (see Burnes, 2020). *Unfreezing* refers to the process of destabilizing a situation that is currently in equilibrium in order to prepare for and achieve later change. This can be done, for instance, by establishing a sense of urgency (e.g., by communicating a threat like a new competitor or a change in government regulations that requires the organization to change) (e.g., Kotter, 1995). Unfreezing is similar to the concept of change readiness which reflects organizational members' beliefs that a change is needed and that the organization is capable of successfully making the changes (Armenakis et al., 1993). *Changing* describes the steps that are taken to move toward the goal of the change initiative, like the introduction of a new organizational structure, the implementation of a new IT system, or the introduction of training activities. It also reflects change recipients' adoption efforts, which are crucial as recipients can also reject a change (Armenakis & Harris, 2002). Interestingly, Lewin (1947b) describes this part as an iterative process, that is, change takes place in several steps with feedback loops at every step that can affect the further changes. This idea of change as an iterative process with feedback loops can also be found elsewhere in the change literature: changes are often implemented sequentially, and change recipients try to make sense of each of these steps (e.g., Jacobs et al., 2008). Finally, *refreezing* describes actions that aim to establish a new equilibrium that is (quasi)stationary. Particularly for this final step, Lewin (1947a) emphasized the importance of participation of change recipients. Indeed, several studies have supported the idea that a participative approach to change creates stronger commitment and support for change projects (see, e.g., the results of a meta-analysis by Oreg et al., 2011).

Unfortunately, Lewin's Three-Step Model is often read in isolation and judged as being overly simplistic and even outdated. Yet, putting the model into the context of Lewin's broader work in field theory, group dynamics, and action research offers additional insights on the change process (e.g., Burnes, 2004). For instance, field theory as a broader theory of behavioral change argues that the status quo of a "field," defined as the totality of coexisting facts, is maintained by certain factors or "forces." An analysis of these forces can inform us what forces need to be reduced or strengthened in order to achieve change. In his works on group dynamics, Lewin (1947c) further suggests that the focus of change should be particularly on the group level as group factors strongly guide human behavior. In this sense, looking at Lewin's broader works provides more concrete information on the three phases and how to achieve transitions between phases.

3.2.2   Ten Evidence-Based Change Management Principles

In addition to Lewin's work, there are several other phase models available in the change management literature that propose a sequence of phases or steps to achieve positive change outcomes and that have received ample support in the scientific literature (for an overview, see Cummings et al., 2016; Stouten et al., 2018). In their recent review, Stouten et al. (2018, p. 756) concur that these models considerably overlap and have integrated seven prominent phase models (including the ones by Lewin and the popular 8-step model by Kotter, 1995) and the empirical literature on change in a 10-step model that summarizes the general temporal flow of a change process and recommends appropriate change management actions that should be taken at the different stages of a change initiative to facilitate change success. These steps are: (1) Gathering facts for a diagnosis to convince change recipients that the change is needed (e.g., organizational needs, Armenakis & Harris, 2009; constraining factors, Rafferty & Restubog, 2017; or discrepancy between present state and desired end-state, Armenakis et al., 1993), (2) Assessing and addressing the organiza-tion's readiness for change (e.g., past change history, Bordia et al., 2011; current stress level of change recipients, Oreg et al., 2011; system and individual change readiness, Armenakis et al., 1993), (3) Implementing evidence-based change interventions (e.g., choosing appropriate interven-tions, Neuman et al., 1989), (4) Developing change leadership (e.g., training change initiators change-related skills, Heyden et al., 2017), (5) Developing and communicating a change vision (e.g., achieving a broadly shared goal, Kleingeld et al., 2011), (6) Working with social networks (e.g., building ties to influential people who support and promote the change, Battilana & Casciaro, 2013), (7) Using enabling practices to support implementation (e.g., participation of change recipients, see Oreg et al., 2011; providing room for learning for recipients; Kao, 2017), (8) Promoting microprocesses and experimentation (e.g., allowing change recipients to experiment with change elements to find out what works best, Reay et al., 2006), (9) Assessing change progress over time (e.g., measuring change commitment and changes in commitment over time, Wiedner et al., 2017), and (10) Institutionalizing the change (e.g., integration in organizational culture and/or HR practices to facilitate recipients' sustainable change adoption, Armenakis et al., 1999).

Even though implicitly included in the 10-steps model, the temporal dimension is not directly mentioned. However, some principles logically apply earlier than others (e.g., diagnosis and planning before implementation, implementation before institutionalization) and some principles can be applied concurrently (polyphony; e.g., working with networks and using enabling practices). At least the general temporal sequence of Lewin's "Change-as-Three-Phases" model applies to the ten change management principles though. Time is also included in the feedback loops that are an explicit part of the model. For instance, principle (8) refers to the importance of experimenting as to which change practices work best, hereby arguing that change is a process. The following principle (9) explicitly acknowledges that change unfolds over time, and that outcomes of change may change over time and need to be monitored. In case of negative developments of change outcomes over time, change interventions need to be adapted or changed (Stouten et al., 2018, p. 777). The final principle, institutionalizing change, similarly explicitly emphasizes the variability and temporal nature of change outcomes.

3.2.3   The Change Curve

The abovementioned process models of change are strongly conceptualized from the perspective of the change initiator, indicating what actions are most important for managing a change process throughout its different phases. An underlying assumption of these managerial phase models seems to be that change recipients' needs and reactions vary during a change project. Thus, to understand the full complexity and richness of organizational change and its dynamics, attention should also be given to other stakeholders, in particular the primary change recipients (see Stouten et al., 2018, p. 778). In line with this, we now focus on approaches modeling the experiences of change recipients which – building on findings from research on individual coping with stressful events as a theoretical basis – explore how these experiences systematically vary during a change process (e.g., Elrod & Tippett, 2002; Fugate et al., 2002). A result of these efforts to identify and describe typical patterns over time in change recipients' reactions to an organizational change process is the curvilinear "change curve" (e.g., Schneider & Goldwasser, 1998; Elrod & Tippett, 2002). The premise of the change curve is that change recipients experience a change project as a crisis that comes with a loss, and their reactions to this crisis can be compared to individuals' reactions to other crisis situations like, for instance, the loss of a loved person. Depending on the scope of the change,

change recipients can perceive change processes as a threat to their professional identity and to "their" organization (Jacobs et al., 2013). Change recipients can bemoan the loss of their work routines or grief about the relationship with colleagues, that were altered or terminated due to new work processes. Most importantly, change recipients might be concerned about the purpose and value of change processes and might perceive that the very purpose of their work gets threatened or, in the worst case, lost (Jacobs & Keegan, 2018). Based on findings from research on coping with traumas (Kubler-Ross, 1969), scholars advocating the change curve therefore argue that individuals are confronted with a serious threat or loss during a change process and pass through different phases of bereavement, and their reactions to the loss become initially more negative over time before adaptation can occur and reactions can become more positive again (see Elrod & Tippett, 2002). A similar development over time has also been advocated by scholars on teamwork (e.g., Katzenbach & Smith, 1993) who argue that the performance of working teams tends to go down in the early phases of a team implementation before increasing again later in time.

"The Peak of Optimism": The "classic change curve" (Schneider & Goldwasser, 1998) depicts a prototypical change process as a sequence of three phases over time. Most change initiatives start out with unrealistically *high expectations* and related positive reactions of change recipients in anticipation of the changes to start. Chung and Choi (2018, p. 1018) note in this respect that, at the initial or anticipatory stages of a change project, change recipients mostly receive information from change initiators which is positively biased and focuses on the benefits and feasibility of the change to increase recipients' change readiness (Armenakis & Harris, 2002). Also, the implications of a change on the strategy and structure of an organization and on job-related processes are not fully predictable (e.g., Bordia et al., 2004). It usually takes time before a change project is implemented at all levels of an organization and its implications and outcomes become clear and impact the direct work environment of change recipients (Pettigrew et al., 2001). As a consequence, the expectations of change recipients are often unrealistically high at the outset of a change initiative.

"The Valley of Despair": These unrealistically high expectations typically result in a mismatch between change recipients' expectations and understandings of the change's implications and the organizational reality during the implementation of the change (Chung & Choi, 2018). The "change curve" is therefore characterized by *increasingly negative reactions* of change recipients in the first part of a change process (Schneider &

Goldwasser, 1998; Elrod & Tippett, 2002). Due to the costs of adaption to the changes, recipients' morale and performance generally decrease. This decline in morale and performance at the early levels of a change project was tested and supported by Elrod and Tippett (1999), who found a curvilinear relationship between team maturity and team performance for the implementation of teamwork. Also, in support of negative reactions at the beginning of a change project, Belschak et al. (2020) found that change recipients' change-related beliefs became increasingly negative in the first half of a large-scale change initiative.

"The Good Ending": Once change recipients have adapted their expectations regarding the change process, that is, they are able to oversee the remaining change efforts needed and develop realistic ideas about the change ("light at the end of the tunnel," Schneider & Goldwasser, 1998, p. 42), and they start to realize positive results of the change, their *change reactions will become more positive again*. This logic is reflected in Kotter's (1995) advice for change managers to create short-term wins. There is also empirical support for this final more positive part of the change curve. For instance, Elrod and Tippett (1999) found that team performance after the introduction of teamwork in an organization increased to levels exceeding those at the start of the change process after an initial decrease in performance. Similarly, Jansen et al. (2016) found that a substantial group of employees start with negative perceptions in the earlier stages of a project and develop more positive change perceptions at the later stages of the project.

Empirical Evidence: While quantitative studies covering the whole process of a change process are scarce (for an exception see the above-mentioned study by Elrod & Tippett, 1999), there is some qualitative research available on sensemaking that directly addresses the temporal aspects of the change curve and supports its general idea (Isabella, 1990; Konlechner et al., 2019). As Konlechner et al. (2019) note, sensemaking during organizational change is a continuous process in which change recipients constantly generate new experiences, compare these experiences to their cognitive frames based on past experiences, and adapt their expectations about the change initiative. In an in-depth interview study investigating how change recipients make sense of organizational changes, Isabella (1990) identified different stages of a change project (e.g., anticipation versus culmination stage) and found that recipients' interpretations of the change initiative varied across these different stages. Before the implementation of a change project ("anticipation stage"), usually there is only limited and disconnected information about the change available for change recipients, which results in biased interpretations of an envisioned distant future. Often recipients engage in "wishful thinking" in anticipation of the change (Fugate et al., 2002; Konlechner et al., 2019) and tend to underestimate the level of required adaptation efforts (Lovallo & Kahneman, 2003). Yet, due to a general positivity and optimism bias regarding events in the distant future, people's evaluations of events tend to become more negative the closer the events get, leading to stress and disappointment as their biased expectations do not materialize (Gilovich et al., 1993). Change recipients compare their current experiences during change to their expectations, and a discrepancy between experiences and expectations leads to feelings of ambiguity that result in negative perceptions of and reactions to change as soon as a person's tolerance to ambiguity is exhausted (Konlechner et al., 2019). During the implementation of the changes ("culmination stage"), recipients are "peppered with double exposures" (Isabella, 1990, p. 23). They come to realize that old behaviors do not work anymore and that they need to learn new ways to interact and do their work. For instance, the introduction of a new shared service center requires that change recipients communicate with new colleagues, build up new networks, and learn how to work with new information (see polychronicity, Kunisch et al., 2017). Due to the novelty of the situation, these efforts needed for adaptation are difficult for recipients to anticipate; as Weick (1988, pp. 305–306) notes, an individual "cannot know what [she/]he is facing until [she/]he faces it." While adapting to the changes and developing new routines, the change project often takes unexpected turns (Jacobs et al., 2008) and change recipients usually encounter performance hindrances (Burke et al., 2006) which further increase the required efforts to successfully maneuver through the change process and make the adaptation needs and costs more salient (Buono et al., 1985). Change recipients' reactions to these adaptation needs are usually negative, and findings by Isabella (1990) suggest that such change resistance should be interpreted as an element inherent to change, that is, as a cognitive transition change recipients need to undergo in order to make sense of changes and create a new frame of reference for their work. Once change recipients have established what a change process means for them and how they fit into the new, changed organization, they are able to realistically see its costs and outcomes and embrace it, resulting in more positive change reactions ("aftermath stage," Isabella, 1990).

Yet, some studies also provide empirical evidence that deviates from the classical change curve. For instance, in their longitudinal qualitative study, Konlechner et al. (2019) find that change recipients' negative experiences of and reactions to the change project they underwent did not become more positive again at the end of the project. Rather, the change initiative was evaluated as a failure by change recipients, expectations about potential positive changes in the future were low, and people were frustrated and demotivated. Similarly, Petrou et al. (2018) did not find evidence of more positive developments of change recipients' reactions in the change project they investigated. These authors studied change recipients' work engagement during a major organizational change project and found that their work engagement one year after the implementation of the changes was at the same level as during the changes. These findings indicate that the shape of the change curve is likely contingent on several variables, like the characteristics of the change recipients (e.g., tolerance of ambiguity; Judge et al., 1999; Konlechner et al., 2019), the characteristics of the change (e.g., success or failure; Konlechner et al., 2019), or the change management activities undertaken by management (Schneider & Goldwasser, 1998). In what follows we, therefore, develop a more comprehensive model of organizational change over time that extends the longitudinal model of the change curve and incorporates findings from the change management literature.

3.3   Developing an Integrative Process Model of Change

The starting point for our process model of organizational change is the classical change curve. The general tenet of the model is that a change process consists of different phases, and change recipients' experiences of and reactions to organizational change vary during these phases of the change project. More specifically, we argue that typically these changes follow a pattern in the sense that change recipients' reactions start out positively in anticipation of the change project, then become more negative in the first stages of the change project before getting more positive again at the later stages. The model also adds individual (e.g., traits) and change characteristics (e.g., duration or complexity of the change project) as variables that affect change recipients' reaction and, hence, the shape of the change curve, and it includes change initiators' activities that have been shown to be effective during the different stages of a change process (see Rafferty et al., 2013). Figure 3.1 shows our process model of change.

The basic development of change recipients' reactions follows the logic of the change curve. People often start out, maybe fueled by promises concerning the change process and results, with too high expectations and positive reactions to change that are disconfirmed after the change project

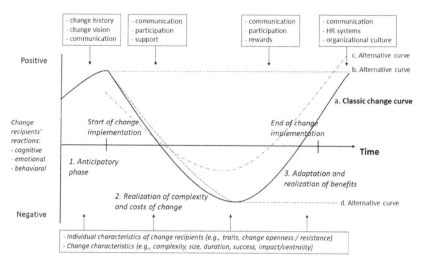

Figure 3.1   An integrative process model of organizational change

has started to unfold, resulting in ambiguities and related increasingly negative change reactions (Konlechner et al., 2019). Once they have adapted their expectations, the uncertainties which arise at the early stages of a change project due to the lack of predictability of the required changes and adaptation efforts (e.g., Schweiger & DeNisi, 1991) are reduced. People are better able to oversee the full amount of the changes and start to experience successful first changes, and their reactions to the change get more positive again. Change recipients' reactions to a change project cover cognitive, emotional, and behavioral aspects (see Oreg et al., 2011), which all systematically vary over time during the different phases of a change project.

Cognitive Reactions: Particularly relevant change-related cognitions are recipients' beliefs about the change project (e.g., Armenakis et al., 2007). These beliefs reflect individuals' knowledge and expectations about the organizational change they are confronted with, which provide a lens to understand, interpret, and give meaning to this change (Armenakis et al., 1993). Beliefs may cover aspects like the value of a change, its appropriateness, or the support from management (Armenakis et al., 2007). As mentioned above, qualitative as well as quantitative studies found evidence that recipients' beliefs vary during a change project. In anticipation of and at the start of a change project beliefs become more positive as change recipients are particularly exposed to positively biased information (Fugate et al., 2002; Konlechner et al., 2019). Next, Belschak et al. (2020) investigated recipients' beliefs in a multi-wave study covering the first half of a change project and found support for increasingly negative beliefs during the initial phase of a change project. More specifically, the perceived impact of a change increased during the implementation phase, due to the cascading effects of adaption processes (Jacobs et al., 2008). At the same time, change recipients' beliefs about the appropriateness and value of the change decreased as adaptation needs and costs become more salient during the implementation (Buono et al., 1985). In support of the idea of more positive beliefs at the end of the change project, Petrou et al. (2018) found that employees' beliefs about the impact of a change had significantly decreased again after the end of the project as compared to during the project.

Affective Reactions: Compared to change recipients' cognitive reactions to change, there is much less research available on their affective reactions. Yet, existing studies seem to support the proposed model. In line with the predictions of the change curve, Giaever and Smollan (2015) found in a longitudinal qualitative study among nurses that, during the anticipation and start of a large change project, recipients' emotional experiences centered around the theme hopefulness, whereas emotions three months after the start of the implementation of the changes were rather characterized by feeling overwhelmed and negative emotions. Similarly, Fugate et al. (2002) found change recipients' negative emotions to increase in the initial phase of a merger as compared to the anticipatory phase, and Kiefer (2005) reports that recipients' negative emotions increase with the number of changes experienced at work (cf. change frequency, Kunisch et al., 2017). Schweiger and DeNisi (1991) suggest, in this regard, that it is particularly the uncertainty and loss of control related to change rather than the changes themselves which lead to negative feelings. This also offers an explanation as to why affective reactions to change become more negative in the initial phases of change, when change recipients cannot fully oversee what is yet to come in terms of additional changes and adaptation needs, and become more positive again when they are able to make such predictions and thereby reduce their uncertainty.

Behavioral Reactions: Next to cognitive and affective reactions to change, individuals also vary in their behavioral reactions to change depending on the stage the project is currently in. As mentioned in Section 3.2.3, Elrod and Tippett (1999) found empirical evidence that group performance decreased in the initial phase after the introduction of a change and increased again at the later stages of the project. Another important behavioral variable that is often investigated as a reaction to change is employee turnover (intention) (e.g., Wanberg & Banas, 2000; Rafferty & Restubog, 2010). Here, Belschak et al. (2020) investigated in a longitudinal study change recipients' turnover intentions and found – in line with earlier results by Begley and Czajka (1993) – that work engagement decreased and turnover intentions increased during the first half of a major change project. In support of a change toward more positive behavioral reactions during the "aftermaths" of the change process, Petrou et al. (2018) found that recipients' adaptation to change was higher after the change than during the change. In sum, there is ample evidence that change recipients' cognitive, affective, and behavioral reactions to change follow the logic of the proposed change curve.

We do not posit though that change recipients' reactions during a change process do *always* follow the proposed shape (see, for instance, Bartunek & Woodman, 2015, on the sequence of events in change projects). Rather, we acknowledge that different variables are likely to affect their reactions over time. More specifically, we argue that particularly characteristics of the change recipients, characteristics of the change project, and change management activities by the organization are likely to affect change recipients' reactions and, hence, the shape of the change curve.

Individual Characteristics of Change Recipients: Several studies have shown that not all change recipients react similarly to change and that their reactions are affected by individual characteristics. These individual characteristics cover change-related dispositions like dispositional change resistance and change self-efficacy (e.g., Oreg, 2003; Herold et al., 2007), as well as broader, more general dispositions like self-esteem, optimism, openness to experience, and tolerance for ambiguity (e.g., Judge et al., 1999; Wanberg & Banas, 2000). It can, thus, be expected that, for example, individuals higher on optimism react generally more positively to organizational changes as their expectations are positively biased, and their change curve should therefore be less steep (see alternative curve c in Figure 3.1) or even does not show a negative development at all (see alternative curve b in Figure 3.1). By contrast, individuals high on change resistance are likely to show even more negative reactions than depicted in the classical change curve, resulting in a stronger negative slope of the curve in the initial stage of a change project and potentially even continued negative reactions rather than a change toward more positive reactions in the later stage of the change project (see alternative curve d in Figure 3.1). In support of these ideas, Belschak et al. (2020) found that people high on Machiavellianism – a "dark" personality trait characterized by a high level of selfishness and a strong focus on the achievement of one's individual goals by using all possible means – reacted even more strongly negatively than low Machiavellians in the initial phases of an organizational change process, resulting in a steeper slope of the change curve for this group of people.

Characteristics of the Change Project: Next to their own individual characteristics, change recipients' reactions during an organizational change project are likely also affected by the characteristics of the change project. For instance, the deterioration in individual reactions during the initial phase of a change project is usually explained by the complexity of the organizational change processes which are difficult to oversee for change recipients due to the high interdependencies, particularly in this phase (Griffin et al., 2007). This unpredictability creates uncertainty and stress for individuals, resulting in negative reactions (Schweiger & DeNisi, 1991). Yet, as Belschak et al. (2020) note, this argument applies specifically to large-scale change projects which are highly complex and take time to unfold (Jacobs et al., 2008). For less complex change trajectories one might expect that change recipients start out with more realistic expectations resulting in a different shape of the curve in anticipation of and as an initial reaction to the change project (e.g., alternative curve c in Figure 3.1). In this regard, Rafferty et al. showed in different studies that change characteristics (e.g., planned change, transformational change, frequency or duration of changes) are closely linked to change recipients' change-related feelings of uncertainty and their cognitive, affective, and behavioral change reactions (Rafferty & Griffin, 2006; Rafferty & Jimmieson, 2017). One specific type of organizational change which likely shows a deviating change curve, particularly in anticipation of the changes, are downsizing activities. Here, change recipients likely develop negative rather than positive expectations at the announcement of the changes as they are afraid to lose their jobs or their valued colleagues. In line with this, Kalimo et al. (2003) found that anticipated downsizing comes with psychological strain and cynicism. As threat-rigidity theory (Staw et al., 1981) argues, individuals react negatively to impending threats (like the potential loss of their job).

Organizational Change Management Activities: When presenting their classical change curve, Schneider and Goldwasser (1998) emphasize that people's reactions to change – and thus the shape of the change curve – can be influenced by organizational change management activities. The authors mention in particular the importance of change initiators' activities (e.g., providing support, vision) and communication which they posit to reduce negative and increase positive reactions to change (see alternative curve c in Figure 3.1). This resonates with the academic literature on change management that particularly mentions three groups of effective change management activities: leadership, communication, and participation (e.g., change process: Oreg et al., 2011; internal context enablers: Rafferty et al., 2013). For example, Rafferty and Restubog (2010) showed that communication and participation activities before the start of the implementation of a change project were able to reduce negative reactions of change recipients during the initial phase of the change implementation. Similarly, recipients' perceptions of a positive past change history of the organization were able to reduce negative reactions in the early phase of a change project (Rafferty & Restubog, 2010), even though this effect is likely stronger for individuals with a temporal focus on the past (Kunisch et al., 2017). These results regarding the effects of participation and communication on individuals' openness to change were also replicated in experimental studies (Devos et al., 2007). Interestingly, these management activities are also mirrored in the managerial step models of change (e.g., Kotter, 1995).

While the proposed integrative process model of change is based on empirical evidence, there is still much more research needed. For instance, it would be interesting to explore whether indeed certain change management activities are particularly effective in specific phases of the change process and less so in others (e.g., Is the existence of a vision more important at the start of a change project than in its later stages?). Next, the model focuses particularly on top-down change projects. It would be interesting to explore the specifics and differences of bottom-up change initiatives and how these affect our model. For instance, actors with multiple conflicting identities (e.g., gender or ethical background) are often well-positioned to trigger changes in their organizations through challenging existing norms, logics, and values and may, hence, play an important role, especially in the first phase of an organizational change process (Horton et al., 2014). Finally, several of the variables mentioned in the model have only been investigated in cross-sectional studies, and longitudinal research that tests the model and the proposed moderating effects is scarce. Similarly, research that covers a whole change process from planning to consequences after completion is hardly to be found. In this sense the argument by Ployhart and Vandenberg (2010, p. 103) still applies, "the critical issue is to have enough measurements to appropriately model the hypothesized form of change."

3.4 Conclusion

Time is highly relevant for the conceptualization of change as it affects the "what" (e.g., Are we investigating the planning and anticipation of a change trajectory or its implementation?), the "how" (e.g., Are antecedents of change influencing the change process equally strong during the different stages of the change process?), and the "why" of change (e.g., How do change recipients interpret and make sense of change given the different information they have at different stages of a change process?). Some of these questions are addressed in step models of the change process, which offer advice for change initiators on how to facilitate successful change by following a certain sequence of change management activities. This suggests an underlying temporal conceptualization of a change process: Change evolves over time and requires different activities at different moments of time as the change process unfolds. The change curve is based on a similar assumption but assumes the perspective of the change recipient, by investigating typical reactions to change at different phases of the change process. We have combined these two approaches in an integrative process model of change and added moderators to the picture to allow for identifying and also understanding change recipients' reactions that deviate from the "classical" change curve. This theoretical model offers a useful framework for scholars and practitioners to show the inherently temporal nature of organizational change and its consequences. We hope that our framework helps to inspire empirical research and informs evaluation trajectories and participation and communication plans to explicitly incorporate the temporal dimension of organizational change.

REFERENCES

Amis, J., Slack, T., & Hinings, C. R. (2004). The pace, sequence, and linearity of radical change. *Academy of Management Journal, 47*(1), 15–39.

Ancona, D. G., Okhuysen, G. A., & Perlow, L. A. (2001). Taking time to integrate temporal research. *Academy of Management Review, 26*(4), 512–529.

Armenakis, A. A., Bernerth, J. B., Pitts, J. P., & Walker, H. J. (2007). Organizational change recipients' beliefs scale: Development of an assessment instrument. *Journal of Applied Behavioral Science, 43*(4), 481–505.

Armenakis, A. A., & Harris, S. G. (2002). Crafting a change message to create transformational readiness. *Journal of Organizational Change Management, 15*(2), 169–183.

(2009). Reflections: Our journey in organizational change research and practice. *Journal of Organizational Change Management, 9*(2), 127–142.

Armenakis, A. A., Harris, S. G., & Feild, H. S. (1999). Making change permanent: A model for institutionalizing change interventions. In W. A. Pasmore & R. W. Woodman (eds.), *Research in organizational change and development*, vol. 12 (pp. 97–128). New York: JAI Press.

Armenakis, A. A., Harris, S. G., & Mossholder, K. W. (1993). Creating readiness for large scale change. *Human Relations, 46*(6), 681–703.

Balogun, J., & Hope Hailey, V. (2004). *Exploring strategic change* (2nd ed.). London: Prentice-Hall.

Bartunek, J. M., & Woodman, R. W. (2015). Beyond Lewin: Toward a temporal approximation of organization development and change. *Annual Review of Organizational Psychology and Organizational Behavior, 2*, 157–182.

Battilana, J., & Casciaro, T. (2013). Overcoming resistance to organizational change: Strong ties and affective cooption. *Management Science, 59*(4), 819–836.

Begley, T. M., & Czajka, J. M. (1993). Panel analysis of the moderating effects of commitment on job satisfaction, intent to quit, and health following organizational change. *Journal of Applied Psychology, 78*(4), 552–556.

Belschak, F. D., Jacobs, G., Giessner, S. R., Horton, K. E., & Bayerl, P. S. (2020). When the going gets tough: Employee reactions to large-scale organizational change and the role of employee Machiavellianism. *Journal of Organizational Behavior, 41*(9), 830–850.

Bordia, P., Hobman, E., Jones, E., Gallois, C., & Callan, V. J. (2004). Uncertainty during organizational change: Types, consequences, and management strategies. *Journal of Business & Psychology, 18*(4), 507–532.

Bordia, P., Restubog, S. L. D., Jimmieson, N. L., & Irmer, B. E. (2011). Haunted by the past: Effects of poor change management history on employee attitudes and turnover. *Group & Organization Management, 36*(2), 191–222.

Buono, A. F., Bowditch, J. L., & Lewis, J. W. III (1985). When cultures collide: The anatomy of a merger. *Human Relations, 38*(5), 477–500.

Burke, C. S., Stagl, K. C., Salas, E., Pierce, L., & Kendall, D. (2006). Understanding team adaptation: A conceptual analysis and model. *Journal of Applied Psychology, 91*(6), 1189–1207.

Burnes, B. (2004). Kurt Lewin and the planned approach to change: A reappraisal. *Journal of Management Studies, 41*(6), 977–1002.

(2020). The origins of Lewin's Three-Step Model of Change. *Journal of Applied Behavioral Science, 56*(1), 32–59.

Chen, G., Ployhart, R. E., Cooper Thomas, H., Anderson, N., & Bliese, P. D. (2011). The power of momentum: A new model of dynamic relationships between job satisfaction change, and turnover intentions. *Academy of Management Journal, 54*(1), 159–181.

Chung, G. H., & Choi, J. N. (2018). Innovation implementation as a dynamic equilibrium: Emergent processes and divergent outcomes. *Group & Organization Management, 43*(6), 999–1036.

Cummings, S., Bridgman, T., & Brown, K. G. (2016). Unfreezing change as three steps: Rethinking Kurt Lewin's legacy for change management. *Human Relations, 69*(1), 33–60.

Devos, G., Buelens, M., & Bouckenooghe, D. (2007). Contribution of content, context, and process to understanding openness to organizational change: Two experimental simulation studies. *Journal of Social Psychology, 147*(6), 607–630.

Elrod, P. D., & Tippett, D. D. (1999). An empirical study of the relationship between team performance and team maturity. *Engineering Management Journal, 11*(1), 7–14.

(2002). The "death valley" of change. *Journal of Organizational Change Management, 15*(3), 273–291.

Fugate, M., Kinicki, A. J., & Scheck, C. L. (2002). Coping with an organizational merger of four stages. *Personnel Psychology, 55*(4), 905–928.

Fugate, M., Prussia, G. E., & Kinicki, A. J. (2012). Managing employee withdrawal during organizational change: The role of threat appraisal. *Journal of Management, 38*(3), 890–914.

George, J. M., & Jones, G. R. (2000). The role of time in theory and theory building. *Journal of Management, 26*(4), 657–684.

Giaever, F., & Smollan, R. K. (2015). Evolving emotional experiences following organizational change: A longitudinal qualitative study. *Qualitative Research in Organizations and Management, 10*(2), 105–123.

Gilovich, T., Kerr, M., & Medvec, V. H. (1993). Effect of temporal perspective on subjective confidence. *Journal of Personality and Social Psychology, 64*(4), 552–560.

Gordon, S. S., Stewart, W. H., Sweo, R., & Luker, W. A. (2000). Convergence versus strategic reorientation: The antecedents of fast-paced organizational change. *Journal of Management, 26*(5), 911–945.

Grant, A. M., Dutton, J. E., & Rosso, B. D. (2008). Giving commitment: Employee support programs and the prosocial sensemaking process. *Academy of Management Journal, 51*(5), 898–918.

Griffin, M. A., Neal, A., & Parker, S. K. (2007). A new model of work performance: Positive behavior in uncertain and interdependent contexts. *Academy of Management Journal, 50*(2), 327–347.

Heracleus, L., & Bartunek, J. (2021). Organization change failure, deep structure, and temporality: Appreciating Wonderland. *Human Relations, 74*(2), 208–233.

Herold, D. M., Fedor, D. B., & Caldwell, S. D. (2007). Beyond change management: A multilevel investigation of contextual and personal influences on employees' commitment to change. *Journal of Applied Psychology, 92*(4), 942–951.

Herscovitch, L., & Meyer, J. P. (2002). Commitment to organizational change: Extension of a three-component model. *Journal of Applied Psychology, 87*(3), 474–487.

Heyden, M. L. M., Fourné, S. P. L., Koene, B. A. S., Werkman, R., & Ansari, S. (2017). Rethinking 'top-down' and 'bottom-up' roles of top and middle managers in organizational change: Implications for employee support. *Journal of Management Studies, 54*(7), 961–985.

Horton, K. E., Bayerl, P. S., & Jacobs, G. (2014). Identity conflicts at work: An integrative framework. *Journal of Organizational Behavior, 35*(S1), S6–22.

Hughes, M. (2011). Do 70 per cent of all organizational change initiatives really fail? *Journal of Change Management, 11*(4), 451–464.

Isabella, L. A. (1990). Evolving interpretations as a change unfolds: How managers construe key organizational events. *Academy of Management Journal, 33* (1), 7–41.

Jacobs, G., Christe-Zeyse, J., Keegan, A., & Polos, L. (2008). Reactions to organizational identity threats in times of change: Illustrations from the German police. *Corporate Reputation Review, 11*(3), 245–261.

Jacobs, G., & Keegan, A. (2018). Ethical considerations and change recipients' reactions: 'It's not all about me'. *Journal of Business Ethics, 152*(1), 73–90.

Jacobs, G., Van Witteloostuijn, A., & Christe-Zeyse, J. (2013). A theoretical framework of organizational change. *Journal of Organizational Change Management, 26*(5), 772–792.

Jansen, K. J., Shipp, A. J., & Michael, J. H. (2016). Champions, converts, doubters, and defectors: The impact of shifting perceptions on momentum for change. *Personnel Psychology, 69*(3), 673–707.

Judge, T. A., Thoresen, C. J., Pucik, V., & Welbourne, T. M. (1999). Managerial coping with organizational change: A dispositional perspective. *Journal of Applied Psychology, 84*(1), 107–122.

Kalimo, R., Taris, T. W., & Schaufeli, W. B. (2003). The effects of past and anticipated future downsizing on survivor well-being: An equity perspective. *Journal of Occupational Health Psychology, 8*(2), 91–109.

Kaltiainen, J., Lipponen, J., Fugate, M., & Vakola, M. (2020). Spiraling work engagement and change appraisals: A three-wave longitudinal study during organizational change. *Journal of Occupational Health Psychology, 25*(4), 255–284.

Kao, R. H. (2017). The relationship between work characteristics and change-oriented organizational citizenship behavior: A multi-level study on transformational leadership and organizational climate in immigration workers. *Personnel Review, 46*(8), 1890–1914.

Katzenbach, J. R., & Smith, D. K. (1993). *The wisdom of teams*. Maidenhead: McGraw-Hill.

Kiefer, T. (2005). Antecedents and consequences of negative emotions in ongoing change. *Journal of Organizational Behavior, 26*(8), 875–897.

Kleingeld, A., van Mierlo, H., & Arends, L. (2011). The effect of goal-setting on group performance: A meta-analysis. *Journal of Applied Psychology, 96*(6), 1289–1304.

Konlechner, S., Latzke, M., Güttel, W. H., & Höfferer, E. (2019). Prospective sensemaking, frames and planned change: A comparison of change trajectories in two hospital units. *Human Relations, 72*(4), 706–732.

Kotter, J. P. (1995). Leading change: Why transformation efforts fail. *Harvard Business Review*, *73*, 59–67.

Kubler-Ross, E. (1969). *On death and dying.* New York: Touchstone.

Kunisch, S., Bartunek, J. M., Mueller, J., & Huy, Q. N. (2017). Time in strategic change research. *Academy of Management Annals*, *11*(2), 1005–1064.

Lewin, K. (1947a). Frontiers in group dynamics: Concept, method and reality in social science, equilibrium and social change. *Human Relations*, *1*(1), 5–41.

(1947b). Frontiers in group dynamics: II. Channels of group life; social planning and action research. *Human Relations*, *1*(2), 143–153.

(1947c). Group decision and social change. In T. M. Newcomb & E. L. Hartley (eds.), *Readings in social psychology* (pp. 330–344). New York: Henry Holt.

Lovallo, D., & Kahneman, D. (2003). Delusions of success. *Harvard Business Review*, *81*(7), 56–63.

McGrath, J. E. (1988). *The social psychology of time.* Newbury Park, CA: Sage.

Neuman, G. A., Edwards, J. E., & Raju, N. S. (1989). Organizational development interventions: A meta-analysis of their effects on satisfaction and other attitudes. *Personnel Psychology*, *42*(3), 461–489.

Oreg, S. (2003). Resistance to change: Developing an individual difference measure. *Journal of Applied Psychology*, *88*(4), 680–693.

Oreg, S., Bartunek, J. M., Lee, G., & Do, B. (2018). An affect-based model of recipients' responses to organizational change events. *Academy of Management Review*, *43*(1), 65–86.

Oreg, S., Vakola, M., & Armenakis, A. (2011). Change recipients' reactions to organizational change: A 60-year review of quantitative studies. *Journal of Applied Behavioral Science*, *47*(4), 461–524.

Petrou, P., Demerouti, E., & Schaufeli, W. B. (2018). Crafting the change: The role of employee job crafting behaviors for successful organizational change. *Journal of Management*, *44*(5), 1766–1792.

Pettigrew, A. M., Woodman, R. W., & Cameron, K. S. (2001). Studying organizational change and development: Challenges for future research. *Academy of Management Journal*, *44*(4), 697–713.

Piderit, S. K. (2000). Rethinking resistance and recognizing ambivalence: A multidimensional view of attitudes toward organizational change. *Academy of Management Review*, *25*(4), 783–794.

Ployhart, R. E., & Vandenberg, R. J. (2010). Longitudinal research: The theory, design, and analysis of change. *Journal of Management*, *36*(1), 94–120.

Rafferty, A. E., & Griffin, M. A. (2006). Perceptions of organizational change: A stress and coping perspective. *Journal of Applied Psychology*, *91*(5), 1154–1162.

Rafferty, A. E., & Jimmieson, N. L. (2017). Subjective perceptions of organizational change and employee resistance to change: Direct and mediated relationships with employee well-being. *British Journal of Management*, *28*(2), 248–264.

Rafferty, A. E., Jimmieson, N. L., & Armenakis, A. A. (2013). Change readiness: A multilevel review. *Journal of Management, 39*(1), 110–135.

Rafferty, A. E., & Restubog, S. L. D. (2010). The impact of change process and context on change reactions and turnover during a merger. *Journal of Management, 36*(5), 1309–1338.

(2017). Why do employees' perceptions of their organization's change history matter? The role of change appraisals. *Human Resource Management, 56*(3), 533–550.

Reay, T., Golden-Biddle, K., & Germann, K. (2006). Legitimizing a new role: Small wins and microprocesses of change. *Academy of Management Journal, 49*(5), 977–998.

Schneider, D. M., & Goldwasser, C. (1998). Be a model leader of change. *Management Review, 87*, 41–45.

Schweiger, D. M., & DeNisi, A. S. (1991). Communication with employees following a merger: A longitudinal field study. *Academy of Management Journal, 34*(1), 110–135.

Staw, B. M., Sandelands, L. E., & Dutton, J. E. (1981). Threat rigidity effects in organizational behavior: A multilevel analysis. *Administrative Science Quarterly, 26*(4), 501–524.

Stouten, J., Rousseau, D. M., & De Cremer, D. (2018). Successful organizational change: Integrating the management practice and scholarly literature. *Academy of Management Annals, 12*(2), 752–788.

Uhlaner, R., & West, A. (2011). McKinsey global survey results: Organizing for M&A. *McKinsey Quarterly*, December, 1–8.

Wanberg, C. R., & Banas, J. T. (2000). Predictors and outcomes of openness to changes in a reorganizing workplace. *Journal of Applied Psychology, 85*(1), 132–142.

Weick, K. E. (1988). Enacted sensemaking in crisis situations. *Journal of Management Studies, 25*(4), 305–317.

(1995). *Sensemaking in organizations*, vol. 3. Thousand Oaks, CA: Sage.

Whetten, D. A. (1989). What constitutes a theoretical contribution? *Academy of Management Review, 14*(4), 490–495.

Wiedner, R., Barrett, M., & Oborn, E. (2017). The emergence of change in unexpected places: Resourcing across organizational practices in strategic change. *Academy of Management Journal, 60*(3), 823–854.

Zimbardo, P., & Boyd, J. (1999). Putting time in perspective: A valid, reliable individual-differences metric. *Journal of Personality and Social Psychology, 77*(6), 1271–1288.

CHAPTER 4

Change Recipients' Emotions during Organizational Change
A Review and Directions for Future Research

Alannah E. Rafferty, Ashlea C. Troth, and Peter J. Jordan

The way in which [our company] treats its employees is an impudence ... This is no merger, it is a takeover [pause], and we feel like employees of second class ... It is *disappointment, resignation*, it is somehow a *disbelief* that they don't take us employees seriously, even though we have done such a good job in recent years.

(Kiefer, 2002b, p. 57; emphasis added)

I think at first we thought (the CEO) was crazy. I was *excited* and I felt *empowered*. I was *afraid* of anything new, and *afraid* of putting myself "out there" into new roles and responsibilities.

(Lawrence et al., 2014, p. 267; emphasis added)

Researchers have argued that change recipients' reactions to organizational change are critically important to the success of transformation efforts (Oreg et al., 2011; Rafferty et al., 2013). Change recipients refer to those individuals or groups who the organization must influence to initiate change (Zaltman & Duncan, 1977). The opening quotes vividly capture the complex beliefs and emotional responses that recipients commonly report when dealing with organizational changes (Kiefer, 2002b; Lawrence et al., 2014). To date, research has primarily focused on employees' cognitive beliefs and subsequent attitudes about change and has paid less attention to their emotional responses to change. Indeed, it is only in the last two decades that researchers have recognized that emotions are an important aspect of individuals' responses to change (Oreg et al., 2011, 2018; Rafferty & Minbashian, 2019). In this chapter, we focus on recipients' emotional responses to organizational change. Based on our review, we develop an integrative framework that can be used to organize thinking about recipients' emotional (and cognitive) reactions to change (see Figure 4.1).

We first clarify the concepts used when discussing emotions and then consider the theoretical frameworks of emotion that have been adopted in the change literature. The most common theoretical approaches used are

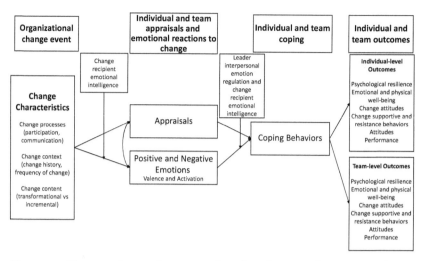

Figure 4.1   The antecedents and outcomes of employees' emotional responses to change

based on appraisal theories of emotions (Agote et al., 2016), such as the transactional model of stress and coping (Lazarus & Folkman, 1984). Other theoretical perspectives that have been adopted include affective events theory (AET; Weiss & Cropanzano, 1996) and Fredrickson's (2001) broaden and build theory of positive emotions. However, several dominant theories in the emotions field, including emotion regulation theories (Gross & John, 2003) and theories of emotional contagion (Kelly, 2001), have not received much attention when studying change. We suggest that these theoretical perspectives offer potential new directions for research on organizational change.

Empirically, a range of topics involving change recipients' emotions have been considered. We identify four key foci of empirical research on recipients' emotional responses to change, including efforts to (1) understand the structure of emotional responses to change, (2) develop process models of emotional responses to change, (3) consider the antecedents and outcomes of emotional responses to change, and (4) explore the impact of change recipient and leader emotional intelligence (EI) on change outcomes. Finally, we summarize existing knowledge and identify strengths and weaknesses of work in these areas.

4.1   Defining Affect, Moods, and Emotions

Prior to discussing the theoretical frameworks used to examine change recipients' emotional responses to change, we distinguish between the various concepts that have been used in the literature when considering emotions. *Affect* is an overarching term that has been used by scholars to encompass affective dispositions, moods, and emotions (Kelly, 2001). Affect is broadly and inclusively defined as a "subjective feeling state" (Ashforth & Humphrey, 1995). *Dispositional affect* consists of a person's affective predispostion toward perceiving the world around them positively or negatively (Lazarus, 1991). It is an individual difference variable that captures the characteristic way that basic emotions are experienced and expressed. In contrast, *moods* are low-intensity, diffuse feeling states that usually do not have a clear antecedent (Forgas, 1995) and can be caused by dispostional affect or emotions. *Emotions* are distinct from dispositional affect and moods in that they have a clear cause or target, are generally shorter in duration, and are more focused and intense (Frijda, 1993). Examples of discrete emotions include fear, anger, happiness, and sadness, while more complex or blended emotions can include feelings of enjoyment and pride or anxiety and excitement (Russell & Barrett, 1999). The terms "dispostional affect," "mood," and "emotion" may be seen to represent the broader notion of "affect" in this chapter.

4.2   Theoretical Focus of Research on Emotions during Change

Many studies in the change literature are based on appraisal theories of emotions, such as the transactional model of stress and coping (Lazarus & Folkman, 1984). Other theoretical perspectives that have been adopted include AET (Weiss & Cropanzano, 1996), the affect infusion model (AIM; Forgas, 1995), and Fredrickson's (2001) broaden and build theory of positive emotions. We describe these theories briefly in this section and identify empirical research that has adopted these perspectives. Later in the chapter, we consider several frameworks that have been less commonly adopted when considering emotional reactions to change, although these perspectives may offer new insights to increase our understanding of this phenomenon.

4.2.1   Appraisal Theories of Emotions

A variety of authors have used appraisal theories of emotions (Fugate et al., 2011; Agote et al., 2016) when considering change recipients' emotional responses to change. The predominant appraisal theory adopted is the transactional model of stress and coping (Lazarus & Folkman, 1984), which assumes that stress occurs because of a transaction between an individual and the environment (Dewe, 1991). Two critical processes mediate the person–environment relationship – cognitive appraisal and coping. The three appraisals identified in the transactional model (Lazarus & Folkman, 1984) – threat, harm, and challenge – have been identified as being followed by emotional responses (Lazarus, 1991). For example, challenge appraisals (i.e., an appraisal that change provides the potential for growth or development) are often followed by positive emotions such as eagerness, excitement, and exhilaration. Empirical tests of appraisal theories in a change context reveal a more complex set of relationships between appraisals, emotions, and coping than was outlined in the initial formulation of the transactional model. While empirical work by Fugate et al. (2008) suggests that emotions are an outcome of the appraisal and coping process rather than an antecedent, in a later study, Fugate et al. (2011) found a synchronous reciprocal relationship between negative appraisal and negative emotions. In summary, empirical tests of appraisal theories in a change context reveal a complex set of relationships between change recipients' appraisals, emotions, and coping during change. Studies suggest that change recipients' emotions may act as both an antecedent and outcome of appraisals and coping. In Figure 4.1, we acknowledge that cognitions and emotional reactions to change are likely to occur contemporaneously and influence each other.

4.2.2   Affective Events Theory (AET)

Another theoretical framework that has been used when considering emotions about change is AET (Weiss & Cropanzano, 1996). This theory proposes that a range of daily events at work (e.g., employee and customer interactions, job design changes) can be conceptualized as affective events that give rise to employees' emotional responses, which in turn influence their attitudinal and behavioral states. In the change field, researchers have used AET in a relatively limited fashion, with a focus on using this theory to argue that organizational changes are affectively charged events that influence outcomes. For example, Chen et al. (2013), in a series of three studies, drew on AET to identify change as an affective event. Based on these studies, Chen et al. concluded that greater leader charisma attribution during organizational change is associated with stronger follower positive emotions and weaker negative emotions about change. Seo et al. (2012) conducted a longitudinal study with an organization undergoing a major structural change. In a study of 906 employees who reported to 217 managers, employees' positive and negative affective experiences during the initial phase of organizational change were strongly related to their commitment to change and their behavioral support and resistance to change and creative behaviors. Managers' transformational leadership was also directly related to employees' positive affective reactions and negatively related to their negative affective reactions. In turn, these affective reactions predicted change commitment and then supportive, resistant, and creative change behaviors.

Paterson and Cary (2002) drew on AET to argue that characteristics of a change implementation process (i.e., communication quality and participation) predicted appraisals about the change that in turn predicted cognitive (justice) and affective (anxiety) responses to change. These responses, in turn, determined change outcomes including acceptance of change, morale, and employee turnover. These authors examined the impact of downsizing in an Australian public organization with a sample of seventy-one employees and found that positive appraisals reduced anxiety about the change directly and indirectly by increasing the perceived fairness of the outcomes (Paterson & Cary, 2002). Perceptions that the procedures were fair and low levels of anxiety, in turn, increased employees' acceptance of the downsizing. Low change anxiety was positively associated with employee morale.

In summary, research adopting an AET perspective has viewed change broadly as an affective event with little consideration of what aspects of the event make change affectively important (for an exception see Paterson and Carey, 2002). This downplays the potential of this theory as AET proposes that characteristics of the workplace environment influence the occurrence of certain affectively laden work events, which lead to specific emotions (affective reactions), which in turn shape work attitudes and behaviors (Weiss & Cropanzano, 1996). Paterson and Cary's focus on identifying characteristics of the implementation process as an important aspect of change that influences whether a change is affectively influential is a step in the right direction. However, it is likely that other aspects of the change, including aspects of the change context such as whether the change has been (un)successfully implemented in the organization in the past, that is the change history of the organization (Rafferty & Jimmieson, 2017), the order in which the key systems in the organization are transformed (Amis et al., 2004), and the content of the change in terms of the degree of transformation experienced by change recipients (Levy, 1986), are also likely to influence the extent to which a change is experienced as an affectively charged event.

In Figure 4.1, we identify the characteristics of the change process, characteristics of the change event itself, and the change context as important aspects of change likely to result in specific affectively laden work events or experiences, which in turn influence emotional responses and cognitive appraisals of change that subsequently influence coping behaviors and, ultimately, change outcomes. We suggest that researchers need to adopt a much more nuanced understanding of what it is about change events that make them affectively influential rather than being satisfied with broadly describing change events as "affective events."

Another criticism of the application of AET in the change field to date is that researchers have primarily adopted a between-persons perspective. However, it is important to note that AET is focused on *within-person* changes in emotions in response to a series of affect eliciting events (or experiences) of varying intensity. As such, there is an opportunity to explore the within-person changes in emotions that occur in response to organizational change events. Most large-scale organizational changes consist of multiple interlocking and interconnected change events. It would be especially interesting to consider the influence of such complex and interconnected change events on both within-person and between-person emotional responses to change.

4.2.3   Broaden and Build Theory

Another theoretical model that has been used to consider emotions during change is Fredrickson's (2001) broaden and build theory, which examines the way in which positive emotions play a role in generating broader ways of thinking and behaving. This theory suggests that multiple, discrete positive emotions are essential aspects of optimal human functioning and that experiencing joy, interest, contentment, and love yield multiple benefits including (a) broadening people's thought–action repertoires (Fredrickson & Branigan, 2005), (b) undoing negative emotions, (c) contributing to psychological resilience, and (d) triggering upward spirals toward enhanced emotional well-being (Fredrickson & Joiner, 2002). Some research in the change field has begun to address the role of positive emotions (Lin et al., 2016; Rafferty & Minbashian, 2019), although to date most attention has been on negative emotional responses to change (Kiefer, 2002a, 2002b). Recognizing the importance of positive emotions during change, Rafferty and Minbashian (2019) argued that the positive emotions experienced in relation to change predict change readiness and promote change supportive behaviors. These authors found support for these arguments and concluded that positive emotions during change directly and indirectly broaden individuals' thought–action repertoires during large-scale organizational changes.

Lin et al. (2016) conducted a study with 40 teams from multiple organizations in Taiwan, including 248 full-time employees and 40 team leaders. Surveys were collected at three time points. Using broaden and build theory as a theoretical basis, these authors identified leader member exchange quality as influencing employee positive affect, which in turn predicted employee psychological capital, and ultimately creative performance and taking charge behaviors during change. Overall, results provided support for a broadening pathway through which LMX promotes employees' psychological capital via positive affect as well as the building pathway through which positive affect drives employees' creative performance and taking charge via psychological capital.

In summary, the broaden and build theory has not been extensively considered in the change field. However, this approach has real potential for identifying how change agents and change recipients can utilize positive emotions to build more positive and proactive approaches to change. In Figure 4.1, we recognize the importance of considering the influence of both positive and negative emotional and cognitive responses to change on the outcomes outlined by broaden and build theory. We identify psychological resilience and well-being, which are outcomes of concern in this theoretical perspective, as well as more traditional outcomes, such as change attitudes and change supportive and resistance behaviors, as important indicators of change success.

4.3 An Overview of Empirical Research on Emotions during Organizational Change

A growing body of empirical work has considered the influence of emotions during organizational change. Reviewing this work, we identify four main areas of research interest. In this section, we discuss these four foci of research on recipients' emotions during organizational change.

4.3.1 The Structure of Emotional Reactions to Change

Early research on recipients' responses to organizational change was focused on the prevalence of negative reactions as captured in the construct of resistance to change (Coch & French, 1948). Today, authors have acknowledged that an individual's responses to change are more nuanced, with ambivalent (Piderit, 2000; Oreg & Sverdlik, 2011) and multifaceted affective, behavioral, and cognitive responses to change (Giæver, 2009;

Giæver & Hellesø, 2010) more likely to occur than simple uniformly negative reactions.

Recent research attention has addressed the theoretical and empirical structure of change recipients' emotional responses to change in a more nuanced way (Oreg et al., 2018; Rafferty & Minbashian, 2019). Research has revealed that employees experience a wide range of negative and positive emotional responses to change. For example, in a qualitative study of Norwegian nurses, Giæver (2009) reported that nurses reported a wide range of negative and positive emotions prior to and after change implementation. Giaever concluded that nurses' emotional responses to change are not only related to their past, present, and anticipated personal and work situation, but are also linked with wider societal beliefs such as those concerning technological progress.

Kirsch et al. (2010) analyzed a database incorporating the responses of over 250,000 individuals from more than 200 organizations experiencing change. These authors reported that change recipients' emotions were primarily differentiated as either positive or negative. Seven categories of emotional responses to change were identified, including passion (excited, creative, feeling good), drive (determined, decisive, humorous, proud), curiosity (curious), defiance (stubborn, impatient), anger (angry, cynical, blaming, struggling, avoiding, disapproving), distress (helpless, fearful, sad), and damage (humiliated, guilty, bored). Clearly, change generated many different emotional responses.

Building on a theoretical model of the antecedents of change readiness (Rafferty et al., 2013), Rafferty and Minbashian (2019) identified employees' positive emotional responses to change as one of two sets of proximal antecedents of employees' change readiness attitude. These authors identified two emotion families (Fredrickson, 2001) as capturing important aspects of individuals' positive emotional experiences during change – joy and interest. The joy emotion family captures high arousal positive emotions including happiness, exhilaration, and joy (Fredrickson, 2001). Frijda (1986) outlines that joy results in an action tendency called free activation, an "aimless, unasked-for readiness to engage in whatever interaction presents itself" (p. 89). The emotion "interest" includes intrigue, excitement, and wonder, and is closely associated with challenge and intrinsic motivation (Fredrickson, 1998). The action tendency associated with interest is a desire to investigate or become involved in or expand the self by incorporating new information or having new experiences with the person or object that stimulated the interest (Izard, 1991). Both these emotions have potential for advancing organizational change efforts.

Recently, Oreg et al. (2018) organized the valence (pleasant–unpleasant) and activation (i.e., passivity–activity) dimensions of change recipients' affective and behavioral responses into a model of responses to change. These authors focused on an *emotional episode* experienced in response to change, which was defined as involving a single event of affective significance that led to a series of subevents. These scholars demonstrated that an emotional episode includes: (1) a feeling component, which can be either positive or negative and activated or deactivated, (2) an appraisal component, and (3) action tendencies.

Overall, the extant research suggests that both negative and positive emotional responses to organizational change are common. However, employees often experience ambivalent or mixed beliefs and emotional responses to organizational change (Giæver, 2009; Giæver & Hellesø, 2010; Smollan, 2014) and these mixed responses to change are more likely to occur than simple uniform positive or negative reactions. Future research would benefit from continuing to focus on identifying the complex patterns of emotions, appraisals, and action tendencies that influence change recipients' attitudes and intentions and behavioral support or resistance to change.

4.3.2 *Process Models of Emotional Reactions to Change*

A range of different process models of individuals' emotional responses to change have been developed (George & Jones, 2001; Liu & Perrewe, 2005; Castillo et al., 2018). We do not seek to conduct a comprehensive review of these models, which outline distinct stages through which individuals' emotions progress over the course of change. Rather, we identify several models that adopt distinctly different approaches to highlight the range of approaches that have been adopted and tested empirically.

In a recent study, Castillo et al. (2018) explored negative organizational change events and applied the Kubler-Ross (1969) model of grieving as a starting point for understanding recipients' emotional responses to change. After interviewing change recipients, Castillo et al. reported that individuals move between denial and anger, bargaining, depression, and revising, but ultimately the change process concluded with individuals either leaving the organization or accepting the change.

George and Jones (2001) proposed that emotions play a central role in initiating the change process. These authors argue that when individuals experience a discrepancy with a pre-existing schema, this results in cognitive discomfort and produces a sense of dissonance. Individuals experience emotions in response to a discrepancy, which provides a signal that there is a problem or issue in need of their immediate attention. As such, emotions ensure that change recipients are in a state of preparedness to deal with any discrepancies and allow an individual to mobilize cognitive processing and behavioral responses. George and Jones argue that, when emotional reactions occur, and do not result in learned helplessness, the change process is initiated for the individual. At this point, George and Jones propose that employees seek to manage their emotional responses. When emotions have subsided into a less intense mood(s), substantive information processing occurs so that individuals can interpret the change (Forgas, 2000).

Drawing on the Affect Infusion Model (AIM) (Forgas, 1995), George and Jones (2001) outlined that individuals pay attention to the information available to them during the change process because the situation is uncertain. In these circumstances people are motivated to accurately assess and incorporate information to form judgments. Judgments made during substantive information processing are especially likely to be influenced by people's concurrent affective states or their moods (Forgas, 2000). Mood influences substantive information processing through affect priming, where people selectively attend to, encode, and retrieve information from memory, and make connections and judgments that are consistent with their current mood state. When the schema is activated in the future, the affect associated with it will also be activated, influencing perceptions, interpretations, and judgments guided by the schema.

Liu and Perrewe (2005) drew on Lazarus and Folkman's (1984) transactional model of stress and coping when developing their process model. Based on this model, they argue that the primary appraisal stage, where an individual assesses the extent to which an event is stressful (i.e., a challenge, threat, or harmful), results in emotions that are high in arousal, mixed in hedonic tones, and is anticipatory. In the secondary appraisal stage, individuals assess coping options and the likelihood of successful coping. Based on this appraisal process, people might decide not to cope or to engage in emotion regulation, for instance to reappraise the situation. Here, the mixed emotional experiences prevalent in the first stage of change give way to either positive or negative emotions. These emotional experiences then affect employees' coping behaviors in the third stage of the model. In the final stage of change, where the outcomes of planned change have become clear, discrete emotions that are evaluative and have distinct action tendencies are induced because of the change outcomes. Liu and Perrewe argue that the emotions of anger and shame are related to exit from the organization; frustration, happiness, and pride are related to voice; sadness is related to neglect; while happiness, pride, and guilt are related to loyalty.

It is interesting to compare these models of recipients' emotional responses to change with Isabella's (1990) cognitively focused process model of change. Based on interviews with change recipients, Isabella identified four distinct stages – anticipation, confirmation, culmination, and aftermath – through which recipients' interpretations of change progress. We suggest that a complete process model of change needs to consider both cognitive and emotional responses that individuals' experience in response to change. George and Jones' (2001) approach – with its focus on both recipients' emotions and cognitions – appears to recognize the complex interplay of emotions and cognitions that operate in organizational change settings and drive change attitudes and behavioral responses to change. In Figure 4.1, as outlined previously, we recognize the complex interplay of emotions and cognitive appraisals by recognizing that they occur contemporaneously and are likely to influence each other (Fugate et al., 2011).

4.3.3 Antecedents and Outcomes of Emotional Responses to Change

Researchers have considered several antecedents of change recipients' emotional responses to change including authentic leadership (Agote et al., 2016), trust in the leader (Agote et al., 2016), psychological capital (Avey et al., 2008), and poor managerial planning (Giæver & Hellesø, 2010). To date, there has not been a consistent theoretical perspective used to identify antecedents of recipients' emotional reactions to change. However, the focus of the extant literature appears to be on change process factors that facilitate positive responses to change such as leadership and planning (Giaever & Hellesø, 2010; Agote et al., 2016) and individual's resources in the form of personality characteristics (Avey et al., 2008).

Several studies (Bartunek et al., 2006; Giæver & Hellesø, 2010; Agote et al., 2016) have considered aspects of the change implementation process, which we identify in Figure 4.1 as one of three different characteristics of change that may influence employees' emotional and cognitive responses to change. Agote et al. conducted a cross-sectional survey of 102 Spanish HR managers and found that authentic leadership was directly positively associated with followers' trust in their leader and the experience of positive emotions during change. Trust mediated the relationship between authentic leadership and negative emotions. Giæver and Hellesø conducted interviews with nursing staff following the introduction of an electronic care planning system. A range of different negative emotional experiences were reported after the change implementation. Emotional reactions were linked to a lack of (poor) managerial planning prior to and during change implementation and a negative impact of change on the quality of professional work as reflected in a reduction in the capacity to provide high quality patient care.

Bartunek et al. (2006) identified employee affect (pleasantness and activation) as mediating relationships between two measures of participation in change and perceived losses and gains from change. These authors reported that employee affect was not impacted by participation. The degree of pleasantness had an impact only on the degree to which the change effort led to gains in professional development, whereas activation had no significant impacts on perceived gains. However, pleasantness and activation were the only variables that strongly showed unit-level effects. Unit-level pleasantness was positively associated with unit level professional development, which was identified as a gain from change.

In contrast, other research has considered employees' personal resources as antecedents of their emotional responses to change. For example, Avey et al. (2008) conducted a study of 132 adults from a wide range of US organizations experiencing change. The results of this study indicated that positive emotions fully mediated the relationship between psychological capital and engagement and citizenship deviance behaviors.

A range of outcomes of positive and negative emotional responses to change have been identified, including engagement and citizenship deviance behaviors (Avey et al., 2008), group-level perceived gains from change (Bartunek et al., 2006), quality of professional work (Giæver & Hellesø, 2010), change readiness   (Rafferty & Minbashian, 2019), and change cooperation and change championing behaviors (Rafferty & Minbashian, 2019). Examining the research around outcomes, we note that one favorable development has been a move to identify specific change-related outcomes such as change attitudes and change supportive behaviors as important dependent variables.

In summary, the literature reveals a broad focus on positive and negative emotions as mediators of relationships between characteristics of the change process and individuals' personality characteristics. Figure 4.1 reflects this thinking, although we identify a broader range of change characteristics than has been currently considered as antecedents of emotional and cognitive responses to change. Our review suggests that most researchers have focused on the valence of the emotions experienced during change (i.e., whether emotions are positive or negative) and, except for work by Bartunek et al. (2006), typically ignore the activation level of change recipients' emotions. We identify both elements of change recipients' emotional responses to change as important in Figure 4.1. In relation to the theoretical underpinning for this research, there has been little consistency in terms of the underlying factors identified as linking recipients' emotional responses to change with antecedents or outcomes. Turning to an assessment of the outcomes of emotional responses to change that have been examined in the literature, we note that there has been a growth in research focused on change-specific outcomes. We see this as a positive development as it will allow a clearer understanding of exactly how change recipients' emotional responses influence attitudes to change, intentions, and behaviors that support or undermine change efforts, and ultimately change success or failure. In turn, this will give both academics and practitioners a greater ability to understand the benefits and costs of focusing on (or ignoring) change recipients' emotional responses to change when seeking to transform organizations.

4.3.4 *The Role of Change Recipient and Change Leader EI during Change*

Mayer and Salovey (1997) define EI as consisting of four basic abilities: (1) the ability to perceive and to recognize emotions in both self and others; (2) the ability to incorporate emotional information in decision-making and thinking; (3) the ability to understand the effects of emotion in self and others; and (4) the ability to use and manage emotion in self and others. Significantly, they focus on EI as an ability, rather than a trait, and on this basis these abilities can be developed by change recipients. There is considerable evidence to show that an individual's level of EI is positively associated with their level of workplace well-being. Miao et al.'s (2017) meta-analysis showed that employees with higher EI have higher job satisfaction, organizational commitment, and lower turnover intentions. These authors concluded that EI improves job satisfaction by helping employees to reduce negative feelings, by increasing positive feelings, and/or improving job performance. We note that these are desired outcomes in any change process. The importance of change recipient EI is reflected in Figure 4.1 by identifying this concept as an individual resource that moderates the relationship between the characteristics of an organizational change and individuals' emotional and cognitive reactions to change. We also recognize that both leader EI and change recipient EI may moderate relationships between recipients' emotional and cognitive responses to change and coping behaviors.

Researchers have theoretically (Huy, 1999) and empirically (Neil et al., 2016) explored the role of EI during change. Jordan and Troth (2002) argued that EI is likely to be important during organizational change because individuals with high EI prefer to seek collaborative solutions when confronted with conflict. Later, Jordan (2005) argued that individuals who can manage and make sense of their own and other's emotions during organizational change are able to influence social relationship outcomes and positively contribute to the change process. Jordan also argued that high EI individuals will be under less stress during organizational change because of their awareness of their own emotions and their ability to control their emotions.

Several empirical studies have examined relationships between EI and change outcomes. Vakola et al. (2004) conducted a cross-sectional study of 137 professionals who completed self-report inventories assessing EI, personality traits, and attitudes toward change. Results revealed that the EI dimension of use of emotions for problem solving was positively associated with an attitude to change measure above and beyond the effect of personality. Ferres and Connell (2004) examined the relationship between leader EI and employee cynicism about change. Results of a cross-sectional study with Australian public servants revealed that three aspects of employee-rated leader EI – empathy, social skills, and motivation – were significantly negatively associated with employee cynicism.

Smollan and Parry (2011) conducted interviews with twenty-four employees from New Zealand organizations experiencing change. These authors reported that when followers perceived that their leaders genuinely responded to their emotions, they reported that they were provided with psychological support and, therefore, tended to adopt more positive attitudes toward the change. Conversely, lack of acknowledgment of their emotions often led change recipients to feel a sense of alienation that contributed to their decision to exit the organization. In addition, leaders perceived as failing to regulate their emotions by their followers were considered to have acted inappropriately. This resulted in negative consequences for the followers' well-being and negative attitudes to change. Finally, Smollan and Parry concluded that employees who reported their leaders as being unable or unwilling to deal with follower's emotions were also more likely to conceal their emotional responses to change.

Groves (2005) conducted a study of 108 leaders from 64 organizations and reported that visionary leaders who possess emotional expressivity skills generated a greater magnitude of organizational change than did leaders without these skills. That is, there was a strong positive relationship between visionary leadership and the magnitude of organizational change under conditions of high leader emotional expressivity. In contrast, conditions of low visionary leadership and high leader emotional expressivity inhibited the magnitude of change.

In earlier research, Huy (1999) argued that an individual's emotional intelligence is positively related to the individual's ability to change and adapt personally. Similarly, at the organizational level, an organization's emotional capability is argued to be positively related to its ability to change. The more emotionally capable an organization, the more successful will be its change efforts. At the organizational level, Huy (2005) defined emotional capability as "the organization's ability to acknowledge, recognize, monitor, discriminate, and attend to emotions at both the individual and the collective levels" (p. 303). This ability is built into the organization's habitual procedures for actions or their routines, which reflect the collective knowledge and skills demonstrated in local contexts to manage emotions related to change. Huy (2005) also introduced the concept of *emotional balancing* when discussing emotion management, which is a group-level process that involves engaging in emotion-related actions that are intended to drive change while also inducing a sense of continuity in a group. Emotional balancing requires developing emotional commitment to proposed changes and attending to employees' emotional responses to change.

In summary, the topic of EI during change has been introduced to advance our understanding of the change phenomenon. We reflect the importance of employee EI in Figure 4.1, by identifying EI as moderating relationships between change characteristics and individuals' and teams' emotional responses to change and individuals' and teams' appraisals of change. We also identify employee EI as a moderator of relationships between individuals' and teams' emotional responses and appraisals of change and individuals' and teams' coping behaviors in responses to change. Overall, we suggest that while a focus on EI has clearly contributed to highlighting the role of change recipients' emotions, broader theoretical perspectives that are more entrenched in the emotions literature could provide further insights into change recipients' responses to change. We discuss these perspectives in Section 4.4.

4.4 Future Research Directions

Consideration of the literature on emotions reveals several influential theoretical perspectives that have not been widely applied in the change field. We argue that attending to emotion regulation theories (Gross & John, 2003) and emotional contagion (Kelly, 2001) may expand our understanding of recipients' emotions during change. We discuss these theories and consider how they could be applied in a change context in this section, as they provide promising areas for future research.

4.4.1   Emotional Regulation Theories

An important focus of research in the literature on emotions at the within-persons and between-persons levels is how individuals manage or modify discrete emotional experiences and expressions to influence subsequent outcomes. Gross's (1998) emotion regulation process model describes "the process by which individuals influence which emotions they have, when they have them and how they experience and express these emotions" (p. 275). Events at work can potentially give rise to a full range of discrete emotions (e.g., happiness, sadness, anger) in line with AET. However, the exact nature of the discrete emotion experienced and expressed also partly depends on the use of different emotion regulation (ER) strategies (Lawrence & Callan, 2011) that ultimately impact coping and well-being.

According to Gross (1998), individuals regulate their emotions using antecedent-focused (prior to the full development of an emotional experi-ence) and response-focused strategies (after the discrete emotion has been experienced). In this regard, Gross identifies five broad emotion regulation categories. The first four comprise antecedent strategies: (1) situation selection, (2) situation modification, (3) attentional deployment, and (4) cognitive change. The fifth strategy is a response-focused response modu-lation strategy (e.g., expressive suppression) that occurs after a discrete emotion has been experienced and is intended to increase, to maintain, or to decrease one or more components of the discrete emotion (experiential or expression). Within Gross's process theory, the choice of strategy depends on an individual's emotion-related goals. The enactment of a strategy can occur consciously, unconsciously, in isolation, or as part of simultaneous regulation attempts (Gross, 1998; Lawrence et al., 2011).

Individuals who typically regulate their emotions through reappraisal report more positive affect, less negative affect, and greater psychological well-being than others (Gross & John, 2003). On the other hand, indi-viduals who typically use suppression report less positive affect, more negative affect, less social support, and more depression (Gross & John, 2003; John & Gross, 2007). It is also increasingly recognized that the outcomes of emotion regulation depend on the intensity and type of emotion being regulated and the context. For example, in terms of anger, there is evidence to suggest, while the use of reappraisal as a regulation strategy should improve employee outcomes, the use of anger expression could result in reciprocal anger and poor outcomes depending on the intensity and target of the anger (Geddes et al., 2020). Furthermore, in the face of excessive anger expressed by others, it might be judicious for an employee to engage in suppression of their emotion, at least in the short-term, even though this may not resolve the anger-inducing situation. Thus, both the discrete emotion and the type of strategy used to regulate a particular emotion in a context is closely linked to outcomes.

In the organizational change literature, the topic of emotional regulation has received little attention (van Dam, 2018). In her consideration of emotional regulation from a change perspective, van Dam addressed how relevant or appropriate the five broad emotion regulation categories are when individuals experience organizational change events. For example, van Dam concluded that, in a change context, situation selection (often inferring avoidance) is not often a viable strategy for emotion regulation when individuals are exposed to large-scale organizational changes. Large-scale changes typically mean that employees have few options to respond if they want to avoid the change, except withdrawing from the organization. When exploring employees' response regulation during organizational change, van Dam suggested that employees in change situations may try to downplay their emotional arousal or feelings through, for instance, relaxation, mindfulness, or other strategies. Overall, van Dam's analysis suggested some interesting possibilities as to the effectiveness or appropriateness of the five different emotional regulation strategies during organizational change.

Huy and Zott (2019) explored the emotional regulation behaviors of the founders of six firms over a period of seven years. After conducting multiple interviews with entrepreneurs and other stakeholders, Huy and Zott identified emotion regulation behaviors that differentiated between managers who displayed a high attention to emotional regulation compared to those who paid only modest attention to emotional regulation. These authors distinguished between emotional regulation behaviors of the self (ERS) and emotional regulation behaviors of others (ERO). ERS involves time-related emotional regulation behaviors such as refusing to look back at past high aims, getting over short-term issues by looking at the longer-term picture, and reappraising current performance by focusing on "what might be" in the future. The second aspect of ERS is reward-related emotional regulation behaviors, including considering downsides of being an employee versus a founder, focusing on emotional benefits of being a founder, not just financial considerations, and expecting more passion from business building than from being employed. In contrast, ERO incorporates three dimensions – maintaining an open dialog about opportunities (e.g., revealing performance to staff members to demonstrate transparency, creating strategic project teams with new employees to make them feel involved), controlling the display of emotions (e.g., displaying certainty-related emotions by behaving calmly under pressure, showing strong enthusiasm for the venture), and showing consideration and support (e.g., showing genuine interest in employees' personal problems, sending gifts, and personalized notes).

In conclusion, our review has revealed recent interest in emotional regulation in an organizational change context. van Dam's (2018) work raises questions about how emotion regulation processes evolve over time, the order in which emotion regulation strategies are used, and whether this order affects employee outcomes such as well-being or attitudes toward the change. Huy and Zott's (2019) work identifies specific emotional regulation behaviors of leaders that contribute to positive outcomes during change. Further investigations of change recipients' and change agent's emotional regulation strategies and processes seem to be an important area for future research to address. We reflect on the importance of leader emotion regulation in Figure 4.1. We include leader interpersonal emotion regulation as a moderator of relationships between individual and team coping behaviors and individual and team change outcomes. A focus on leader interpersonal emotion regulation offers possibilities for identifying new training opportunities to support leaders when managing individuals' and teams' emotional responses to change.

4.4.2   Emotional Contagion

Emotional contagion occurs when individuals "catch" or transfer emotions unconsciously and unintentionally to each other (Hatfield et al., 1993). Bartel and Saavedra (2000) suggest that emotional contagion occurs through behavioral mimicry and synchrony, which can lead individuals to become emotionally in tune with others in two ways. First, individuals tend to feel emotions consistent with the facial, postural, and vocal expressions they mimic. These expressions are generated unconsciously and promote emotional contagion in social settings. Second, a conscious self-perception process may also occur, such that people make inferences about their own emotional states based on their own expressive behavior.

When internal physiological cues about one's emotions and feelings are weak or ambiguous, an individual relies on behavioral cues to infer mood. This is highly relevant during change, as psychological uncertainty abounds in these contexts (Bordia et al., 2006).

Research has revealed that emotional contagion is important in work groups. For example, Kelly and Barsade (2001) show that emotional contagion is key to the dissemination of moods in work teams and in the formation of group affective tone (George, 1990). This latter construct has been defined as occurring when individuals in workgroups tend to experience highly similar levels of affect (excitement, frustration, etc.). In the change field, Rafferty et al. (2013) argued that several theoretical processes including emotional contagion are likely to contribute to the development of shared affective responses to change events (Bartel & Saavedra, 2000; Sanchez-Burks & Huy, 2009). Rafferty et al. argued that collective positive emotional responses to change are a direct proximal antecedent of collective change readiness. Building on this work, we suggest that emotional contagion processes are likely to be important during organizational change in influencing group level affect (Collins et al., 2013), which we expect are positively related to outcomes such as change supportive behaviors and negatively related to change resistance behaviors.

Research findings also reveal that shared positive moods in teams are positively related to team satisfaction (Kelly & Spoor, 2007), team goal commitment (Chi et al., 2011), and negatively related to group absenteeism (Mason & Griffin, 2003). We suggest that positive group affective tone helps team members build enduring social resources (e.g., cooperation, helping), psychological resources (e.g., optimism, resilience) and physical resources (e.g., more energy) by increasing supportive and encouraging communication during team interactions, which then in turn positively influence team and change outcomes. High levels of group positive affect build social, psychological, and physical resources during change, which in turn enhance change outcomes, including supportive behaviors and positive change attitudes.

Research also indicates that negative group affective states are more likely to be linked to team conflict, absenteeism (George, 1990), exhaustion, and sick days (Knight et al., 2018). We argue that, in a change context, groups that report high levels of shared negative affect will report poorer team support and more negative change outcomes. An examination of research does not reveal any studies of shared negative affect or emotions. DeCelles et al. (2013) examined a collective cynicism about change construct, which was defined as employees' pessimistic beliefs about organizational improvement. As such, collective cynicism focused on shared negative beliefs and did not incorporate negative emotional responses to change.

In summary, we suggest that emotional contagion is likely to be an important antecedent of shared positive and negative team/group affect during organizational change. There is a real need to consider whether and when a work group's shared positive and negative affect influence change outcomes. Theoretically, there is a strong case that emotional contagion is likely to occur during organizational change due to the heighted levels of uncertainty that characterize such events. However, researchers have not yet demonstrated this or explored the influence of shared group affect on team change outcomes and team change implementation success. Overall, research on emotional contagion may help us to develop a theoretical understanding of how to create positive collective emotional responses to change and minimize negative emotional responses to change. We see real potential for emotional contagion to enhance our understanding of a team's emotional responses to change and the subsequent impact on team-level outcomes. A focus on emotional contagion makes it clear that teams can develop shared or collective responses to change. We reflect this in Figure 4.1 by focusing on both individual- and team-level constructs in the model. For example, research suggests that team emotional responses to change can and do develop and influence individual and team coping behaviors, and individual and team change outcomes. However, it is also likely that team appraisals about change develop and influence individual and team coping behaviors and outcomes. This latter topic has yet to be explored though and offers exciting new possibilities for research in the change field.

4.5   Conclusion

Our review of research on recipients' emotional reactions to change reveals growing interest in this topic. Based on our review, we present an integrative theoretical framework in Figure 4.1, which we hope will guide thinking on the relationships of key theoretical frameworks and concepts that have been identified when considering employees' emotional responses to change. We first considered the major emotion theoretical perspectives that have been adopted in the change literature. The predominant approach adopted is appraisal theories of emotion such as Lazarus and Folkman's (1984) transactional model. Our review highlighted that studies using appraisal theories in a change context as an explanation reveal mixed findings as to whether change recipients' emotions during change are antecedents or consequences of appraisals. A second theoretical approach that has been examined is AET (Weiss & Cropanzano, 1996). We suggest that this approach has real potential for identifying what characteristics of change events influence change recipients' emotional responses to change. However, there is a need to identify more clearly which aspects of a change event make it affectively meaningful. There is also a need to consider *within-person* changes in emotions in response to a series of affect eliciting events. Finally, some researchers have considered Fredrickson's (2001) broaden and build theory of positive emotions. This theoretical perspective offers interesting possibilities regarding how to build change recipients' resources, which should be further explored.

Next, we considered empirical work on change recipients' responses to change. We identify four areas of research foci. One of the limitations of work in the area is that many researchers have not clearly outlined the theoretical framework(s) guiding their empirical research. We hope that our review encourages researchers to locate their research more clearly in the emotions literature and to explain how their research builds our understanding of change recipients' emotional responses to change. We concluded our review by identifying two emotion theoretical frameworks that have not been widely applied in the change field: emotional regulation and emotion contagion. In terms of emotional regulation, little work has been done. van Dam (2018) identified this as an important omission in the change field and outlined a range of directions for future research. Huy and Zott's (2019) work identifies specific emotional regulation behaviors of leaders that contribute to positive outcomes during change. Further investigations of change recipients' and change agent's emotional regulation strategies and processes seem to be an important area for future research to address. Finally, we identified emotional contagion as an important theoretical model that has not been widely considered in the change field. We hope that the integrative framework presented in this chapter can be used to better understand and further explore this interesting aspect of change.

REFERENCES

Agote, L., Aramburu, N., & Lines, R. (2016). Authentic leadership perception, trust in the leader, and followers' emotions in organizational change processes. *The Journal of Applied Behavioral Science*, 52(1), 35–63.

Amis, J., Slack, T., & Hinings, C. R. (2004). The pace, sequence, and linearity of radical change. *Academy of Management Journal, 47*(1), 15–39.

Ashforth, B. E., & Humphrey, R. H. (1995). Emotion int he workplace: A reappraisal. *Human Relations, 48*(2), 97–125.

Avey, J. B., Wernsing, T. S., & Luthans, F. (2008). Can positive employees help positive organizational change? Impact of psychological capital and emotions on relevant attitudes and behaviors. *Journal of Applied Behavioral Science, 44*, 48–68.

Bartel, C. A., & Saavedra, R. (2000). The collective construction of work group moods. *Administrative Science Quarterly, 45*(2), 197–231.

Bartunek, J. M., Rousseau, D. M., Rudolph, J. W., & DePalma, J. A. (2006). On the receiving end: Sensemaking, emotion, and assessments of an organizational change initiated by others. *The Journal of Applied Behavioral Science, 42*(2), 182–206.

Bordia, P., Jones, E., Gallois, C., Callan, V. J., & DiFonzo, N. (2006). Management are aliens! Rumors and stress during organizational change *Group and Organization Management, 31*(5), 601–621.

Castillo, C., Fernandez, V., & Sallan, J. M. (2018). The six emotional stages of organizational change. *Journal of Organizational Change Management, 31*(3), 468–493.

Chen, C. C., Belkin, L. Y., McNamee, R., & Kurtzberg, T. R. (2013). Charisma attribution during organizational change: The importance of followers' emotions and concern for well-being. *Journal of Applied Social Psychology, 43*(6), 1136–1158.

Chi, N. W., Chung, Y. Y., & Tsai, W. C. (2011). How do happy leaders enhance team success? The mediating roles of transformational leadership, group affective tone, and team processes. *Journal of Applied Social Psychology, 41* (6), 1421–1454.

Coch, L., & French, J. R. P. (1948). Overcoming resistance to change. *Human Relations, 1*, 512–532.

Collins, A. L., Lawrence, S. A., Troth, A. C., & Jordan, P. J. (2013). Group affective tone: A review and future research directions. *Journal of Organizational Behavior, 34*(Supp 1), S43–S62.

van Dam, K. (2018). Feelings about change: The role of emotions and emotion regulation for employee adaptation to organizational change. In M. Vakola & P. Petrou (eds.), *Organizational change: Psychological effects and strategies for coping* (pp. 67–77). London: Routledge.

DeCelles, K. A., Tesluk, P. E., & Taxman, F. S. (2013). A field investigation of multilevel cynicism about change. *Organization Science, 24*(1), 154–171.

Dewe, P. J. (1991). Primary appraisal, secondary appraisal and coping: Their role in stressful work encounters. *Journal of Occupational Psychology, 64*, 331–351.

Ferres, N., & Connell, J. (2004). Emotional intelligence in leaders: An antidote for cynicism towards change? *Strategic Change, 13*(2), 61–71.

Forgas, J. (1995). Mood and judgment: The affect infusion model (AIM). *Psychological Bulletin*, *117*(1), 39–66.

(2000). Affect and information processing strategies: An interactive relationship. In J. P. Forgas (ed.), *Feeling and thinking: The role of affect in social cognition* (pp. 253–282). Cambridge: Cambridge University Press.

Fredrickson, B. L. (1998). What good are positive emotions? *Review of General Psychology*, *2*(3), 300–319.

(2001). The role of positive emotions in positive psychology. *American Psychologist*, *56*(3), 218–226.

Fredrickson, B. L., & Branigan, C. (2005). Positive emotions broaden the scope of attention and thought-action repertoires. *Cognition & Emotion*, *19*(3), 313–332.

Fredrickson, B. L., & Joiner, T. (2002). Positive emotions trigger upward spirals toward emotional well-being. *Psychological Science*, *13*(2), 172–175.

Frijda, N. H. (1986). *The emotions*. Cambridge: Cambridge University Press.

(1993). The place of appraisal in emotion. *Cognition & Emotion*, *7*(3–4), 357–387.

Fugate, M., Harrison, S., & Kinicki, A. J. (2011). Thoughts and feelings about organizational change: A field test of appraisal theory. *Journal of Leadership & Organizational Studies*, *18*, 421–437.

Fugate, M., Kinicki, A. J., & Prussia, G. E. (2008). Employee coping with organizational change: An examination of alternative theoretical perspectives. *Personnel Psychology*, *61*, 1–36.

Geddes, D., Callister, R. R., & Gibson, D. E. (2020). A message in the madness: Functions of workplace anger in organizational life. *Academy of Management Perspectives*, *34*(1), 28–47.

George, J. M. (1990). Personality, affect, and behavior in groups. *Journal of Applied Psychology*, *75*(2), 107–116.

George, J. M., & Jones, G. R. (2001). Towards a process model of individual change in organizations. *Human Relations*, *54*(4), 419–444.

Giæver, F. (2009). Looking forwards and back: Exploring anticipative versus retrospective emotional change-experiences. *Journal of Change Management*, *9*(4), 419–434.

Giæver, F., & Hellesø, R. (2010). Negative experiences of organizational change from an emotions perspective. *Nordic Psychology*, *62*(1), 37–52.

Gross, J. (1998). Antecedent- and response-focused emotion regulation: Divergent consequences for experience, expression, and physiology. *Journal of Personality and Social Psychology*, *74*(1), 224–237.

Gross, J., & John, O. P. (2003). Individual differences in two emotion regulation processes: Implications for affect, relationships, and well-being. *Journal of Personality and Social Psychology*, *85*(2), 348–362.

Groves, K. S. (2005). Linking leader skills, follower attitudes, and contextual variables via an integrated model of charismatic leadership. *Journal of Management*, *31*(2), 255–277.

Hatfield, E., Cacioppo, J. T., & Rapson, R. L. (1993). Emotional contagion. *Current Directions in Psychological Science*, 2(3), 96–99.

Huy, Q., & Zott, C. (2019). Exploring the affective underpinnings of dynamic managerial capabilities: How managers' emotion regulation behaviors mobilize resources for their firms. *Strategic Management Journal*, 40(1), 28–54.

Huy, Q. N. (1999). Emotional capability, emotional intelligence, and radical change. *Academy of Management Review*, 24(2), 325–345.

  (2005). Emotion management to facilitate strategic change and innovation: How emotional balancing and emotional capability work together. In C. Hartel, N. M. Ashkanasy, & W. Zerbe (eds.), *Emotions in organizational behavior* (pp. 295–316) New York: Psychology Press.

Isabella, L. A. (1990). Evolving interpretations as a change unfolds: How managers construe key organizational events. *Academy of Management Journal*, 33 (1), 7–41.

Izard, C. E. (1991). *The psychology of emotions*. New York: Springer Science & Business Media.

John, O. P., & Gross, J. (2007). Individual differences in emotion regulation. In J. J. Gross (ed.), *Handbook of emotion regulation* (pp. 351–372). New York: Guildford Press.

Jordan, P. (2005). Dealing with organizational change: Can emotional intelligence enhance organizational learning. *International Journal of Organizational Behaviour*, 8(1), 456–471.

Jordan, P. J., & Troth, A. C. (2002). Emotional intelligence and conflict resolution: Implications for human resource development. *Advances in Developing Human Resources*, 4(1), 62–79.

Kelly, J. R. (2001). Mood and emotion in groups. In M. A. Hogg & R. S. Tindale (eds.), *Blackwell handbook of social psychology: Group processes* (pp. 164–181). Oxford: Blackwell.

Kelly, J. R., & Barsade, S. G. (2001). Mood and emotions in small groups and work teams. *Organizational Behavior and Human Decision Processes*, 86(1), 99–130.

Kelly, J. R., & Spoor, J. R. (2007). Naïve theories about the effects of mood in groups: A preliminary investigation. *Group Processes & Intergroup Relations*, 10, 203–222.

Kiefer, T. (2002a). Managing emotions in the workplace. In N. M. Ashkanasy, W. J. Zerbe, & C. E. J. Hartel (eds.), *Managing emotions in the workplace* (pp. 45–69). New York: M. E. Sharpe.

  (2002b). Understanding the emotional experience of organizational change: Evidence from a merger. *Advances in Developing Human Resources*, 4, 39–61.

Kirsch, C., Parry, W., & Peake, C. (2010). The underlying structure of emotions during organizational change. In W. J. Zerbe, C. E. J. Hartel, & N. M. Ashkanasy (eds.), *Emotions and organizational dynamism. Research on emotions in organizations* (pp. 113–138). Bingley: Emerald.

Knight, A., Menges, J., & Bruch, H. (2018). Organizational affective tone: A meso perspective on the origins and effects of consistent affect in organizations. *Academy of Management Journal*, 61(1), 191–219.

Kubler-Ross, E. (1969). *On death and dying*. New York: Macmillan.

Lawrence, E., Ruppel, C. P., & Tworoger, L. C. (2014). The emotions and cognitions during organizational change: The importance of the emotional work for leaders. *Journal of Organizational Culture, Communications and Conflict, 18*(1), 257–273.

Lawrence, S. A., & Callan, V. J. (2011). The role of social support in coping during the anticipatory stage of organizational change: A test of an integrative model. *British Journal of Management, 22*(4), 567–585.

Lawrence, S. A., Troth, A. C., Jordan, P. J., & Collins, A. L. (2011). A review of emotion regulation and development of a framework for emotion regulation in the workplace. In P. L. Perrewe & D. C. Ganster (eds.), *Research in occupational stress and well-being* (Vol. 9, pp. 197–263). Bingley: Emerald.

Lazarus, R. S. (1991). Progress on a cognitive-motivational-relational theory of emotion. *American Psychologist, 46*(8), 819–834.

Lazarus, R. S., & Folkman, S. (1984). *Stress, appraisal, and coping*. New York: Springer.

Levy, A. (1986). Second-order planned change: Definition and conceptualization. *Organizational Dynamics, 15*, 5–20.

Lin, C.-C., Kao, Y.-T., Chen, Y.-L., & Lu, S.-C. (2016). Fostering change-oriented behaviors: A broaden-and-build model. *Journal of Business and Psychology, 31*(3), 399–414.

Liu, Y., & Perrewe, P. L. (2005). Another look at the role of emotions in organizational change: A process model. *Human Resource Management Review, 15*, 263–280.

Mason, C. M., & Griffin, M. A. (2003). Group absenteeism and positive affective tone: A longitudinal study. *Journal of Organizational Behavior, 24*, 667–687.

Mayer, J. D., & Salovey, P. (1997). What is emotional intelligence. In P. Salovey & D. J. Sluyter (eds.), *Emotional development and emotional intelligence: Educational implications* (Vol. 3, p. 31). New York: Basic Books.

Miao, C., Humphrey, R. H., & Qian, S. (2017). A meta-analysis of emotional intelligence and work attitudes. *Journal of Occupational and Organizational Psychology, 90*(2), 177–202.

Neil, R., Wagstaff, C. R., Weller, E., & Lewis, R. (2016). Leader behaviour, emotional intelligence, and team performance at a UK government executive agency during organizational change. *Journal of Change Management, 16*(2), 97–122.

Oreg, S., Bartunek, J. M., Lee, G., & Do, B. (2018). An affect-based model of recipients' responses to organizational change events. *Academy of Management Review, 43*(1), 65–86.

Oreg, S., & Sverdlik, N. (2011). Ambivalence toward imposed change: The conflict between dispositional resistance to change and the orientation toward the change agent. *Journal of Applied Psychology, 96*(2), 337–349.

Oreg, S., Vakola, M., & Armenakis, A. (2011). Change recipients' reactions to organizational change: A sixty-year review of quantitative studies. *Journal of Applied Behavioral Science, 47*(4), 461–524

Paterson, J. M., & Cary, J. (2002). Organizational justice, change anxiety, and acceptance of downsizing: Preliminary tests of an AET-based model. *Motivation and Emotion*, *26*(1), 83–103.

Piderit, S. K. (2000). Rethinking resistance and recognizing ambivalence: A multidimensional view of attitudes toward an organizational change. *Academy of Management Review*, *25*(4), 783–794.

Rafferty, A. E., & Jimmieson, N. L. (2017). Subjective perceptions of organizational change and employee resistance to change: Direct and mediated relationships with employee well-being. *British Journal of Management*, *28*, 248–264.

Rafferty, A. E., Jimmieson, N. L., & Armenakis, A. (2013). Change readiness: A multilevel review. *Journal of Management*, *39*(1), 110–135.

Rafferty, A. E., & Minbashian, A. (2019). Cognitive beliefs and positive emotions about change: Relationships with employee change readiness and change-supportive behaviors. *Human Relations*, *72*(10), 1623–1650.

Russell, J. A., & Barrett, L. F. (1999). Core affect, prototypical emotional episodes, and other things called emotion: Dissecting the elephant. *Journal of Personality and Social Psychology*, *76*(5), 805–819.

Sanchez-Burks, J., & Huy, Q. N. (2009). Emotional aperture and strategic change: The accurate recognition of collective emotions. *Organization Science*, *20*(1), 22–34.

Seo, M. G., Taylor, M. S., Hill, N. S., Zhang, X., Tesluk, P. E., & Lorinkova, N. M. (2012). The role of affect and leadership during organizational change. *Personnel Psychology*, *65*, 121–165.

Smollan, R. K. (2014). The emotional dimensions of metaphors of change. *Journal of Managerial Psychology*, *29*(7), 794–807.

Smollan, R. K., & Parry, K. (2011). Follower perceptions of the emotional intelligence of change leaders: A qualitative study. *Leadership*, *7*(4), 435–462.

Vakola, M., Tsaousis, I., & Nikolaou, I. (2004). The role of emotional intelligence and personality variables on attitudes toward organisational change. *Journal of Managerial Psychology*, *19*(2), 88–110.

Weiss, H. M., & Cropanzano, R. (1996). Affective events theory: A theoretical discussion of the structure, causes and consequences of affective experiences at work. *Research in Organizational Behavior*, *18*, 1–74.

Zaltman, G., & Duncan, R. (1977). *Strategies for planned change*. New York: Wiley.

PART III

Change in Context
Exploring Types and Contexts of Change

CHAPTER 5

Exploring Types of Organizational Change and Differential Effects on Employee Well-Being and Personal Development

Joris Van Ruysseveldt, Karen van Dam, Hans De Witte, and Irina Nikolova

5.1 Introduction

Organizational change can have negative as well as positive outcomes for change-recipients. Reviewing the literature on organizational change, Michel and Gonzáles-Morales (2013) conclude that organizational change can have a negative impact on mental and physical health, across organizational levels and positions; and that this health-damaging or energy-depleting impact is due not only to downsizing, but also to other types of change, such as mergers, reorganizations, and restructuring. In addition, there is mounting evidence that change also has positive effects on employees, for instance when employees experience challenges and learning opportunities (Fugate, 2013; Michel & Gonzáles-Morales, 2013; Oreg et al., 2013). In short, there is mixed evidence as to whether organizational change positively and/or negatively affects employee well-being and personal development (e.g., Nikolova et al., 2014; Kiefer et al., 2015; Solinger et al., 2021).

The impact of change on recipients might depend on the kind or type of organizational change (Kiefer et al., 2015; Solinger et al., 2021). For example, innovations in production processes can challenge employees, provide interesting learning opportunities, and thus promote their well-being and motivation (Skule, 2004; Cerasoli et al., 2018). In contrast, changes that involve the closing of departments and the lay-off of a large number of staff can have devastating consequences for health, well-being, trust, motivation, and organizational commitment (Michel & Gonzáles-Morales, 2013). However, while the past two decades have seen an increase in research into employee responses to organizational change, little attention has been paid to the role of the type of change. Often, changes, whether it is a merger or a technological innovation, are classified under the heading of organizational change, thus turning change into an unspecified container concept that includes all types of change. Yet, some studies clearly indicate that different types of change will affect the well-being and learning of the recipients of a change in different ways (e.g., Kiefer et al., 2015). This implies a shift away from researching the effects of *any kind of change* (Kiefer et al., 2015, p. 19) to approaches that investigate the impact on attitudes, emotions, behavior, and well-being of employees in the light of the specific type of ongoing change.

In this study, we elaborated on the idea that change can have different impacts on change recipients, and that these differences are associated with the nature, content, or specific objectives, that is, the type, of change. The main research question was whether and how employees' responses to change in their organization depend upon the type of organizational change and its core characteristics. Our goal was to identify different types of organizational change and investigate whether these organizational change types are differentially associated with employee well-being and personal development. To this end, we first extended and refined existing dichotomies of organizational change found in the literature, using and combining multiple dimensions, both quantitative (e.g., staff numbers) and qualitative (e.g., process innovation). The resulting six organizational change types were empirically tested with a large sample of employees who were undergoing different changes. In a next step, we investigated whether these organizational change types are differentially associated with positive (active learning as an indicator of personal development) and negative (emotional exhaustion as an indicator of employee well-being) outcomes. Through identification and differentiation of organizational change types, this study aims to provide a deeper and more balanced insight into the organizational change–employee outcomes relationship, and to contribute to the effectiveness of the management of organizational change processes.

5.1.1   Approaches in Studying the Organizational Change–Employee Reactions Relationship

Researchers use different approaches when studying the effects of organizational change on attitudes, emotions, behaviors, and well-being of change recipients. Some focus on general, context independent aspects of organizational change, such as the frequency of change (Rafferty & Griffin, 2006), the level of planning of change (planned versus emergent) (Rafferty & Griffin, 2006; Myers et al., 2012), or the extent of change and its impact on the individual's job (Fedor et al., 2006). For example, Rafferty and Griffin (2006) found that the frequency of change was negatively and indirectly related to employee well-being (job satisfaction and turnover intentions). This line of research provides interesting insights into the extent to which these characteristics are important precursors of employee outcomes. However, these change characteristics are investigated independent of the kind of organizational change or the content of the change objectives, for example, whether this change entails downsizing or the introduction of digitalized services.

Other approaches focus on "how" the change is implemented, and highlight the role of change process characteristics such as participation, communication, and leadership (Michel & Gonzáles-Morales, 2013), or change-related fairness, trust in management, and perceived organizational support (Fedor et al., 2006; Fugate, 2013). As Fedor et al. (2006, p. 4) state: "how organizations do what they do matters a great deal. This can sometimes be as or more important even than what is done." Not surprisingly, many researchers in the areas of organizational development and change management focused on the role of these change process characteristics (Fedor et al., 2006).

Both research on "general, transcending" change characteristics and change process characteristics have greatly increased our understanding of employee responses to change (Oreg et al., 2011). Yet, there is still a key question to be answered, relating to the impact of the *content* of ongoing changes on employee outcomes. Therefore, our study takes the type of ongoing change as an important setting for studying the consequences of organizational change for employee well-being and personal development. Our approach is oriented toward "what" changes instead of "how" this change is implemented. A focus on specific types of organizational change may complement our knowledge on the organizational change–employee reactions relationship based on existing research and may produce more variegated insights. We propose that a nuanced insight in change outcomes requires a contextualized approach, which assumes that the impact of organizational change on employee well-being depends on the type of ongoing organizational change. Consequently, employee outcomes have to be studied in relation to this specific change context.

While this study strictly focusses on types of change at the *organizational* level, it contributes to future research into employee change outcomes in yet another way. It has already been suggested that change at the organizational level affects work characteristics and subsequently attitudes, emotions, behaviors, and well-being of change recipients. For example, Fedor et al. (2006) propose a "cascading" mechanism, arguing that changes that have proximal impact, that is, those affecting job requirements or work group characteristics, entail a greater influence on organizational and change commitment than changes with a more distal impact. This cascading mechanism presumes that most organizational level changes affect work situations and work lives to some extent, and this lower level (work situations) impact of higher level changes (at the organizational level) subsequently explains employee outcomes such as change commitment and well-being (Fedor et al., 2006; Solinger et al., 2021). However, understanding experiences of the most proximal change situation and its impact on change recipients' reactions first requires an accurate understanding of the organization-level change context that nurtures these experiences. In this regard, our classification of organizational change types may contribute to this research effort, as it provides an approach for the systematic identification of organization-level changes.

5.1.2 *Exploration of Types of Organizational Change*

As a first step, we explored different types of change at the organizational level, that is, the change content, building on previous research that distinguished interesting dichotomies of organizational change. For instance, Kiefer et al. (2015) differentiated in their study between cutback-related and innovation-related change at the organizational level. Cutback-related change is described as "organizational change towards lower levels of resource consumption" (Kiefer et al., 2015, p. 1282), aimed at reducing expenditure, for example, downsizing, recruitment freezes, and mergers. In contrast, innovation-related change "refers to changes that focus on doing something new in the organization by generating or adopting new practices and services" (Kiefer et al., 2015, p. 1282), for example, new ways of working, organizing, or evaluating. Kiefer et al. (2015) identify these two kinds of organizational change in the context of different public sector responses to a national announcement of budget reductions in the United Kingdom, which also explains why they distinguished these two (and not others). Differentiation of both kinds of organizational change enabled them to investigate the differential impact on employee well-being. Cutback-related organizational change showed predominantly negative effects (negative emotional well-being), while innovation-related organizational change was associated with positive outcomes (job satisfaction, engagement), and also with less negative outcomes.

Investigating the role of job crafting in the context of organizational change, Petrou et al. (2017) applied a similar dichotomy, distinguishing regular change and cutback-related change. Regular organizational change refers to the change an organization implements in order to improve organizational functioning, whereas cutback-related organizational change is implemented "to cope with the financial recession and concerns resource reservation or restraints in the organization" (Petrou et al., 2017, p. 63). In their meta-analysis, Solinger et al. (2021) distinguish between cost-oriented change (with an emphasis on cost cutting and improvements of operational efficiency, e.g., downsizing and restructuring) and people-oriented change (a form of strategic renewal oriented toward targeted investments in people, e.g., introduction of high-performance HR systems and practices). They found cost-oriented changes to be associated with sustained reductions in job attitudes, and people-oriented changes with sustained increases in job attitudes (e.g., job satisfaction).

These classifications of different types of change show considerable similarities, but also share some shortcomings, especially because of their somehow limited focus. They all refer to the change content or its main orientation and objectives. Moreover, all three distinguish between change oriented toward cost reduction and change which is more oriented toward investments, innovation, or some kind of (organizational) renewal. However, they lack clarity, because the same kind of change can be targeted at both cost reduction and renewal, for example, technological innovations can be used to cut staff levels, and hence costs reductions, but also in the light of organizational renewal and expansion. Finally, they limit themselves to cost reductions in the context of decline and organizational survival but surpass growth and expansion as an important type of organizational change.

For these reasons, we developed our types of organizational change using two important and not mutually exclusive dimensions. This enabled us to disentangle important aspects of ongoing change and then recombine them to identify relevant types of organizational change. In principle, organizations can adapt – whether reactively or proactively – to environmental developments, threats, challenges, or opportunities by changing qualitative (e.g., ways of working) and/or quantitative (e.g., staff numbers) aspects of the organization. Hence, in building our types of organizational change, we distinguished and combined these two dimensions (see Table 5.1):

- a "qualitative" axis representing the prevalence of process and/or product innovation within the organization (low versus high); and
- a "quantitative" axis that distinguishes between growth and decline (plus low versus high restructuring).

Table 5.1 *Framework for the identification of organizational change types*

Qualitative change dimension	Quantitative change dimension		
		Decline	
	Growth	No restructuring	With restructuring
Low innovation	Type 1	Type 2	Type 3
High innovation	Type 4	Type 5	Type 6

The qualitative axis of Table 5.1 refers to organizational change efforts targeted at improvement and optimization of organizational performance through innovation-oriented policies and practices. These include techno-logical innovations in production processes (e.g., robotics), service development and delivery (e.g., banking apps), and the innovation of products and services (e.g., electric cars). Kiefer et al.'s (2015) innovation-related change can be situated on this qualitative axis. Organizations can be low or high in investments in innovative efforts.

The quantitative axis of Table 5.1 distinguishes between growth and decline. Indeed, quantitative organizational change does not only entail decline, failure, and setbacks, resulting in collective lay-offs, downsizing, or reorganizations (e.g., merging departments), as previous approaches (Kiefer et al., 2015; Petrou et al., 2017; Solinger et al., 2021) have emphasized. Growth and expansion are also part of organizational life and organizational success may result in quantitative changes such as increasing staff and other resources or expanding production volumes. Hence, the opposites on the quantitative axis should be growth versus decline. Within a situation of decline, we additionally differentiate between cases where decline is a result of or is accompanied by restructuring. Quantitative downward adjustments of organizations may result from purely volume-driven decisions such as lay-offs without accompanying restructuring efforts, or these quantitative changes may be the result of restructuring efforts such as the closing or merging of departments. Distinguishing between a decline scenario with or without restructuring events may be important to gain a better understanding of the change outcomes for change recipients. For example, in a decline situation without restructuring a survivors' syndrome may become apparent, but these survivors are not faced with further changes in the organizational structure; in a decline situation with restructuring events, survivors must also cope with ongoing organizational change which may additionally impact their well-being.

In a next step, both axes are combined because qualitative and quantitative change can occur simultaneously. Organizations may respond to environmental developments by introducing both qualitative and quantitative kinds of organizational change. For instance, growth (increasing staff and production volumes) may be accompanied by innovation of products, or not. As Kiefer et al. (2015, p. 1280) note "cutback- and innovation-related changes are not mutually exclusive." Organizational change is often a complex process in which different aspects of organizational realities are affected. By combining the qualitative and quantitative axis, we can obtain a better, more refined, and multifaceted image of organizational change, identifying and distinguishing not only "pure" (e.g., only decline through cost reductions, but *without* innovation), but also "mixed" types of organizational change (e.g., decline *with* innovation). Table 5.1 represents both axes and their combinations and, within this classification, six organizational change types emerge.

Our classification puts an emphasis on qualitative and quantitative aspects of organizational change. Organizational change may imply renewal and innovation (in the quest for better performance, higher adaptive capacities, engagement in market competition, or assimilation to technological and scientific developments), and/or may represent cyclical trends such as decline or growth and expansion. It is multidimensional in the sense that the two dimensions – quantitative and qualitative – are combined in order to identify relevant "mixed" types of organizational change. It supports a contextualized approach: it enables the investigation of the impact of organizational change on employee well-being and personal development in relation to the specific change context, that is, the content of ongoing organizational change.

5.1.3   Exploring the Differential Well-Being Outcomes Associated with the Types of Change at the Organizational Level

But how are our organizational change types related to different employee outcomes? With respect to negative outcomes of change, we investigated the association between the organizational change types and employees' emotional exhaustion, an indicator of employee well-being. Emotional exhaustion is a concept derived from theories about stress and burnout, and refers to feelings of being overextended and exhausted by the job demands of one's work (Schaufeli et al., 1996). With respect to positive outcomes of change, we focus on the association between the organizational change types and employees' active learning at work (indicating personal development), which can be defined as the extent to which employees acquire new or deepen existing knowledge, skills and competences (Nikolova et al., 2013). In general, we assumed that organizational change types characterized by decline and restructuring without innovation are associated with higher levels of emotional exhaustion, while organizational change types characterized by innovation and/or growth will stimulate active learning.

These assumptions are largely based on theoretical propositions drawn from the Job Demands-Resources (JD-R) model (Demerouti et al., 2001) and the challenge-hindrance framework (Cavanaugh et al., 2000; LePine et al., 2004). In the JD-R model, demanding work situations (characterized by stressful circumstances such as high work load, cognitive and emotional demands) install an energy-depletion process: prolonged exposure to high job demands may result in higher risk of burn-out (e.g., emotional exhaustion) (Bakker & Demerouti, 2007). Meanwhile, resourceful work situations (characterized by supportive and motivating circumstances such as autonomy, social support, and learning opportunities) stimulate a motivational process which results in higher work engagement (Bakker & Demerouti, 2007) and more active learning in the workplace (Van Ruysseveldt et al., 2011). Building on these two processes, ongoing change may be considered to act as an energy-demanding stressor that increases emotional exhaustion among change recipients. But ongoing change may also – under favorable conditions – positively contribute to resource development and subsequently advance active learning in the workplace. Moreover, not all demands are "created" equal (Van den Broeck et al., 2010), meaning that the consequences of demanding work characteristics depend on their appraisal as either challenging or hindering; both challenging and hindering demands require energy investment from employees but only challenging demands advance work engagement and active learning (Cavanaugh et al., 2000; LePine et al., 2004).

Moreover, even organizational level changes with favorable outcomes for change recipients, for example, jobs with more challenging tasks and more learning opportunities, instigate adaptation mechanisms such as a need to restore a misfit between demands and abilities (Dawis, 2005). These mechanisms entail adaptation requirements and subsequently put pressure on employees as they need to invest energy and resources in adaptive efforts (Hobfoll & Freedy, 2017) and cope with uncertainty, unpredictability, fear of failure, and loss of control (Fedor et al., 2006). Consequently, in all organizational change types, even those with high challenging and at first sight appealing change characteristics, change recipients may experience emotional exhaustion as a consequence of demanding adaptation efforts.

Building on these theoretical perspectives, we expect that organizational change types characterized by decline are associated with higher levels of emotional exhaustion because this change context implies cutting costs through staff and resources reductions and hence higher (hindering) job demands such as increasing workload. If this decline is accompanied by restructuring events (e.g., merger of departments), the extra adaptation efforts required of change recipients contribute to even higher levels of energy depletion and emotional exhaustion. Previous research provides some clues for these expectations. Kiefer et al. (2015) found cutback-related change to increase negative well-being and decrease positive well-being. Solinger et al. (2021) concluded that cost-oriented changes negatively impacted job attitudes, while mergers, acquisitions, and restructuring had a sustained negative impact on job attitudes.

With respect to positive change outcomes for change recipients, we expect innovation-driven organizational change types to be characterized by higher challenging demands and resource development. Employees are introduced to new ways of working, new technologies, products, and services, and this may add to higher motivating cognitive job demands and learning opportunities. These organizational change types require energy in order to engage in adaptive efforts (e.g., development of new skills) but also entail a high motivational potential to actively participate in work-related learning processes. Conversely, the organizational change types which are low in innovation will entail less challenging and resourceful properties and will be associated with less active learning. In line with these expectations, Kiefer et al. (2015) found innovation-related change to increase positive well-being, job satisfaction, and work engagement. Solinger et al. (2021) concluded that people-oriented changes positively impacted job attitudes, while technological changes and learning and growth-related changes had a sustained positive impact on job attitudes. Nikolova et al. (2019) found qualitative organizational change (e.g., new ways of working) to be associated with increased workplace learning.

As a consequence, the organizational change type that combines innovation and growth may be the most beneficial type for employees (lower emotional exhaustion and higher active learning). The organizational change type that combines decline, restructuring, and innovation represents a highly demanding change context, requiring substantial adaptive efforts from change recipients and, therefore, can be considered the most detrimental type for employees (higher emotional exhaustion and lower active learning).

In sum, we developed two hypotheses on direct relationships between organizational change type and employee outcomes:

Hypothesis 1: Organizational change types with more negative quantitative aspects (i.e., decline, restructuring) will be negatively related to negative employee reactions (emotional exhaustion).

Hypothesis 2: Organizational change types with more qualitative aspects (i.e., innovations) will be positively related to positive employee reactions (active learning).

Finally, we developed two hypotheses on combinations between organizational change type dimensions (mixed organizational change types).

Hypothesis 3: Organizational change types combining negative quantitative aspects (decline, restructuring) with qualitative aspects (i.e., innovations) are highest on negative employee reactions (emotional exhaustion). We expect to find the highest levels of emotional exhaustion in the type "Innovative restructuring," which combines decline, restructuring, and innovation.

Hypothesis 4: Organizational change types combining positive quantitative aspects (growth, expansion) with qualitative aspects (e.g., innovations) are highest on positive employee reactions (active learning). We expect to find the highest levels of active learning in the types "Thriving" and "Innovative expansion," which combine growth and innovation.

5.2 Method

5.2.1 Data Collection and Respondents

To identify organizational change types, a representative sample of private sector employees (both industrial sectors and private services) from a longitudinal survey was used. Data were collected by a professional ISO (International Organization for Standardization) certified market research company conducting internet research in the Netherlands (the company is registered under the Dutch Data Protection Authority (CBP) in The Hague). The total sample of Dutch private sector employees (both industrial sectors and private services) had been stratified by gender, age, and education. A comparison was conducted between the group obtained in our study and data on the total working Dutch population in the private sector (gender, age, education, and location) provided by the Central

Office for Statistics of the Netherlands, showing that our sample was representative. Approximately 2,500 employees in the age group between 18 and 64 years were invited via the internet to take part in this study. The survey was sent in the last week of March 2012 and was available to the respondents for one week. After three days, a reminder was sent in order to ensure an optimal response. The respondents completed the survey voluntarily and could discontinue their participation at any point during data collection; they were informed that the data would be used for research purposes only, that the collected data would be handled confidentially, and no identifying personal information (e.g., names or contact information) would be made available to the researchers or other parties. In total, 1,010 respondents completed the first questionnaire

At T1, respondents were asked whether their organization was characterized by (any) organizational change. The respondents who completed the questionnaire at T1 were invited to take part in the second data collection, which took place six months later (T2). At the beginning of October 2012, a total of 787 respondents completed the questionnaire at T2 (78 percent response rate). Similar to the procedure followed during the first data collection, a reminder was sent three days after the initial invitation. Each participant was assigned a unique survey number (code), which was used during the two points of data collection. Each participant's responses were matched over time using this code.

At T2, respondents who indicated that organizational change was present in their organization (n = 511) were asked to describe the kind of changes that took place in this six-month reference period: changes in staff numbers, the occurrence of restructuring events (e.g., fusion of departments), expansion in production capacity, introduction of new products, the level of process innovation (i.e., changes in production technology, work procedures, working methods, . . .). This sample was used to perform cluster analysis. Respondents at T2 who again indicated that organizational change was absent, were included in the sample as a control group (n = 276). The total sample of 787 respondents was used to validate the identification of clusters, by comparing data on the selected organizational change characteristics between those who didn't experience change and those who did experience the specific kind of change characteristic of each cluster/type. This sample (N = 787) was also used to test Hypotheses 1–4. At T2, respondents' age ranged between 18 and 64 years (M = 43.0 years; SD = 10.5 years). Educational level ranged from lower educational training (20 percent), to mid-level educational training (49 percent) and higher educational training (31 percent); 63 percent were male.

5.2.2   Measures

To empirically identify organizational change types through a cluster analysis, we asked respondents for information about five organization-level change characteristics. Change in staff numbers and expansion in production capacity indicated quantitative change aspects (decline versus growth), whereas introduction of new products and process innovation (i.e., changes in production technology, work procedures, working methods, ...) represented qualitative organizational change. The number of restructuring events indicated the experience of ongoing organizational restructuring.

Change in staff level was measured as the extent to which the number of employees increased or decreased during the past six months. A seven-point response scale was used, ranging from 1 (*very strongly increased*) to 7 (*very strongly decreased*).

Expansion of production capacity was measured with one question: "Did, during the last six months, your organization expand production capacity?", which could be answered with 0 (*no*) or 1 (*yes*).

The *occurrence of restructuring events* was measured as the number of restructuring events that were experienced. Each respondent could indicate whether or not – 0 (no) or 1 (yes) – he/she experienced a number of change events, such as downsizing, internal fusion of departments, closure of departments.

The *introduction of new products or services* was measured with one question: "Did your organization, during the last six months, introduce new products or services?" which could be answered with 0 (*none*), 1 (*yes, but only one*), or 2 (*yes, more than one*).

The extent of *process innovation* was measured with four items based on existing scales on work changes and innovation (Jiménez-Jiménez & Sanz-Valle, 2011; Petrou et al., 2012; Nikolova et al., 2014; Kiefer et al., 2015). Each item indicated the extent to which a specific process innovation was experienced and was preceded by the phrase "In my department, during the past six months, changes occurred regarding ..." Sample items were "... the work methods for producing goods or delivering services." and "... technology such as ICT, automation, digitization." A 5-point response scale was used ranging from 1 (= to a very small degree) to 5 (= to a very large degree). Cronbach's α was .81.

Change type. In order to test Hypotheses 1–4, and based on the results of the cluster analysis, we constructed a new nominal variable "change type." This independent variable reflected whether change occurred and what kind of change occurred based on our classification of organizational change types: 0 (no change), 1 (expansion), 2 (shrinkage), 3 (lean restructuring), 4 (thriving), 5 (innovative restructuring), and 6 (innovative expansion).

We used validated measurement scales for the dependent variables: emotional exhaustion, and newly acquired KSAOs.

Emotional exhaustion was measured with the five-item scale of a Dutch version of the Maslach Burnout Inventory (Schaufeli et al., 1996). A sample item is "I feel mentally exhausted from my work." The response scale ranged from 1 (never) to 6 (always). Cronbach's alpha was .94.

Active learning was assessed with Nikolova et al.'s (2013, 2014) four-item scale that probed into newly-acquired KSAOs. The expression "in the past six months" was used as an introduction to the questions of this scale in order to ensure that participants' responses referred to the period in which changes under investigation took place. A sample item is "In the past six months, I have obtained new competences, which help me to function better at my work." The response scale ranged from 1 (strongly disagree) to 5 (strongly agree). Cronbach's alpha was .96.

5.2.3   Analysis

The statistical software program SPSS was used to perform non-hierarchical cluster analysis applying K-means clustering (Kent, 2015). Five variables were used, each representing an organizational change characteristic reflecting the quantitative or qualitative change dimensions from our classification framework: changes in staff numbers, the occurrence of restructuring events, expansion of production capacity, introduction of new products, and process innovation. All variables were standardized.

To test Hypotheses 1–4, we conducted a one-way between-groups analysis of covariance (ANCOVA), using SPSS, and controlling for age (in years), gender (0 = male; 1 = female) and educational level (ranging from 1 = no or primary education to 7 = university). These demographic variables were included as control variables, since they could potentially influence both emotional exhaustion (e.g., Maslach et al., 2001), and active learning (e.g., Nikolova et al., 2016).

5.3   Results

The results of the cluster analysis are shown in Table 5.2.

K-means cluster analysis largely confirmed our expectations, as we found six clusters representing five of the types we identified within our

Table 5.2 *Cluster analysis: six clusters representing types of organizational change*

Qualitative change dimension	Quantitative change dimension		
		Decline	
	Growth	No restructuring	With restructuring
Low innovation	C1: EXPANSION	C2: SHRINKAGE	C3: LEAN RESTRUCTURING
High innovation	C4: THRIVING C5: INNOVATIVE EXPANSION		C6: INNOVATIVE RESTRUCTURING

classification framework (see Table 5.1). One cell in our framework was not represented by a cluster, that is, the mixed type representing decline without restructuring on the quantitative axis and high innovation on the qualitative axis. Instead, two clusters fell within one cell in our framework; both clusters represented growth in combination with innovation, but in cluster/type 4 innovations involved *products/services* whereas in cluster/type 6 innovations related to *production processes*.

In total, 35 percent of the respondents experienced no change in their organization during the past six months; 65 percent experienced a specific kind of organizational change or combinations thereof. We labeled and qualified the six clusters as follows:

1. "Expansion" (cluster/type 1): this type of organizational change is characterized by growing staff numbers in combination with production capacity expansion. This type reflects (quantitative) growth without innovation; 20 percent of respondents belonged to this cluster. This type appears to include organizations that are successful and are expanding in terms of staff numbers, but this success is not due to or associated with innovation efforts.

2. "Shrinkage" (cluster/type 2): one clear-cut characteristic dominated this type of change, that is, decreasing staff numbers. This type reflected (quantitative) decline without innovation and included 10 percent of respondents. This type appears to include organizations that are no longer successful and innovative, and that need to cut resources such as staff in order to survive.

3. "Lean restructuring" (cluster/type 3): this type of change embraced decreasing staff numbers associated with organizational restructuring. It resembled the "Shrinkage" type 2, because it reflected decline but this was accompanied by restructuring events (without innovations); 8 percent of respondents belonged to this cluster. This type appears to include struggling organizations that try to become successful again through cutting costs and restructuring.

4. "Thriving" (cluster/type 4): this type is characterized by growing staff numbers in combination with increases in production capacity (such as type 1 "Expansion") but also by product innovation; it included 14 percent of respondents. This type appears to include flourishing organizations that are able to expand both quantitatively (staff, production capacity), and qualitatively through launching new products.

5. "Innovative restructuring" (cluster/type 5): this type of change is characterized by staff reductions in combination with restructuring and process innovation; it combines decline and restructuring with innovating production processes. Only 3 percent of respondents belonged to this cluster. Even more than type 3 (lean restructuring) this type appears to include organizations that strive for their survival, through staff reductions in combination with restructuring, but also through efforts to innovate their production processes.

6. "Innovative expansion" (cluster/type 6): this type is characterized by growing staff numbers and capacity expansion in combination with process innovation; 11 percent of respondents belonged to this cluster. In contrast to type 5 (Innovative restructuring), process innovation is implemented in the context of growth, and this growth may also be a result of innovation efforts.

Table 5.3 represents average scores on the five organizational change characteristics per cluster and for the "no change" group. For each characteristic, the "no change" group showed the lowest average compared to the clusters. Moreover, each cluster showed highest averages for the organizational change characteristics which typified this cluster. For example, types 5 (Innovative restructuring) and 6 (Innovative expansion) were highest on process innovation ($M = 3.07$ and $M = 2.87$, respectively) and this was significantly higher than the "no change" group, as well as higher than each other cluster ($F(6,772) = 112.80, p < .01$).

After controlling for age, gender, and education, a significant effect of change type on emotional exhaustion was shown, $F(6,787) = 3.02$,

Table 5.3 *Average of organizational change characteristics per cluster, no change group, and total*

Cluster/type Change characteristic	1 Expansion	2 Shrinkage	3 Lean restructuring	4 Thriving	5 Innovative restructuring	6 Innovative expansion	No change	Total
Changes in staff numbers	0.41*	−1.18*	−0.81*	0.49*	−1.57*	0.55*	−0.07	0.00
Restructuring events	0.26	0.74*	2.84*	0.73*	1.85*	0.56*	0.33	0.67
Expansion of production capacity	0.08	0.03	0.15	0.22*	0.08	0.20*	0.07	0.11
Product innovation	0.10*	0.19*	0.47*	1.00*	0.73*	0.51*	0.03	0.40
Process innovation	2.12*	2.28*	2.36*	2.31*	3.07*	2.87*	1.85	2.12

Note: * significantly different from the "no change" group

$p < .01$. Significantly higher levels of emotional exhaustion appeared in the "Innovative restructuring" (M = 3.15; SD = .23) and "Innovative expansion" (M = 2.94; SD = .13) types compared to the "no change" group (M = 2.46; SD = .07), the "Expansion" (M = 2.48; SD = .09), "Shrinkage" (M = 2.57; SD = .13), and "Thriving" (M = 2.54; SD = .11) types.

Also, and after controlling for age, gender, and education, a significant effect of change type on newly-acquired KSAO's (active learning) was shown $F(6,787)$ = 4.37, $p < .01$. Significantly higher levels of active learning were observed in the "Thriving" (M = 2.86; SD = .09) and "Innovative expansion" (M = 2.99; SD = .10) types compared to the "no change" group (M = 2.51; SD = .05), and the "Shrinkage" (M = 2.56; SD = .10) type. The "Innovative expansion" type also demonstrated higher levels of active learning compared to the "Expansion" (M = 2.69; SD = .07) type.

Figure 5.1 shows average levels of emotional exhaustion and active learning for each change type. These results most strongly supported our Hypotheses 3 and 4 on combinations between organizational change type dimensions on the dependent variables. Comparing the six organizational change types and the "no change" group, as expected,

1. Organizational change types combining negative quantitative aspects (decline, restructuring) with qualitative aspects (i.e., innovations) are highest on negative employee reactions (emotional exhaustion). The

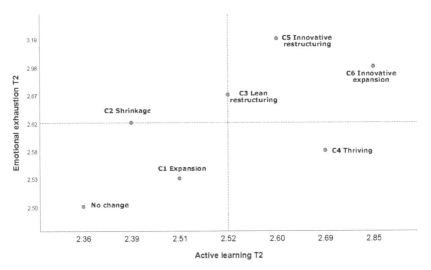

Figure 5.1   Average level of emotional exhaustion and active learning by organizational change type

"Innovative restructuring" type represents the most detrimental situation: high levels of emotional exhaustion and medium levels of active learning. Pairwise comparisons revealed that the "Innovative restructuring" type showed significantly higher levels for emotional exhaustion compared to the other types (including the no change group), except for the "Lean restructuring" and "Innovative expansion" type.

2. Organizational change types combining positive quantitative aspects (growth, expansion) with qualitative aspects (e.g., innovations) are highest on positive employee reactions (active learning). The "Thriving" type showed to be the most advantageous type: relatively low on emotional exhaustion, but high levels of active learning. The "Innovative expansion" type combined a relatively high level of emotional exhaustion with high active learning. Pairwise comparisons revealed that the "Thriving" and "Innovative expansion" types showed significantly higher levels for active learning compared to the other types (including the no change group), except for the "Lean restructuring" and "Innovative restructuring" type.

5.4   Discussion

5.4.1   Conclusions

Our study identified six organizational change types that largely fit the framework that deductively extended existing dichotomies in the organizational change literature (e.g., cost-oriented and innovation-oriented change; Kiefer et al., 2015). Only one cell in our theoretical framework was not represented by a cluster, that is, the type which represents decline in combination with innovation. Although it is theoretically conceivable that some organizations apply innovative strategies and practices while at the same time cutting costs through decreasing staff, this mixed kind of change was not empirically supported. Possibly, organizations in decline do not have the capacity to innovate at the same time, or management operating in an organizational context of decline fear that innovative efforts cannot be very effective or successful.

The focus was strictly on the change content (the "what"), and more specifically on quantitative and qualitative aspects of ongoing change. On the quantitative change dimension, growth and decline (with or without restructuring) defined the opposite positions, while the qualitative change dimension distinguished between ongoing change which is low versus high in innovation of products and/or process. Combining these dimensions enabled us to identify "mixed" types of organizational change which embraced innovation efforts with quantitative changes such as growth or decline. The importance of investigating these combinations of change types is underlined by two outcomes. First, almost half of our sample had to deal with one of the mixed change types when confronted with organizational change. Second, our findings showed that these mixed change types had the strongest impact on both positive (active learning) and negative (emotional exhaustion) outcomes for change recipients. Overall, our classification demonstrates that organizational change is seldom straightforward, but often complex, multi-dimensional and multifaceted. Recognizing the diverse and varied realities of organizational change can advance us in gaining a deeper understanding of change recipients' reactions toward change and the underlying mechanisms and processes.

Indeed, our findings revealed the importance of combinations of change dimensions for employee outcomes. In general, the strongest reactions of change recipients, both negative and positive, were observed in *mixed* types of organizational change: the "Innovative restructuring" type – combining decline, restructuring, and innovation – represents the most detrimental change situation, with high levels of emotional exhaustion and only medium levels of active learning. The "Thriving" type – combining product innovation and growth – is shown to be the most advantageous type, with relatively low levels of emotional exhaustion and high levels of active learning. The "Innovative expansion" type combined relatively high levels of emotional exhaustion with high active learning. In Section 5.4.2, we will elaborate on some theoretical implications of these findings.

5.4.2   *Theoretical Relevance and Suggestions for Future Research*

Our research contributes in several ways to the organizational change literature. This study builds upon existing classifications (Kiefer et al., 2015; Petrou et al., 2017; Solinger et al., 2021) and enabled us to verify these. At the same time, it elaborates and extends these (dichotomous) classifications of organizational change. Our study not only distinguishes qualitative and quantitative forms of organizational change but also combines these in order to reach a more realistic view of ongoing change in practice. In many cases ongoing change embraces or aims for both quantitative (e.g., cost reductions) and qualitative (e.g., process and/or product innovation) objectives.

Moreover, our findings contribute to gaining a better understanding of the differential effects of organizational change on employee well-being and personal development. Organizational change in itself is neither intrinsically good nor bad, but its impact on change recipients depends on the kind of ongoing change. Our study provides more insight into which effects are most likely to be associated with a particular kind of organizational change or a specific combination of organizational change aspects. It highlight the relevance of distinguishing between quantitative and quantitative changes and investigating the impact of combinations of these kind of changes. The findings indicate that change is often complex and multifaceted with different substantial targets, such as cost reductions in combination with product innovation, with the aim of sustainable organizational survival, and might stimulate a more nuanced debate on organizational change – employee well-being relationships and underlying mechanisms. These latter mechanisms and processes still have to be investigated in greater detail and should be subject to future research efforts. We hope that our approach is inspiring for further research in this area. Most importantly, future research should address the potential mechanisms underlying the impact of the kind of ongoing organization-level change and change recipients' reactions toward this change.

A suggestion for this kind of research might be to investigate the relationship between the organizational change types and associated shifts in work characteristics (Fedor et al., 2006). How do quantitative and qualitative changes (and combinations of these) at the organizational level subsequently affect changes in the working lives of change recipients through changes in the workplace? As Michel and Gonzáles-Morales (2013) note, change is stressful because it creates pressure for employees in a direct way (through aspects of the change itself) but also indirectly through affecting other aspects of work (e.g., work characteristics such as workload and autonomy). Building upon the JD-R model (Demerouti et al., 2001), Michel and Gonzáles-Morales (2013) propose that organizational change is associated with job demands and resources and that these affect the way change recipients appraise the ongoing organizational change (as challenging, threatening, or non-threatening). In particular, they posit that increased demands resulting from organizational change may augment negative health-related consequences of organizational change, whereas resources may buffer against these, provided that they are not eroded in the face of ongoing change. In sum, research is needed that investigates the impact of types of organizational change on employee well-being through changes in work characteristics such as job demands (e.g., cognitive and emotional demands) and job resources (e.g., autonomy, learning opportunities). Our classification of organizational change types may contribute in this research effort because it provides an approach to the systematic identification of organization-level changes.

5.4.3 Limitations and Further Suggestions for Future Research

The empirical investigation of our classification of organizational change types is based on subjective perceptions of the recipients of ongoing organizational change; and personal assessments were used to measure indicators of well-being (emotional exhaustion) and personal development (active learning). Consequently, our studies are subject to common method bias.

Our classification of organizational change types has a clear and specific focus but unavoidably entails certain limitations. It has a strict orientation at the organizational level and not at lower levels such as departments or work units. As Fedor et al. (2006) argue, assessments of change at different levels and their interrelationships may contribute highly to a better understanding of and explanation for individual level responses to change. Future research should aim to encompass different organizational levels in order to unravel interrelationships and underlying dynamics.

The focus on qualitative and quantitative aspects of organizational change implies that other aspects of change, such as cultural change aspects or HRM-related types of change (e.g., high performance HR systems or practices; Solinger et al., 2021) are disregarded. In view of Kiefer's (2005, p. 877) definition of ongoing organizational change as "incremental or substantial alterations to an organization's structures, processes, or social systems," our classification focuses specifically on structures (e.g., restructuring) and processes (e.g., growth, decline and innovation), and not on social systems (e.g., organizational culture). This follows from our aim to develop a more complex model in which organizational level changes are linked to change recipients' reactions through their impact on lower level changes, e.g., the team or the workplace (i.e., a "cascading" mechanism; see Fedor et al., 2006, p. 7). We assume that understanding these change recipients' reactions requires an insight into how organizational level changes affect specific work situations, in particular job demands and resources (Michel & Gonzáles-Morales, 2013; Petrou et al., 2017). For this reason, our focus is on systemic/structural and processual aspects of organizational change, as we assume these aspects to have the largest influence on change recipients' job demands and resources. However, this does not imply that other relevant organizational changes pertaining to the social system should be overlooked. Future research could address the question of whether and how cultural and HR aspects of organizational change can be included; which may eventually lead to an extension of our classification. Alternatively, the impact of organizational change types on change recipients' reactions may be studied in relation to simultaneous cultural or HR-related changes.

Our approach focuses on "what" changes, disregarding "how" change is implemented or without taking the role of change process characteristics such as participative decision-making into account (Fedor et al., 2006). Our findings underpin the idea that the kind of ongoing change impacts change recipients' reactions toward this change in terms of their well-being and personal development. However, Fedor et al. (2006, p. 4) suggest that "how organizations do what they do matters a great deal. This can sometimes be as or more important even than what is done." Not surprisingly, many researchers in the areas of organizational development focused on the role of the change process (Fedor et al., 2006; Fugate, 2013). Negative change recipients' reactions may result from poor implementation of change projects such as ineffective communication, low participation in change processes, unfair change procedures or outcomes. Future research could focus on the relative contribution of and interaction between "what" and "how" aspects of ongoing change for change recipients' reactions. In this respect, tackling exclusively change process characteristics may be less productive in several ways. As our research shows: what organizations change matters; and it may be more effective to deal with negative consequences of organizational level change directly by adjusting the kind of ongoing change instead of relying solely on "smoothing" fairness perceptions of change recipients. Based on their findings, Fedor et al. (2006, p. 23) conclude that "doing a good job on the process side," such as advancing fairness aspects of the change process, may not be enough. They are "not sufficient to override the favorableness of the change or the change's impact on the individual's job situation." In line with Fedor, we propose that more complex models need to be built to better understand reactions of employees toward ongoing change. This not only implies the inclusion of different levels in the organization and of cultural and HR-related change aspects, but also characteristics of change implementation processes. Future research could deal with the role and effectiveness of change process characteristics within each organizational change type. The effectiveness of change management initiatives and practices may depend on the specific type of change. For instance, genuine participation could be essential in organizational change types character-ized by innovation and expansion, while fairness and trust in management may be pivotal in cases of organizational decline. Future research could investigate the influence of procedural or operational change characteristics in a more contextualized manner, that is, in the context of ongoing change.

REFERENCES

Bakker, A., & Demerouti, E. (2007). The job demands-resources model: State of the art. *Journal of Managerial Psychology, 22*, 309–328.

Cavanaugh, M. A., Boswell, W. R., Roehling, M. V., & Boudreau, J. W. (2000). An empirical examination of self-reported work stress among US managers. *Journal of Applied Psychology, 85*, 65–74.

Cerasoli, C. P., Alliger, G. M., Donsbach, J. S., Mathieu, J. E., Tannenbaum, S. I., & Orvis, K. A. (2018). Antecedents and outcomes of informal learning behaviors: A meta-analysis. *Journal of Business and Psychology, 33*(2), 203–230.

Dawis, R. V. (2005), The Minnesota theory of work adjustment. In S. Brown and R. Lent (eds.), *Career development and counseling: Putting theory and research to work* (pp. 3–23). Hoboken: John Wiley and Sons.

Demerouti, E., Bakker, A. B., Nachreiner, F., & Schaufeli, W. B. (2001). The job demands-resources model of burnout. *Journal of Applied Psychology, 86*, 499–512.

Fedor, D. B., Caldwell, S., & Herold, D. M. (2006). The effects of organizational changes on employee commitment: A multilevel investigation. *Personnel Psychology, 59*(1), 1–29.

Fugate, M. (2013). Capturing the positive experience of change: Antecedents, processes, and consequences. In S. Oreg, A. Michel, & R. T. By (eds.), *The psychology of organizational change: Viewing change from the employee's per-spective* (pp. 15–39). Cambridge: Cambridge University Press.

Hobfoll, S. E., & Freedy, J. (2017). Conservation of resources: A general stress theory applied to burnout. In T. Marek, W. B. Schaufeli, & C. Maslach (eds.), *Professional burnout: Recent developments in theory and research* (pp. 115–129). New York: Routledge.

Jiménez-Jiménez, D., & Sanz-Valle, R. (2011). Innovation, organizational learn-ing, and performance. *Journal of Business Research, 64*, 408–417.

Kent, R. (2015). *Analysing quantitative data. Variable-based and case-based approaches to non-experimental datasets*. London: Sage.

Kiefer, T. (2005). Feeling bad: Antecedents and consequences of negative emo-tions in ongoing change. *Journal of Organizational Behavior, 26*, 875–897.

Kiefer, T., Hartley, J., Conway, N., & Briner, R. (2015). Feeling the squeeze: Public employees' experiences of cutback- and innovation-related organiza-tional changes following a national announcement of budget reductions. *Journal of Public Administration Research and Theory, 14*, 1279–1305.

LePine, J. A., LePine, M. A., & Jackson, C. L. (2004). Challenge and hindrance stress: Relationships with exhaustion, motivation to learn, and learning performance. *Journal of Applied Psychology*, *89*, 883–891.

Maslach, C., Schaufeli, W. B., & Leiter, M. P. (2001). Job burnout. *Annual Review of Psychology*, *52*, 397–422.

Michel, A., & González-Morales, M. G. (2013). Reactions to organizational change: An integrated model of health predictors, intervening variables, and outcomes. In S. Oreg, A. Michel, & R. T. By (eds.), *The psychology of organizational change: Viewing change from the employee's perspective* (pp. 65–91). Cambridge: Cambridge University Press.

Myers, P., Hulks, S., & Wiggins, L. (2012). *Organizational change: Perspectives on theory and practice*. Oxford: Oxford University Press.

Nikolova, I., Van Dam, K., Van Ruysseveldt, J., & De Witte, H. (2019). Feeling weary; feeling insecure? Are workplace changes all bad news? *International Journal of Environmental Research and Public Health*, *16*, 1842.

Nikolova, I., Van Ruysseveldt, J., De Witte, H., & Syroit, J. (2013). Work-based learning: Development and validation of a scale measuring the learning potential of the workplace (LPW). *Journal of Vocational Behavior*, *84*, 1–10.

(2014). Employee well-being in times of task restructuring: The buffering role of workplace learning. *Work & Stress*, *28*, 217–235.

Nikolova, I., Van Ruysseveldt, J., Van Dam, K., & De Witte, H. (2016). Learning climate and workplace learning: Does work restructuring make a difference? *Journal of Personnel Psychology*, *15*, 66–75.

Oreg, S., Michel, A., & By, R. T. (eds.) (2013). *The psychology of organizational change: Viewing change from the employee's perspective*. Cambridge: Cambridge University Press.

Oreg, S., Vakola, M., & Armenakis, A. A. (2011). Change recipients' reactions to organizational change: A 60-year review of quantitative studies. *Journal of Applied Behavioral Science*, *47*, 461–524.

Petrou, P., Demerouti, E., Peeters, M. C., Schaufeli, W. B., & Hetland, J. (2012). Crafting a job on a daily basis: Contextual correlates and the link to work engagement. *Journal of Organizational Behavior*, *33*, 1120–1141.

Petrou, P., Demerouti, E., & Xanthopoulou, D. (2017). Regular versus cutback-related change: The role of employee job crafting in organizational change contexts of different nature. *International Journal of Stress Management*, *24*(1), 62–85.

Rafferty, A. E., & Griffin, M. A. (2006). Perceptions of organizational change: A stress and coping perspective. *Journal of Applied Psychology*, *91*, 1154–1162.

Schaufeli, W. B., Leiter, M. P., Maslach, C., & Jackson, S. E. (1996). Maslach burnout inventory: General survey. In C. Maslach, S. E. Jackson, & M. P. Leiter (eds.), *The Maslach burnout inventory*, 3rd ed. – Test Manual. Palo Alto, CA: Consulting Psychologists Press.

Skule, S. (2004). Learning conditions at work: A framework to understand and assess informal learning in the workplace. *International Journal of Training and Development*, *8*(1), 8–20.

Solinger, O., Joireman, J., Vantilborgh, T., & Balliet, D. P. (2021). Change in unit-level job attitudes following strategic interventions: A meta-analysis of longitudinal studies. *Journal of Organizational Behavior, 42*(7), 964–986.

Van den Broeck, A., De Cuyper, N., De Witte, H., & Vansteenkiste, M. (2010). Not all job demands are equal: Differentiating job hindrances and job challenges in the job demands-resources model. *European Journal of Work and Organizational Psychology, 19*, 735–759.

Van Ruysseveldt, J., Verboon, P., & Smulders, P. (2011). Job resources and emotional exhaustion: The mediating role of learning opportunities. *Work & Stress, 25*(3), 205–223.

CHAPTER 6

Employee Responses to Technological Change
A Retrospective Review

Katerina Gonzalez and Rouven Kanitz

Technology and its use – fast-tracked by the recent global pandemic – is transforming organizational life in a meaningful manner. Today many organizational changes are focused on or accompanied by the introduction of new technologies. Organizations implement technologies for different reasons (e.g., to increase efficiency, enhance collaboration, or become more innovative). These technologies can come in various forms, such as an enterprise resource planning system, collaboration software, or an AI-based medical diagnostic system. Some employees may perceive these new technologies positively but others may perceive them as hindrances, influencing adoption processes and outcomes. Yet, these technologies can only reach their intended goals if individuals accept and adopt them. This insight has led to an increasing body of research that examines how employees respond to technological change in organizations. In this review, we integrate this work and provide a retrospective account of the variety of factors that influence the psychology of technological change, which can be of value for those driving technological change in organizational reality.

   In empirical investigations of how individuals process and respond to technological change in their workplaces, researchers have considered various types of technologies, employed a broad range of theoretical approaches, and examined different responses, such as technology acceptance and resistance. However, in many studies, technological change has been treated as a setting. In other words, considering aspects related to the type and design of the technology has not had a primary role in theoretical models (Landers & Marin, 2021). Thus, we have outlined the perspectives used to study this type of change specifically, using change response frameworks to gain a better holistic understanding of technology change. We hope that this review of prior work on this topic assists scholars in developing a more nuanced view of how the technology itself might be included in theory building and study design. Additionally, a second limitation with this body of work is that there is only limited exchange between scholars across disciplines. We undertake this synthesis of the literature base in part because the exchange from scholars from organizational behavior to information systems (e.g., Rivard & Lapointe, 2012) and those from information systems to organizational behavior (e.g., Marler et al., 2006) can be reciprocal and fruitful. Thus, instead of focusing on research within a single discipline (e.g., organizational behavior), we focus broadly on the psychology of change where technology implementation has been a central point of a study. Complementing the focus of this book (on the psychology of change), in this chapter, we focus on what is known about how employees respond to *technological* changes.

In this chapter, we review and synthesize relevant research on the psychology of technological change, integrating work from various disciplines (information systems, organizational behavior, operations management, and strategy). We organize our review into four main parts. First, we briefly review the types of technological changes that have been studied and discuss these in relation to broader dimensions of organizational change (i.e., scale and degree). Second, we describe the theoretical perspectives used to examine responses to technology implementation. We elaborate on and compare several well-established, technology-specific theoretical models (e.g., Venkatesh & Davis, 2000; Venkatesh et al., 2003) to broader theoretical approaches that have been adopted. Third, we describe the antecedent-change response relationships that have been examined during technological change, and some more distal outcomes that have been considered. Finally, we highlight limitations in our current understanding and describe opportunities for future research.

6.1 Method

We began by searching within journals that regularly publish articles on the psychology of technological change. After identifying relevant articles through an electronic search, we scanned the abstracts and removed articles that did not meet specific search criteria. Then, we extracted information from the articles that were relevant using a coding procedure. We used a controlled vocabulary (e.g., *new system, technolog* implementation, response* to change*, attitud* toward change, technology acceptance*) to search within specific journals on the Web of Science database. We searched within several journals that regularly publish articles on the psychology of technological change: journals from the *Financial Times'* journal list (FT 50). Articles published between 1998 and 2020 were considered in order to complement a previous review on responses to change (Armenakis & Bedeian, 1999).

Article abstracts were then screened based on several inclusion criteria. Studies (1) were empirical with primary data, (2) contained some component of a cognitive, emotional, or behavioral response (e.g., resistance), (3) included a technological change that was a central (and not an auxiliary) part of the investigation, (4) included a sample of employed adults (18+ years of age), and (5) contained variables that were measured immediately before, during, or immediately after a technological change. Sixty-seven articles met these criteria. We used a coding system that would allow us to examine the psychology of technological change in light of existing frameworks of response antecedents and longer-term consequences (e.g., Oreg et al., 2011; Rafferty et al., 2013). We coded the articles based on the theoretical perspective, the variables studied (dependent, independent, mechanisms, moderators), and the type of technological change.

6.2   Technological Change

Technology implementations are a subset of broader organizational changes (culture change, strategic change, reorganization, etc.), ranging from complex, transformational projects to relatively simple updates to existing technology infrastructure. We categorize the types of technological changes that emerge from our article database based on two dimensions of change: (1) the *scale* of change (i.e., broad versus narrow) and (2) the *degree* of change (radical versus incremental). We focus on these two dimensions because they have very different implications for employee psychology within the context of technological change. Some of the implementations that have been studied have been broad in *scale*, often spanning across the organization. In contrast, others are narrow and only impact a single division, business unit, or department. The scale of the technological change (ranging from organization-wide/core to peripheral) influences the level of disturbance to the status quo (Nadler & Tushman, 1989).

Another factor that can cause a disturbance to the status quo is the *degree* of change or the extent to which the new system diverges from the existing system or practices, ranging from radical to incremental (Ettlie et al., 1984). That is, a new technology can introduce a drastic, even risky departure from the way that activities are carried out (i.e., a radical change) or can impart only a slight deviation from the status quo (i.e., an incremental change). This distinction can be due to the magnitude of the organization's investment in the implementation or due to a substantive

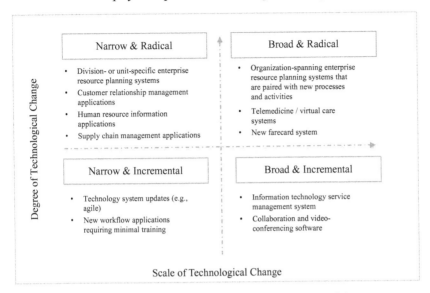

Figure 6.1   Technological change examples by dimension of change

shift in the input, throughput, and output (Ettlie et al., 1984). These dimensions of organizational changes can play a role in how individuals perceive and respond to new technologies. Examples of technological changes categorized into these two dimensions can be found in Figure 6.1.

6.2.1   Broad and Radical

Some technology implementations are associated with high levels of disturbance because they are wide-reaching and radical simultaneously, such as an industry shift to telemedicine technology that promoted physicians to consider adopting virtual care methods (Chau & Hu, 2002). One commonly studied technological change fitting within this category relates to the introduction of enterprise resource planning (ERP) systems, so long as they are organization-wide initiatives. ERP systems can be hosted on a cloud and/or on-premise and facilitate and support various business activities across organizational functions (e.g., supply chain, financial, manufacturing, and services management), often in real-time. Such implementations are often considered to be radical because they require adaptations to core activities, processes, and structures. Several studies included in this review have included an examination of acceptance and resistance processes within broad-reaching and radical ERP implementations (e.g., Robey et al., 2002; Boudreau & Robey, 2005; Marler et al., 2006; Kim & Kankanhalli, 2009; Morris & Venkatesh, 2010). ERP systems can store, manage, and assist with the interpretation of data, and can be transformational for an organization.

ERP system implementations have been studied across various industries, including in healthcare. In an early example, the introduction of electronic medical records in a hospital setting (Lapointe & Rivard, 2005) allowed hospital staff to access patient records in real-time and from various locations. More recently, technological changes in hospital settings have included enterprise-wide health care solutions that support a holistic view of patient care (Venkatesh et al., 2011), and are predecessors to virtual care systems currently in place. Such implementations have the potential to enhance employee and customer (patient) outcomes.

6.2.2   Broad and Incremental

Another technological change that is broad in scale is the implementation of an information technology service management system (Leonardi, 2007). Although this can help increase efficiency in providing information technology support services to employees and customers, the discontinuity caused is likely to be incremental for this technological change because it does not require a redesign of core processes and structures.

Similarly, the introduction of collaboration software affects members across the organization. Still, it may vary in terms of their degree of discontinuity, depending on the deviation from the way members collaborated previously. These are used for knowledge sharing and interacting with others in real-time (Devaraj et al., 2008; Brown et al., 2010, 2014) or can even allow individuals to telecommute, mimicking a conventional office setup (Venkatesh, 1999). The introduction of video conferencing software represents an organization-wide change but is often thought of as an incremental deviation from the status quo in terms of the activities that change recipients are responsible for. Such implementations can also facilitate hybrid and remote work arrangements for employees.

6.2.3   Narrow and Radical

Other more peripheral (i.e., narrow in scale) technological changes that have been studied are those designed to support or enhance business activities but that are limited to a specific business unit, division, or department. ERP systems can be limited to a specific business unit or division (e.g., Sykes, 2015) but still have the potential to cause a disturbance to the status quo. Another technological change fitting in this grouping that has been examined is the introduction of customer relationship management (CRM) applications, also termed sales force automation (Homburg et al., 2010), which can yield large performance benefits to those in sales roles in particular (Ahearne et al., 2010). These allow those in sales and relationship management roles to more effectively keep track of accounts (Gefen & Ridings, 2002; Ahearne et al., 2010; Beaudry & Pinsonneault, 2010; Hsieh et al., 2011). These systems often have a radical impact on recipients because they redesign the nature of many job tasks.

Another type of technological change that is narrow but can be considered as radical is the introduction of human resource information systems. Such a technology implementation is limited in scale (Venkatesh & Goyal, 2010) but can significantly impact practice for human resource professionals. Moreover, supply chain management (SCM) application implementation projects fall into this category. They offer benefits for optimizing the supply chain and inventory management (Autry et al., 2010; Bala, 2013; Bendoly, 2014). Often, SCM implementations are coupled with business process reengineering programs that complement each other (Stensaker & Falkenberg, 2007). Combining SCM implementations with wider-sweeping process changes allows for more discontinuous or radical modifications to governance, structure, control systems, and work processes for change recipients.

6.2.4   Narrow and Incremental

A fourth type relates to technological changes that are narrow in scale and incremental in terms of their disturbance of the status quo. Such changes may occur quite frequently in organizational reality (e.g., a new system update). Examples of peripheral or narrow changes that are more incremental are smaller-scale process technology updates for specific manufacturing plants (Cua et al., 2001) or the introduction of business unit workflow applications (Santhanam et al., 2007) to specific divisions or departments that require minimal training. Incremental changes can also occur frequently using agile information system updates, characterized by frequent updates with limited features in each release (Brown et al., 2010; Hong et al., 2011).

6.2.5   Further Characteristics of Technological Change

Apart from the dimensions discussed within Sections 6.2.1–6.2.4, a few other distinctions can be made between the ways that scholars have approached the study of technology implementations. First, new systems studied are either developed in-house (Beaudry & Pinsonneault, 2010) or provided by vendors (Morris & Venkatesh, 2010). A more expansive and complex social network web (i.e., the inclusion of vendors and other consulting partners) can have implications for how employees respond and for an implementation's success. Second, scholars have also studied diverging user belief systems associated with making technology adoptions voluntary (Malhotra & Galletta, 2005; Beaudry & Pinsonneault, 2010) and mandatory (Hardgrave et al., 2003). Third, they have also diverged in their implementation of hardware and software. In a few earlier articles, scholars examined how individuals respond to new workstations and PCs (Gallivan et al., 2005; Symon, 2005) as organizations migrated to PCs from paper. Similarly, scholars of earlier work have examined the transition to what are now considered as less-advanced technologies, such as the implementation of electronic trading and internet-based technologies in finance and banking (Heracleous & Barrett, 2001). Contrasting the early changes (e.g., moving from paper to electronic databases; migrating to PCs) against the later ones (ERP systems, new technologies that enhance work effectiveness, machine learning, etc.) underscores the increasing frequency and pace of the implementation of new technologies in the workplace. Next, we turn to specific theoretical lenses and frameworks that have been used.

6.3   Theoretical Perspectives and Frameworks

Scholars have used a variety of lenses to explore how individuals respond to new technology implementation. In the following sections, we delve into some of the works representative of each of the theoretical approaches scholars have used to better understand the psychology of technological change.

6.3.1   Cognitive Perspectives

Theories that shed light on why specific attitudes are linked to technology acceptance and use behaviors were the most prevalent. These include broad cognitive approaches rooted in psychology theories and those that have been developed specifically to explain the acceptance and use of technology systems.

Intentions and Attitudes: Some studies have been rooted in cognitive psychology broadly, including studies where a broad theoretical approach has been taken, such as those employing the theory of planned behavior (Ajzen, 1991) or cognitive dissonance theory (Festinger, 1957). Those applying the theory of planned behavior assume that attitudes about the system are predictive of intention to use the system and actual use behaviors (e.g., Bendoly & Cotteleer, 2008). Studies where general attitudes, subjective norms, and belief systems about the technology influence adoption processes are also common (e.g., Karahanna et al., 1999). How individuals form expectations (cognitive dissonance theory; Festinger, 1957) about system characteristics (e.g., switching costs) have also been found to influence individuals' acceptance of a new technology (Brown et al., 2008; Kim & Kankanhalli, 2009; Venkatesh & Goyal, 2010). Other theoretical models and frameworks have been further tailored to better understand individual responses to technological change, such as the technology acceptance model.

Technology Acceptance Model (TAM) and Extensions: Another cluster of technology-centric frameworks has been developed cumulatively since the 1980s, with each extension building on earlier models. Each incremental contribution in this area has promised enhanced predictive validity regarding technology use behaviors. The seminal technology acceptance model (TAM) is focused on two factors of new technology implementation – *perceived ease of use* (i.e., does the individual believe they will need to exert relatively low effort associated with use?) and *usefulness* (i.e., does the individual believe usage will enhance their job performance?) – that facilitate use through increasing behavioral intentions (Davis, 1989). This model continues to be applied by scholars to understand various types of technological change (e.g., Hu et al., 1999; Venkatesh, 2000; Venkatesh & Morris, 2000; Chau & Hu, 2002; Hardgrave et al., 2003; Marler et al., 2006; Brown et al., 2008, 2014; Devaraj et al., 2008; Autry et al., 2010; Homburg et al., 2010). However, it has been criticized for its lack of consideration of the individual motivational factors and broader social (e.g., cultural, relational) factors influencing technology acceptance (e.g., Bagozzi, 2007). Thus, this model has been extended several times, primarily via the addition of predictors and moderators.

Venkatesh and Davis (2000) proposed an extended model (TAM2) by including new antecedents of perceived usefulness. Specifically, they introduced several variables which represented two factors – social influence and cognitive perceptions (instrumental perceptions about the system) – that predicted perceived usefulness and ultimately adoption, drawing from classic work on social influence and power (e.g., Kelman, 1958) for the former factor, and on work on motivation and decision-making for the latter factor (e.g., Vroom, 1964). They also found a path from perceived ease of use to perceived usefulness. Venkatesh and Davis supported this model across four longitudinal field studies.

In a separate study, Venkatesh (2000) expanded the predictors to TAM's perceived ease of use factor using an anchoring and adjustment-based theoretical model. This group of variables related to "anchoring and adjustment" fell into two sections: anchors (general beliefs associated with computer use, such as computer self-efficacy and computer anxiety) and adjustments (perceptions of the system based on hands-on experience with the system, such as perceived enjoyment). This model enhanced TAM by combining motivational components with individual differences to better understand technology-oriented cognitions. The authors supported this model across several longitudinal field studies. In TAM3, Venkatesh and Bala (2008) developed a nomological network from the prior models. Hands-on experience with the system was included as a moderator of a few of the relationships. Additionally, they added different predictors for each perceived ease of use and usefulness.

Unified Theory of Acceptance and Use of Technology (UTAUT): One of the most highly cited models in the group of more comprehensive models is the UTAUT (Venkatesh et al., 2003); for a broad review of the applications, integrations, and extensions of the UTAUT, see Venkatesh, Thong, et al. (2016). The early models (TAM, TAM2), along with other competing theoretical frameworks, inspired the development of the UTAUT. In this work, Venkatesh et al. (2003) develop and test several competing theoretical models, identifying four key factors (i.e., performance expectancy, effort expectancy, social influence, and facilitating conditions) that predict behavioral intention and, ultimately, actual technology use. The first three factors predicted behavioral intention, while the latter factor (along with behavioral intentions) predicted actual technology use. They also explored several moderators of the relationships (i.e., age, gender, experience, and the degree of voluntariness). Several studies have also used the UTAUT to explain the extent of use of various technologies after implementation (Venkatesh et al., 2008; Brown et al., 2010).

Researchers have considered the UTAUT to have reached saturation in terms of explaining technology use, given that it has explained almost

80 percent of the variance in intention to use a technology and approximately half of the variance in actual technology use (Venkatesh, Thong, et al., 2016) and are now calling for further extensions and replication studies (Blut et al., 2021). Thus, building on previous models used to predict technology adoption, the authors used a cognitive approach (e.g., Ajzen, 1991) and work on social influence and motivation (e.g., Bandura, 1986) to develop the UTAUT.

Situated Cognition Models: Other complex theoretical models have been developed to examine individual reactions to technological change. One cluster of these studies is centered around the juxtaposition of cognition, the technological change itself, and work characteristics. This perspective assumes that individuals are situated within their workplace, and thus cognitions related to the technological change will have a reciprocal relationship with cognitions related to the job. For example, the authors of one study (Morris & Venkatesh, 2010) point to individual outcomes being predicted by how individuals perceive their jobs in relation to the technology implementation by relying on job characteristics theory (Hackman et al., 1980) in addition to cognitive dissonance theory (Festinger, 1957). In another example, Bala and Venkatesh (2013) built a theoretical framework to predict why employees will experience changes in their perceptions of the characteristics of their jobs, in turn influencing their behaviors; changes in perceptions of job characteristics were found to be predicted by both technology and work process characteristics. They termed this the job characteristics change model based on the premise that job characteristics shift during technology implementations, which influences individual perceptions of the job.

Triadic (technology-job-cognition) work rooted in socio-technical systems theory has also contributed a more situated approach. Socio-technical systems theorists (Bostrom & Heinen, 1977) acknowledge that organizational design is a complex process consisting of non-linear interactions between social and technical factors, and this theory has been applied by several scholars to understand technological change (Cua et al., 2001; Bala, 2013; Seidel et al., 2013; Sykes et al., 2014). This line of thought is centered around the idea that the design and functionality of new technology must also keep in mind the responses and expectations of the end-users. Ultimately, there is a co-dependency between the tasks individuals perform and information systems (Lauterbach et al., 2020). After all, achieving optimal performance depends on practices that are both socially- and technically-oriented (Cua et al., 2001). In one study, a combination of socio-technical systems theory with goal-setting theory has been applied to understand the relationships between individual motivations and meaning-making during transformational changes (Seidel et al., 2013). In addition to contributing a situated-cognitive perspective, systems theories also contribute a processual lens to our understanding of technological change.

Sensemaking: Another cognitive lens used to study responses to technological change is sensemaking (Weick, 1995; Langley, 1999). Sensemaking research emphasizes the social construction process through which change recipients try to find meaning in technology change. Sensemaking studies often use qualitative-interpretive methods to gain deep insights into the schemas people use to work through change ambiguity. For instance, some use a sensemaking lens to study the obstacles recipients experience regarding technology adoption over the course of a change (Dawson & Buchanan, 2005). Managers make sense of environmental turbulence (Autry et al., 2010) and can use this information to alter an implementation approach and reduce tensions. This lens has enabled scholars to gain insight into the psychological processes of managers and employees over time (Stensaker & Falkenberg, 2007; Hsieh et al., 2011). The sensemaking lens adds value by offering a processual and social constructivist lens to a cognition perspective.

6.3.2   Stress and Coping Perspectives

Another perspective that has been used to examine responses to technological change focuses on how employees experience stress and cope with new technology. Therefore, the transactional model of stress and coping (Lazarus & Folkman, 1984; Lazarus, 1991) has been applied to understand how individuals appraise and adapt to new technologies. In one work rooted in this theory, Beaudry and Pinsonneault (2010) argue that emotions (not just cognitions) are essential drivers in the acceptance of new technology application implementations. They also studied the role of discrete emotions (anger, anxiety, happiness, and excitement) in coping mechanisms (e.g., venting, seeking support, distancing). Building on Beaudry and Pinsonneault's (2010) work, Bala and Venkatesh (2016) applied the transactional model of stress and coping to understand how the appraisal process (primary: perceived opportunity, perceived threat; secondary: perceived controllability), influenced by various implementation characteristics, leads to different forms of technology adaptation (i.e., exploration-to innovate, exploration-to-revert, exploitation, avoidance) during implementations. As anxiety associated with technology can present as a significant obstacle to adopting new technologies (e.g., Venkatesh, 2000), examining the role of techno-stress in technological change will continue to be an important area of study. The stress and coping lenses emphasize the role of cognition *and* emotion during appraisals to better understand responses to technological change.

6.3.3   Learning Perspectives

Learning theories highlight how individuals' knowledge and skill development shapes how they respond to technological change. Such lenses have been applied to enhance our understanding of when and why individuals are motivated to engage with technologies. Although an individual's existing information technology knowledge is a predictor of technology use (Aggarwal et al., 2015), how individuals learn new processes and when and why they are open to training have been given attention. For instance, dialectic learning processes have been applied to understand how individuals overcome knowledge barriers (Robey et al., 2002). Additionally, theories about how specific individual needs drive motivation (e.g., self-determination theory; Ryan & Deci, 2000) have been applied across various studies (e.g., Cadwallader et al., 2010). In one study, the Lewin-Schein theory of change was used to understand the longitudinal influences of salesperson goal orientations (i.e., learning and performance) on their performance (Ahearne et al., 2010), highlighting the need to identify the motivational orientations that can enhance individual learning during technological change.

However, learning is a social process. Thus, other scholars have explored how knowledge is shared (Santhanam et al., 2007) and transferred to others, embedding in their work learning theories such as Bandura's (1986) social cognitive theory (e.g., Aiman-Smith & Green, 2002; Bruque et al., 2008). In studies using social cognitive theory, the authors assume that behavioral engagement with technology is a product of the reciprocal interaction of both personal (i.e., internal) and environmental (i.e., external) factors. Learning can also be accelerated with more structural changes (i.e., work practices) (Avgar et al., 2018), complementing investments in training and information sharing during new technological changes.

Psychological safety theory has also been applied to understand how knowledge is shared in teams during technology implementations (Edmondson et al., 2001; Stevens & van Schaik, 2020). Findings suggest that successful implementers used practice sessions to create psychological safety, which facilitated collective learning and new technology adoption

(Edmondson et al., 2001). Learning a new system in a holistic way has also been found to have benefits for psychological safety. An individual's understanding of system dynamics and features (e.g., feedback loops and delays) predicted the quality of information shared among members and perceptions of psychological safety in another study (Bendoly, 2014). A learning lens on the study of responses to technological change offers a developmental rather than static view of technology adoption.

6.3.4   Leader–Follower Perspectives

Managers can frame new technology in different ways to appeal to change recipients. In one study, social power principles and influencing tactics were applied to understand how some users delegate tasks within the system to other users (i.e., indirect use) (Tong et al., 2017). Still, individuals can also choose to frame their responses to managers in ways that align (or misalign) with the original framing to contest aspects of the change (Chreim, 2006). The dyadic relationship between manager and employee can also impact how an employee perceives a change. In addition to influence tactics from managers, leader–follower relationship quality (i.e., leader–member exchange) can shape employee resistance to technological change (Furst & Cable, 2008). The congruency in perceptions and communications between leaders and followers has also been examined as a predictor of employee outcomes during implementations (Narayanaswamy et al., 2013).

Communication and support from management and organizational leaders (as opposed to managers) have also been linked to technology adoption. Applying a social influence lens, in one study, the authors explore how resistance from employees responsible for implementing a change and the public (the users of the new technology) shaped the success of an implementation of a country-wide farecard transportation system in Singapore (Sutanto et al., 2008). Sutanto et al. (2008) find that communication from senior managers can help reduce internal resistance, and public opinions from external leaders can also stimulate widespread acceptance of the system. However, opposingly, social influence frameworks (Kelman, 1958) have also been used to understand why certain types of social pressures can cause behavioral resistance from users in the long term (Malhotra & Galletta, 2005). Arguments for and against a technology implementation represent interpretations of the change, and such persuasive rhetoric is also used to construct identities and negotiate political power (Symon, 2005); technological change is an evolving process involving different actors with varying politically-oriented motivations. Overall, leader–follower perspectives emphasize how social embeddedness and social interactions with others can impact how employees respond to technological change.

6.3.5 Summary of Theoretical Perspectives and Frameworks

Scholars have used various lenses to study responses to technological change. The lenses emphasize different psychological processes that are important to enhance our understanding of the psychology of change. First, cognitive models consist of the majority studied. We include in this grouping the more holistic and widely studied technology models (e.g., TAM, UTAUT) because of their focus on intent to use as an antecedent to the actual use of new technologies; some of these models include components of some of the other approaches we discuss in this section (e.g., social influence). Second, a few studies have explored how emotions and appraisal processes shape coping with technological change. Third, learning perspectives highlight individual development and have also been applied to understand when individuals will be more likely to engage in a meaningful way with the technology. Fourth, leader–follower approaches place particular emphasis on the influence of social support and social networks and point to the importance of social-psychological processes.

6.4 Antecedent-Response Relationships

In this section, we discuss the various antecedent-response sets studied, grouped by the common responses to a new technology (i.e., acceptance and resistance). We then elaborate on some of the more distal outcomes that have been studied. A framework with these relationships is depicted in Figure 6.2.

6.4.1 Technological Change Acceptance

Technological change acceptance can take the form of an affective response (e.g., anger, excitement, coping), a cognitive response (e.g., intent to use, expectations of a system, support for a system), or a behavioral response (e.g., actual adoption/use duration, frequency, and intensity) (e.g., Venkatesh et al., 2008; Brown et al., 2014). Affect, cognition, and behavior in response to technological implementations have been found to have been influenced by (1) individual characteristics (e.g., traits, skills,

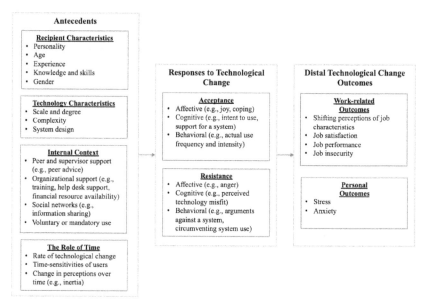

Figure 6.2   Antecedents and consequences of technology acceptance and resistance
Note: Model adapted from Oreg et al. (2011).

demographics), (2) technology characteristics (e.g., system design, complexity), (3) the internal context (e.g., social support, organizational support, social networks), and (4) temporal factors.

Acceptance as a Function of Change Recipient Characteristics: Traits, demographic characteristics, experiences, and other individual differences influence acceptance of a new technology. In one study, the authors report relationships between each personality factor in the five-factor model and acceptance cognitions (Devaraj et al., 2008). Age and experience with technology have been found to predict usage behaviors (Brown et al., 2010). Experience can even overcome some of the structural obstacles associated with change (Alexy et al., 2013). Individual users' comfort level with constant changes is also a strong predictor of acceptance (Hong et al., 2011). Relatedly, having knowledge about a new technology is also predictive of individual usage (Aggarwal et al., 2015). Gender is also related to acceptance behaviors (Brown et al., 2010). According to Venkatesh and Morris (2000), men and women differed in their cognitions about a new technology. They find that the usage decisions for men are predicted by perceptions of usefulness, whereas, for women, these are mostly predicted by perceptions of ease of use and subjective norms. Thus, individuals differ in terms of their perceptions of a new technology (Venkatesh, 2000), which can shape adoption processes. Although there are several factors unique to individuals that can facilitate acceptance, organizations can also shape system characteristics so that they are conducive to acceptance.

Acceptance as a Function of Technology Characteristics: System design can increase an individual's motivation to engage with the technology. For instance, findings suggest that new system acceptance and sustained use can increase when individuals interact with gamification-based training (Venkatesh, 1999). In one study, the authors find that technology characteristics (i.e., radicalness and complexity) explain speed to user competence (Aiman-Smith & Green, 2002). Designing system implementations so that users can engage with them on a voluntary basis (instead of mandatory) may also help with adoption. After all, usage behaviors and intent to use a system can also be an emotionally-laden decision (e.g., Malhotra & Galletta, 2005) and discrete emotions resulting from specific implementation-related events can directly and indirectly facilitate (or hinder) user acceptance (Beaudry & Pinsonneault, 2010). Indeed, understanding change recipient emotions during implementations are essential for managers to consider.

Acceptance as a Function of the Internal Context: The extent to which an individual feels supported by their peers, managers, and the organization in general also influences their propensity to engage with technological change (Marler et al., 2006). In fact, in several of the seminal works in this area, user acceptance has been examined in relation to social influence factors in addition to motivational factors (e.g., Venkatesh & Davis, 2000; Venkatesh et al., 2003). Individuals may also seek social support as part of coping (Beaudry & Pinsonneault, 2010). Support provided by the organization can include traditional support structures, such as system training, online support, help desk support, and change management support, as well as informal support structures, such as peer advice (Sykes, 2015). Sykes (2015) found that these support structures led to user satisfaction with the system. Financial resource availability and management support are associated with high-quality implementation practices, which in turn have contributed to consistent and effective system use (Klein et al., 2001).

Additionally, the social support received also influences the acceptance of new technology. Specifically, the type of network ties (Venkatesh et al., 2011) – ingroup versus outgroup – and information gleaned from a social network (Bruque et al., 2008) – supportive versus informational – also have different effects on individual system use and adaptation behaviors during change. Network density (reflecting "get-help" ties) and network centrality (reflecting "give-help" ties) are also both predictors of system use (Sykes et al., 2009). Evidence suggests that the weight of social influences is greater than that of individual influences (Gallivan et al., 2005), but there is also evidence to the contrary (Alexy et al., 2013). The relative importance of each factor may depend on the context and type of user (Chau & Hu, 2002).

Overall, internal contextual factors and social interactions contribute to individuals' technology acceptance. There are several reasons for this. The transfer of knowledge during implementations has been shown to influence how users interface with new technology and are also crucial for learning processes (Santhanam et al., 2007). The collective learning process can also facilitate change diffusion and determine whether or not routines incorporating the new technologies become part of organizational life (Edmondson et al., 2001). Such social interactions facilitate help-seeking behaviors (e.g., Leonardi, 2007; Beaudry & Pinsonneault, 2010), reducing the possibility that the technology change is perceived as a threat.

6.4.2 Technological Change Resistance

The nature of resistance to technological change has been dissected and conceptualized, suggesting it is not simply the opposite of acceptance. Although several sources of resistance have been studied (for example, switching costs; Kim & Kankanhalli, 2009), scholars have also examined the dynamics and different forms of resistance. Apart from its affective, cognitive, and behavioral components, various forms of resistance exist: aggressive resistance, active resistance, passive resistance, and apathy (Lapointe & Rivard, 2005). Counter-arguments used as persuasive rhetoric against a technology implementation have been considered a manifestation of resistance (Symon, 2005). Furthermore, Lapointe and Rivard (2005) point out that resistance to a technological change is (a) a social process and (b) influenced by time.

Resistance as a Function of the Internal Context: The recursive and dialogic nature of resistance has been explored to some degree. Symon (2005) demonstrated that resistance is used in identity construction and political maneuvers. In a later study, Rivard and Lapointe (2012) analyzed how change implementers (i.e., managers or technology professionals) responded to instances (events) of user resistance and found that the responses fell into four categories (i.e., inaction, acknowledgment, rectification, and dissuasion). These findings helped explain why some forms of resistance among users are perpetuated, and how implementers' responses may interact with some of the antecedents of resistance. Power can also help with persuasion when resistance arises; senior management can decrease resistance by using appropriate communication tactics (Sutanto et al., 2008).

Resistance as a Function of Time: The influence of time on outcomes during technological change has also been a theme in a few studies. The rate of change of perceptions of a system over time (and that the system is misaligned with user expectations) can have implications for user resistance (Venkatesh & Goyal, 2010). Similarly, perceived task technology misfit among managers and users creates time-sensitivities in intentions to circumvent a new technology (a form of resistance) such that, when opportunities for resistance are presented, more circumvention attempts are made (Bendoly & Cotteleer, 2008). In addition, the forms of resistance recipients use have been found to change over time. Boudreau and Robey (2005) find that users will initially avoid using a system due to inertia. However, over time (when it seems unlikely that the implementation will fail), users use workarounds to deal with constraints, which the authors term "reinvention." Thus, resistance can generate other more creative responses and behaviors aligned with the evolution of a technology transformation.

6.4.3   Distal Technological Change Outcomes

Finally, more distal job outcomes, or change consequences, have also been studied. One stream of research has examined how technology change can impact perceptions and behaviors of the workplace. For instance, Bala and Venkatesh (2013) examined how the introduction of an ERP system shaped shifting employee perceptions of job characteristics through their perceptions of work process characteristics and technology characteristics. Other distal work outcomes that have been studied during technological change include job satisfaction (Morris & Venkatesh, 2010; Bala, 2013; Sykes, 2015; Venkatesh, Bala, et al., 2016), job performance (Ahearne et al., 2010; Hsieh et al., 2011; Sykes, 2015), work engagement (Petrou et al., 2018), and job insecurity (Bala, 2013). Another stream of research has also included an examination of well-being-related outcomes, such as stress (Bala, 2013; Sykes, 2015) and anxiety (Bala, 2013). Taken together, this is particularly important to consider because new technology can have a substantial impact on work environments with downstream consequences for distal work and well-being of employee outcomes.

6.5   Future Directions

Our review has brought to light some glaring limitations in our current understanding of the psychology of technological change, which we outline below.

6.5.1   Unpacking the Role of Technology Characteristics

First, and in line with recent calls for research (Landers & Marin, 2021), the technology itself and its distinguishing characteristics should have a central role in theory building and study design. To date, most studies treat the specific type of technological change as secondary. This lack of research on how the type of change shapes employee change responses has also been criticized by scholars (Oreg et al., 2011). In fact, it remains less clear how technological changes differ from one another and differ from other organizational changes such as re-organizations. We have outlined a few insights into the implications of various types of technological changes (e.g., incremental-narrow versus radical-broad changes) and their related psychological processes. Yet, we see ample opportunities, particularly with the rise of artificial intelligence (AI) and machine learning-based applications augmenting and even replacing workers in many work domains. Moreover, more work is needed to understand the implications of the congruency between the type of technology and the process of change (i.e., training needed, type of activities that should be performed). Understanding how individuals think, feel, and behave in relation to change can be regarded as a product of both the type of technology and the change process.

6.5.2   Broadening Our View of Process-Response Relationships

More work is needed to understand the implementation process and design choices that encourage individuals to embrace change. More evidence-based insights are needed on how different process levers (e.g., forms of communication, support, or involvement) can encourage support or mitigate resistance in different implementation phases. Related to how forms of communication influence responses, stories or individual accounts of a change have been studied as part of the complex political process of exercising and gaining power (Dawson & Buchanan, 2005), but more work is needed on the role of persuasive rhetoric at different phases of technological change. Related to social support, future work might explore the nuanced hierarchical relationships between leaders and followers at the various phases of change (e.g., during the anticipatory phase versus during the implementation phase), and how this shapes responses to new technology implementation. In terms of change recipient involvement, gamification has been found to increase acceptance (Venkatesh, 1999), but more work is needed on how technology-based interventions are accepted or resisted at the various phases of change.

Relatedly, another exciting area of research is how digital technology can facilitate and support the change process itself. Many organizations experiment with technology-enabled process interventions such as digital nudges to trigger support or digitally-mediated involvement (e.g., through social media). Hence, we advocate for more empirical work on technology-mediated change management (Kanitz & Gonzalez, 2021) – meaning how managers can leverage digital technology to enhance change processes – which can serve as a means to achieve personalization and broad employee involvement during change implementations.

6.5.3   Examining Ambivalent Responses to Technology Change

Understanding how individuals form these responses requires more in-depth examinations of technology resistance and acceptance. In most studies, particularly for acceptance, more simplistic and homogenous responses have been examined thus far, with little attention to ambivalent responses (i.e., simultaneously positive and negative thoughts or feelings about a technological change). It remains unclear what types of ambivalent responses exist and what the unique consequences of those are. In particular, many people may feel ambivalent about the rise of AI-based assistance systems in many work domains. Indeed, ambivalence may be the norm rather than the exception and gaining a better understanding of the underlying psychological processes that characterize such ambivalent responses remains generally uncharted territory. Although some initial work in the OB domain has started to examine ambivalence in the context of organizational change (e.g., Oreg & Sverdlik, 2011), much more needs to be done. Recent developments in latent profile analyses may be particularly beneficial to identify typologies of ambivalence in the context of technological change. Moreover, we believe that experimental and qualitative work could be beneficial to shed light on more complex responses of technological change.

6.5.4   Extension and Integration of Collective and Individual Level Research

There is room to integrate the rich theoretical models that have been developed (e.g., TAM, UTAUT) across hierarchical levels similar to work on change readiness more broadly (e.g., Rafferty et al., 2013). The majority of work has examined relationships at the individual level. However, there have been a few multi-level studies that have made significant strides. Chau and Hu (2002) propose a multi-level framework for technology acceptance by layering various contexts and examining the interplay between each layer. In another notable study, the authors provide a multi-level, longitudinal theory to explain the process of technological change across the individual- (cognitive absorption), group- (political interactions), and organization-levels (configurations) (Lapointe & Rivard, 2007). The authors acknowledge that integration of theory across levels of analysis allows for insights to be gleaned from what may have been contradictory results initially. Collective responses toward new technologies (e.g., Stensaker & Falkenberg, 2007) will be essential to consider going forward. In the same vein, it will be important to understand how heterogeneity or homogeneity in responses across individuals forms collective responses.

6.5.5   Using Ethical Perspectives on Responses to Technological Change

In addition to understanding the factors that contribute to these other outcomes, we encourage work that integrates the ethics of technological change with desired broader societal and environmental changes. (For an overview, see Grint & Woolgar, 2013; also see Kaplan, 2009). How can the introduction of certain new technologies in organizations improve employee engagement with and perceptions of desirable societal and environmental change? In one noteworthy study, Seidel et al. (2013) explore how information systems can enable environmentally sustainable transformations, and how individuals use those to implement environmentally sustainable work practices. It is possible that knowledge generated by new technologies can facilitate transformations in other parts of the organization (Leonardi, 2007) or, indeed, in other organizations. Work that unpacks the psychology of ethics in the context of technological change is scarce. This is surprising because, in the organizational behavior discipline more generally, ethical perspectives have been studied extensively (e.g., Kaltiainen et al., 2017).

6.6 Conclusion

In this review chapter, we took a backward-looking approach and elaborated on the existing work on how individuals perceive and respond to technological change within organizations. We identified and reviewed sixty-seven articles where a technological change was reported and clustered the articles based on the (1) types of technological changes, (2) theoretical perspective, and (3) antecedent-response relationship studied. First, we discussed the various technology contexts regarding their scale and degree – two dimensions of organizational change. We next described the broad theoretical perspectives, as well as technology-specific theoretical models, that have been applied to the study of technological change. Third, we showed that the conceptualizations of acceptance and resistance responses to technological change have taken distinct directions, and we discussed some of the other antecedents of these and more distal responses that have been studied. In light of our findings, we point to several areas where more investigation is warranted to continue to shed light on the psychology of technological change.

REFERENCES

Aggarwal, R., Kryscynski, D., Midha, V., & Singh, H. (2015). Early to adopt and early to discontinue: The impact of self-perceived and actual IT knowledge on technology use behaviors of end users. *Information Systems Research, 26* (1), 127–144.

Ahearne, M., Lam, S. K., Mathieu, J. E., & Bolander, W. (2010). Why are some salespeople better at adapting to organizational change? *Journal of Marketing, 74*(3), 65–79.

Aiman-Smith, L., & Green, S. G. (2002). Implementing new manufacturing technology: The related effects of technology characteristics and user learning activities. *Academy of Management Journal, 45*(2), 421–430.

Ajzen, I. (1991). The theory of planned behavior. *Organizational Behavior and Human Decision Processes, 50*(2), 179–211.

Alexy, O., Henkel, J., & Wallin, M. W. (2013). From closed to open: Job role changes, individual predispositions, and the adoption of commercial open source software development. *Research Policy, 42*(8), 1325–1340.

Armenakis, A. A., & Bedeian, A. G. (1999). Organizational change: A review of theory and research in the 1990s. *Journal of Management, 25*(3), 293–315.

Autry, C. W., Grawe, S. J., Daugherty, P. J., & Richey, R. G. (2010). The effects of technological turbulence and breadth on supply chain technology acceptance and adoption. *Journal of Operations Management, 28*(6), 522–536.

Avgar, A., Tambe, P., & Hitt, L. M. (2018). Built to learn: How work practices affect employee learning during healthcare information technology implementation. *MIS Quarterly, 42*(2), 645–660.

Bagozzi, R. P. (2007). The legacy of the technology acceptance model and a proposal for a paradigm shift. *Journal of the Association for Information Systems, 8*(4), 244–254.

Bala, H. (2013). The effects of IT-enabled supply chain process change on job and process outcomes: A longitudinal investigation. *Journal of Operations Management, 31*(6), 450–473.

Bala, H., & Venkatesh, V. (2013). Changes in employees' job characteristics during an enterprise system implementation: A latent growth modeling perspective. *MIS Quarterly, 37*(4), 1113–1140.

(2016). Adaptation to information technology: A holistic nomological network from implementation to job outcomes. *Management Science, 62*(1), 156–179.

Bandura, A. (1986). *Social foundations of thought and action: A social cognitive theory.* Hoboken, NJ: Prentice Hall.

Beaudry, A., & Pinsonneault, A. (2010). The other side of acceptance: Studying the direct and indirect effects of emotions on information technology use. *MIS Quarterly, 34*(4), 689–710.

Bendoly, E. (2014). System dynamics understanding in projects: Information sharing, psychological safety, and performance effects. *Production and Operations Management, 23*(8), 1352–1369.

Bendoly, E., & Cotteleer, M. J. (2008). Understanding behavioral sources of process variation following enterprise system deployment. *Journal of Operations Management, 26*(1), 23–44.

Blut, M., Chong, A., Tsiga, Z., & Venkatesh, V. (2021). Meta-analysis of the unified theory of acceptance and use of technology (UTAUT): Challenging its validity and charting a research agenda in the Red Ocean. *Journal of the Association for Information Systems, 23*(1), 13–95.

Bostrom, R. P., & Heinen, J. S. (1977). MIS problems and failures: A sociotechnical perspective. Part I: The causes. *MIS Quarterly, 1*(3), 17–32.

Boudreau, M.-C., & Robey, D. (2005). Enacting integrated information technology: A human agency perspective. *Organization Science, 16*(1), 3–18.

Brown, S. A., Dennis, A. R., & Venkatesh, V. (2010). Predicting collaboration technology use: Integrating technology adoption and collaboration research. *Journal of Management Information Systems, 27*(2), 9–54.

Brown, S. A., Venkatesh, V., & Goyal, S. (2014). Expectation confirmation in information systems research: a test of six competing models. *MIS Quarterly, 38*(3), 729–756.

Brown, S. A., Venkatesh, V., Kuruzovich, J., & Massey, A. P. (2008). Expectation confirmation: An examination of three competing models. *Organizational Behavior and Human Decision Processes, 105*(1), 52–66.

Bruque, S., Moyano, J., & Eisenberg, J. (2008). Individual adaptation to IT-induced change: The role of social networks. *Journal of Management Information Systems, 25*(3), 177–206.

Cadwallader, S., Jarvis, C. B., Bitner, M. J., & Ostrom, A. L. (2010). Frontline employee motivation to participate in service innovation implementation. *Journal of the Academy of Marketing Science, 38*(2), 219–239.

Chau, P. Y. K., & Hu, P. J. (2002). Examining a model of information technology acceptance by individual professionals: An exploratory study. *Journal of Management Information Systems, 18*(4), 191–229.

Chreim, S. (2006). Managerial frames and institutional discourses of change: Employee appropriation and resistance. *Organization Studies, 27*(9), 1261–1287.

Cua, K. O., McKone, K. E., & Schroeder, R. G. (2001). Relationships between implementation of TQM, JIT, and TPM and manufacturing performance. *Journal of Operations Management, 19*(6), 675–694.

Davis, F. D. (1989). Perceived usefulness, perceived ease of use, and user acceptance of information technology. *MIS Quarterly, 13*(3), 319–340.

Dawson, P., & Buchanan, D. (2005). The way it really happened: Competing narratives in the political process of technological change. *Human Relations, 58*(7), 845–865.

Devaraj, S., Easley, R. F., & Crant, J. M. (2008). Research note: How does personality matter? Relating the five-factor model to technology acceptance and use. *Information Systems Research, 19*(1), 93–105.

Edmondson, A. C., Bohmer, R. M., & Pisano, G. P. (2001). Disrupted routines: Team learning and new technology implementation in hospitals. *Administrative Science Quarterly, 46*(4), 685–716.

Ettlie, J. E., Bridges, W. P., & O'Keefe, R. D. (1984). Organization strategy and structural differences for radical versus incremental innovation. *Management Science, 30*(6), 682–695.

Festinger, L. (1957). *A theory of cognitive dissonance.* Evanston, IL: Row Peterson.

Furst, S. A., & Cable, D. M. (2008). Employee resistance to organizational change: Managerial influence tactics and leader-member exchange. *Journal of Applied Psychology, 93*(2), 453–462.

Gallivan, M. J., Spitler, V. K., & Koufaris, M. (2005). Does information technology training really matter? A social information processing analysis of coworkers' influence on IT usage in the workplace. *Journal of Management Information Systems, 22*(1), 153–192.

Gefen, D. R., & Ridings, C. M. (2002). Implementation team responsiveness and user evaluation of customer relationship management: A quasi-experimental design study of social exchange theory. *Journal of Management Information Systems, 19*(1), 47–69.

Grint, K., & Woolgar, S. (2013). *The machine at work: Technology, work and organization.* Hoboken, NJ: John Wiley & Sons.

Hackman, J. R., Hackman, R. J., & Oldham, G. R. (1980). *Work redesign.* Reading, MA: Addison-Wesley.

Hardgrave, B. C., Davis, F. D., & Riemenschneider, C. K. (2003). Investigating determinants of software developers' intentions to follow methodologies. *Journal of Management Information Systems*, *20*(1), 123–151.

Heracleous, L., & Barrett, M. (2001). Organizational change as discourse: Communicative actions and deep structures in the context of information technology implementation. *Academy of Management Journal*, *44*(4), 755–778.

Homburg, C., Wieseke, J., & Kuehnl, C. (2010). Social influence on salespeople's adoption of sales technology: A multilevel analysis. *Journal of the Academy of Marketing Science*, *38*(2), 159–168.

Hong, W., Thong, J. Y., Chasalow, L. C., & Dhillon, G. (2011). User acceptance of agile information systems: A model and empirical test. *Journal of Management Information Systems*, *28*(1), 235–272.

Hsieh, J. P.-A., Rai, A., & Xu, S. X. (2011). Extracting business value from IT: A sensemaking perspective of post-adoptive use. *Management Science*, *57*(11), 2018–2039.

Hu, P. J., Chau, P. Y., Sheng, O. R. L., & Tam, K. Y. (1999). Examining the technology acceptance model using physician acceptance of telemedicine technology. *Journal of Management Information Systems*, *16*(2), 91–112.

Kaltiainen, J., Lipponen, J., & Holtz, B. C. (2017). Dynamic interplay between merger process justice and cognitive trust in top management: A longitudinal study. *Journal of Applied Psychology*, *102*(4), 636–647.

Kanitz, R., & Gonzalez, K. (2021). Are we stuck in the predigital age? Embracing technology-mediated change management in organizational change research. *The Journal of Applied Behavioral Science*, *57*(4), 447–458.

Kaplan, D. M. (ed.). (2009). *Readings in the philosophy of technology*. Lanham, MD: Rowman & Littlefield Publishers.

Karahanna, E., Straub, D. W., & Chervany, N. L. (1999). Information technology adoption across time: A cross-sectional comparison of pre-adoption and post-adoption beliefs. *MIS Quarterly*, *23*(2), 183–213.

Kelman, H. C. (1958). Compliance, identification, and internalization three processes of attitude change. *Journal of Conflict Resolution*, *2*(1), 51–60.

Kim, H.-W., & Kankanhalli, A. (2009). Investigating user resistance to information systems implementation: A status quo bias perspective. *MIS Quarterly*, *33*(3), 567–582.

Klein, K. J., Conn, A. B., & Sorra, J. S. (2001). Implementing computerized technology: An organizational analysis. *Journal of Applied Psychology*, *86*(5), 811–824.

Landers, R. N., & Marin, S. (2021). Theory and technology in organizational psychology: A review of technology integration paradigms and their effects on the validity of theory. *Annual Review of Organizational Psychology and Organizational Behavior*, *8*, 235–258.

Langley, A. (1999). Strategies for theorizing from process data. *Academy of Management Review*, *24*(4), 691–710.

Lapointe, L., & Rivard, S. (2005). A multilevel model of resistance to information technology implementation. *MIS Quarterly, 29*(3), 461–491.

(2007). A triple take on information system implementation. *Organization Science, 18*(1), 89–107.

Lauterbach, J., Mueller, B., & Kahrau, F. (2020). Achieving effective use when digitalizing work: The role of representational complexity. *MIS Quarterly, 44* (3), 1023–1048.

Lazarus, R. S. (1991). Progress on a cognitive-motivational-relational theory of emotion. *American Psychologist, 46*(8), 819–834.

Lazarus, R. S., & Folkman, S. (1984). *Stress, appraisal, and coping*. New York: Springer.

Leonardi, P. M. (2007). Activating the informational capabilities of information technology for organizational change. *Organization Science, 18*(5), 813–831.

Malhotra, Y., & Galletta, D. (2005). A multidimensional commitment model of volitional systems adoption and usage behavior. *Journal of Management Information Systems, 22*(1), 117–151.

Marler, J. H., Liang, X., & Dulebohn, J. H. (2006). Training and effective employee information technology use. *Journal of Management, 32*(5), 721–743.

Morris, M. G., & Venkatesh, V. (2010). Job characteristics and job satisfaction: Understanding the role of enterprise resource. *MIS Quarterly, 34*(1), 143–161.

Nadler, D. A., & Tushman, M. L. (1989). Organizational frame bending: Principles for managing reorientation. *Academy of Management Perspectives, 3*(3), 194–204.

Narayanaswamy, R., Grover, V., & Henry, R. M. (2013). The impact of influence tactics in information system development projects: A control-loss perspective. *Journal of Management Information Systems, 30*(1), 191–226.

Oreg, S., & Sverdlik, N. (2011). Ambivalence toward imposed change: The conflict between dispositional resistance to change and the orientation toward the change agent. *Journal of Applied Psychology, 96*(2), 337–349.

Oreg, S., Vakola, M., & Armenakis, A. (2011). Change recipients' reactions to organizational change: A 60-year review of quantitative studies. *The Journal of Applied Behavioral Science, 47*(4), 461–524.

Petrou, P., Demerouti, E., & Schaufeli, W. B. (2018). Crafting the change: The role of employee job crafting behaviors for successful organizational change. *Journal of Management, 44*(5), 1766–1792.

Rafferty, A. E., Jimmieson, N. L., & Armenakis, A. A. (2013). Change readiness: A multilevel review. *Journal of Management, 39*(1), 110–135.

Rivard, S., & Lapointe, L. (2012). Information technology implementers' responses to user resistance: Nature and effects. *MIS Quarterly, 36*(3), 897–920.

Robey, D., Ross, J. W., & Boudreau, M.-C. (2002). Learning to implement enterprise systems: An exploratory study of the dialectics of change. *Journal of Management Information Systems, 19*(1), 17–46.

Ryan, R. M., & Deci, E. L. (2000). Self-determination theory and the facilitation of intrinsic motivation, social development, and well-being. *American Psychologist, 55*(1), 68–78.

Santhanam, R., Seligman, L., & Kang, D. (2007). Postimplementation knowledge transfers to users and information technology professionals. *Journal of Management Information Systems, 24*(1), 171–199.

Seidel, S., Recker, J., & Vom Brocke, J. (2013). Sensemaking and sustainable practicing: Functional affordances of information systems in green transformations. *MIS Quarterly, 37*(4), 1275–1299.

Stensaker, I., & Falkenberg, J. (2007). Making sense of different responses to corporate change. *Human Relations, 60*(1), 137–177.

Stevens, M., & van Schaik, J. (2020). Implementing new technologies for complex care: The role of embeddedness factors in team learning. *Journal of Operations Management, 66*(1–2), 112–134.

Sutanto, J., Kankanhalli, A., Tay, J., Raman, K. S., & Tan, B. C. (2008). Change management in interorganizational systems for the public. *Journal of Management Information Systems, 25*(3), 133–176.

Sykes, T. A. (2015). Support structures and their impacts on employee outcomes: A longitudinal field study of an enterprise system implementation. *MIS Quarterly, 39*(2), 473–496.

Sykes, T. A., Venkatesh, V., & Gosain, S. (2009). Model of acceptance with peer support: A social network perspective to understand employees' system use. *MIS Quarterly, 33*(2), 371–393.

Sykes, T. A., Venkatesh, V., & Johnson, J. L. (2014). Enterprise system implementation and employee job performance: Understanding the role of advice networks. *MIS Quarterly, 38*(1), 51–72.

Symon, G. (2005). Exploring resistance from a rhetorical perspective. *Organization Studies, 26*(11), 1641–1663.

Tong, Y., Tan, C.-H., & Teo, H.-H. (2017). Direct and indirect information system use: A multimethod exploration of social power antecedents in healthcare. *Information Systems Research, 28*(4), 690–710.

Venkatesh, V. (1999). Creation of favorable user perceptions: Exploring the role of intrinsic motivation. *MIS Quarterly, 23*(2), 239–260.

(2000). Determinants of perceived ease of use: Integrating control, intrinsic motivation, and emotion into the technology acceptance model. *Information Systems Research, 11*(4), 342–365.

Venkatesh, V., & Bala, H. (2008). Technology acceptance model 3 and a research agenda on interventions. *Decision Sciences, 39*(2), 273–315.

Venkatesh, V., Bala, H., & Sambamurthy, V. (2016). Implementation of an information and communication technology in a developing country: A multimethod longitudinal study in a bank in India. *Information Systems Research, 27*(3), 558–579.

Venkatesh, V., Brown, S. A., Maruping, L. M., & Bala, H. (2008). Predicting different conceptualizations of system use: The competing roles of behavioral intention, facilitating conditions, and behavioral expectation. *MIS Quarterly, 32*(3), 483–502.

Venkatesh, V., & Davis, F. D. (2000). A theoretical extension of the technology acceptance model: Four longitudinal field studies. *Management Science, 46* (2), 186–204.

Venkatesh, V., & Goyal, S. (2010). Expectation disconfirmation and technology adoption: Polynomial modeling and response surface analysis. *MIS Quarterly, 34*(2), 281–303.

Venkatesh, V., & Morris, M. G. (2000). Why don't men ever stop to ask for directions? Gender, social influence, and their role in technology acceptance and usage behavior. *MIS Quarterly, 24*(1), 115–139.

Venkatesh, V., Morris, M. G., Davis, G. B., & Davis, F. D. (2003). User acceptance of information technology: Toward a unified view. *MIS Quarterly, 27*(3), 425–478.

Venkatesh, V., Thong, J. Y., & Xu, X. (2016). Unified theory of acceptance and use of technology: A synthesis and the road ahead. *Journal of the Association for Information Systems, 17*(5), 328–376.

Venkatesh, V., Zhang, X., & Sykes, T. A. (2011). "Doctors do too little technology": A longitudinal field study of an electronic healthcare system implementation. *Information Systems Research, 22*(3), 523–546.

Vroom, V. H. (1964). *Work and motivation.* Hoboken, NJ: Wiley.

Weick, K. E. (1995). *Sensemaking in organizations,* vol. 3. Thousand Oaks, CA: Sage.

CHAPTER 7

Identification Change in Chinese Acquisitions in Europe
The Social Identity Approach

Anna Lupina-Wegener, Rolf van Dick, and Shuang Liang

7.1 Introduction

Over the last ten years, we have increasingly observed small, local Chinese firms emerging as global players. In 2010, 9 percent of the Fortune Global 500 firms were Chinese (Money, 2010). Just one decade later, this number had almost tripled to 24 percent (Forbes, 2019). We argue that Chinese firms aspiring to change from a local to a global firm might require an in-depth identification change of their employees (Mathews, 2006). However, identification processes underpinning the transition from a local Chinese to a global firm, and the factors contributing to these change processes remain unknown. Indeed, research on China remains undertheorized (Kostova & Hult, 2016), and qualitative investigations could help generate new theoretical breakthroughs (Barkema et al., 2015). Therefore, the identification change needs to be better understood in such a context as it is an important success factor of Mergers and Acquisitions (M&As).

To address this gap, we will build on the social identity theory and examine the underexplored identification change of employees of those Chinese firms which strive to become global players. We will present a model of organizational identification change among Chinese employees after overseas acquisitions and will provide an illustration with a case study of a Chinese acquisition in Europe wherein identification change was difficult. The chairman lacked identity leadership and was distracted by the Chinese government's internationalization and innovation fostering policies. This resulted in low identity congruence between pre- and post-merger identification and transition from pre-merger and post-merger identification did not take place successfully. The chapter helps advance the social identity theory in the context of Chinese culture and also addresses a gap in the international management literature wherein identification change in collectivist and high power distance cultures are under-investigated. We will be guided by the following research question: How do managers in acquiring firms deal with identification change in failed Sino-Western acquisitions?

7.2 Theoretical Background: The Social Identity Approach to M&As

We will rely on the social identity theory (SIT) centered on individuals, not acting on the basis of their personal identities, but rather as members of their ingroup(s) in relation to members of other groups (Tajfel & Turner, 1979; van Dick et al., 2004). Self-categorization theory explains how and when people will define themselves as group members and examines the impact of this variability on self-perception ("I" vs. "we") to better understand individual and group behavior (Turner, 1985; Turner et al., 1987). Building on SIT and self-categorization theory (SCT), organizational identification is defined as the individual's perception of the sharedness of this organizational identity, one which helps an individual define him or herself by sharing aspects of the organization's identity with other members (Ashforth & Mael, 1989). When organizational identification is strong, the organizational identity is salient and incorporated in what the individual believes is distinctive, central, and enduring about him or herself (Albert & Whetten, 1985). Thus, organizational identification is "the extent to which people define themselves as members of a particular group or organization," and it "indicates whether people engage in a process of self-stereotyping whereby their behaviour is oriented towards, and structured by, the content of that group or organization's defining characteristics, norms and values" (Haslam et al., 2003, p. 360). Organizational identification is one important form of relationship between individuals and their organization, wherein members adopt the defining characteristics of the organization as defining characteristics for themselves (Dutton et al., 1994).

Similarly, identification is at the heart of change processes wherein psychological bonds between employees and the employing organization might become weaker (van Dick, 2004). Thus, identification mechanisms in the context of change have received extensive attention from scholars seeking to understand how organizational identification can sustain the frequent organizational changes which follow M&As (Rousseau, 1998). Organizational identification change in M&As has received significant attention in organizational studies (Giessner, 2011; Lupina-Wegener, Karamustafa et al., 2015). There is empirical evidence showing that changing organizational identification is often not easy for employees in both the acquiring and acquired organizations. For example, in a qualitative study, Wei and Clegg (2018) found that identity change takes place gradually throughout the post-merger integration. First, employees might show resistance to the identity change and they might accept the change over time only after appropriate managerial interventions (van Dijk & van Dick, 2009). In cross-border M&As, identification change may be particularly complex as members of the acquired organization may need time to figure out how they differ from the acquirer and sister organizations in the parent network. For example, in a longitudinal qualitative case study in Mexico, Lupina-Wegener, Schneider et al. (2015) show that, although the head office may facilitate identification change at the post-merger subsidiary level, there is ultimately a need for a shared identity to incorporate and unite the subsidiary on the national, regional, and global levels. Similarly, in a qualitative case study of a Finnish–Swedish merger, Vaara (2003) explains that the identity change process is difficult because of employees' attachment to their pre-merger identities and negative stereotypes of their new colleagues.

Second, in cross-border M&As, multiple identities are salient and their inter-relationships are characterized by high complexity (Sarala et al., 2017), especially as they are often accounting for different forms of identification such as identification, neutral/ambivalent identification, and disidentification (Kreiner & Ashforth, 2004). There is evidence from previous empirical investigations that Europeans might disidentify from a Chinese acquirer due to perceived lower quality and, overall, a lower status. Further, those studies show that identification processes change over time, with – for example – neutral identification changing into ambivalent identification   (Lupina-Wegener et al., 2020; Liang et al., 2021;). Despite those insights, organizational identification change remains underexplored in Sino-Western M&As. The investigation presented in this chapter provides insights into the complexity of identification change of a small Chinese firm through overseas acquisitions, which may advance further theory development.

7.3   The Social Identity Approach in the Chinese Context

Understanding the identification processes underpinning the transition of a local Chinese into a global firm together with the contributing factors provides a unique theoretical opportunity (Lupina-Wegener & van Dick, 2016). Over the last ten years, we have increasingly observed small, local Chinese firms emerging as global players. In 2010, 9 percent of the Fortune Global 500 firms were Chinese (Money, 2010). Just one decade later, this number had almost tripled to 24 percent (Forbes, 2019). The transformation into global players has often taken place through inward (IFDI) and outward foreign direct investment (OFDI) which increased exponentially. Initially, many Chinese firms grew through IFDI, intending to provide their foreign partner with access to the Chinese market while the Chinese partner benefited from access to strategic assets such as innovative technology. For example, Chinese automotive and pharmaceutical firms have grown through international joint ventures, strategic alliances, and acquisitions with firms from advanced markets (Zhao et al., 2005). Following joint ventures and M&As, Chinese firms and their "copy-cat" competitors have been exposed to foreign competition, were able to improve their governance structure, and gain financial and managerial capabilities. This increased competitive advantage acquired through IFDI is an important factor motivating Chinese competitors to subsequently focus on the acquisition of strategic assets through OFDI in order to close the development gap with their Western competitors (Cui et al., 2014). A renowned example is Lenovo's acquisition of IBM personal computers or Geely's acquisition of Volvo. In 2018, Chinese OFDI flows reached $130 billion, making China the world's second largest outward investor after Japan (UNCTAD, 2019). These Chinese OFDIs aim to acquire strategic and critical assets from developed markets in order to overcome their latecomer disadvantage on the global stage (Luo & Tung, 2007). Not all cases are successful. For example, the cash intensive overseas acquisitions conducted by HNA Group with targets in different industries (IT, hotels, catering, etc.) resulted in financial difficulties and ultimately the founder's suicide. Such failures might result from the fact that many firms which were actually not ready, engaged into international acquisitions as encouraged by Chinese governments' internationalization and innovation fostering policies. The goal was to provide access to overseas markets through a pro-OFDI incentive structure for local firms such as easy access to bank loans or domestic guarantees for foreign currency (Li & Hendrischke, 2020). Indeed, government policies and regulations importantly shape the direction of Chinese OFDI (Buckley et al., 2018).

Identification processes in acquisitions in China are under-investigated, therefore this context provides a unique opportunity for further theory building (Deng, 2009). Along the same lines, Kostova and Hult (2016, p. 27) call for the development of "more theoretically derived parameters that define a particular environment in a comprehensive and refined way and allow for a deeper examination of contextual effects on company strategies and behaviours." Similarly, Barkema et al. (2015) realize that management research in China requires more qualitative, inductive methods for theory building, accounting for culture, institutions and organizational change to help generate new theoretical breakthroughs.

There is evidence that, in Eastern and Western cultures, people have different ways to manage their interpersonal relationships, which can be understood by the two cultural dimensions of collectivism and power distance (Barkema et al., 2015). A meta-analysis by Lee et al. (2015) reveals that organizational identification has stronger effects on work behavior in collectivist rather than individualistic cultures. In the same vein, a quantitative study by Chung et al. (2014) on change at a Chinese retailer after an unexpected US acquisition reveals that the Chinese "Zhongyong" value (Confucian doctrine prescribing harmonious interpersonal relationships) is an important driver of Chinese employees' reaction to change. Particularly, Chinese employees tend to support change initiatives which they view as positive for the organization and peers, rather than those that are driven by self-interest, that is, concerned with "me" issues. Chinese employees do not want to be seen as "self-oriented" to avoid social isolation. Indeed, change in identification after the merger can be supported by Chinese employees if they are clear about the benefits for the collective and fit in with peers and the organization, as well as a larger stakeholder network.

Further, there are few studies that explore how power distance matters in identification change processes. In high power distance countries, there is high respect and admiration for leaders. Thus, leadership can be linked more strongly with employees' attitudes and behaviors. van Dick and Kerschreiter (2016) propose that a leader's behavior helps to create strong identities, particularly in China and other collectivistic societies with pronounced paternalism. In light of these characteristics of the Chinese culture and the overall high ambivalence triggered by multiple identities in Sino-European M&As (Lupina-Wegener et al., 2020), we argue that identity leadership might help manage multiple identities and foster transition from pre-merger to post-merger identification.

The identity leadership model (Haslam et al., 2020) focuses on leaders' management of a shared sense of "we" and "us," wherein this shared identity development results from a process of social influence involving the followers' willingness to contribute to collective action (Steffens et al., 2014). Identity leadership comprises four-dimensions. Identity prototypicality involves representing the unique qualities that define the group or organization. Acts of identity entrepreneurship create a shared sense of "we" and "us" by words and deeds, that is, the boundaries and content of who we are. Acts of identity advancement promote core interests of the group/organization, for example, by standing up for the group or defending it. Finally, acts of identity impresarioship create material reality for the group or organization, building on structures that facilitate shared understanding, coordination, and collective success.

Furthermore, the political context might be relevant for Chinese firms' identification change. The literature reveals that central and municipal governments often have a powerful impact on Chinese firms (Deng, 2009). For instance, the central government policies can influence both Chinese firms' M&A decisions and IFDI by increasing or decreasing the financial support to the relevant companies. Increased financial support may encourage Chinese firms to seek strategic assets through overseas acquisitions. Indeed, the Chinese OFDI initiatives, "China 2025" and Belt Road Initiative were set to promote the international competitiveness of Chinese companies. Finally, the socio-political history of China, such as the Cultural Revolution, and immature institutions contribute to a lower level of trust outside the family and network circle. Trust remains reserved to *guanxi*, that is, interpersonal relationships (Fukuyama, 1995; Buckley et al., 2006).

7.4   Framework of Identification Change in Chinese Overseas Acquisitions

After this introduction, we will now present a framework and illustrate our arguments by presenting findings from a qualitative study guided by the following research question: How do managers in acquiring firms deal with identification change in failed Sino-Western acquisitions? Figure 7.1 presents a framework of the identification change process in Chinese overseas acquisitions.

Figure 7.1 depicts identity-related mechanisms and boundary conditions that take place during the transition from a pre-merger to a post-merger identification, that is, the processes of becoming an international. The impact of leadership on identification processes can be particularly strong in Chinese acquisitions due to a strong power distance combined with high collectivism described in Section 7.3; culture as a moderator and a boundary condition (see van Dick and Kerschreiter, 2016). Acts of identity leadership influence both congruence and continuity which are both mediators that support or prevent the transition from pre- (or current) to post- (or desired) identification. Identity congruence received attention on the individual level of analysis chiefly from the person–environment fit theory which focuses on congruence with regard to identity categories between individuals and their teams or organizations (Junker et al., 2021). Similarly, congruence between pre-merger and post-merger identification may provide organizational members with a reliable

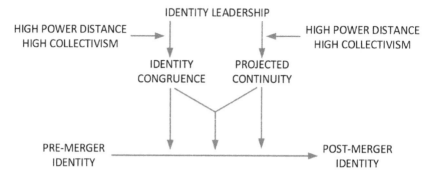

Figure 7.1   The framework of identification change in Chinese overseas acquisitions

source of self-definition (Dutton et al., 1994). Foreman and Whetten (2002) define identity congruence as a comparison between ideal and current identity, which further impacts organizational members' attitudes and behaviors, such as cooperation and altruism, involvement, loyalty, and acceptance of the change. Similarly, identity congruence in our framework is conceptualized as a degree of fit between pre- and desired post-merger identification in terms of content (who we are) and processes (the degree to which we identify). High fit facilitates the transition from pre- to post-merger identification. The low fit makes such a transition difficult.

While identity congruence is necessary for the transition, it is not enough. As depicted in our model, we argue that identity congruence and projected continuity interact. Projected continuity captures employees' understanding of where their organization is going and how they can personally contribute to this path ahead (Ullrich et al., 2005; Liang et al., 2021; Lupina-Wegener et al., 2014). For example, in their paper, Liang et al. (2021) feature a case of a Chinese acquisition, wherein its' members experienced dramatic changes, and they sought to keep changing as "change was their continuity." Through continuous transformation and identification change, this firm got rid of its inferior status of a "copy-cat" and members transferred their pre-merger to post-merger identification. Thus, identity congruence can involve change, but requires projected continuity. Identity congruence without projected continuity or projected continuity without identity congruence is not sufficient, as compared to both being high. Only in such conditions can employees effectively transfer pre-merger to post-merger identification.

We will illustrate our framework based on the case of ChinaCorp (here and in the following, names are disguised to maintain the organizations' anonymity). It is a representative case as it is similar to other conglomerates (such as Wanda or HNA Group) which are actively acquiring western firms. ChinaCorp was founded in the early 1990s. Motivated by the Chinese "go global" policy, ChinaCorp was an active and aggressive acquirer by getting access to necessary financial resources. Through its acquisitions, it grew from a small, local retail shop to a large conglomerate with an international presence. Currently, the ChinaCorp business areas focus on retail, finance, real estate, and collectibles. It is a shareholder in Shanghai-listed Red-City based ChinaMall, which purchased the Europe-based department store chain EuroMall.

We stepped into ChinaCorp with our research, twenty-six months after the acquisition took place. It was shortly after the Grand Opening of EuroMall in Red-City and further overseas acquisitions of EuroMall2 and EuroMall3. We conducted seven interviews, one focus group, and many off-the-record-discussions with senior executives from ChinaCorp. We thoroughly studied available information on the acquisition available in the European and Chinese press as well as the social media. We continued collecting the secondary data over five years. The majority of the primary and secondary data collection was conducted in Chinese.

We chose to focus on the EuroMall acquisition, as its identity was aligned with ChinaCorp DNA "retail," and it was the largest among ChinaCorp's acquisitions in the retail industry – all of those acquisitions in retail failed within four-to-five years, with overseas targets going into bankruptcy. ChinaCorp further grew in the Chinese domestic healthcare industry, leveraging its overseas acquisitions facilitated by Chinese government policies fostering innovation in health and international expansion. We will explain the acquisition's failure from an identity perspective. This will answer our research question: How do managers in acquiring firms deal with identification change in failed Sino-Western acquisitions?

7.5   The Case of EuroMall Acquisition by ChinaCorp

7.5.1   *The Political Context of ChinaCorp's Overseas Acquisitions*

The goal of the government has been to develop China as an international and innovation-driven economy rather than a manufacturing powerhouse. Chinese overseas acquisitions are often aligned with the relevant government policies for catching up with western MNCs in terms of technological and managerial competencies. For instance, the government's Belt Road Initiative provides an enormous opportunity for ChinaCorp's overseas acquisitions. The Chinese government also put in place a system wherein Chinese firms' overseas acquisitions can receive support by a special "credit system" for financing future overseas acquisitions.

7.5.2   *The Chairman's Identity Leadership*

Chairman Xuming Zhu was a business and a state political leader. Before starting his own business, Chairman Zhu had been a government official. He held various honorary roles in government-related bodies and was a member of the most important patriotic organization "RedProvince First." In addition, he was the founder and the chairman of ChinaCorp. Chairman Zhu started his entrepreneurial journey with a small shop before he moved into a diversified, large retail business. In 2018, Chairman Zhu was rated one of the richest Chinese, with a fortune of over a billion USD. However, within two years, ChinaCorp grew its' debt to several billion USD.

As a business leader, he had a strong opportunity-driven approach to business development, leading his teams with limited strategic planning. Chairman Zhu was described by our interviewees as hard-working but not easy to collaborate with. He tended to take all decisions, expected the management to follow, and often applied sanctions for those who refused. He was viewed as autocratic, harsh, and unpredictable. One interviewee said:

> He grew up as a small self-employed person. Back then, he had to manage customers, money, government relations, and everything else. So even though he has now a company of this size, he still maintains the same kind of leadership as before.

As a political leader, Chairman Zhu displayed a strong identification with the Chinese government and Chinese international development plans for innovation through overseas acquisitions. He was an outspoken leader who liked contact with the press and sharing insights on the development of his businesses as well as on China's successes. In the light of his political background, he said:

> In the past five years, the "RedProvince First" has handled and responded to the issues concerning many fields to which it paid attention with high efficiency, conducted in-depth consultations and made accurate suggestions in various fields such as poverty alleviation, medical reform and rule of law, and helped to establish the close and clear relationship between politics and business, fully playing its roles of political consultation, democratic supervision, and participation in the administration and discussion of state affairs. I personally also raised a dozen proposals in the past five years and all of them had been seriously answered and handled. This fully shows that the "RedProvince First" members earnestly participate in the great practice of socialism with Chinese characteristics.

Table 7.1 summarizes Chairman Zhu's identity leadership acts.

Table 7.1 *Summary of Chairman Zhu's weak identity leadership acts*

Identity prototypicality	- Business and political player - Autocratic and unpredictable
Identity entrepreneurship	- Focuses on making a contribution to China's growth, e.g., China 2025, BRI - Opportunity-driven and low strategic thinking - Actual: fear culture vs. desired identity: positivity, kindness, and introspection
Identity advancement	- Misses important opportunities for the Chinese and European organizations, e.g., e-commerce - Follows Chinese government policies, but does not ensure firms' profitability
Identity impresarioship	- Fails to create structure for synergies between the acquirer and the target - Makes false promises to the European target, and high, undesired turnover takes place in both EuroMall and ChinaMall - Lacking action plan for EuroMall and ChinaMall integration

7.5.3   *The Motive of the EuroMall Acquisition and the Subsequent Acquisitions*

The Chairman was good at playing with his dual identities in the government and in business. He thoroughly studied Xi Jinping's thoughts on socialism with Chinese characteristics. He strived to fulfil his duties as a "RedProvince First" member and to improve the lives and collaboration of Chinese and foreign people. He was committed to making China great and to contributing to China's positive image in Western economies. He wanted his business to contribute to building a strong China. To this end, in the last ten years, Chairman Zhu aimed to buy overseas assets. He said:

> In the past five years, we have actively responded to the great initiative of the Party and State in building "the Belt and Road" and vigorously implemented the "going global and bringing in" strategy with gratifying results … At the same time, we have also actively participated in charity activities abroad, demonstrating the good international image of Chinese enterprises and realizing a multi-win result. I think "the Belt and Road" initiative is amazing and serves as a road of cooperation for promoting common development and achieving common prosperity in the world!

Until his first acquisition (of EuroMall), Chairman Zhu had no clear business strategy for ChinaCorp's overseas expansion. Following "China 2025" and BRI, he decided to focus on the following three segments:

healthcare, consumption, and finance, as he claimed: "The development of ChinaCorp today won't be possible without reform and opening up, and we won't have a tomorrow without the concern and care of the party and state."

By responding to the government's call actively with various business activities, Chairman Zhu was a recipient of various achievement awards. His first acquisition – EuroMall, was an opportunity acquisition that was proposed by his banker. EuroMall was a department store chain with an over 100-year heritage, located in Europe. It had found itself at the brink of bankruptcy. On the acquirer's side, there was ChinaMall, part of ChinaCorp's holding and located in the city center of Red-City. Both ChinaMall and EuroMall operated in industries in transformation due to an increasing role played by e-commerce. Chairman Zhu considered it interesting to buy EuroMall as e-commerce was not developed in Europe and customers preferred the traditional way of shopping as compared to Chinese customers. Moreover, he identified more business growth opportunities in China rather than in Europe. Thus, the post-merger plan was that ChinaMall and EuroMall would focus on business growth in China whereas, in Europe, EuroMall would maintain its stability. Soon after acquiring EuroMall, Chairman Zhu engaged in further acquisitions in both retail and healthcare industries. Retail acquisitions were aimed at ChinaMall's core domestic business improvement and healthcare acquisitions aimed at business development in new areas. Table 7.2 summarizes those overseas acquisitions.

Table 7.2 *ChinaCorp's overseas acquisitions*

Month[1]	Target	Bankruptcy date	Industry
M1	EuroMall	M65: sold again for 25% of the original value	Retail
M4	EuroMall2	M53: sold again for 30% of the original value	Retail
M9	EuroHealth1		Healthcare services
M19	EuroMall2	M63: sold again with a large value decrease	Retail
M26	Data collection		
M26	EuroHealth2		Healthcare
M26	EuroHealth3		Healthcare
M27	EuroHealth4		Healthcare

[1] The timeline for the overseas acquisitions. The first one started in M1 (EuroMall1), the second one started in M4 (EuroMall2), the third one in M19 (EuroMall3), etc.

7.5.4   Pre-merger Identity

ChinaCorp's DNA is diverse, which includes not only the original retail business. One of the interviewees said:

> Before I joined ChinaCorp, I thought ChinaCorp was a local retail business. Really, after I came here, I think there are two words that are very good. One is diversification. It's really … we have been involved in so many fields, consumer retail, finance, culture and entertainment, real estate, industrial construction, medical, hospital management, etc.

ChinaMall was a local gallery with mid-to-low end products. The mall was not very attractive to Chinese customers due to its outdated offers and image. The need for improvement and change was evident for the mall to retain its competitive advantage in China. Moreover, like many fast-growing conglomerates in China, ChinaMall was viewed as flexible, fast, changing, Chinese/local, and cost-driven, as for example revealed by one of our interviewees: "Chinese organization structure is full of flexibility, the structure can be changeable, and the employees can be changeable, even the top management team." EuroMall was viewed as organized, stable, not flexible, conservative/old fashioned, professional, but not sensitive to costs and lacking innovation. In China, EuroMall would target the upper-middle class, the younger generation interested in fashion and loving overseas products.

Throughout its development, ChinaCorp had instilled a unique corporate culture centered on diversity, openness, positivity, introspection, and insight. It was mentioned that the Group was committed to value creation for customers as well as to providing opportunities for employees, which contributed to the enterprise's unique charisma and cohesive culture. However, employees seemed to be relatively neutral with regard to identification with ChinaCorp; they neither identified with or disidentified from their organization. When the Chairman intended to set a kindergarten in the shopping mall, one employee claimed that he and his colleagues didn't want to judge it, they would only see how it will go.

At the same time, ChinaMall interviewees displayed a limited attractiveness of EuroMall, which was viewed as a company in trouble and with a low degree of innovation. Its financial problems and changing ownership within the last three decades (since the 1990s) were giving EuroMall a view as a company in failure. Indeed, both EuroMall and ChinaMall were characterized by a low degree of innovation and a low degree of advancement in e-commerce.

7.5.5   *Identity Congruence*

Our interviewees were convinced of many potential synergies and opportunities for both EuroMall and ChinaMall. Chairman Zhu's ideal vision for the post-merger organization was strongly disconnected from the actual identities of ChinaMall and the EuroMalls.

7.5.5.1   *Short-Term Ideal Identity Incongruence with Pre-merger Identity*

EuroMall was a renowned department store in Europe and embedded in the European heritage. It was acquired for the expertise and knowledge in retail, reputation in brand and supply chain management, which had been well developed over 150 years. EuroMall would improve ChinaCorp retail, which was old fashioned and not very popular among the Chinese young people. Through the acquisition, ChinaCorp's management strove to improve ChinaMall's image and obtain a reputational endorsement. ChinaMall's management would also learn from EuroMall about the international supply chains to sell Chinese products in overseas markets.

However, ChinaCorp's management viewed EuroMall to have a low degree of innovation and a low growth potential in Europe due to high market saturation. Thus, further developments in Europe were not viewed as necessary. Instead, EuroMall would internationalize into China, starting in Red-City and then open circa fifty shops worldwide. As Chinese customers were more attracted to European heritage and culture, it was expected that EuroMall in China would be a success. EuroMall would become a cultural landmark in Red-City, attracting tourists and local customers. Making the Chinese proud of EuroMall in Red-City would be a collective effort of ChinaCorp with Red-City. The opening ceremony of EuroMall's first shopping mall in Red-City was a big success. It took place in Chinese style and the top management team from Europe came to participate in this event.

Moreover, ChinaMall would leverage EuroMall's expertise in its other department stores. EuroMall would aim to serve the upper class of rich Chinese customers and ChinaMall would aim to serve middle class customers. In Europe, EuroMall would aim to maintain its stable position and increase its profitability. In China, ChinaMall and EuroMall would build together on a scenario shopping experience, that is, a retail business model based on the customers coming to malls with families for unique experiences and leisure rather than shopping per se. EuroMall's management, however, hoped that the acquisition would allow them to get back to EuroMall's historic glory.

Very soon after acquiring EuroMall, ChinaCorp pursued further retail acquisitions to create a "new consumption industry group," wherein ChinaMall, together with the acquired retail firms, would become one single industry group of branded companies managed by ChinaCorp.

7.5.5.2   Mid-Term Ideal Identity Incongruence with Pre-merger Identity

Under Chairman Zhu's leadership, ChinaCorp strove to become a global conglomerate with Chinese characteristics – a blend of traditional Chinese philosophy and modern Western management concepts. Chairman Zhu was committed that ChinaCorp would contribute to making China successful internationally, along with the Belt Road Initiative and "China 2025." The aim was to move into an innovation-driven industry through internationalization. To this end, the EuroMall acquisition would be leveraged to pursue more innovation-driven, overseas takeovers – as in the strategy for the Chinese healthcare industry but also for the development of an integrated, modern service platform that embraces the benefits of Big Data. Besides retail and healthcare, ChinaCorp moved into finance and real estate. EuroMall would provide ChinaCorp management with international experience and the capacity to work with overseas executive teams. It would be an endorsement of ChinaCorp's global mindset.

7.5.6   Projected Continuity

The Chinese management team (ChinaCorp) did not know how to work toward the acquisition's objectives, as they had little experience in managing overseas operations. The post-merger integration was based on trial-and-error, which made the process complicated and inefficient. For example, one interviewee revealed: "I think no matter from business to people, we are moving and testing and moving again and testing again, constantly updating, then gradually gather our experiences. This process is challenging, I think we paid some 'tuition fees,' too."

Indeed, reaching the acquisition's goals was challenging due to the high conflict between EuroMall and ChinaMall's top management teams. Firstly, EuroMall and ChinaMall had different pre-merger identities, which were embedded in the different cultural (Europe, China) and institutional (e.g., different customers' expectations) contexts, which made collaboration difficult. More specifically, the two companies had different business models: a systematic approach at EuroMall and a high flexibility at ChinaCorp. In addition, ChinaCorp implemented performance-based management and financial incentives to motivate Europe-based top management teams. According to our interviewees, this led to tensions as European management managers did not appreciate such an approach.

Secondly, EuroMall did not obtain the financial support promised by Chairman Zhu to develop the business. This fact resonates with our interviewees' testimonies that Chairman Zhu was an autocratic leader. Indeed, back in Month 1, ChinaCorp had agreed to inject a certain amount of money into EuroMall, which never happened. Instead, EuroMall had to use its own cash to pay for the business developments in Europe and China. In effect, the European top management lost their trust in the Chairman and ChinaCorp.

Thirdly, ChinaCorp's top management was disappointed by EuroMall not being willing to collaborate. EuroMall's management was frustrated by Chairman Zhu's lack of understanding of the retail industry, and his continual changes to the post-merger plan. There were many shopping malls planned to open first in Red-City and then across China. Initially, EuroMall's European HQs were in charge of the business development in China. However, due to the conflicts, the autonomy of EuroMall Europe was reduced and the mandate to open malls in China was withdrawn. ChinaMall took over the EuroMall internationalization project in China, as the Chinese team had a better customer knowledge. The EuroMall team thus oversaw the European market and the Chinese EuroMall team the Chinese market. One of our interviewees said that "this change costs both organizations time and money..."

7.5.7   Post-merger Identification

As described, EuroMall and ChinaMall had separated structures as, instead of creating a shared team to foster the post-merger integration, both organizations put in place an autonomous boundary spanning "synergy" teams (in Europe these were called the "strategy team" and in China they were called the "retail strategy department"). EuroMall became ChinaCorp's "additional business." This structural separation came in the way to the integration and shared identity development. One inter-viewee said:

> Every acquisition is led by the Chairman. He will basically point the team and thereafter form the synergy team. We call it synergy, but there's no official form of synergy. We call it synergy, it's a philosophy, a concept but we do have different departments like HR, finance, international finance, branding, or sectors. We synergize, we team up and we launch our 100 days

plan. So, we form a plan, we form a plan, we form a team, and then we start going case by case, day by day.

Due to this structural separation, the planned merger objectives were not reached. Our interviewees lamented that synergies cannot be reached if both organizations had nothing to do with each other. ChinaCorp was not able to start building its own strategic teams and deploying expertise from EuroMall and also from the other acquired retails firms in Europe. Moreover, EuroMall's expansion in China was supposed to be based on the "greenfield investment." However, in the end, one existing shopping mall, belonging to Chairman Zhu, was re-branded into EuroMall in Red-City. Further, due to the conflicts, a high turnover took place in EuroMall's top management team. The CEO, CFO, COO, head of the supply chain, and other top executives left EuroMall. Some executives left voluntarily and others were fired.

The planned transformation of ChinaMall was not implemented. For instance, the retail system upgrading and the advanced EuroMall "technology" (business models transferring) did not take place (the western business model in retail, which is more developed than the typical one in China). In addition, at ChinaCorp, serial acquisitions were viewed to "cover" many different issues and inefficiencies. Some interviewees and the press described those frequent acquisitions and the fast expansion by Chairman Zhu as too risky and cash intensive as high capital needed to be injected. People realized that synergies between different businesses were impossible. At the end, EuroMall and ChinaCorp failed to follow the e-commerce developments and thus failed to catch up with innovation in the industry. Consequently, in 2018, EuroMall went into administration and ChinaCorp focused on other strategic goals, that is, healthcare. Further retail overseas acquisitions also went bankrupt and were sold (cf. Table 7.2). However, ChinaCorp kept the China-based operations of those overseas firms: EuroMall1, EuroMall2, EuroMall3. Chairman Zhu revealed that if he could go back in time, he wouldn't have gone down the same path. From the time perspective, he viewed that he took a too difficult path for ChinaCorp, he mentioned that: "We should reflect on our business strategy. In the past, we were greeding for big. In the future, we should be completely profit-oriented. We should be specialized in one thing as the first priority, and only followed by scale."

He also disclosed that, for everyone who looks at his brilliance, they must see his deep scars, and for everyone who looks at his deep scars, there must also be fruitful results. For the sake of his career he claimed to have given up a lot of things and made many sacrifices he would not have done again. Two years after EuroMall and all other retail bankruptcies he said: "These two years, I day and night have reflected deeply, deeply ashamed. From the bottom of my heart I recognize my mistakes, admit what I did wrong, and I will correct my mistakes."

7.6   Discussion

We refer to the social identity theory and examine how Chinese managers deal with identification change in becoming international players. We argue that identity leadership impacts identity congruence and projected continuity which are necessary for Chinese firms to become global players (Mathews, 2006; Luo & Tung, 2007). We focus on identity leadership, which might be especially important in the context of a high power distance and collectivist culture. In China, the chairman is a key figure with his or her access to resources and centralized decision making power. Thus, the leader's behavior might have an even stronger impact on identification processes than in Western firms, characterized by a lower power distance culture (cf. van Dick and Kerschreiter, 2016).

In terms of identity entrepreneurship, Chairman Zhu gave a long-term vision in terms of what ChinaCorp stands for (pre-merger identity): positivity, kindness, introspection, reason, balance, insight, and what ChinaCorp should become through overseas acquisitions (projected continuity): new consumption but also new finance and new healthcare. However, his identity advancement was not aligned with his acts of entrepreneurship. Instead of strategically developing his business, Chairman Zhu was distracted by the Chinese government's internationalization and innovation fostering policies. With access to financial resources of overseas acquisitions, he failed to protect key interests of the firm, with risky and costly acquisitions, which led to high debt. He also missed opportunities related to e-commerce in Europe and China. Chairman Zhu did not keep his promises made to employees both at ChinaCorp and EuroMall. Decreased autonomy of the acquired firm is one of the key sources of identity threat in M&As (Lupina-Wegener, Karamustafa et al., 2015). Finally, he also did not create structures that fostered collaboration between teams based in Europe and China. There was no action plan, which hints at limited identity impresarioship acts.

The identity leadership model can be further extended by the Chinese paternalistic leadership model characterized by a combination of discipline and authority, fatherly benevolence, and moral integrity (Lau et al., 2020).

Benevolence focuses on caring and protecting followers and showing holistic concern for followers, which is related to identity advancement. Moral integrity with unselfishness and leading by example is complementing identity prototypicality. Authoritarianism focused on the accentuation of authority and control might be considered legitimate and appreciated, mainly by individuals who value power distance (Lin & Sun, 2018). This can shed light on the application of the identity leadership model in high power distance cultures (Haslam et al., 2020). Accordingly, individual actors' use of power and control is considered to create a divide and decrease trust between leaders and their followers (van Dick et al., 2018). A quantitative study by Tian and Sanchez (2017) revealed that authoritarian leadership leads to Chinese followers' decreased trust in the leader, but only if unaccompanied by benevolent leadership. Chairman Zhu was an authoritarian, but not a benevolent leader (cf. identity advancement acts, being distracted by the Chinese government's internationalization and innovation fostering policies, which involved risky and costly acquisitions, and led to high debt). Authoritarianism might be considered as the fifth dimension of the identity leadership model in high power and collectivistic cultures. This, however, requires further investigations.

Inappropriate identity leadership acts of Chairman Zhu led to identity incongruence and low projected continuity in the case of EuroMall's acquisition by ChinaCorp. The pre-merger identity (traditional retail) was not congruent with the desired post-merger identity characterized by new consumption, new finance, and new healthcare. Many organizational changes took place and ChinaCorp grew from a small, local retail shop to a large conglomerate. Those changes were triggered by the Chairman's distraction from the Chinese government's policies which encourage internationalization and innovation. The conglomerate lacked strategic focus and its extensive growth was debt based. Summing up, organizational changes took place, but both identity congruence and projected continuity were low. Hoped for pre-merger identity transfer into post-merger identity – change identity from a local to an international firm – did not take place.

As a result, ChinaCorp maintained its limited international presence despite acquisitions. Turnover was high both among Chinese and European management team members. Synergies between ChinaCorp's key business (B2C) areas retail and healthcare were also not leveraged. The EuroMall acquisition was, however, leveraged into support from the state stakeholders who provided funding for further acquisitions by ChinaCorp. EuroMall, as well as all other of ChinaCorp's acquisitions in retail, failed, and the foreign targets were sold with significant losses (cf. Table 7.2).

In terms of overseas collaboration, ChinaCorp focused on healthcare. Chairman Zhu admitted his mistakes and explicitly admitted that his autocratic leadership and low participation from ChinaCorp's management was a mistake he has conducted. He committed publicly to change his leadership and, with creditor backing for restructuring received from state-owned financial enterprises, he hoped that the healthcare business could be rescued.

7.7 Conclusions

Our research reveals difficulties for small, local Chinese firms to become large international players, despite access to financial resources, long-term planning and benefiting from the government's support for innovation and internationalization. We theorized on the role of identity leadership and extended it with the Chinese paternalistic leadership model in order to explain the conditions under which the transfer from pre-merger to post-merger identification could work successfully.

REFERENCES

Albert, S., & Whetten, D. A. (1985). Organizational identity. *Research in Organizational Behavior, 7,* 263–295.

Ashforth, B. E., & Mael, F. (1989). Social identity theory and the organization. *Academy of Management Review, 14*(1), 20–39.

Barkema, H. G., Chen, X.-P., George, G., Luo, Y., & Tsui, A. S. (2015). West meets East: New concepts and theories. *Academy of Management Journal, 58* (2), 460–479.

Buckley, P. J., Clegg, J., & Tan, H. (2006). Cultural awareness in knowledge transfer to China: The role of guanxi and mianzi. *Journal of World Business, 41*(3), 275–288.

Buckley, P. J., Clegg, L. J., Voss, H., Cross, A. R., Liu, X., & Zheng, P. (2018). A retrospective and agenda for future research on Chinese outward foreign direct investment. *Journal of International Business Studies, 49*(1), 4–23.

Chung, G. H., Du, J., & Choi, J. N. (2014). How do employees adapt to organizational change driven by cross-border M&As? A case in China. *Journal of World Business, 49*(1), 78–86.

Cui, L., Meyer, K. E., & Hu, H. W. (2014). What drives firms' intent to seek strategic assets by foreign direct investment? A study of emerging economy firms. *Journal of World Business, 49*(4), 488–501.

Deng, P. (2009). Why do Chinese firms tend to acquire strategic assets in international expansion? *Journal of World Business, 44*(1), 74–84.

van Dick, R. (2004). My job is my castle: Identification in organizational contexts. In C. L. Cooper, & I. T. Robertson (eds.), *International review of industrial and organizational psychology* (pp. 171–203) Chichester: Wiley.

van Dijk, R., & van Dick, R. (2009). Navigating organizational change: Change leaders, employee resistance and work-based identities. *Journal of Change Management, 9*(2), 143–163.

van Dick, R., & Kerschreiter, R. (2016). The social identity approach to effective leadership: An overview and some ideas on cross-cultural generalizability. *Frontiers of Business Research in China, 10*(3), 363–384.

van Dick, R., Lemoine, J. E., Steffens, N. K., Kerschreiter, R., Akfirat, S. A., Avanzi, L., Dumont, K., Epitropaki, O., Fransen, K., & Giessner, S. (2018). Identity leadership going global: Validation of the Identity Leadership Inventory across 20 countries. *Journal of Occupational and Organizational Psychology, 91*(4), 697–728.

van Dick, R., Wagner, U., Stellmacher, J., & Christ, O. (2004). The utility of a broader conceptualization of organizational identification: Which aspects really matter? *Journal of Occupational and Organizational Psychology, 77*(2), 171–191.

Dutton, J. E., Dukerich, J. M., & Harquail, C. V. (1994). Organizational images and member identification. *Administrative Science Quarterly, 39*(2), 239–239.

Forbes. (2019). World's 500 largest corporations in 2019: China matches America. Available online at: Forbes.com.

Foreman, P., & Whetten, D. A. (2002). Member's identification with multiple-identity organizations. *Organization Science, 13*(6), 618–635.

Fukuyama, F. (1995). *Trust: The social virtues and the creation of prosperity.* New York: Free Press.

Giessner, S. (2011). Is the merger necessary? The interactive effect of perceived necessity and sense of continuity on post-merger identification. *Human Relations, 64*(8), 1079.

Global 500. (2010). 2010: Companies – C – FORTUNE. Available online at: CNNMoney.com

Haslam, S. A., Postmes, T., & Ellemers, N. (2003). More than a metaphor: Organizational identity makes organizational life possible. *British Journal of Management, 14*(4), 357–369.

Haslam, S. A., Reicher, S. D., & Platow, M. J. (2020). *The new psychology of leadership: Identity, influence and power* (2nd ed.). London: Routledge.

Junker, N. M., van Dick, R., Häusser, J. A., Ellwart, T., & Zyphur, M. J. (2021). The I and we of team identification: A multilevel study of exhaustion and (in)congruence among individuals and teams in team identification. *Group & Organization Management, 47*(1), 10596011211004789.

Kostova, T., & Hult, G. T. M. (2016). Meyer and Peng's 2005 article as a foundation for an expanded and refined international business research agenda: Context, organizations, and theories. *Journal of International Business Studies, 47*(1), 23–32.

Kreiner, G. E., & Ashforth, B. E. (2004). Evidence toward an expanded model of organizational identification. *Journal of Organizational Behavior*, *25*(1), 1–27.

Lau, W. K., Li, Z., & Okpara, J. (2020). An examination of three-way interactions of paternalistic leadership in China. *Asia Pacific Business Review*, *26*(1), 32–49.

Lee, E.-S., Park, T.-Y., & Koo, B. (2015). Identifying organizational identification as a basis for attitudes and behaviors: A meta-analytic review. *Psychological Bulletin*, *141*(5), 1049–1080.

Li, W., & Hendrischke, H. (2020). Local integration and co-evolution of internationalizing Chinese firms. *Thunderbird International Business Review*, *62* (4), 425–439.

Liang, S., Lupina-Wegener, A., Ullrich, J., & van Dick, R. (2021). "Change is our continuity": Chinese managers' construction of post-merger identification after an acquisition in Europe. *Journal of Change Management*, *22*(1), 59–78.

Lin, C.-H. V., & Sun, J.-M. J. (2018). Chinese employees' leadership preferences and the relationship with power distance orientation and core self-evaluation. *Frontiers of Business Research in China*, *12*(1), 1–22.

Luo, Y., & Tung, R. L. (2007). International expansion of emerging market enterprises: A springboard perspective. *Journal of International Business Studies*, *38*(4), 481–498.

Lupina-Wegener, A., & van Dick, R. (2016). Multiple shared identities in cross-border M&As. In S. Tarba, S. C. L. Cooper, R. M. Sarala, & M. F. Ahammad (eds.), *Mergers and acquisitions in practice* (pp. 182–191). London: Routledge.

Lupina-Wegener, A., Drzensky, F., Ullrich, J., & van Dick, R. (2014). Focusing on the bright tomorrow? A longitudinal study of organizational identification and projected continuity in a corporate merger. *British Journal of Social Psychology*, *53*(4), 752–772.

Lupina-Wegener, A., Liang, S., Ullrich, J., & van Dick, R. (2020). Multiple organizational identities and change in ambivalence: The case of a Chinese acquisition in Europe. *Journal of Organizational Change Management*, *33*(7), 1253–1275.

Lupina-Wegener, A., Schneider, S. C., & van Dick, R. (2015). The role of outgroups in constructing a shared identity: A longitudinal study of a subsidiary merger in Mexico. *Management International Review*, *55*(5), 677–705.

Lupina-Wegener, A. A., Karamustafa, G., & Schneider, S. C. (2015). Causes and consequences of different types of identity threat: Perceived legitimacy of decisions in M&As. In A. Risberg, D. King, & O. Meglio (eds.), *M&A Companion* (pp. 354–366). London: Routledge.

Mathews, J. A. (2006). Dragon multinationals: New players in 21st century globalization. *Asia Pacific Journal of Management*, *23*(1), 5–27.

Money, C. (2010). Global 500. Retrieved 4 April from https://money.cnn.com/magazines/fortune/global500/2010/countries/China.html

Rousseau, D. (1998). Why workers still identify with organizations. *Journal of Organizational Behavior, 19*(3), 217–233.

Sarala, R. M., Vaara, E., & Junni, P. (2017). Beyond merger syndrome and cultural differences: New avenues for research on the "human side" of global mergers and acquisitions (M&As). *Journal of World Business, 54*(4), 307–321.

Steffens, N. K., Haslam, S. A., Reicher, S. D., Platow, M. J., Fransen, K., Yang, J., Ryan, M. K., Jetten, J., Peters, K., & Boen, F. (2014). Leadership as social identity management: Introducing the Identity Leadership Inventory (ILI) to assess and validate a four-dimensional model. *Leadership Quarterly, 25*(5), 1001–1024.

Tajfel, H., & Turner, J. C. (1979). An integrative theory of intergroup conflict. In W. G. Austin, & S. Worchel (eds.), *The social psychology of intergroup relations* (pp. 33–47). Monterey, CA: Brooks/Cole.

Tian, Q., & Sanchez, J. I. (2017). Does paternalistic leadership promote innovative behavior? The interaction between authoritarianism and benevolence. *Journal of Applied Social Psychology, 47*(5), 235–246.

Turner, J. C. (1985). Social categorization and the self-concept: A social cognitive theory of group behavior. *Advances in Group Processes: Theory and Research, 2*, 77–122.

Turner, J. C., Hogg, M. A., Oakes, P. J., Reicher, S. D., & Wetherell, M. S. (1987). *Rediscovering the social group: A self-categorization theory*. Oxford: Basil Blackwell.

Ullrich, J., Wieseke, J., & Dick, R. V. (2005). Continuity and change in mergers and acquisitions: A social identity case study of a German industrial merger. *Journal of Management Studies, 42*(8), 1549–1569.

UNCTAD. (2019). *World investment report, special economic zones*. New York: United Nations Conference on Trade and Development (UNCTAD).

Vaara, E. (2003). Post-acquisition integration as sensemaking: Glimpses of ambiguity, confusion, hypocrisy, and politicization. *Journal of Management Studies, 40*(4), 859–894.

Wei, T., & Clegg, J. (2018). Effect of organizational identity change on integration approaches in acquisitions: Role of organizational dominance. *British Journal of Management, 29*(2), 337–355.

Zhao, Z., Anand, J., & Mitchell, W. (2005). A dual networks perspective on inter-organizational transfer of R&D capabilities: International joint ventures in the Chinese automotive industry. *Journal of Management Studies, 42* (1), 127–160.

CHAPTER 8

Social Identity Processes in Sino-Western Mergers and Acquisitions

*Shuang Liang, Rolf van Dick, Johannes Ullrich, and
Anna Lupina-Wegener*

8.1 Introduction

For over two decades, Chinese firms have expanded into international markets and accessed technology, innovation, and know-how, often through acquisitions of high technology firms based in advanced economies (Schüler-Zhou & Schüller, 2009). In 2022, China's OFDI had reached $153.7 billion (National Bureau of Statistics of China, 2021). In 2018, Chinese cross-border M&A activities increased by 379.4 percent, making up 54.0 percent of the total outward foreign direct investment (OFDI) as compared to 2017 (Wang & Miao, 2020); although, in 2020, the value of Chinese outbound M&As decreased due to COVID-19 (PwC Report, 2021). While some Chinese cross-border M&As have been successful, many others have not lived up to the expected performance. For instance, in 2018, the Chinese Sanpower Group had to sell the acquired House of Fraser (UK); this acquisition failed because Sanpower did not deliver on its promises to House of Fraser and imposed hierarchical controls on the acquired UK-based company. In contrast, the Chinese Joyson Group successfully integrated German Preh GmbH and achieved the expected synergies (de Oliveira & Rottig, 2018).

Social identity processes influence mergers and acquisitions (M&A) outcomes (Ullrich & van Dick, 2007) but they remain under-investigated in the context of Chinese M&As (Lupina-Wegener et al., 2020; Liang, Lupina-Wegener et al., 2021), often due to restricted access to empirical data (Liu & Deng, 2014). We address this gap in a research program that includes three empirical investigations which reveal how changes can be facilitated in M&As. The results are relevant beyond this specific phenomenon, and they can particularly apply to other forms of interorganizational or intergroup collaboration which require knowledge transfer or learning.

8.2 Three Studies on Social Identity Processes in M&As

We will rely on the social identity theory (SIT) centered on individuals' acting as members of their group(s) in relation to members of other groups, rather than acting on the basis of their personal identities (Tajfel & Turner, 1986; van Dick et al., 2004). The self-categorization theory explains how and when people define themselves as group members (Turner, 1985; Turner et al., 1987). Building on SIT and the self-categorization theory, organizational identification is defined as "the extent to which people define themselves as members of a particular group or organization," and it "indicates whether people engage in a process of self-stereotyping whereby their behaviour is oriented towards, and structured by, the content of that group or organization's defining characteristics, norms and values" (Haslam et al., 2003, p. 360). When organizational identification is strong, these identities are salient and incorporated into what the individual believes is distinctive, central, and enduring about him or herself (Albert & Whetten, 1985).

By combining two organizations into one, M&As redraw organizational boundaries which employees might experience as a threat to the continuity of their pre-merger organizational identity (Lupina-Wegener, Karamustafa, et al., 2015). This hinders knowledge transfer (Sarala et al., 2016). For example, a qualitative case study conducted by Karamustafa-Köse et al. (2022) reveals that interpretations of the takeover through pre-merger identity lenses might interfere with the acquisition of the target's unique capabilities during post-merger integration.

We present a research program to advance our understanding of the social identity processes in Chinese M&As. We conducted three studies investigating M&As motivated by learning. In the first study, we quantitatively examined the responses to criticism that are vital for innovation, learning, and facilitating change processes (Nemeth & Owens, 1996). Our results confirm that the ingroup sensitivity effect is high in M&As, even when motivated by learning; employees from the acquiring organization respond negatively to the criticism given by employees from the acquired organization. Consequently, we further investigated social identity processes in a qualitative case study, accounting for the experiences of both the acquirer and acquired employees who tend to deal differently with organizational changes (Lipponen et al., 2017). Constructing post-merger identification can be more difficult for members of the acquired organization because of a perceived discontinuity between pre-merger and post-merger identities (van Knippenberg et al., 2002). In the second study, we investigated social identity processes underlying changes, as they were experienced by European members of the acquired organization. In the third study, we looked at how Chinese members of the acquiring organization changed and constructed their post-merger identification. The insights from these three studies complement the previous chapter that features a failed Chinese acquisition (Chapter 7).

8.2.1   Study 1: The Intergroup Sensitivity Effect in M&As

Our investigation of social identity processes focused on individuals' responses to criticism in M&As (Liang, Ullrich et al., 2021). When learning is the motive, constructive criticism can help identify blind spots in group decision-making (Nemeth & Owens, 1996) and, overall, it might be a valuable driver of innovation and learning (Sommer & Kulkarni, 2012). Research has shown that people act more defensively toward criticism from an outgroup as compared to an ingroup member (intergroup sensitivity effects, ISEs; e.g., Hornsey et al., 2004). We argued that the ISE might be particularly present in the context of M&As as ingroup–outgroup demarcation is salient.

There is evidence that merger motives significantly influence employees' attitudes toward the other group and the merger (Rentsch & Schneider, 1991). M&As can be focused on achieving economies of scale (Schweizer, 2005) or synergies, relying on the effective collaboration between members of formerly distinct organizations (Damoah et al., 2015). We hypothesized that ISEs might be lower when M&As are driven by synergy through effective collaboration, rather than by growth for achieving economies of scale. Synergy motives provide an opportunity for the acquiring firm to access valuable know-how held by the acquired firm (Hitt et al., 2009). This might create a stronger learning orientation and make employees more open to receiving criticism (Shimizu et al., 2004).

We conducted three experiments examining whether people would show lower ISEs when the merger motive is synergy through collaboration. Adapting vignettes that had been designed to understand ISEs in M&As (Hornsey & Imani, 2004; Hornsey et al., 2007), we asked participants to imagine themselves as employees from an acquiring organization and to respond to criticism from an ingroup member (i.e., another employee from the acquiring organization) or an outgroup member (i.e., an employee from the acquired organization, the fictitious Moon Group). We also manipulated the motives underlying the acquisition by presenting various CEO statements. In the synergy condition, the CEO was saying, "if we are open to the fresh perspectives offered by the newly acquired Moon Group, our company will have a great future." In contrast, in the growth condition, the CEO indicated, "if the newly acquired Moon Group keeps their great work, our company will have a great future."

Results of the experiments indicate that ISEs occur in the context of M&As; people responded more defensively to criticism when it stemmed from an outgroup than from an ingroup member. Consistent with previous research, we obtained evidence that the ISE is mediated by the extent to which the criticism is attached to his or her workplace identity (Hornsey et al., 2004), the legitimacy (i.e., whether the criticism is seen as more qualified to criticize the group) and the constructiveness of criticism (i.e., whether the criticism is rated as fair, well-informed, and constructive; Hornsey et al., 2002). However, there was no evidence of a moderating effect of the merger motive. This suggests that employees' negative perceptions of criticism originating from the outgroup might be an obstacle to intergroup learning in M&As.

8.2.2 Introduction to Studies 2 and 3

We further investigated social identity processes in a Chinese learning motivated acquisition in Europe. Alpha-Owner was a multidivisional Chinese holding; Alpha-Prod was its key division focused on the manufacturing of low-end machinery in China. To improve Alpha-Prod's technology and managerial know-how, Alpha-Owner acquired Beta-West, a boutique manufacturer with state-of-the-art capacities. Beta-West employees viewed the acquisition by Alpha-Owner as an opportunity to access the growing Chinese market and to benefit from Alpha's financial support for the development of new products. In Study 2, we investigated the experiences of European members, and in Study 3 we focused on Chinese members from the acquiring organization.

8.2.3 Study 2: European Experiences in the Chinese Acquisition

We studied European members of the target organization, focusing on the following two research questions (Lupina-Wegener et al., 2020): (1) how do members of a European organization construct their multiple identities over time after being acquired by a Chinese organization? and (2) what are the key factors in the changing dynamics of multiple organizational identities? To answer the two questions, we interviewed European managers across different levels at the acquired company in Europe.

We conducted fifteen interviews at Time 1 (T1) and twenty interviews at Time 2 (T2).

Five identities were salient for European managers at T1: Beta-West (the historical identity of the acquired European company), Gamma (the previous owner of Beta-West), Sino-Beta (the Chinese subsidiary of Beta-West), Alpha-Owner (the Chinese acquirer), and Alpha-Prod (the key division of Alpha-Owner). Employees showed different forms of organizational identification (cf. Kreiner & Ashforth, 2004), identifying with Beta-West, disidentifying from Gamma and Alpha-Prod, and ambivalently identifying with Sino-Beta and Alpha-Owner. More specifically, disidentification with Alpha-Prod – which was seen as a low-quality manufacturer – created a negative orientation toward the acquisition. However, their disidentification from the previous owner (Gamma) and identification with Beta-West historical identity (leveraged by Alpha-Owner) fostered a positive orientation toward the acquisition. Thus, at T1, the overall orientation toward the acquisition was ambivalent. However, the ambivalence decreased over time. At T2, negative and ambivalent forms of identification had changed into positive (e.g., disidentification had changed to identification). This was possible through two structural interventions: concurrent identity separation and integration. First, a newly-constructed boundary-spanning organization (AB-Tech) separated the European target organization (positive identity) from the sub-category of the acquirer from which Europeans disidentified Alpha-Prod. Second, between T1 and T2, task and human integration interventions fostered the development of a post-merger identity, aligned with the historical identity of Beta-West. European interviewees considered the Chinese acquisition as an opportunity to return to the glory days of the early times of Beta's inception. Consequently, by T2, ambivalence decreased which resulted in European managers' willingness to share knowledge with a specific sub-group in the acquiring firm, namely with Chinese members of the boundary-spanning organization – AB-Tech. Also, criticisms by the Chinese chairman, initially perceived as posing a threat to the target's pre-merger identity (T1), were ultimately considered to be relevant for the post-merger integration changes and contribute to acquisition success (T2).

8.2.4   Study 3: Chinese Experiences in a Chinese Acquisition

We investigated the same case but considered the experiences of Chinese managers' from the acquiring organization, based in China (Liang,

Lupina-Wegener et al., 2021). Our goal was to identify how Chinese managers construct their post-merger identification after acquiring a European innovative company. Focusing on the following research question "How do Chinese managers adapt to frequent changes after an acquisition?" we conducted thirty-five interviews and analyzed archival data. The comprehensive data collected presents a rare opportunity to explore Chinese employees' identity construction and acquisition of the unique capability of the target. At the early stage of the post-merger integration, Chinese managers considered their inferior status legitimate because of lower technological know-how and business expertise. They addressed the acquired European company as "Goddess," wanted to improve their innovation capability, and were open to changes coming from the European colleagues. However, they considered collaboration with them challenging.

The study results reveal that an agile organizational identity (AOI) helped members of the Chinese organization cope effectively with organizational changes. AOI "guides employees' collective actions towards change and their belief that their organization is able to move swiftly in a changing environment" (Liang, Lupina-Wegener et al., 2021:73). Chinese managers realized that direct collaboration might pose a threat to European managers. To reduce this threat, they created a new organization in Europe (AB-Tech, see Section 8.2.3 on the European perspective) that enabled them to collaborate directly with their European colleagues. Fundamental and frequent organizational changes were occurring after the creation of AB-Tech, but the Chinese managers did not experience threat to their pre-merger identity. They stated that the new organization was "a milestone intervention for the collaboration between two companies" and described agility as the main characteristic of their organization. For example, one manager stated: "If I could choose one word, I would choose 'agile' to describe our organization." Chinese managers viewed the acquisition as an opportunity to enhance their inferior pre-merger identity. They constructed their post-merger identification successfully by leveraging the AOI. Although organizational changes were occurring, the DNA of Chinese managers (agility and change) stayed the same. Maintaining pre-merger identity continuity was equal to the continuing changes. Chinese managers were embracing, rather than being threatened by, fundamental and frequent organizational changes, because *agility* was the main characteristic of their organizational identity.

8.3 Discussion

The results of our research program relying on quantitative and qualitative methods contribute to the M&A literature by uncovering social identity processes in Chinese acquisitions. First, we conducted experiments to test whether people would respond less negatively to criticisms of outgroup members when the acquisition had a learning motive. The hypothesis was not confirmed; we found that employees in merging organizations have greater difficulties in accepting criticism from an outgroup rather than an ingroup member, independently of the motive.

With an increasing number of Chinese takeovers motivated by access to knowledge in advanced markets (Zhou et al., 2020), we further investigated social identity processes in this context. Our qualitative case study explores social identity processes in a Chinese takeover wherein the acquirer successfully accessed the unique capabilities of the European target. Learning took place through changes chiefly on the Chinese acquirer and less on the acquired company side. Indeed, when the unique capabilities of the target are the motive of an acquisition, the routines of the acquirer need to change, which might be challenging due to social identity processes (Karamustafa-Köse et al., 2022).

The investigation of experiences of European managers confirms that identity construction processes in M&As might not uniquely rely on ingroup and outgroup identities (Sarala et al., 2019). In our case study, employees showed different forms of organizational identification which initially triggered ambivalence toward the acquisition but which decreased over time. As a result of managerial interventions, pre-merger organizational boundaries were blurred and initial outgroup members became part of the ingroup. Thus, even when the Chinese acquisition is perceived negatively due to asymmetries in technology and knowhow (Riad et al., 2012), knowledge can effectively be shared across organizational and cultural boundaries (Moore, 2016).

Our third study presents the experiences of Chinese members of the acquiring organization. Our results reveal that, similarly to their European colleagues, they viewed their firm to be in a low-status position due to inferior technological know-how and business expertise. Research on M&As refers to those deals as reverse takeover which might not be viewed as illegitimate by members of the acquiring organization (Lupina-Wegener, Schneider, et al., 2015). In our case, employees made sense of their organization as the one that can move swiftly in a rapidly changing environment, and so viewed their inferior status as legitimate. Consequently, they welcomed changes which allowed them to successfully acquire the European target's unique capabilities. These findings complement results from a quantitative study conducted by Zhou et al. (2020), on a sample of acquired Chinese subsidiaries by international multinational firms, who found that knowledge transfer from the acquirer to the target required important changes in the Chinese acquired organizations.

The influence of social identity processes on willingness to change and learning might be particularly strong in the context of a collective culture in which organizational identification will have more salient effects on work behavior (Chung et al., 2014; Lee et al., 2015). This might explain why Chinese managers embraced changes focusing on the future of their organization, rather than being preoccupied by "me-issues." Further, being from the acquiring organization makes it easier to develop post-merger identification due to a higher projected continuity, that is, understanding the future direction of the firm after an acquisition (Ullrich et al., 2005; Lupina-Wegener et al., 2014).

The comparison of the Chinese and European perspectives between Studies 2 and 3 reveals that granting autonomy to the target might not be enough to ensure learning in M&A (Junni & Sarala, 2014). Instead leaders responsible for M&A execution might want to take a gradual approach to post-merger integration (Zhou et al., 2020). At the early stage of integration, Alpha and Beta started with an indirect integration (e.g., the creation of a shared collaborative platform – AB-Tech). Only later, they deployed integration initiatives at AB-Tech, aimed at the transfer of technology and acquisition of the target's unique capability. This alters initial pre-merger organizational boundaries so that the groups initially perceived as outgroups can become ingroups. This re-categorization might facilitate a decrease in the ISEs (Study 1) and readiness to change and contribute to interorganizational learning (Studies 2 and 3).

8.4 Conclusion

The results of our studies together contribute to a better understanding of change processes as experienced by different groups. We chose the context of Chinese acquisitions in Europe to gain insights into complex intergroup dynamics, influenced by status asymmetries and cultural characteristics. Our insights confirm that intergroup sensitivity effects (ISEs) can be an important obstacle in M&As and other strategic change initiatives.

However, with multiple identities being salient, who is the ingroup and outgroup can change over time. With blurred pre-merger organizational boundaries, positive intergroup change can be facilitated and initial ISEs can decrease with increased legitimacy for post-merger integration initiatives and commitment to shared, post-merger identification.

REFERENCES

Albert, S., & Whetten, D. A. (1985). Organizational identity. *Research in Organizational Behavior, 7*, 263–295.

Chung, G. H., Du, J., & Choi, J. N. (2014). How do employees adapt to organizational change driven by cross-border M&As? A case in China. *Journal of World Business, 49*(1), 78–86.

Damoah, O. B. O., Opoku, L., & Acquah-Coleman, R. (2015). Understanding the relative strength of the motives that influence acquisition strategy: Evidence from an emerging market. *African Journal of Management Research, 23*(1), 55–72.

van Dick, R., Christ, O., Stellmacher, J., Wagner, U., Ahlswede, O., Grubba, C., Hauptmeier, M., Hohfeld, C., Moltzen, K., & Tissington, P. A. (2004). Should I stay or should I go? Explaining turnover intentions with organizational identification and job satisfaction. *British Journal of Management, 15*(4), 351–360.

Haslam, S. A., Postmes, T., & Ellemers, N. (2003). More than a metaphor: Organizational identity makes organizational life possible. *British Journal of Management, 14*(4), 357–369.

Hitt, M. A., King, D., Krishnan, H., Makri, M., Schijven, M., Shimizu, K., & Zhu, H. (2009). Mergers and acquisitions: Overcoming pitfalls, building synergy, and creating value. *Business Horizons, 52*(6), 523–529. https://doi.org/10.1016/j.bushor.2009.06.008

Hornsey, M. J., Grice, T., Jetten, J., Paulsen, N., & Callan, V. (2007). Group-directed criticisms and recommendations for change: Why newcomers arouse more resistance than old-timers. *Personality and Social Psychology Bulletin, 33*(7), 1036–1048.

Hornsey, M. J., & Imani, A. (2004). Criticizing groups from the inside and the outside: An identity perspective on the intergroup sensitivity effect. *Personality and Social Psychology Bulletin, 30*(3), 365–383.

Hornsey, M. J., Oppes, T., & Svensson, A. (2002). "It's OK if we say it, but you can't": Responses to intergroup and intragroup criticism. *European Journal of Social Psychology, 32*(3), 293–307.

Hornsey, M. J., Trembath, M., & Gunthorpe, S. (2004). "You can criticize because you care": Identity attachment, constructiveness, and the intergroup sensitivity effect. *European Journal of Social Psychology, 34*(5), 499–518.

Junni, P., & Sarala, R. M. (2014). The role of leadership in mergers and acquisitions: A review of recent empirical studies. *Advances in Mergers and Acquisitions, 13*, 181–200.

Karamustafa-Köse, G., Schneider, S. C., & Davis, J. D. (2022). Unpacking the dynamics in acquisition of capabilities: The role of identities during post-merger integration. *Journal of Organizational Change Management*, *35*(8), 13–38.

van Knippenberg, D., van Knippenberg, B., Monden, L., & Lima, F. (2002). Organizational identification after a merger: A social identity perspective. *British Journal of Social Psychology*, *41*(2), 233–252.

Kreiner, G. E., & Ashforth, B. E. (2004). Evidence toward an expanded model of organizational identification. *Journal of Organizational Behavior*, *25*(1), 1–27.

Lee, E.-S., Park, T.-Y., & Koo, B. (2015). Identifying organizational identification as a basis for attitudes and behaviors: A meta-analytic review. *Psychological Bulletin*, *141*(5), 1049–1080.

Liang, S., Lupina-Wegener, A., Ullrich, J., & van Dick, R. (2021). "Change is our continuity": Chinese managers' construction of post-merger identification after an acquisition in Europe. *Journal of Change Management*, *22*(1), 59–78.

Liang, S., Ullrich, J., van Dick, R., & Lupina-Wegener, A. (2021). The intergroup sensitivity effect in mergers and acquisitions: Testing the role of merger motives. *Journal of Applied Social Psychology*, *51*(8), 769–778.

Lipponen, J., Wisse, B., & Jetten, J. (2017). The different paths to post-merger identification for employees from high and low status pre-merger organizations. *Journal of Organizational Behavior*, *38*(5), 692–711.

Liu, Y., & Deng, P. (2014). Chinese cross-border M&A: Past achievement, contemporary debates and future direction. In C. L. Cooper & S. Finkelstein (eds.), *Advances in mergers and acquisitions* (Vol. 13, pp. 85–107). Bingley: Emerald.

Lupina-Wegener, A., Drzensky, F., & Van Dick, R. (2014). Focusing on the bright tomorrow? A longitudinal study of organizational identification and projected continuity in a corporate merger. *British Journal of Social Psychology*, *53*(4), 752–772.

Lupina-Wegener, A., Schneider, S. C., & van Dick, R. (2015). The role of outgroups in constructing a shared identity: A longitudinal study of a subsidiary merger in Mexico. *Management International Review*, *55*(5), 677–705.

Lupina-Wegener, A. A., Karamustafa, G., & Schneider, S. C. (2015). Causes and consequences of different types of identity threat: Perceived legitimacy of decisions in M&As. In A. Risberg, D. King, and O. Meglio (eds.), *M&A Companion* (pp. 354–366). London: Routledge.

Lupina-Wegener, A. A., Liang, S., van Dick, R., & Ullrich, J. (2020). Multiple organizational identities and change in ambivalence: The case of a Chinese acquisition in Europe. *Journal of Organizational Change Management*, *33*(7), 1253–1275.

Moore, F. (2016). Flexible identities and cross-border knowledge networking. *Critical Perspectives on International Business*, *12*(4), 318–330.

National Bureau of Statistics of China. (2021). China statistical yearbook. *China Statistics Press.* Available online at: www.stats.gov.cn/tjsj/ndsj/2021/indexch .htm, last accessed May 18, 2022.

Nemeth, C., & Owens, P. (1996). Making work groups more effective: The value of minority dissent. In M. A. West (ed.), *Handbook of work group psychology* (pp. 125–142). Chichester: John Wiley.

de Oliveira, R. T., & Rottig, D. (2018). Chinese acquisitions of developed market firms: Home semi-formal institutions and a supportive partnering approach. *Journal of Business Research, 93,* 230–241.

PwC Report. (2021). *2020 China M&A Market Review and Outlook* (pp. 12–16). Available at: www.pwccn.com/zh/deals/publications/ma-2020-review-and-2021-outlook.pdf. Last accessed May 18, 2022.

Rentsch, J. R., & Schneider, B. (1991). Expectations for postcombination organizational life: A study of responses to merger and acquisition scenarios. *Journal of Applied Social Psychology, 21*(3), 233–252.

Riad, S., Vaara, E., & Zhang, N. (2012). The intertextual production of international relations in mergers and acquisitions. *Organization Studies, 33*(1), 121–148.

Sarala, R. M., Junni, P., Cooper, C. L., & Tarba, S. Y. (2016). A sociocultural perspective on knowledge transfer in mergers and acquisitions. *Journal of Management, 42*(5), 1230–1249.

Sarala, R. M., Vaara, E., & Junni, P. (2019). Beyond merger syndrome and cultural differences: New avenues for research on the "human side" of global mergers and acquisitions (M&As). *Journal of World Business, 54*(4), 307–321.

Schüler-Zhou, Y., & Schüller, M. (2009). The internationalization of Chinese companies: What do official statistics tell us about Chinese outward foreign direct investment? *Chinese Management Studies, 3*(1), 25–42.

Schweizer, L. (2005). Organizational integration of acquired biotechnology companies into pharmaceutical companies: The need for a hybrid approach. *Academy of Management Journal, 48*(6), 1051–1074.

Shimizu, K., Hitt, M. A., Vaidyanath, D., & Pisano, V. (2004). Theoretical foundations of cross-border mergers and acquisitions: A review of current research and recommendations for the future. *Journal of International Management, 10*(3), 307–353.

Sommer, K. L., & Kulkarni, M. (2012). Does constructive performance feedback improve citizenship intentions and job satisfaction? The roles of perceived opportunities for advancement, respect, and mood. *Human Resource Development Quarterly, 23*(2), 177–201.

Tajfel, H., & Turner, J. C. (1986). The social identity theory of intergroup behavior. In S. Worchel & W. G. Austin (eds.), *Psychology of intergroup relations* (pp. 7–24). Chicago: Nelson-Hall.

Turner, J. C. (1985). Social categorization and the self-concept: A social cognitive theory of group behavior. *Advances in Group Processes, 2,* 77–122.

Turner, J. C., Hogg, M. A., Oakes, P. J., Reicher, S. D., & Wetherell, M. S. (1987). *Rediscovering the social group: A self-categorization theory*. Oxford: Basil Blackwell.

Ullrich, J., & van Dick, R. (2007). The group psychology of mergers & acquisitions: Lessons from the social identity approach. *Advances in Mergers and Acquisitions*, 6, 1–15.

Ullrich, J., Wieseke, J., & Van Dick, R. (2005). Continuity and change in mergers and acquisitions: A social identity case study of a German industrial merger. *Journal of Management Studies*, 42(8), 1549–1569.

Wang, H., & Miao, L. (2020). *The globalization of Chinese enterprises: Trends and characteristics*. Singapore: Springer Singapore.

Zhou, A. J., Fey, C., & Yildiz, H. E. (2020). Fostering integration through HRM practices: An empirical examination of absorptive capacity and knowledge transfer in cross-border M&As. *Journal of World Business*, 55(2), 1–14.

PART IV

The Development of Change Leadership

CHAPTER 9

Developing Change Competencies
An Examination of Sensemaking Processes in a Change Management Competency Intervention

Johan Simonsen Abildgaard, Karina Nielsen, and Esben Langager Olsen

The important role of management in change processes has been well established (Higgs & Rowland, 2011; Lundmark et al., 2017; Andersen, 2018). Evidence in the scientific literature on organizational change has shown that if change processes are managed poorly, they present a risk to both productivity and employee wellbeing (Armenakis & Bedeian, 1999; Todnem By, 2005; de Jong et al., 2016). Key elements in any organizational change process are the competencies of the managers responsible for implementing the change.

In addition to being change agents, line, middle, and senior managers must also manage daily business operations (Kieselbach et al., 2009). This dual role places managers at all levels under pressure to implement change processes efficiently. Accordingly, Bickerich et al. (2018) found that managers experienced a need for support to achieve change success and manage their own reactions to change.

The key role of managers requires them to use a range of tools, techniques, and approaches for implementing change. However, managers need to acquire the competencies required to apply these tools, techniques, and methods. Such change management competencies have been defined in various ways in the literature (Higgs & Rowland, 2000; Battilana et al., 2010; Have et al., 2015). Change management competencies comprise behavioral repertoires and ways of thinking that foster successful change management, including managers' readiness for change (Krummaker & Vogel, 2013), understanding of change (Have et al., 2015), change communication (Battilana et al., 2010), mobilization of subordinates (Higgs & Rowland, 2000), and handling resistance (Higgs & Rowland, 2000). Have et al. (2015) underscored the complexity of change competencies by emphasizing the inter-relatedness of sub-competencies and their context dependence. According to a functional definition, change competencies are change-related attitudes and behaviors "underpinning successful performance; what it is people do in order to meet their objectives; how they go about achieving the required outcomes; what enables their competent performance" (Kurz & Bartram, 2002, p. 235).

Change management training is commonly conducted to foster change competencies. We therefore need to understand how change management training affects managers' competencies and how they make sense of change.

In this chapter, we focus on a specific change management training initiative, the Change Management Competency Intervention (CMCI), in which a series of workshops using serious game simulations are conducted to develop managers' change competencies. To analyze how line, middle, and senior managers find new ways to make sense of change after participating in the CMCI, we apply a sensemaking-based analysis to qualitative case examples.

The results of the analysis shed light on the sensemaking processes that underpin how change management training enables the development of change competencies and paves new ways for participating managers to make sense of change management. The findings show that the CMCI led to sensemaking processes in which managers used the CMCI workshops and their experiential elements, particularly serious game simulations, as occasions to make sense of change management and their change competencies in novel ways.

First, the managers became aware of and preoccupied with key notions relating to change management in serious gameplaying, such as differing change-related needs among change recipients. Second, self-reflection, fueled by participation in the CMCI, led to the managers' reconsideration of how change was currently managed, and how it could be done differently. Third, sensemaking, and learning in the CMCI, appeared to be not only incorporated into change management competencies but also combined with learning about other training techniques. These three findings demonstrate that the content of the serious game simulations and personal reflections on change and other initiatives were combined to form a new foundation for change. The findings also show that elements in the CMCI became incorporated in managers' sensemaking of change processes. The analysis provided in this chapter shows that preexisting managerial sensemaking was challenged by the managers' participation in the CMCI activities, and new ways of making sense of change, personal change, and employee change reactions emerged from the intervention.

9.1 Change Management Training

In the literature, there has been substantial debate about the effectiveness of management training programs in general. For example, the extent to which learning in formal management training leads to improved management practice has been explored (Tafvelin et al., 2021), and the overall applicability of abstract classroom training to real-world management situations has been questioned (Vignoli et al., 2021). Despite such criticism, management training in general and change management training in particular have remained popular. Moreover, previous studies have found that training initiatives can support organizational change processes (Nielsen et al., 2010). Change management training has been found to be effective in providing competencies that are lacking, as well as innovative support and development (Sartori et al., 2018).

9.2 Sensemaking as a Theoretical Framework for Analyzing Learning in the Change Management Competency Intervention

To provide a theoretical framework for analyzing the development of change competencies in the CMCI, we drew on sensemaking theory (Weick, 1995; Weick et al., 2005). Sensemaking has been defined as "creating intersubjective meaning through cycles of interpretation and action, and thereby enacting a more ordered environment from which further cues can be drawn" (Maitlis & Christianson, 2014, p. 67).

Sensemaking occurs in all forms of training. It is tied to cognitive social and cultural processes, and it guides the actions of individuals and groups (Weick et al., 2008; Jordan et al., 2009; Weick, 2010; Iveroth & Hallencreutz, 2015). The concept of sensemaking has been applied to analyses of change processes to investigate managers', change agents', and employees' sensemaking during change processes (Balogun & Johnson, 2005; Lüscher & Lewis, 2008; Teulier & Rouleau, 2013; Ala-Laurinaho et al., 2017; Abildgaard & Nielsen, 2018). Similarly, the process through which managers influence their subordinates has been theorized as a process of collective sensemaking (Ala-Laurinaho et al., 2017; Olsen et al., 2020). Although the CMCI is not based on sensemaking theory, it provides a useful framework for conducting detailed analyses of the ongoing reshaping of meaning during the CMCI. The relevance of sensemaking as a framework for theorizing the processes through which the CMCI affects the participating managers is fourfold. First, the sensemaking framework emphasizes the ongoing interactions between perception and enactment. Though it is not necessarily labeled as a "learning" framework (Schwandt, 2005), processes theorized as sensemaking function as linchpins between perceptions and behaviors (Corley & Gioia, 2003; Wilson & Beard, 2013). The sensemaking framework suggests that perceptions of a current situation affect what the actors perceive to be sensible actions. Because change management is a discipline that requires managing complex change processes as they take place, a shift in focus from basic learning (i.e., learning the change management model) to the goal of sensemaking (i.e., learning to make sense of change processes) may be more relevant (Weick, 2007). The form of learning addressed in this chapter concerns continuous sensemaking processes both during and after training (Guiette & Vandenbempt, 2016).

Second, although sensemaking is an ongoing process in the present context (Weick, 1995), it is also a retrospective process in which previous experiences, collective cultural norms, and cognitive schemata affect how a person makes sense of their current situation. Similarly, sensemaking is also prospective and directed toward a future situation.

Regarding dialogue and interaction with cases and simulations during change management training, the temporal emphasis on the sensemaking framework is highly relevant. Change management training offers learners an opportunity to reflect on previous events and enables them to develop new sensemaking strategies and forms of action (Olsen et al., 2020).

Third, sensemaking emphasizes the importance of identity and self-perception. The structures inherent in a specific profession or hierarchical position can affect perceptions (Weick, 1993; Weick et al., 2005; Olsen et al., 2020). Self-identification as a particular form of manager or having a distinct approach to change management is both influenced by and influences sensemaking and learning in management training (Corley & Gioia, 2003).

Fourth, an additional aspect of sensemaking is that it is shared. The implementation of change often requires collective action, which requires collective sensemaking. Collective sensemaking emphasizes the complexity involved in developing shared beliefs as well as the reasons that it is necessary (Weick et al., 2005) vis-à-vis the three points previously mentioned. Change management training potentially provides a space for experiencing shared sensemaking and fostering the subsequent potential for action and organizational learning (Corley & Gioia, 2003).

9.3   Experiential Learning Elements

In addition to a curriculum that includes change management theories, models, and phases, most, if not all, change management training programs rely on experiential learning to influence participants (Kolb & Kolb, 2005). Experiential learning includes exercises that are aimed at letting the participant experience and enact learning. They include a broad range of techniques, such as roleplaying, reflective dialogue, case studies, and simulations (Wilson & Beard, 2013). Experiential learning can be broadly defined as "the sensemaking process of active engagement between the inner world of the person and the outer world of the environment" (Wilson & Beard, 2013, p. 26).

Experiential learning elements of change management training involve exposing participants to actual or fictional change processes and change dilemmas and encouraging them to discuss and reflect on such material (Kolb & Kolb, 2005; Moon, 2013). The goal is to influence the sensemaking processes of managers who participate in the training in relation to themselves and how they conduct change management. We argue that experiential elements in change management training are an integral component of such programs, and they play a key role in affecting the participating managers and their sensemaking processes. In contrast to classroom training and lectures, experiential components do not necessarily involve questions about how to act in specific situations and change phases. Instead, they are focused on managers experiencing and enacting elements of change processes. These experiential components support the development of change competencies, such as attitudes and behaviors in relation to change processes. Hence, they comprise a key element in raising managers' awareness of how change management could be done differently, thus leading to new perceptions of sensemaking.

9.4 Serious Game Simulations

The CMCI employs a particular type of experiential element, namely, the serious game simulation. Serious games "have an explicit and carefully thought-out educational purpose and are not intended to be played primarily for amusement" (Abt, 1987, p. 9). In the context of this chapter, "serious" refers to the game's intention to improve managers' change competencies. Simulations of reality have been used extensively in both military and business contexts to develop the competences of managers and leaders (Faria et al., 2009). Present-day simulations borrow elements, such as game-mechanics and narrative aspects, from roleplaying games, board games, and computer games to present complex, rich, and realistic learning environments to participants in training programs (Agger & Møller, 2018).

As experiential learning tools, simulations are constructed to provide a safe context for experimenting with course content and exposure to alternative ways of making sense of change processes. This implies that, although serious game simulations are fictitious, they encourage self-reflection and new ways of making sense of change management. In the present chapter, we argue that experiential components, specifically serious game simulations, are key elements in encouraging training participants to perceive how change can be managed differently. In the CMCI, serious game simulations function as complex and challenging change events, of which managers are required to make sense. In our study, we brought novel perspectives to the analysis of the development of change competencies of managers participating in change management training in our analyses of how the participants made sense of the CMCI and its serious game simulations.

9.5   The Case: Lean Implementation and CMCI in Novozymes

Our case study focused on the Danish biochemical enzyme company Novozymes A/S, where the CMCI project was initiated to develop the change management competencies of their managers and support their implementation of "Lean" in their production and supply chain departments. Novozymes supplies products to the global market. The competitive market for enzyme production has led to a demand for increasing the efficiency of production processes, something Novozymes aims to achieve by the strategic implementation of several Lean production tools. These tools have included techniques, meetings, visualizations, and boards that have been applied to support production monitoring, subsequent problem-solving, and implementing initiatives (Womack et al., 1991).

Novozymes previously attempted to implement Lean in some departments, but the company struggled with convincing employees to adhere to the implemented Lean tools and comply with agreements and new work standardizations, which were mandated through the Lean management system. Consequently, there was an increased focus on how to improve managers' change management competencies to support the implementation of Lean and increase the value potential of the Lean activities that emerged. The Lean office and the supply chain senior management in Novozymes saw the potential to improve the competencies of the managers in approaching their Lean-related tasks with greater sensitivity to the dimensions of change management, which is understood as the human side of change. This led to the development of the CMCI, which is based on serious game simulations that were developed and facilitated by the change agency Workz A/S.

9.5.1 *The Change Management Competency Intervention (CMCI)*

The CMCI consisted of four days of workshops that focused on developing an understanding and vocabulary for the human side of change management. Because managers influence each other and middle management interacts with line management in implementing change, it was decided that the participants in the CMCI were drawn from existing managerial groups. The head and all line managers of the participating departments were invited. The five participating departments were under the management of three senior managers (i.e., plant managers), two of whom also participated in the workshops. The core content of the CMCI was developed by the consultancy Workz A/S, which included a range of change-related topics aimed at understanding, identifying, and addressing resistance (Maurer, 2010), understanding the different phases of change, balancing stability and change (Kotter, 1996), as well as influencing and managing stakeholders (Thomas, 1988).

Box 9.1 Wallbreakers: a change management serious game simulation

The core serious game simulation used was the game Wallbreakers, which is a decision-making game that was run within two days of the workshop. The game is based on the fictitious case of a merger-acquisition involving the buyout of an older, small IT company named Nordicon by a larger and more modern international company named TLA. In the game, the participants were divided into groups and tasked with making decisions as managers of a merged department. The game included extensive background material on the case, such as the bios of the ten employees in the department.

The simulation uses metaphors of change in which the departments were represented as moving buses and the employees as play pieces either on or off the bus; those not on the bus exhibited some level of change resistance. The learning mechanisms in the game primarily involve decision-making. The participant groups are presented with the choice of prioritizing either change or stability in each of three change phases: start-up, implementation, and anchoring. In each phase, the participants are also tasked with choosing four of twelve management actions. These actions affect the level of resistance of employees in the simulation and progress of the change.

Several times during the game, facilitators linked the events in the game to the participants' actual change management challenges by asking questions such as "How does the choice you made in the game reflect the way you usually manage change?" At the end of the game, the participating managers were asked to develop both a personal and a detailed departmental action plan of what they planned to do differently with regard to change management when they returned to their departments after the workshops.

Box 9.2 Structured dialog exercises: Backtalk and role playing

In the CMCI, specific structured dialog exercises were used to encourage the participants to think about their change management practices. A key tool that was used multiple times was a backtalk exercise, which was derived from narrative psychological techniques of using outsider-witnesses (Carey & Russell, 2003). During the exercise, the participants were organized into smaller groups of three to four participants. One participant functioned as an interviewee who talked about their change dilemmas; another participant interviewed the interviewee and posed illuminating questions; and the third and fourth persons in the group remained silent during the interview. After the interview, the silent observer(s) disclosed their reflections and perspectives on the interview they had just witnessed.

Another dialog tool used in the training was roleplaying exercises. In one workshop, the participants roleplayed an interaction between a manager and an employee, the premise of which was that the employee had some degree of resistance to change. During the roleplay, the participant playing the manager was tasked with identifying the level and form of resistance in the participant who roleplayed the employee. As in the backtalk exercise, one or two participants functioned as observers. The participant who played the role of manager had the option of declaring timeouts during the roleplay to discuss the situation with the observers.

The workshops comprised a combination of change management serious game simulations (notably the serious game simulation Wallbreakers (see Box 9.1)), reflective interviewing, roleplay exercises, and theory lectures (see Box 9.2). The simulations also focused on individual differences in both change reactions and change management, and personality and managerial typologies were used to illustrate them (Myers et al., 1998; Owen et al., 2017).

The researchers participated in the planning of the workshops and observed the training sessions. The Novozymes Lean consultant participated in the workshops by bringing a Lean perspective to the discussions, and consultants from Workz facilitated the workshops.

9.6   Methods

The evaluation was designed to provide comprehensive data on the participants' experiences of the CMCI. A focused data collection strategy (Abildgaard, 2018) was applied. Interview data were collected both immediately after the workshops and after a follow-up period. The participants

Table 9.1 *Data sources*

Data source	Data type	Amount of data
Telephone interviews	Recordings of interviews with training participants 1–2 days after training	27 interviews, avg. length 30 minutes
Follow-up interviews	Recordings of interviews with training participants 4–6 months after training	29 interviews, avg. length 40 minutes

included three senior managers (i.e., plant managers), five middle managers (i.e., department heads), and nineteen line managers.

9.6.1   Data Sources

An overview of the data sources is presented in Table 9.1.

We conducted semi-structured (Brinkmann & Kvale, 2015) telephone interviews with around three to four participants one to two days after each workshop in the CMCI. The telephone interviews focused on experiences in the workshop, the managers' evaluations of the workshop components, and their learning from the workshop. All participating managers were interviewed in-person, in semi-structured follow-up interviews four-to-six months after the last training session. The follow-up interviews focused on how the participants had applied the learning from the training course in practice, their experiences in change management in general, and Lean implementation in particular. The interviews were transcribed verbatim in Danish and translated by the authors from Danish to English.

9.6.2   Data Analysis

A thematic analysis was conducted on the data collected (Boyatzis, 1998). An iterative process was used to first code the data corpus, identify salient themes in the coded data, review and refine themes, and define them (Braun & Clarke, 2012). In identifying themes, we went through stages of coding. We first conducted topic coding (Saldaña, 2015) to identify relevant passages in the data in which change management competencies were exposed or addressed. In this stage, the output was a corpus of data that was analyzed in more depth in the subsequent stages.

Inductive coding was conducted in the second stage of the data analysis (Saldaña, 2015). The interview and workshop data were reviewed to identify relevant themes. In this stage, the relevance of applying a sensemaking perspective became apparent. In the second stage of coding, the conceptualization of the sensemaking lens led to the identification of three specific themes for further analysis: "Learning that change perceptions are situated and individual"; "Learning to make sense of your own role in change processes"; and "Reflections on learning and changed change management competencies."

In the third stage, the entire data corpus was re-examined to identify situations in which these three themes appeared and a finer-grained and sensemaking theory-based analysis of the data was conducted, which focused on how the roles played in sensemaking processes in the CMCI led to the development of change management competencies. This process led to the inclusion of further examples and the retheorization of some case examples compared with other examples.

The presentation of the interviews drew inspiration from a narrative approach (Riessman, 1993, 2002; Czarniawska, 1998), specifically by applying a thematic narrative style (Riessman, 1993). The managers were encouraged to talk about phenomena related to the three themes. This allowed the researchers to follow the thoughts and arguments of the interviewees in relation to the themes identified in the analysis. The presentation of themes in the results is structured so that two themes that focus on immediate sensemaking processes are presented first and the third theme, which focuses on sensemaking and retrospective reflections on learning and change competencies, is presented last. The chronology allows the readers to follow the sensemaking processes of the managers from their initial reflections shortly after the CMCI to subsequent reflections on the applicability of the training to their own change management practice.

9.7   Results

9.7.1   Theme 1: Learning That Change Perceptions Are Situated and Individual

One learning experience that had a profound impact on the participants in the CMCI concerned the following: sentiments regarding the change process are highly individualized phenomena rooted in the context and identity of the change recipients. Experiencing the individualized sentiments of employees, which were caricaturized in the serious game simulations, shifted the sensemaking of the participants from trying to make sense of a homogeneous group of employees to trying to make sense of a collective of individuals. One participant explained the following:

LINE MANAGER: Well, I think, when I was there, I actually thought it was very beneficial, but perhaps not completely new to me, the theories, that is, but I still think I got something with me that I have used afterwards . . . because we have made a lot of changes. For some, they might seem small, but when you think about that it is people's daily lives, you are changing. So, the changes are actually larger than they initially appear. That is actually what I took with me from the course. That is, I got a better understanding of what is hard for people, and why they don't move.

This shift in sensemaking was an important step toward developing change management competencies. Understanding and internalizing that each employee and manager had their own ongoing processes of making sense of the organizational change was part of the foundation of a change management position that was more sensitive to the complexity of the ongoing processes of organizing. Such shifts do not simply involve learning pieces of information. They result from a process that involves a change in perception and sensemaking. Experiencing and making sense of the complexity of individual change reactions were central components of the sensemaking processes that occurred after the CMCI.

The finding that participating managers understood that individuals react differently to change was evidenced by a plant manager who explained that his primary takeaway from the course had been a heightened awareness of the causes of resistance and, crucially, how some employees might be more reluctant to change than they were.

PLANT MANAGER: I think, on my behalf, because I have been a driver in this development, I have gained a slightly better understanding of what keeps people from jumping on the bus. The things that inhibit you from stepping in front of your co-workers and talking about stuff are in reality everyday things and work stuff and how it can be difficult for some. I think I got a broader understanding of those dynamics.

INTERVIEWER: Can you elaborate on that understanding?

PLANT MANAGER: Ehm [long pause] Yeah, I think some of it [the course content] I knew already, resistance to change and its causes, and how it is often about insecurity. It's also about personality, some people have a personality of – what to call it – "maintain" [uses the English word] – that you stay in the same patterns. Then it is a much bigger step to do something different, and it almost takes a certain degree of – almost threats [laughs] of discomfort in order to make people move. An image that I find enticing is not necessarily one that others find appealing. That is the lesson that I took with me from the training course. What I gave most thought when I came back to the plant was what it is that keeps people from participating. Yeah, I thought a lot about that.

A substantial sensemaking process occurred in how the managers reflected on change management after the workshops. Even though the managers knew much of the formal curriculum in advance, playing the serious game simulations and reflecting on change with fellow managers affected their sensemaking and initiated a process of reflecting on their own management practices. The results showed not only the awareness of individual differences but also how this awareness contributed to self-awareness and developing change management competencies. Specifically, the managers on the production site improved by being attentive to individual and context-specific processes that underpinned change reactions.

9.7.2   Theme 2: Learning to Make Sense of Your Own Role in Change Processes

The second line of learning and reflections was related to managers shifting their attention from making sense of their employees' change reactions to reflecting on their own roles and positions in change processes. As the managers developed nuanced understandings of employees' reactions, they began to question and reflect on their own roles in change processes. These reflections included questions about self-identity as change managers and an understanding of how to manage change. The experiences in the CMCI presented the managers with new ways of making sense of change, which they integrated in nuanced ways to make sense of what change management entails. One manager articulated the following:

HEAD OF DEPARTMENT: ... I'm pretty sure – I can only speak for myself, but I also hope that the others feel this way – that we have become more aware that people are different. People need to be treated differently to get them involved. And this is something we have reflected a lot on afterwards – the thing about making sure to also just take a chat with those who were sitting in the back of the bus.

Here, the understanding that people are different and that some are likely to enact degrees and forms of resistance was coupled with the direct imperative that managers should ensure that they communicate with change-resistant employees. This excerpt illustrates the link between sensemaking, that is, becoming more aware that people are different, and enacting change management competencies (i.e., communicating with those who are resistant to change). When sensemaking has changed, perceptions and actions are likely to change accordingly. Asked specifically what had changed in his managerial behavior, the department head elaborated as follows:

HEAD OF DEPARTMENT: So, personally, then I think that it is very strong, that picture, when you have made some decisions [in the simulation] and you move the bus on, and say "okay, I got two men with a pure heart with the rest they are foot-dragging," right? That really gives rise to reflection on the way you usually think . . . I know very well that when I get a good start, when I start the engine up and then run full throttle, and things run smoothly, then we reach our goals. But maybe it would be better if I got some more people on board, because then – what do you call it – "the sustainability" [uses English term], the process of change itself, would give something. . . . So, I have worked a lot afterwards with myself, just trying to tone down my need to constantly say, "it's that way!" and be directive, and then just spend a little more time understanding, "where are you at?" and "What do you say to this?" "I know I think it's awesome, but where are you?," right?

The head of department clearly experienced the training as relevant and became more aware of how he could implement changes in a more sustainable manner. Although he may still be directive and driven in his managerial style, he appeared to have become more attentive to the fact that others might not always be responsive to this management style. He exemplified that changing perceptions of the role of change manager could lead to conducting change more effectively and ensuring that the process itself could be a positive experience that would lead to sustainable results. This development clearly demonstrated that his sensemaking of both change management and himself as a manager had shifted. This change in sensemaking led him to articulate the need to improve his change management competencies in relation to communication and involvement was apparent when he was asked further about a key learning takeaway from the workshop:

INTERVIEWER: Can you recount specific episodes where you have rediscovered some more reflections and it has led to other decisions or . . .?

HEAD OF DEPARTMENT: I would guess so! I'm having a hard time pinpointing one specific thing right now because it's been so damn long since [the training] . . . but when I mass communicate to the [production] site I think a little more about it now, for instance thinking; okay, maybe not everyone is equally motivated by the fact that I think this change is damn cool. But then I try to give a little more background, right? when I communicate. Another thing is that when I happen to be on the shop floor, I ask more questions. And then I try to listen a bit more because that's also what I think it takes, if you want to have more people on the bus, right? Then you also have to understand what goes on. Then you can sometimes think "it's damn foolish" and so on, but you have to understand it. It's where people are, right. So, I think it's mostly like, if I have to summarize on the personal level, then it's probably that it has shaken up my habits and way of communicating that I've been through this.

Such reflections demonstrate that, although the department head found it difficult to recollect specific episodes, he perceived that changes had occurred in how he communicated and how he regarded his employees and himself. In relation to learning to manage change, this highly relevant example illustrates the complexity of disagreeing with employees and the ability to accept that employees perceive things differently and act or communicate in ways that foster change. Learning to make sense of employees' perceptions and managers' self-perceptions, as well as acting collectively and developing shared sensemaking all serve as competencies of change.

9.7.3   Theme 3: Reflections on Learning and Changed Management Competencies

Although the experiences and shifts in sensemaking presented in the first two themes comprised personal experiences, they consistently pointed in the direction of an increased awareness of employee diversity and recognizing the need to improve change communication. Becoming aware of nuances in change reactions and their diversity led the participating managers to arrive at various positions in learning to better manage change and develop change competencies. One manager articulated these developments clearly:

LINE MANAGER: ... concretely much, much more skilled managers by having been through those thoughts of "why do people react like that" ...
I recognize the patterns when I think of situations where I have been involved in implementing major changes.

Other managers reported that they did not think much about the CMCI after the workshops and they had mostly forgotten the personal action plans they had developed. However, these managers recounted situations that led them to recall and draw on their experiences at the CMCI. This exemplifies that the change management competencies learned at the workshop were tied to sensemaking processes, in contrast to learning about theories and models. The ongoing process of making sense of the world had been slightly adjusted, and experiences in the CMCI had shifted their focus to being attentive to managing changes more competently. One manager articulated the fleeting nature of takeaways from the change management training intervention:HEAD OF DEPARTMENT: There are probably some elements I take with me; right now, we are actually right now facing a mega-size change in my department. So, there are some things that pop-up when we're just talking about the changes, – "oh, there was something about a game," and "there's something about communication here," and so on. So, I also filled out [the action plan] at the workshop. But I simply have not looked at it subsequently.

A complication of analyzing the sensemaking processes in the CMCI is that it was difficult for the participants to separate which aspect of management practice and Lean implementation stemmed from the CMCI, and which were due to other initiatives in the workplace. Although the findings indicated that the participants combined learning and development, a distinct change in sensemaking regarding the complexity of change and change management appeared to have originated in the CMCI. For example, one manager explained that, even though she was unable to separate various initiatives, she had a clear understanding that the CMCI had increased her awareness of change management and hence made her better equipped to ensure that her employees took part in change processes.

LINE MANAGER: It's unclear what is [the CMCI's] fault, and what is due to all the other activities; but the employees have been made aware of the fact that "well, you actually have a role and you have to provide something to show that you are taking initiative and you have to be involved and be a part of this." And you could say that if we had not had [the change management training intervention], then we might not have thought about what is happening in the process, and then we might not have been so aware of it.

These examples of how experiences from the CMCI affected change management demonstrate that the link between learning and sensemaking is complex. Moreover, although it is an individual endeavor, it is tied to cultural cues and ongoing social processes. When most of the managers in a team reflected on similar themes, a collective shift in sensemaking emerged, and learning of change management competencies took place in both individuals and the organization. The experiences of another line manager illustrated this shift and how it, in his opinion, had led to the successful implementation of change while taking employee wellbeing into account:

LINE MANAGER: What I have reflected most on, since I came back [to the department from the course] has been that stuff about, what is it that keeps people from supporting change ... Yeah, I have given it much thought.

INTERVIEWER: Yes, and when I ask about the outcome, *you* have thought a lot about it, but what has it given the department?

LINE MANAGER: It has at least given the department that I have ... My approach to change has become more nuanced than what I would normally have done. I think we can call it something we have gained as a department. We have successfully implemented [Lean] without a long line of sick and injured afterwards.

The line manager making the connections between a more nuanced approach to change management, and how it led to implementation success without sacrificing employee wellbeing is a clear example of the important role of sensemaking processes for the CMCI to foster a development in change management competencies.

9.8   Discussion

The results of the analysis shed light on the sensemaking processes at play in the CMCI. First, we demonstrated that the participants experienced a heightened awareness of employees' individual change reactions as a result of participating in the CMCI and reflecting on the serious game simulations. Experiencing change reactions as both individual and collective phenomena increased the managers' awareness of nuances in employee change reactions. Second, we followed the managers in their reports of having become more aware of their own change management practices. The reflexivity led to possibilities of managing change differently, specifically by making sense of one's own change management behavior and its link to change competencies. Third, the findings demonstrated that learning from the CMCI manifested in a complex of developments that were intertwined with other initiatives.

A common denominator in the participants' experiences was that the CMCI had led them to become more attentive to change and develop change competencies through reflecting on change management. The findings of our study showed that change management training initiatives, such as the CMCI, can foster learning and improve managers' change management competencies by affecting the ways in which they reflect on their subordinates, themselves, their managerial practices, and therefore their sensemaking processes.

9.8.1   Sensemaking and Learning in the CMCI

Our findings indicated that the participants' sensemaking processes began with reflections on the CMCI and their current situations. In line with sensemaking theory (Weick, 1995), sensemaking can be seen as a link between reflections on the past and behavior, cognition, and thinking in the future. The combination of reflection, dialog, and serious game simulations appeared to be a fruitful platform for sensemaking and for the managers to attain new change management competencies. As mentioned in the literature and exemplified in the results of the data analysis, sensemaking and learning are closely connected phenomena (Colville et al., 2016). The learning–sensemaking link observed in the CMCI is evidence for the efficacious use of serious game simulations and other experiential learning tools in change management training (Wilson & Beard, 2013). The managers in our study experienced that learning was closely tied to personal experience. They used reflections on the serious game simulations and other experiential elements to facilitate subsequent sensemaking. The implications for change management training are that serious game simulations and other experiential learning elements comprise useful strategies for ensuring that even experienced managers can internalize learning and develop change competencies (Argyris, 1991).

9.8.2 Link between Reflexive Sensemaking and Change Management

A consistent point made by the participating managers was that the CMCI has made them aware that employees react individually when change occurs. The participants had experienced the destabilization of their assumptions about employee reactions to change, which made them aware of the complexity and diversity of meaning-making among employees. Destabilization may be undesirable but, in the case of change management competencies, it is arguably a positive development. According to the classic "unfreeze–change–refreeze" model of change (Lewin, 1947), a substantial force is needed to destabilize status quo reasoning (Burnes, 2012). Unfreezing can, in itself, be a complicated task, as entrenched opinions and positions often support current opinions and reasoning. The fact that the findings of the present study demonstrated that the change management training intervention increased not only the managers' attentiveness to nuances in change management but also their interest in better ways of managing change management is a substantial argument for change management training.

The CMCI managers did not report that they took standardized solutions home from playing the serious game simulations. However, they reported being more aware of and having new perspectives on change. Subsequently, based on their new, wider repertoire of change management competencies, they could be able to face change management challenges and improvise accordingly. Raising the managers' awareness of a diverse repertoire of change management actions and perspectives is an important part of the sensemaking processes at play in the CMCI. While the CMCI seemingly "unfroze" the participants' perspectives on change management competencies and led them to new sensemaking, their direction and "refreezing" was less controllable.

9.8.3   Implications for Change Management Training

The results of the change management training presented in the present chapter had both agential and reflective effects on the participants' change management competencies. The initial intention of the CMCI, and potentially other change management programs, was to help managers learn how to achieve better change implementation and reduce employee resistance. A pervasive finding in this study was that the participants reflected primarily on their practice and their employees rather than simply internalizing the behaviors presented in the training. Even though reflection may not seem attractive when change is taking place, it may form a foundation for continuing the development of change management practices (Weick, 1991; Corley & Gioia, 2003). Sensemaking is inextricably bound to perceptions, relations, and identity (Weick, 1995). The process of destabilizing managerial sensemaking is a necessary stepping stone to achieving novel change competencies. The subsequent possibilities of increased curiosity about employees and themselves both motivate and facilitate psychologically sound change (Ala-Laurinaho et al., 2017).

A further implication of the findings concerns the relevance of initiatives, such as the CMCI. Discussing and reflecting on change with a managerial group is not necessarily possible during a hectic workday. In this study, the participating managers were given the opportunity to discuss and reflect on how they and their organization managed change. Such reflections are an important vehicle for learning through sensemaking processes (Colville et al., 2016). As the findings of this study demonstrated, the participants experienced changes related to sensemaking, which led to the development of various aspects of change management competencies, both individually and collectively.

Individual and collective sensemaking may foster an increased focus on change management and more nuanced approaches to handling employee reactions to organizational change. Managers who participate in change management training have the potential to develop their change competencies by making sense of their roles in change management and increasing their awareness of how their employees react to changes.

Sensemaking is a crucial component in ensuring that managers participating in change management training arrive at a nuanced understanding of the psychology of the employees for whom they are responsible. A key example is the manager who emphasized that he had become more aware that he tended to appreciate new initiatives more than the employees did. Learning to integrate such sensemaking into managerial practice is clearly part of the foundation for developing change competencies and good change management.

9.9 Conclusion

In this chapter, we analyzed the sensemaking processes at play in change management training. We emphasized that the CMCI led to changes by utilizing experiential learning and sensemaking processes to facilitate learning about and developing change competencies. Sensemaking processes and interactions with experiential elements in change management training can lead to surprising and personal learning that helps participants make sense of their own roles in change and find ways forward regarding the development of their change management competencies. Finally, as the findings of our study demonstrated, sensemaking processes in the CMCI were collective because learning and sensemaking were congruent across the participants, and they were individual and based on each manager's reflection on their own practice. The participating managers made sense of how they currently performed change management and how they wanted to perform change management in the future as both individual managers and as members of a managerial group.

REFERENCES

Abildgaard, J. S. (2018). Tricks of the trade: Practical advice from the PIPPI project for evaluating organizational interventions. In K. Nielsen & A. Noblet (eds.), *Organizational Interventions for Health and Well-being: A Handbook for Evidence-Based Practice* (pp. 144–166). Oxford: Routledge.

Abildgaard, J. S., & Nielsen, K. (2018). The interplay of sensemaking and material artefacts during interventions: A case study. *Nordic Journal of Working Life Studies, 8*(3). https://doi.org/10.18291/njwls.v8i3.109538

Abt, C. C. (1987). *Serious games*. Lanham, MD: University Press of America.

Agger, A., & Møller, M. (2018). Leadership development simulations from the best of intention to real-life balance. In S. Gudiksen & J. Inlove (eds.), *Why innovators and changemakers use games to break down silos, drive engagement and build trust* (pp. 139–154). London: Kogan Page.

Ala-Laurinaho, A., Kurki, A.-L., & Abildgaard, J. S. (2017). Supporting sense-making to promote a systemic view of organizational change: Contributions from activity theory. *Journal of Change Management, 17*(4), 367–387.

Andersen, T. K. (2018). Understanding the success or failure of organizational ICT integration: The criticality of managerial involvement. *Journal of Change Management, 18*(4), 327–343.

Argyris, C. (1991). Teaching smart people how to learn. *Harvard Business Review, 69*(3), 99–109.

Armenakis, A. A., & Bedeian, A. G. (1999). Organizational change: A review of theory and research in the 1990s. *Journal of Management, 25*(3), 293–315.

Balogun, J., & Johnson, G. (2005). From intended strategies to unintended outcomes: The impact of change recipient sensemaking. *Organization Studies, 26*(11), 1573–1601.

Battilana, J., Gilmartin, M., Sengul, M., Pache, A.-C., & Alexander, J. A. (2010). Leadership competencies for implementing planned organizational change. *The Leadership Quarterly, 21*(3), 422–438.

Bickerich, K., Michel, A., & O'Shea, D. (2018). Executive coaching during organisational change: A qualitative study of executives and coaches perspectives. *Coaching: An International Journal of Theory, Research and Practice, 11* (2), 117–143.

Boyatzis, R. E. (1998). *Transforming qualitative information: Thematic analysis and code development.* Thousand Oaks, CA: Sage.

Braun, V., & Clarke, V. (2012). Thematic analysis. In *APA Handbooks in Psychology. APA handbook of research methods in psychology, Vol 2: Research designs: Quantitative, qualitative, neuropsychological, and biological* (pp. 57–71). Washington, DC: American Psychological Association.

Brinkmann, S., & Kvale, S. (2015). *Interviews: Learning the craft of qualitative research interviewing.* Thousand Oaks, CA: Sage.

Burnes, B. (2012). Kurt Lewin and the origins of OD. In D. M. Boje, B. Burnes, & J. Hassard (eds.), *The Routledge companion to organizational change* (pp. 29–44). Oxford: Routledge.

Carey, M., & Russell, S. (2003). Outsider-witness practices: Some answers to commonly asked questions. *The International Journal of Narrative Therapy and Community Work, 1*, 1–22.

Colville, I., Pye, A., & Brown, A. D. (2016). Sensemaking processes and Weickarious learning. *Management Learning, 47*(1), 3–13.

Corley, K. G., & Gioia, D. A. (2003). Semantic learning as change enabler: Relating organizational identity and organizational learning. In M. Easterby-Smith & M. Lyles (eds.), *The Blackwell handbook of organizational learning and knowledge management* (pp. 621–636). Malden, MA: Blackwell.

Czarniawska, B. (1998). *A narrative approach to Oorganization studies.* Thousand Oaks, CA: Sage.

Faria, A. J., Hutchinson, D., Wellington, W. J., & Gold, S. (2009). Developments in business gaming: A review of the past 40 years. *Simulation & Gaming, 40*(4), 464–487.

Guiette, A., & Vandenbempt, K. (2016). Learning in times of dynamic complexity through balancing phenomenal qualities of sensemaking. *Management Learning, 47*(1), 83–99.

Have, S. ten, Have, W. ten, Huijsmans, A.-B., & Eng, N. van der. (2015). *Change competence, implementing effective change* (1st ed.). New York: Routledge.

Higgs, M., & Rowland, D. (2000). Building change leadership capability: "The quest for change competence". *Journal of Change Management, 1*(2), 116–130.

(2011). What does it take to implement change successfully? A study of the behaviors of successful change leaders. *The Journal of Applied Behavioral Science, 47*(3), 309–335.

Iveroth, E., & Hallencreutz, J. (2015). *Effective organizational change: Leading through sensemaking*. London: Routledge.

de Jong, T., Wiezer, N., de Weerd, M., Nielsen, K., Mattila-Holappa, P., & Mockałło, Z. (2016). The impact of restructuring on employee well-being: A systematic review of longitudinal studies. *Work & Stress, 30*(1), 91–114.

Jordan, M. E., Lanham, H. J., Crabtree, B. F., Nutting, P. A., Miller, W. L., Stange, K. C., & McDaniel, R. R. (2009). The role of conversation in health care interventions: Enabling sensemaking and learning. *Implementation Science, 4*(1), 15.

Kieselbach, T., Armgarth, E., Bagnara, S., Elo, A.-L., Jefferys, S., Joling, C., et al. (2009). *Health in restructuring: Innovative approaches and policy recommendations (HIRES)*. Bremen, Germany: Universität Bremen.

Kolb, A. Y., & Kolb, D. A. (2005). Learning styles and learning spaces: Enhancing experiential learning in higher education. *Academy of Management Learning & Education, 4*(2), 193–212.

Kotter, J. P. (1996). *Leading change*. Boston, MA: Harvard Business Press.

Krummaker, S., & Vogel, B. (2013). An in-depth view of the facets, antecedents, and effects of leaders' change competency: Lessons from a case study. *The Journal of Applied Behavioral Science, 49*(3), 279–307.

Kurz, R., & Bartram, D. (2002). Competency and individual performance: Modelling the world of work. In I. T. Robertson, M. Callinan, & D. Bartram (eds.) *Organizational effectiveness: The role of psychiatry* (pp. 227–255). Chichester: John Wiley & Sons, Ltd.

Lewin, K. (1947). Frontiers in group dynamics: Concept, method and reality in social science; social equilibria and social change. *Human Relations, 1*(1), 5–41.

Lundmark, R., Hasson, H., Schwarz, U. von T., Hasson, D., & Tafvelin, S. (2017). Leading for change: Line managers' influence on the outcomes of an occupational health intervention. *Work & Stress, 31*(3), 276–296.

Lüscher, L. S., & Lewis, M. W. (2008). Organizational change and managerial sensemaking: Working through paradox. *The Academy of Management Journal*, *51*(2), 221–240.

Maitlis, S., & Christianson, M. (2014). Sensemaking in organizations: Taking stock and moving forward. *The Academy of Management Annals*, *8*(1), 57–125.

Maurer, R. (2010). *Beyond the wall of resistance: Why 70% of all changes still fail and what you can do about it*. Austin, TX: Bard Press.

Moon, J. A. (2013). *A handbook of reflective and experiential learning: Theory and practice*. Oxford: Routledge.

Myers, I. B., McCaulley, M. H., Quenk, N. L., & Hammer, A. L. (1998). *MBTI manual: A guide to the development and use of the Myers-Briggs Type Indicator*, vol. 3. Palo Alto, CA: Consulting Psychologists Press.

Nielsen, K., Randall, R., & Christensen, K. B. (2010). Does training managers enhance the effects of implementing team-working? A longitudinal, mixed methods field study. *Human Relations*, *63*(11), 1719–1741.

Olsen, E. L., Wåhlin-Jacobsen, C. D., & Abildgaard, J. S. (2020). Reconceptualizing job control in participatory interventions: Collective sensemaking as a missing link. *Nordic Journal of Working Life Studies*, *10*(4). https://doi.org/10.18291/njwls.122137

Owen, J. E., Mahatmya, D., & Carter, R. (2017). Dominance, influence, steadiness, and conscientiousness (DISC) assessment tool. In V. Zeigler-Hill & T. K. Shackelford (eds.), *Encyclopedia of personality and individual differences* (pp. 1–4). Cham: Springer International.

Riessman, C. K. (1993). *Narrative analysis*. Newbury Park, CA: Sage.

(2002). Narrative aAnalysis. In A. Huberman & M. Miles (eds.), *The qualitative researcher's companion* (pp. 216–270). Thousand Oaks, CA: Sage.

Saldaña, J. (2015). *The coding manual for qualitative researchers* (3rd ed.). Thousand Oaks, CA: Sage.

Sartori, R., Costantini, A., Ceschi, A., & Tommasi, F. (2018). How do you manage change in organizations? Training, development, innovation, and their relationships. *Frontiers in Psychology*, *9*, 313.

Schwandt, D. R. (2005). When managers become philosophers: Integrating learning with sensemaking. *Academy of Management Learning & Education*, *4*(2), 176–192.

Tafvelin, S., Hasson, H., Nielsen, K., & von Thiele Schwarz, U. (2021). Integrating a transfer perspective into evaluations of leadership training. *Leadership & Organization Development Journal*, *42*(6), 856–868.

Teulier, R., & Rouleau, L. (2013). Middle managers' sensemaking and inter-organizational change initiation: Translation spaces and editing practices. *Journal of Change Management*, *13*(3), 308–337.

Thomas, K. W. (1988). The conflict-handling modes: Toward more precise theory. *Management Communication Quarterly*, *1*(3), 430–436.

Todnem By, R. (2005). Organisational change management: A critical review. *Journal of Change Management*, *5*(4), 369–380.

Vignoli, M., Nielsen, K., Guglielmi, D., Mariani, M. G., Patras, L., & Peirò, J. M. (2021). Design of a safety training package for migrant workers in the construction industry. *Safety Science, 136*, 105124.

Weick, K. E. (1991). The nontraditional quality of organizational learning. *Organization Science, 2*(1), 116–124.

(1993). The collapse of sensemaking in organizations: The Mann Gulch disaster. *Administrative Science Quarterly, 38*(4), 628.

(1995). *Sensemaking in organizations.* Thousand Oaks, CA: Sage.

(2007). Drop your tools: On reconfiguring management education. *Journal of Management Education, 31*(1), 5–16.

(2010). Reflections on enacted sensemaking in the Bhopal disaster. *Journal of Management Studies, 47*(3), 537–550.

Weick, K. E., Sutcliffe, K. M., & Obstfeld, D. (2005). Organizing and the process of sensemaking. *Organization Science, 16*(4), 409–421.

(2008). Organizing for high reliability: Processes of collective mindfulness. *Crisis Management, 3*, 81–123.

Wilson, J. P., & Beard, C. (2013). *Experiential learning: A handbook for education, training and coaching.* London: Kogan Page.

Womack, J., Jones, D., & Roos, D. (1991). *The machine that changed the world: The story of lean production.* New York: Harper Perennial.

CHAPTER 10

Mindsets for Change Leaders
Exploring a Cognitive Approach for Leadership Development

Bradley Hastings, Dave Bouckenooghe, and Gavin M. Schwarz

10.1 The Need for a Dynamic Approach to Develop Leader Behavior

In change leadership settings, leader behaviors are a known influence on change outcomes – for better or for worse (Ford & Ford, 2012; Oreg & Berson, 2019). Descriptions of desired leader behaviors are typically allied with the type of change process, referring to the activities that enable change. Top-down change processes described planned approaches to change, where future states are envisaged and prescriptive actions are undertaken with the aim to transition the organization toward these new states (Kotter, 1995; Stouten et al., 2018). Correspondingly, leaders – referring to those responsible for change outcomes – play a key role in determining desired outcomes, then plan the execution of activities to achieve these stated aims. In contrast, for bottom-up change processes, change is an emergent phenomenon, where new possibilities emerge organically as a result of interactions between those involved (Bushe & Marshak, 2015; Burnes, 2017). With these processes, leaders should set open-ended goals, facilitate the emergence of innovations, and foster environments where new possibilities are learned.

Yet, whereas change leadership literature describes change processes as *either* top-down or bottom-up (see Weick & Quinn, 1999; Bushe & Marshak, 2009; Burnes, 2017), a body of evidence points to successful change requiring switching between these two processes (see Graebner, 2004; Graetz & Smith, 2008; Collins & Hansen, 2011; Hastings & Schwarz, 2021). For example, bottom-up processes can be used to facilitate the discovery of new ideas, then top-down for the implementation of the best ideas. This combined application presents a need for leaders to switch their behaviors dynamically, as change unfolds (see Battilana et al., 2010; Feser et al., 2017). With this basis, missing from the change leadership literature is a leader development approach that emphasizes leaders' capacity to match their behavior to top-down and bottom-up change processes. In this chapter, as a step toward addressing this gap, we explore how the activation of mindsets can be harnessed as a leader development approach for change leadership contexts.

Leader development refers to the intrapersonal interventions with the purpose to expand the capacity of leaders to perform leadership roles (Day et al., 2014). With respect to understanding development interventions, one approach has focused on the role of the big five personality traits (e.g., extraversion, conscientiousness, agreeableness, neuroticism, and emotional stability) in promoting leader behavior (Derue et al., 2011; Gottfredson & Reina, 2020). Leader development researchers who have taken this approach have been interested in identifying desired personality traits and, as such, either selecting leaders with these traits, or developing leaders to foster them. However, this focus on personality contains a key limitation for change leadership settings: traits manifest themselves as behaviors consistently and stably across a variety of contexts (see Gottfredson & Reina, 2020), thus allowing limited scope for switching behaviors as change unfolds. It is our view that this perspective on leader development is targeted toward developing leader behaviors *before* an instance of change, such as via a training intervention, and is less suited for explaining the adaptation of leader behaviors to situations, such as the *evolution* of the change processes they lead.

In contrast to traits, mindsets are more malleable and are thus more useful for explaining how a given leader can exhibit different behaviors across contexts (see Heslin et al., 2019; Gottfredson & Reina, 2020). Mindsets are assumptions that people hold about the plasticity of personal attributes – such as ability, intelligence and personality – that guide behaviors (Dweck, 1986, 2006). In particular, the fixed and growth mindsets guide how people frame, approach, and react to challenges and change. The fixed mindset stems from beliefs that success reflects a level of natural abilities. Leaders with this mindset approach change with a performance-orientation, with correspondingly individualistic, task-focused behaviors (see Elliott & Dweck, 1988; Dweck & Sorich, 1999; Hong et al., 1999). In contrast, the growth mindset stems from belief that success is a result of the quality of strategies employed and/or the effort applied. As such, leaders with a growth mindset will approach challenges and change with a learning orientation, exhibiting behaviors of openness, coaching others, and seeking feedback. Key to our interest in leader development, mindset theory explains how situational cues activate mindsets. For instance, cues provided by framing an event as "we are learning what to do," is a known cue that activates a growth mindset, whereas framing a situation with a performance outcome (i.e., "this is the goal that we will achieve") activates a fixed mindset (Dweck, 2000; Heslin et al., 2006; Nussbaum & Dweck, 2008).

Mindset activation posits a leader development intervention that can be more readily applied – when compared to traits – in the field. Whereas a development focus on traits may target activities that seek to promote traits that leaders don't have (i.e., helping an introverted leader become more extroverted), mindsets represent latent capabilities that stand "ready to fire" following allied situational cues (see Burnette et al., 2013). For instance, where an introverted person would tend to perceive social situations as unmotivating, Heslin et al. (2019) explain that holding a growth mindset can compensate for this lack of intrinsic motivation by construing social situations as opportunities to learn. Social behavior can, thus, become a desirable activity. Further, research by psychologists has identified a variety of simple, effective, and proven approaches to operationalize situational cues and, as such, activate the fixed and growth mindsets (see Dweck, 2006).

We believe that better understanding mindsets in change leadership contexts, as well as the situational cues that drive them, can help develop more precise leader development guidance that enables leaders to dynamically match their behavior to the chosen change process. To do so, we develop Mindset Activation Theory (MAT) as a new development approach for change leadership. Specifically, MAT explains how fixed and growth mindsets foster behaviors that are congruent with desired leader behaviors of top-down and bottom-up change processes – as represented by diagnostic and dialogic practices (as per Bushe & Marshak, 2009, 2015).

With this outlook, we offer a revelatory approach for leader development that enables leaders to calibrate their mindset and, as such, take more precise control of how their behaviors manifest as change unfolds. This approach provides not only a new approach for developing desired change leader behaviors, it also informs leaders about the change-related advantages of switching between change processes (see Hastings & Schwarz, 2021). To conclude, we propose that, for change leadership scholarship, mindsets offer a realistic and practical means for leader development. In what follows, we first detail the building blocks of MAT. Next, we discuss how MAT contributes to change leadership discussion and conclude with outlining areas for future research.

10.2   Mindset Activation Theory

In Mindset Activation Theory (MAT, Figure 10.1) we aim to extend insights from the psychological literature about how situational cues foster the fixed and growth mindsets, with allied behaviors (see connections 1, 2, and 3 for the fixed mindset and connections 5, 6, and 7 for the growth mindset, Figure 10.1). Key to our contribution is drawing parallels between the known behaviors of a fixed mindset and desired leader behaviors of top-down change processes (connection 4, Figure 10.1), as well as between a growth mindset and the desired leader behaviors of bottom-up change processes (connection 8, Figure 10.1).

In presenting MAT, we make two key assumptions regarding change processes. First, we assume that top-down and bottom-up change processes present the primary means to enable change. In taking this assumption, we follow prior work that classifies change processes into these two perspectives (e.g., Weick & Quinn, 1999; Burnes, 2004). For instance, Weick and Quinn (1999) delineate episodic and continuous change, with the former being a top-down planned and intentional activity

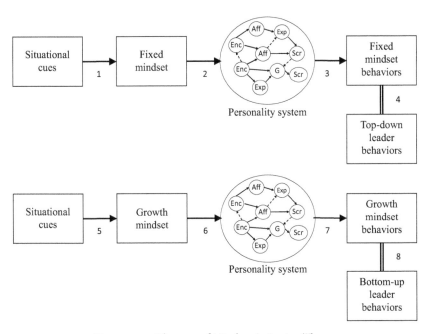

Figure 10.1   Elements of Mindset Activation Theory

implemented by leaders and the latter a bottom-up process, where leaders unblock barriers, promote learning, and make sense of new ideas. This bifurcated perspective on change processes is also adopted by March (1991), who conceptualized exploration – bottom-up processes that facilitate the discovery of new ideas – and exploitation, where successful ideas are implemented in a top-down manner. Continuing this theme, Burnes (2004) and Livne-Tarandach and Bartunek (2009) use the terms planned and emergent change to classify top-down and bottom-up change processes, respectively.

Second, we assume that Bushe and Marshak's (2009, 2015) representation of change processes and change leadership represents the desired leader behaviors for the leadership of top-down and bottom-up change processes. We do so with acknowledgement of Bushe and Marshak's synthetization of over forty years of research on the underlying theories of change and in recognition that, to our knowledge, this work gives the most thorough side-by-side comparison of the key differences between top-down and bottom-up approaches to lead change. Supporting this assumption, we note that prior research on the topic of switching between change processes has used this same representation of change processes (see Gilpin-Jackson & Crump, 2018; Hastings & Schwarz, 2021). In taking this assumption, we differentiate our view of desired leader behaviors from two additional categorizations. Change leadership scholars, with the view to catalog leader behavior, have identified task-orientated behaviors, where leaders shape and implement change top-down, and person-orientated behaviors, where leaders foster change bottom-up (Helmich, 1975; Bass & Bass, 2009; Currie et al., 2009; Battilana et al., 2010). We have chosen to use descriptions of leader behavior described by Bushe and Marshak (2009, 2015) because this offers a side-by-side comparison of leader behaviors that synthesizes the mentioned change leadership research.

Additionally, in establishing the relevance of the fixed and growth mindsets for change leadership, we make three clarifications that are consistent with prior theorizing of mindsets in leadership settings (as per Heslin et al., 2019; Gottfredson & Reina, 2020). First, we highlight that mindsets act subconsciously. In practice, this means that situational cues can cause leaders unwittingly to cue inappropriate mindsets for the context and subsequently exhibit sub-optimal behaviors. This understanding of the subconscious activation of mindsets is an important consideration for MAT because it directs leaders' attention not only to the consciously applied situational cues but also toward the situational cues that can activate mindsets without conscious awareness. Second, consistent with prior theories on how situations and personality interact, we clarify that the environment a leader operates within usually provides substantial degrees of freedom to exhibit behavior authentically (e.g., Tett & Burnett, 2003; Barrick et al., 2013). This means that change leaders have some discretion in how they respond to situations, guided by their internal cognitive processing, as opposed to a strict rules-based approach of "you must do it this way." Third, we distinguish our work from descriptions of mindsets that Bushe and Marshak (2015) have used to illustrate the leadership change processes. Although use of the term "mindset" in the context of leadership of change processes can be confusing with respect to the purpose of this chapter, we note this description does not reference the available mindset theories as developed by psychologists. Further, the authors who proposed the terms "dialogic" and "diagnostic mindset" stated that their terminology "loosely categorizes a mindset" (Bushe & Marshak, 2014, p. 56). As such, hereafter the term "mindset" refers solely to mindset theory, and we take the guidance by Bushe and Marshak (2015) to be a helpful illustration of change leader behaviors.

10.3 From Static to Dynamic Precursors of Leader Behavior

A long-standing theme in the science of leadership has focused on inter-leader differences; specifically, on how personal attributes (i.e., gender, intelligence), personality traits, and behaviors explain leadership effectiveness (Derue et al., 2011; Zaccaro et al., 2018). Within this discussion, personality traits are the most widely studied – conceptualized as broad, stable characteristics (e.g., extraversion, conscientiousness, agreeableness, openness to experience, and emotional stability). Of this set, extraversion, emotional stability, and conscientiousness have been linked with leader effectiveness (Derue et al., 2011; Do & Minbashian, 2014). Alongside this history of research on precursors to leader effectiveness there is a comparatively smaller amount of research on the topic of leader development (Avolio et al., 2009; Day et al., 2014). As Day et al. (2014) note, this tendency to overlook leader development is due to a commonly held premise that, by understanding precursors, a means to develop these characteristics would inevitably follow. Unsurprisingly, change leadership research follows a similar theme, where there has been a considerable focus connecting leader behaviors and change outcomes (see Ford & Ford, 2012; Oreg & Berson, 2019), and correspondingly less focus on development of desired behaviors within leaders.

10.3.1   The Trait Approach

When leader development discussion has explored the precursors of leader behaviors, it has mainly drawn from psychology theories on behavioral antecedents. Within psychological settings, there are two primary psychological explanations for precursors of human behavior: the situation and personality (Mischel, 2009). The leader development literature is based on the dispositional approach, with an interest in identifying the personality traits that determine desired leader behaviors (Derue et al., 2011; Gottfredson & Reina, 2020). The overall aim is to identify the desired traits and either select leaders with these traits or develop leaders to exhibit traits that they do not inherently possess.

The underlying assumption of this approach is that traits manifest themselves as behaviors consistently across situations. However, at the same time, empirical findings show that situations also have a large influence on behavior. As such, the most comprehensive models that explain behavior incorporate both situation and personality antecedents (see Mischel, 2009; Rauthmann et al., 2015). For instance, where the trait of extraversion is associated with highly social behaviors, situation cues moderate the association between extraversion and these behaviors. An inter-company networking session, for example, will be more likely to accentuate the relationship between extraversion and social behaviors than will a religious service.

10.3.2   The Trait–Situation Approach

With a view to more completely understand the dynamics between situations, personality, and behaviors, Mischel and Shoda (1995) developed the cognitive affective processing system (CAPS) framework. This model attempts to explain how traits, as an aspect of an individual's personality system, can remain relatively constant over time and through different contexts, whereas behaviors can vary substantially between situations (Mischel & Shoda, 1995, 2008). CAPS takes a process-orientated perspective on personality, viewing it as a system of interconnections between cognitive units. The process begins when people interact with a situation which is full of features and cues, far too many to process. A reading of the situation occurs via the identification and interpretation of a select number of situational cues. These cues activate a number of affective and cognitive units – described as a personality system – resulting in behaviors that are aimed at guiding the individual to best navigate the situation. Five units of the personality system are described (see Mischel & Shoda, 1995, 2008): (1) encoders, described as the ways in which people categorize information from external stimuli, (2) expectancies, representing the tendency to predict the outcomes of engaging in, or avoiding, specific behaviors, (3) affective responses, reflecting the feelings and emotions about situations, for instance where positive mood-inducing events, such as a success, result in positive behavioral responses (Weiss & Cropanzano, 1996), (4) goals, providing an objective to aim at and a source of motivation, as well as a yardstick for measuring one's progress (Locke & Latham, 2013), and (5) behavioral scripts, presenting both the potential behaviors as well as the organizing action for enabling outcomes (both internal and external). This framework explains that exhibited behaviors are shaped by complex and interwoven interactions between situational cues, dispositions, self-imposed standards, and anticipated consequences.

Particularly relevant for leader development is the role of encoders, because the way in which people categorize information from external stimuli is foundational to leader development models (Mischel & Shoda, 2008; Rauthmann et al., 2015). As Gottfredson and Reina (2020) explain, encoders initiate the personality processes – because it is inefficient for leaders to interpret all of the available information, instead encoders act by filtering and interpreting the information that appears salient. Consequentially, it is selective information that both activates and interacts with the other units of the personality system, in ways unique to selected information and entirely unique to a different selection. For instance, encoding a situation as an opportunity selectively filters information related to new possibilities at the same time as framing affective responses of determination, enthusiasm excitement, and inspiration (Robins & Pals, 2002). In contrast, encoding a situation as a threat filters information related to problems which, in turn, can elicit feelings of distress.

This knowledge developed by psychologists resonates with a wider leadership discussion where it has been known for some time that leaders – like all individuals – are highly selective in the information that they perceive in situations (Starbuck & Milliken, 1988). It has also been recognized that the information that captures a leader's attention is a key determinate of their resulting behavior and, ultimately, their success (Hambrick, 2007). The knowledge that the CAPS framework brings to leadership settings is an understanding of how this selectiveness (studied as encoding schema) influences individual elements of the personality system and, as such, guides leader behavior.

10.3.3   Mindsets

Mindset theory describes two types of mindsets: (1) the fixed mindset and (2) the growth mindset. Leaders with a fixed mindset approach challenges and change with a performance orientation (e.g., "this is what we will do differently"). They prefer to set defined goals – typically ones that they know they have the ability to achieve – avoid feedback and are less focused on coaching others (Heslin et al., 2006). Like the growth mindset, the fixed mindset has also been found to be beneficial in performance situations (Plaks & Stecher, 2007; Park & Kim, 2015). This is because leaders with a fixed mindset will work harder, when compared to growth mindset leaders, to achieve their desired outcomes in contexts where they are trying to validate pre-existing perceptions of ability. In contrast, leaders with a growth mindset maintain a learning orientation (e.g., "we are learning how to do things differently"), with allied behaviors of openness to ideas on how to do things differently (Nussbaum & Dweck, 2008), seeking feedback as a useful source of information (Mueller & Dweck, 1998), and the willingness to coach others (Heslin et al., 2006). Meta analyses have identified positive correlations between a growth mindset and performance in sport, educational achievement, and leadership effectiveness (Burnette et al., 2013; Van Yperen et al., 2014).

Although it is commonly perceived that leaders have either a fixed or growth mindset, these two prototypes represent latent capabilities that are malleable. Although individuals can have a dominant mindset, they can also switch between the fixed and growth mindsets following situational cues (Burnette et al., 2013). This is because mindsets act in two ways: First they scan contexts selectively for relevant information, filling in the gaps and highlighting information pertinent for the task. For instance, leaders with a fixed mindset will observe a failure as a problem – something to be avoided – whereas for those with a growth mindset, failures are seen as an opportunity to learn. Second, as Heslin et al. (2019) illuminate, mindsets act as encoders for all aspects of the personality system described by the CAPS framework. For instance, for the expectancies aspect, the growth mindset is a source of self-efficacy (Bandura, 1986). The fixed mindset is also associated with feelings of distress, shame, and being upset, whereas the growth mindset, in contrast, fosters feelings of enthusiasm, excitement, and inspiration (Robins & Pals, 2002). For goals, the fixed mindset facilitates performance-orientated goals toward maintaining self-esteem (Nussbaum & Dweck, 2008), whereas the growth mindset fosters goals that develop capabilities (Burnette et al., 2013). Further, mindsets shape the practice of strategies to achieve goals, with the growth mindset exhibiting a rigorous approach of learning, whereas the fixed mindset avoids learning (Smith, 2005). With this context, for leader development, the possibility to influence mindsets becomes an effective and immediate approach to influence a leader's personality system and guide their behavior.

10.3.3.1 Mindset Activation Techniques

Psychologists have advanced a variety of mindset activation techniques that operationalize situational cues (see Heslin & Keating, 2017), which have been shown to consciously shift individuals between fixed and growth mindsets (Burnette et al., 2013). The growth mindset can be promoted by engaging in one or more of the following activities: framing a task as a learning outcome (Wood & Bandura, 1989), reading scripts, such as scientific testimonials written from a growth mindset perspective (Kray & Haselhuhn, 2007), praising performance with respect to effort (Mueller & Dweck, 1998) or through self-talk (i.e., "I am learning how to be a better leader"; see Heslin et al., 2006; Heslin & Keating, 2016). For a fixed mindset, situational cues include framing tasks in terms of performance outcomes, reading scripts from a fixed mindset perspective, praising performance with respect to personal attributes (e.g., "you're so smart"), and self-talk that indicates a fixed set of abilities (e.g., "I am not cut out to be a negotiator").

Multiple studies show that situational cues result in, at the least, a short-term shift in behavior (Hong et al., 1999; Blackwell et al., 2007; Kray & Haselhuhn, 2007). Some research identifies the duration of this shift as long lasting; Heslin et al. (2005) showed that MBA students maintained a growth mindset for six weeks, and a nationally-focused one-hour training intervention to activate growth mindsets in school-aged students demonstrated improved academic performance for a full school year (Yeager et al., 2019).

Within this context, mindsets provide an alternative leader development approach for fostering the emergence of desired change process behaviors. Key to harnessing mindsets as a leader development approach is the understanding that encoding typically occurs automatically and subconsciously, without an individual's awareness (Bargh & Chartrand, 1999; Wilson, 2004). Thus, a focus on mindsets provides the opportunity to increase awareness of and, in fact, deliberately promote situational cues as a means to guide a leader's personality system toward exhibiting desired behaviors. For example, in instances where people-orientated leadership is desired, a trait-based approach would focus on either selecting leaders with high extraversion or developing this trait within leaders. In contrast, a mindset-based approach focuses on operationalizing the situational cues that are allied with a growth mindset, thereby fostering behaviors of openness and enhanced working with others. Given these properties of mindsets, a focus on the situational cues allied with the fixed and growth mindsets presents an approach for leader development in change settings. A mindset activation approach to leader development therefore provides a ready and immediate approach to switch between mindsets, thus calibrating leader's behavior to the change process applied.

10.4   Connecting Desired Leader Behavior with Mindsets

Top-down and bottom-up change processes are categorized based on four dimensions, each with allied suggestions for desired leader behavior: (1) the type of goals that are targeted; (2) the temporal frame adopted; (3) the activities that enable transformation; and (4) how leaders interact with followers (adapted from Bushe & Marshak, 2015; p. 19). Table 10.1 offers an overview of these dimensions and how desired leader behaviors for each dimension connect with the fixed and growth mindset behaviors. In Table 10.1, the four dimensions are located in the middle column (Column 3). For ease of comparison between desired leader behaviors for the leadership of change processes and the behaviors promoted by mindsets, top-down change processes and the fixed mindset are illustrated in the left columns (Columns 2 and 1, respectively) and bottom-up change processes and growth mindsets are shown in the right columns (Columns 4 and 5, respectively). Next, we highlight the relevant arguments that inform these connections for each dimension in turn.

10.4.1   Goals

Top-Down Goals and the Fixed Mindset: This perspective of top-down change processes targets developmental goals, categorized as pre-determined, desired changes in organizational states that, in some way, advance the organization and/or the people within it (Bushe & Marshak, 2009). Examples include targeting the elimination of a problem or an expression of where the change process is expected to lead (Kanter et al., 1992). Similarly, people cued with a fixed mindset approach change by asking, "what can we achieve?" – a perspective often termed a performance-orientation (Dweck, 1986; Dweck & Leggett, 1988; Heslin & Keating, 2017). Doing so, they typically set a defined goal which is perceived as within their set of abilities, which is similar to the very nature

Table 10.1 *Connecting leadership and mindset behaviors*

Top-down change processes		Dimension	Bottom-up change processes	
Fixed mindset behaviors	Desired leader behavior		Desired leader behavior	Growth mindset behaviors
Set performance outcomes (i.e., "what can we achieve?") Set less-challenging goals Motivation to achieve goals – if goals reinforce preconceived abilities	Pre-determined (i.e., setting of desired end-state) Developmental	**Goals**	Open-ended (i.e., discover new possibilities) Transformational	Set learning outcomes (i.e., "what can be learned?") Set more challenging goals Motivation towards learning from both success and failure
Finite and tied with outcomes (e.g., "I need to implement this action") Self-worth related to achievement of outcomes; exhibit achievement-focused behaviors	Episodic	**Temporal frame**	Continuous	Open-ended: learning is the priority (e.g., "I am learning to be a better leader") Self-worth related to learning and developing new skills; exhibit learning behaviors
Performance orientation Seek out performance opportunities Motivated to achieve outcomes	Pre-planned Execution of pre-defined steps	**Activities**	Learning new possibilities Focused on emergence of new ideas	Learning orientation Seek comparisons to aid learning Motivated to learn new possibilities
Create performance environments Less likely to provide feedback Less willing to enter social situations Engage in downward comparisons to see if they outperform others Less likely to coach or develop others	Hierarchical, start at top and work down Leaders are prescriptive experts	**How leaders interact with followers**	Heterarchical, ideas can emerge from anywhere Leaders are facilitators and coaches	Create learning environments View feedback as valuable More likely to provide feedback Engage in upward comparisons to learn from top performers More likely to develop/coach followers

of developmental goals as a focus on implementing what is already known to be possible.

For leaders with a fixed mindset, this type of goal-setting is underpinned by a preference to avoid failure. In this context, they are more likely to set goals that encompass specific outcomes and, crucially, where these same people have a preconceived notion that their ability and skills are sufficient to reach these stated aims (Elliott & Dweck, 1988; Dweck & Sorich, 1999; Hong et al., 1999; Mueller & Dweck, 1998). A fixed mindset is sometimes characterized by a lack of effort toward achieving goals, when contrasted to a growth mindset. However, research demonstrates that this is not always the case (Plaks & Stecher, 2007; Park & Kim, 2015). When a task is seen as outside preconceptions of ability, effort is seen as futile; whereas if the task falls within perceptions of one's ability, people with a fixed mindset will work harder than those with a growth mindset, to achieve the desired outcomes because they are trying to validate their preconceived notions that they are able.

Bottom-Up Goals and the Growth Mindset: In contrast to top-down change processes, bottom-up processes take the premise that organizations are in a constant state of flux (Bushe & Marshak, 2009, 2015). Within this perspective, change is less about targeting new organization states and putting in plans to achieve these states, instead it is viewed as redirecting the change that is already underway. Bottom-up processes feature goals that are open-ended. In contrast to the pre-defined goals of top-down processes, leaders engage with stakeholders with the view to disrupt existing ways of working without a defined view of what this engagement will ultimately achieve. In bottom-up processes, leaders are encouraged to let go of the outcome of change and instead focus on the purpose of change, such as establishing a purpose of learning new ways of working. With this approach, outcomes are typically more transformational, because what emerges from such processes are new ideas that support fresh and innovative ways of working.

People cued with a growth mindset are more likely to pursue questions to which they do not know the answer (Elliott & Dweck, 1988; Mueller & Dweck, 1998; Dweck & Sorich, 1999; Hong et al., 1999). This mindset accordingly promotes the approaching of challenges and change with a learning-orientation; by setting learning goals, or asking "what can I learn?" Being more comfortable with failure, people with a growth mindset are more comfortable with setting goals that are outside their pre-conceived levels of ability, when compared to those with a fixed mindset (Tabernero & Wood, 1999). Growth mindset individuals express a willingness to exert increased effort in the face of obstacles (Blackwell et al., 2007). They see effort as the means by which they improve their talent and abilities (Mueller & Dweck, 1998; Blackwell et al., 2007). As such, they are more inclined to persist with tasks because they know that success is a product of hard work (Hong et al., 1999; Blackwell et al., 2007; Nussbaum & Dweck, 2008).

10.4.2 Temporal Frame

Top-Down Temporal Frame and the Fixed Mindset: The temporal perspective of top-down processes is episodic, with a defined start and finish (Weick & Quinn, 1999). With this perspective, change has a specific time boundary related to goal-achievement (Van de Ven, 2004). In parallel, people cued with a fixed mindset establish goals that are finite, such as "we need to implement this action by time X." In other words, the fixed mindset promotes a temporal frame that is finite, bounded by a view of success. With self-worth tied to the achievement of goals, people with this mindset set both a goal and a timeframe to achieve this goal (Kamins & Dweck, 1999). Achieving such goals validates their self-worth.

Bottom-Up Temporal Frame and the Growth Mindset: For bottom-up change processes the temporal frame is continuous. Change does not have a defined beginning, middle, or end – instead it is an ongoing phenomenon (Weick & Quinn, 1999; Bushe & Marshak, 2009). In parallel to this perspective of bottom-up change processes, people cued with a growth mindset set goals that are open-ended. For instance, they say, "I am learning to be a better leader." This learning orientation frames goals as an ongoing endeavor, implying a more continuous temporal frame that spans multiple outcomes.

10.4.3 Activities

Top-Down Activities and the Fixed Mindset: For top-down change processes, change is managed as a sequence of activities (Kotter, 1996; Stouten et al., 2018). Each activity contains desired outcomes, such as establishing a vision or setting in place a guiding coalition. Change process literature provides guidance for how leaders should approach each of these activities, in turn, and progress toward change outcomes is accomplished through the successful completion of these activities. In parallel, people cued with a fixed mindset gain their self-worth from achievement; they believe that if they achieve the targets they set, then they are of value

(Kamins & Dweck, 1999). These fixed mindset individuals are predisposed to approach change as a series of outcomes and opportunities to demonstrate achievement, they also measure their performance with respect to their prior expectations because this validates their preconceptions about their ability (Mangels et al., 2006; Burnette et al., 2013).

Bottom-Up Activities and the Growth Mindset: Bottom-up change processes describe activities that foster the emergence of new possibilities, with a heavy emphasis on learning what works and, additionally, learning from failure (Marion & Uhl-Bien, 2001; Bushe & Marshak, 2015; Jabri, 2017). These activities are primarily conversation-based, with a focus on "how conversations unfold, what narratives currently define the way things are and ways that might lead to new interactions" (Marshak et al., 2015, p. 83). The overall purpose is to identify "strengths," facilitate disruption in existing patterns of organizing, and generate the discovery of new futures (Cooperrider & Srivastva, 1987; Bushe & Marshak, 2015). Because people cued with a growth mindset approach change with a learning orientation, they are more likely to seek out development opportunities, monitor and measure their performance through this development, and are more sensitive to cues that indicate that a situation provides opportunities for learning.

10.4.4   How Leaders Interact with Followers

Top-Down Interaction and the Fixed Mindset: When describing how leaders interact with followers, top-down processes assume an ontological separation of leader and followers, dictating a hierarchical interaction. Leaders inquire about organizational reality objectively (i.e., "what is true?") and design and implement transformation plans top-down. Leaders are seen as the prescriptive experts; they build stories and narratives as a means to influence participants with the view to progress to desired organizational states (Gioia & Chittipeddi, 1991; Barrett et al., 1995). People cued with a fixed mindset adopt a performance orientation, where the completion of change tasks and goals is paramount. They seek out opportunities to engage in activities and engage in downward comparisons to see if they outperform others (Nussbaum & Dweck, 2008).

Bottom-Up Interaction and the Growth Mindset: With bottom-up change processes, leaders are directed to adopt heterarchical structures, where ideas for new possibilities can emerge from anywhere. In contrast to top-down processes, where leaders' role is to design new organizational states, bottom-up processes direct leaders to work as facilitators, fostering environments where learning takes place, and participants contribute to change leadership with ideas, innovations, and new possibilities (Bushe & Marshak, 2015). In parallel, people cued with a growth mindset adopt a learning orientation, where learning is more important than achievement of outcomes. They are more willing to coach employees, more willing to receive coaching themselves, as well as being open to ideas on how to do things differently. Whereas people with a fixed mindset compare themselves to others, those with a growth mindset undertake this comparison with the view to aid learning. With this perspective, a growth mindset encourages feedback from any source, including subordinates, as an essential source of information.

In sum, by establishing connections between the four dimensions of top-down and bottom-up change processes and the known behaviors that the fixed and growth mindsets promote, we extend the relevance of mindset knowledge to change leadership settings. With a view to promoting behaviors allied with change processes, when leaders target change as a top-down process, we suggest that they activate a fixed mindset. Further, for bottom-up change processes, they should activate a growth mindset. For leader development, this connection means that the activation mechanisms for the fixed mindset become a relevant leader development approach for the leadership of top-down change processes. Similarly, cues allied with the growth mindset become pertinent for bottom-up change processes.

10.5 Discussion

In this chapter, by establishing a connection between mindsets and the leadership of change processes, we show how change leadership knowledge can be substantially enriched by consideration of mindsets as a driver of desired leader behaviors. In doing so we present Mindset Activation Theory as a new development approach for change leaders. MAT shifts the target of leader development from the established focus on traits, to one that fosters the fixed and growth mindsets and, as such, the behaviors that result from them. We propose this approach as an addition to prior approaches that foster traits, providing a new approach for practice and a source of new avenues of scholarly inquiry.

10.5.1 A New Leader Development Approach

Presenting mindsets as a target for leader development is aimed at helping leaders increase awareness of and take control of their mindset. The current behavioral focus of change leadership scholarship has advanced explanations of desired leader behaviors that are allied with the change process applied (Bushe & Marshak, 2015; Burnes, 2017). However, with this approach, Johnson (2002) explains that developing leaders so that they are able to switch from top-down and bottom-up leadership behaviors requires years of training and effort. In contrast, MAT advances leader development approaches by providing a means to enable this development on an as-needed basis, as change unfolds.

Taking control of the mindsets they exhibit enables leaders to reap the benefits of switching back and forth between top-down and bottom-up change processes. Doing so requires leaders to both increase their awareness of how situational cues influence their mindset as well as undertake mindset activation activities which, in their nature, provide situational cues that calibrate desired mindsets. Extending knowledge of how situational cues influence mindset will provide greater within-leader stability of desired behaviors plus a dynamic ability to alter leader behavior to match their choice of change processes. By engaging in mindset activation activities, leaders can switch between the fixed and growth mindsets as they lead top-down and bottom-up change processes, respectively, and, crucially, ensure that they maintain desired behaviors, regardless of the situational cues to which they are exposed. Examples of mindset activation techniques include explaining how negative self-talk or initiating change with a performance goal fosters a fixed mindset and, correspondingly, how positive self-talk or commencing with a learning goal fosters a growth mindset. These relatively straightforward activities provide a powerful means for leaders to understand and take control of the automatic processes that guide their behavior.

For leaders, reaping full advantage of mindset knowledge requires first building an awareness of the typically subconscious and automatic influence of cognition. To do so, leaders should engage in a practical experiment, whereby they measure their own mindset, using a self-reported survey (see Chiu et al., 1997), then undertake any of the mindset activation activities listed in this chapter to alter their mindset, followed by a repeat of this survey. This observation extends to leaders an understanding of how a relatively straightforward process of situational cues has immediate consideration for shifting their mindset. When leaders understand how these subconscious processes affect how they operate, it provides them with the opportunity for greater control of the situation–mindset interaction. MAT provides an explanation for practitioners on the operationalization of situational cues, via mindset activation activities, that enable leaders to better control their mindset.

10.5.2 Shifting Focus from Traits to Mindsets

With the trait-based approach for leader development, the change leadership scholarship provides only limited leader development guidance. Instead, research on change processes has preferred to carefully delineate desired behaviors. Although useful, the current behavior-based approach is limited by the assumption that leaders can manifest desired behaviors in practice. As a step toward providing more precise leader development guidance, we draw upon the theories of CAPS and mindsets (Mischel & Shoda, 1995; Dweck, 2000) to illuminate how situational cues and mindsets promote desired behaviors for the leadership of top-down and bottom-up change processes. We propose that, when choosing a change process, the extent to which leaders adopt desired leader behaviors is mediated by their prevailing mindset. For instance, for leaders cued to adopt the growth mindset, this mindset plays a vital role, via their personality system, to guide behaviors allied to effective leadership of top-down change processes. Similarly, the fixed mindset guides behaviors allied with bottom-up change processes. This understanding of how situational cues foster behaviors, via mindsets, enables an understanding of a key antecedent to leader behaviors. Thus, we propose mindsets as a more practical and relevant target for leader development.

The benefits of this shift from a traditional trait-based perspective on leader development to mindset activation are threefold: First, we move the target of leader development to a dynamic focus on situational cues, and thus offer better insights on how desired leader behaviors can be triggered by activating the appropriate mindset. Hence, we move away from a perspective of selecting leaders based on underlying traits to one where leaders can more flexibly foster the appropriate mindset as needed. Second, in doing so we raise awareness of the cognitive antecedents of behaviors. By increasing awareness to mindsets, which are typically subconscious, we direct leaders to take greater control of the situation–mindset interaction, thus providing them with greater control of their behaviors. Third, this focus allows for a more dynamic perspective on change leadership, moving from the traditional focus on a static set of enduring behaviors during change to a focus on leadership that acknowledges that behaviors are a dynamic outcome of personality and situational cues. This is a perspective that we feel is closer to the reality of how change and its leadership unfold.

10.5.3 Practical Considerations

It is worth noting that, whereas the growth mindset is commonly referred to as a preferred mindset, many successful leaders have been said to hold a fixed mindset (e.g., Lee Iacocca from Chrysler and Al Dunlap from Sunbeam; see Dweck, 2006). One of the underlying reasons why these leaders are successful is that they have a preconceived notion of success. As an example, Al Dunlap believed that he should be the chief executive of an American automobile company. However, when he was overlooked for the top role at Ford, in an effort to prove his abilities, he left to take the chief executive job at Chrysler. Although his initial time in the new company was incredibly successful, in his later years he was known for firing employees that came up with better ideas than him – an attribute that Dweck (2006) relates to a fixed mindset view, where a perception of high performance (i.e., "I am the boss") needs to be asserted, even at the expense of opportunities to learn and take the company forward. With this context, we propose that the fixed mindset is beneficial for achievement situations – such as change – with the caveat that leaders must have a preconceived perception that their own abilities are sufficient to achieve successful outcomes.

For change leadership, the extant approach of focusing on traits means either selecting leaders who exhibit traits or focusing on the development of these traits. MAT provides insight for both approaches. For leader selection, the recruitment of a new leader when change is targeted is a common process. However, it is fraught with the possibility of a poor choice or bad luck (Yukl, 2012; Burnes, 2017). Mindset knowledge explains how situational cues, either environmental or social in nature (Murphy & Dweck, 2010), influence leader behavior. Therefore, when selected for a new role, leaders who may appear successful in their current environment may be less exposed to the situational cues that guided their mindset and, as such, their success. There may be no benefit in recruiting new leaders at all (as per Groysberg et al., 2004).

To address this issue, MAT presents a shift in focus from leader selection to the development of talent from within. The current explanations of leader behaviors provide insight into the ingredients for successful change leadership. However, a key limitation is that they require conscious effort – through application and learning – to adopt them. MAT harnesses the subconscious to aid this development. There is a growing body of evidence supporting how conscious interventions can help to take control of the subconscious and improve effectiveness with respect to ethical decision-making (Welsh & Ordóñez, 2014), goal attainment (Gollwitzer, 2012), and employee performance (Bargh et al., 2001; Shantz & Latham, 2009). Our theorizing extends these benefits to leaders in change leadership settings.

10.5.4   Extending Mindset Knowledge

MAT is also useful for extending the discussion of the mindset concept. The fixed and growth mindsets have been traditionally studied in educational settings. More recently, scholars have extended their applicability to a wider leadership context (see Heslin & Keating, 2017; Hoyt et al., 2012). Mindset knowledge is yet to be directly applied for considering how leaders' mindsets affect the outcomes of change. Further, for change practice discussion, MAT extends and clarifies existing notions of mindsets. It is consistent with perspectives by Bushe and Marshak (2015) and Weick and Quinn (1999), whereby the leadership of top-down and bottom-up change processes requires separate and allied mindsets. MAT extends this consideration from one that describes mindsets as how leaders should engage with the processes they lead, to one that regards mindsets as malleable cognitive constructs that aid change leadership. In doing so, this new approach presents mindsets as a quantifiable construct that can be measured and altered. Thus, it provides the possibility for future scholarship of change processes to directly study mindsets as change unfolds and opens the possibility to expand the scope of knowledge on how situational cues influence mindsets in change settings.

10.5.5   Directions for Future Exploration

In addition to the aforementioned MAT extension, with our modeling we provide several pathways for future scholarship and exploration. Taking a MAT perspective of leadership opens a wealth of further research possibilities on subconscious antecedents of change leadership. One possibility is studying additional mindsets. For instance, Gottfredson and Reina (2020) propose deliberative and implemental mindsets as separate encoding schemas. So far, the relevance of these mindsets has yet to be fully understood in change leadership contexts, presenting a future avenue of exploration. Furthermore, research has explored other types of encoding processes inherent to the personality system, such as goal orientation (Vandewalle et al., 2019) and regulatory focus (Lanaj et al., 2012). As such, the fixed and growth mindsets represent only the start of the journey to harness the full potential of the subconscious for change leadership.

REFERENCES

Avolio, B. J., Reichard, R. J., Hannah, S. T., Walumbwa, F. O., & Chan, A. (2009). A meta-analytic review of leadership impact research: Experimental and quasi-experimental studies. *The Leadership Quarterly, 20* (5), 764–784.

Bandura, A. (1986). *Social foundation of thought and action: A social-cognitive view.* Englewood Cliffs: Prentice Hall.

Bargh, J. A., & Chartrand, T. L. (1999). The unbearable automaticity of being. *American Psychologist, 54*(7), 462–479.

Bargh, J. A., Gollwitzer, P. M., Lee-Chai, A., Barndollar, K., & Trötschel, R. (2001). The automated will: Nonconscious activation and pursuit of behavioral goals. *Journal of Personality and Social Psychology, 81*(6), 1014.

Barrett, F. J., Thomas, G. F., & Hocevar, S. P. (1995). The central role of discourse in large-scale change: A social construction perspective. *The Journal of Applied Behavioral Science, 31*(3), 352–372.

Barrick, M. R., Mount, M. K., & Li, N. (2013). The theory of purposeful work behavior: The role of personality, higher-order goals, and job characteristics. *Academy of Management Review, 38*(1), 132–153.

Bass, B. M., & Bass, R. (2009). *The Bass handbook of leadership: Theory, research, and managerial applications.* New York: Free Press.

Battilana, J., Gilmartin, M., Sengul, M., Pache, A.-C., & Alexander, J. A. (2010). Leadership competencies for implementing planned organizational change. *The Leadership Quarterly, 21*(3), 422–438.

Blackwell, L. S., Trzesniewski, K. H., & Dweck, C. S. (2007). Implicit theories of intelligence predict achievement across an adolescent transition: A longitudinal study and an intervention. *Child Development, 78*(1), 246–263.

Burnes, B. (2004). Emergent change and planned change: Competitors or allies?: The case of XYZ construction. *International Journal of Operations & Production Management, 24*(9), 886–902.

(2017). *Managing change* (7th ed.). Harlow: Pearson Education.

Burnette, J. L., O'Boyle, E. H., VanEpps, E. M., Pollack, J. M., & Finkel, E. J. (2013). Mind-sets matter: A meta-analytic review of implicit theories and self-regulation. *Psychological Bulletin, 139*(3), 655.

Bushe, G. R., & Marshak, R. J. (2009). Revisioning organization development: Diagnostic and dialogic premises and patterns of practice. *The Journal of Applied Behavioral Science, 45*(3), 348–368.

(2014). The dialogic mindset in organization development. In R. S. Abraham & D. A. Noumair (eds.), *Research in organizational change and development* (Vol. 22, pp. 55–97). Bingley: Emerald Group.

(2015). Introduction to the dialogic organization development mindset. In G. R. Bushe & R. J. Marshak (eds.), *Dialogic organization development: The theory and practice of transformational change* (pp. 11–32). Oakland, CA: Berrett-Koehler.

Chiu, C.-Y., Hong, Y.-Y., & Dweck, C. S. (1997). Lay dispositionism and implicit theories of personality. *Journal of Personality and Social Psychology*, 73(1), 19.

Collins, J., & Hansen, M. T. (2011). *Great by choice: Uncertainty, chaos and luck: Why some thrive despite them all*. New York: HarperCollins.

Cooperrider, D. L., & Srivastva, S. (1987). Appreciative inquiry in organizational life. In *Research in organizational change and development*, vol. 1 (pp. 129–169). Bingley: Emerald Group.

Currie, G., Lockett, A., & Suhomlinova, O. (2009). The institutionalization of distributed leadership: A "Catch-22" in English public services. *Human Relations*, 62(11), 1735–1761.

Day, D. V., Fleenor, J. W., Atwater, L. E., Sturm, R. E., & McKee, R. A. (2014). Advances in leader and leadership development: A review of 25 years of research and theory. *The Leadership Quarterly*, 25(1), 63–82.

Derue, D. S., Nahrgang, J. D., Wellman, N. E. D., & Humphrey, S. E. (2011). Trait and behavioral theories of leadership: An integration and meta-analytic test of their relative validity. *Personnel Psychology*, 64(1), 7–52.

Do, M. H., & Minbashian, A. (2014). A meta-analytic examination of the effects of the agentic and affiliative aspects of extraversion on leadership outcomes. *The Leadership Quarterly*, 25(5), 1040–1053.

Dweck, C. (1986). Motivational processes affecting learning. *American Psychologist*, 41(10), 1040.

(2006). *Mindset: The new psychology of success* (1st ed.). New York: Random House.

Dweck, C. S. (2000). *Self-theories: Their role in motivation, personality, and development*. Hoboken, NJ: Taylor & Francis.

Dweck, C. S., & Leggett, E. L. (1988). A social-cognitive approach to motivation and personality. *Psychological Review*, 95(2), 256.

Dweck, C. S., & Sorich, L. (1999). Mastery-oriented thinking. In C. R. Snyder (ed.), *Coping: The psychology of what works*, vol. 11 (pp. 232–251). New York: Oxford University Press.

Elliott, E. S., & Dweck, C. S. (1988). Goals: An approach to motivation and achievement. *Journal of Personality and Social Psychology*, 54(1), 5.

Feser, C., Nielsen, N., & Rennie, M. (2017). What's missing in leadership development? *McKinsey Quarterly*, 2017(3), available online at: www.mckinsey.com/featured-insights/leadership/whats-missing-in-leadership-development, last accessed February 6, 2023.

Ford, J. D., & Ford, L. W. (2012). The leadership of organization change: A view from recent empirical evidence. In R. S. Abraham, W. A. Pasmore, & R. W.

Woodman (eds.), *Research in organizational change and development* (pp. 1–36). Bingley: Emerald Group.

Gilpin-Jackson, Y., & Crump, M. (2018). Practicing in the grey area between dialogic and diagnostic organization development: Lessons from another healthcare case study. *Organization Development Practitioner, 50*, 41–47.

Gioia, D. A., & Chittipeddi, K. (1991). Sensemaking and sensegiving in strategic change initiation. *Strategic Management Journal, 12*(6), 433–448.

Gollwitzer, P. (2012). Mindset theory of action phases. In P. A. van Lange (ed.), *Handbook of theories of social psychology* (pp. 526–545). Thousand Oaks: Sage.

Gottfredson, R. K., & Reina, C. S. (2020). Exploring why leaders do what they do: An integrative review of the situation-trait approach and situation-encoding schemas. *The Leadership Quarterly, 31*(1), 101373.

Graebner, M. E. (2004). Momentum and serendipity: How acquired leaders create value in the integration of technology firms. *Strategic Management Journal, 25*(8–9), 751–777.

Graetz, F., & Smith, A. C. T. (2008). The role of dualities in arbitrating continuity and change in forms of organizing. *International Journal of Management Reviews, 10*(3), 265–280.

Groysberg, B., Nanda, A., & Nohria, N. (2004). The risky business of hiring stars. *Harvard Business Review, 82*(5), 92–101.

Hambrick, D. C. (2007). Upper echelons theory: An update. *Academy of Management Review, 32*(2), 334–343.

Hastings, B., & Schwarz, G. (2021). Leading change for success: A dynamic application of diagnostic and dialogic organization development. *The Journal of Applied Behavioral Science, 58*(1), 120–148.

Helmich, D. L. (1975). Corporate succession: An examination. *Academy of Management Journal, 18*(3), 429–441.

Heslin, P. A., & Keating, L. A. (2016). Stuck in the muck? The role of mindsets in self-regulation when stymied during the job search. *Journal of Employment Counseling, 53*(4), 146–161.

(2017). In learning mode? The role of mindsets in derailing and enabling experiential leadership development. *The Leadership Quarterly, 28*(3), 367–384.

Heslin, P. A., Keating, L. A., & Minbashian, A. (2019). How situational cues and mindset dynamics shape personality effects on career outcomes. *Journal of Management, 45*(5), 2101–2131.

Heslin, P. A., Latham, G. P., & VandeWalle, D. (2005). The effect of implicit person theory on performance appraisals. *Journal of Applied Psychology, 90*(5), 842.

Heslin, P. A., Vandewalle, D., & Latham, G. P. (2006). Keen to help? Managers implicit person theories and their subsequent employee coaching. *Personnel Psychology, 59*(4), 871–902.

Hong, Y.-Yi, Chiu, C.-Y., Dweck, C. S., Lin, D. M.-S., & Wan, W. (1999). Implicit theories, attributions, and coping: A meaning system approach. *Journal of Personality and Social Psychology, 77*(3), 588.

Hoyt, C. L., Burnette, J. L., & Innella, A. N. (2012). I can do that: The impact of implicit theories on leadership role model effectiveness. *Personality and Social Psychology Bulletin, 38*(2), 257–268.

Jabri, M. (2017). *Managing organizational change: Process, social construction and dialogue.* Basingstoke: Palgrave.

Johnson, S. (2002). *Emergence: The connected lives of ants, brains, cities, and software.* New York: Simon and Schuster.

Kamins, M. L., & Dweck, C. S. (1999). Person versus process praise and criticism: Implications for contingent self-worth and coping. *Developmental Psychology, 35*(3), 835.

Kanter, R. M., Stein, B. A., & Jick, T. D. (1992). *The challenge of organizational change: How companies experience it and leaders guide it.* New York: The Free Press.

Kotter, J. (1996). *Leading change.* Boston: Harvard Business School Press.

Kotter, J. P. (1995). Leading change: why transformation efforts fail. *Harvard Business Review, 73*(2), 59–67.

Kray, L. J., & Haselhuhn, M. P. (2007). Implicit negotiation beliefs and performance: Experimental and longitudinal evidence. *Journal of Personality & Social Psychology, 93*(1), 49–64.

Lanaj, K., Chang, C.-H., & Johnson, R. E. (2012). Regulatory focus and work-related outcomes: A review and meta-analysis. *Psychological Bulletin, 138*(5), 998.

Livne-Tarandach, R., & Bartunek, J. M. (2009). A new horizon for organizational change and development scholarship: Connecting planned and emergent change. In *Research in organizational change and development* (pp. 1–35). Bingley: Emerald Group.

Locke, E. A., & Latham, G. P. (2013). *New developments in goal setting and task performance.* New York: Routledge.

Mangels, J. A., Butterfield, B., Lamb, J., Good, C., & Dweck, C. S. (2006). Why do beliefs about intelligence influence learning success? A social cognitive neuroscience model. *Social Cognitive and Affective Neuroscience, 1*(2), 75–86.

March, J. G. (1991). Exploration and exploitation in organizational learning. *Organization Science, 2*(1), 71–87.

Marion, R., & Uhl-Bien, M. (2001). Leadership in complex organizations. *The Leadership Quarterly, 12*(4), 389–418.

Marshak, R. J., Grant, D. S., & Floris, M. (2015). Discourse and dialogic organization development. In G. R. Bushe & R. J. Marshak (eds.), *Dialogic organization development: The theory and practice of transformational change* (pp. 77–100). Oakland, CA: Berrett-Koehler.

Mischel, W. (2009). From personality and assessment (1968) to personality science, 2009. *Journal of Research in Personality, 43*(2), 282–290.

Mischel, W., & Shoda, Y. (1995). A cognitive-affective system theory of personality: Reconceptualizing situations, dispositions, dynamics, and invariance in personality structure. *Psychological Review, 102*(2), 246.

(2008). Toward a unified theory of personality. *Handbook of Personality: Theory and Research, 3,* 208–241.

Mueller, C. M., & Dweck, C. S. (1998). Praise for intelligence can undermine children's motivation and performance. *Journal of Personality and Social Psychology, 75*(1), 33.

Murphy, M. C., & Dweck, C. S. (2010). A culture of genius: How an organization's lay theory shapes people's cognition, affect, and behavior. *Personality and Social Psychology Bulletin, 36*(3), 283–296.

Nussbaum, A. D., & Dweck, C. S. (2008). Defensiveness versus remediation: Self-Theories and modes of self-esteem maintenance. *Personality and Social Psychology Bulletin, 34*(5), 599–612.

Oreg, S., & Berson, Y. (2019). Leaders' impact on organizational change: Bridging theoretical and methodological chasms. *Academy of Management Annals, 13*(1), 272–307.

Park, D., & Kim, S. (2015). Time to move on? When entity theorists perform better than incremental theorists. *Personality and Social Psychology Bulletin, 41*(5), 736–748.

Plaks, J. E., & Stecher, K. (2007). Unexpected improvement, decline, and stasis: A prediction confidence perspective on achievement success and failure. *Journal of Personality and Social Psychology, 93*(4), 667.

Rauthmann, J. F., Sherman, R. A., & Funder, D. C. (2015). Principles of situation research: Towards a better understanding of psychological situations. *European Journal of Personality, 29*(3), 363–381.

Robins, R. W., & Pals, J. L. (2002). Implicit self-theories in the academic domain: Implications for goal orientation, attributions, affect, and self-esteem change. *Self and Identity, 1*(4), 313–336.

Shantz, A., & Latham, G. P. (2009). An exploratory field experiment of the effect of subconscious and conscious goals on employee performance. *Organizational Behavior and Human Decision Processes, 109*(1), 9–17.

Smith, B. P. (2005). Goal orientation, implicit theory of ability, and collegiate instrumental music practice. *Psychology of Music, 33*(1), 36–57.

Starbuck, W. H., & Milliken, F. J. (1988). Executives' perceptual filters: What they notice and how they make sense. In D. C. Hambrick (ed.), *The executive effect: Concepts and methods for studying top managers* (pp. 33–65). Greenwich, CT: JAI Press.

Stouten, J., Rousseau, D. M., & De Cremer, D. (2018). Successful organizational change: Integrating the management practice and scholarly literatures. *Academy of Management Annals, 12*(2), 752–788.

Tabernero, C., & Wood, R. E. (1999). Implicit theories versus the social construal of ability in self-regulation and performance on a complex task. *Organizational Behavior and Human Decision Processes, 78*(2), 104–127.

Tett, R. P., & Burnett, D. D. (2003). A personality trait-based interactionist model of job performance. *Journal of Applied Psychology, 88*(3), 500.

Van de Ven, A. (2004). Organizational change. *Blackwell encyclopedic dictionary of organizational behavior.* London: Blackwell Publishers.

Van Yperen, N. W., Blaga, M., & Postmes, T. (2014). A meta-analysis of self-reported achievement goals and nonself-report performance across three achievement domains (work, sports, and education). *PloS One, 9*(4), e93594.

Vandewalle, D., Nerstad, C. G. L., & Dysvik, A. (2019). Goal orientation: A review of the miles traveled and the miles to go. *Annual Review of Organizational Psychology and Organizational Behavior, 6*(1), 115–144.

Weick, K. E., & Quinn, R. E. (1999). Organizational change and development. *Annual Review of Psychology, 50*(1), 361–386.

Weiss, H. M., & Cropanzano, R. (1996). Affective events theory: A theoretical discussion of the structure, causes and consequences of affective experiences at work. *Research in Organization Behavior: Annual Series of Analytical Essays and Critical Reviews, 18*(1), 34–74.

Welsh, D. T., & Ordóñez, L. D. (2014). Conscience without cognition: The effects of subconscious priming on ethical behavior. *Academy of Management Journal, 57*(3), 723–742.

Wilson, T. D. (2004). *Strangers to ourselves.* Cambridge, MA: Harvard University Press.

Wood, R., & Bandura, A. (1989). Impact of conceptions of ability on self-regulatory mechanisms and complex decision making. *Journal of Personality and Social Psychology, 56*(3), 407–415.

Yeager, D. S., Hanselman, P., Walton, G. M., Murray, J. S., Crosnoe, R., Muller, C., Tipton, E., Schneider, B., Hulleman, C. S., & Hinojosa, C. P. (2019). A national experiment reveals where a growth mindset improves achievement. *Nature, 573*(7774), 364–369.

Yukl, G. A. (2012). *Leadership in organizations* (8th ed.). Boston: Pearson Education.

Zaccaro, S. J., Green, J. P., Dubrow, S., & Kolze, M. (2018). Leader individual differences, situational parameters, and leadership outcomes: A comprehensive review and integration. *The Leadership Quarterly, 29*(1), 2–43.

PART V

The Process of Change Leadership

CHAPTER 11

Building Commitment to Organizational Change
The Important Role of Leadership

John P. Meyer and Leonid V. Beletski

Although it is a given that effective organizational change requires cooperation on the part of those charged with enacting it, the willingness of these individuals to behave in a way that supports the change is not (Armenakis & Harris, 2009). It is not surprising, therefore, that a great deal of research has been directed at understanding the different ways that employees react to change, including readiness (Eby et al., 2000; Madsen et al., 2005), openness (Wanberg & Banas, 2000; Axtell et al., 2002), commitment (Conner & Patterson, 1982; Herscovitch & Meyer, 2002), resistance (Shapiro & Kirkman, 1999; Oreg, 2006), and cynicism (Reichers et al., 1997; Stanley et al., 2005) as well as the conditions that help to explain these reactions (see Oreg et al., 2013). In this chapter we focus on employees' commitment as an important proximal predictor of their behavioral support for organizational change initiatives (Jaros, 2010; Bouckenooghe et al., 2015).

Initial interest in employee commitment stemmed from its implications for retention (Mowday et al., 1982). However, in their need to remain competitive in a turbulent world economy in the last decades of the twentieth century, many organizations underwent extensive restructuring (e.g., mergers and acquisitions, re-engineering, downsizing), leading to disruption of the traditional employer–employee relationship. With increasing instability and uncertainty in the economy, organizations were less likely to seek a long-term commitment from their employees (Baruch, 1998). At the same time, change experts were advising that one of the keys to effective organizational change was the commitment of those called upon to enact it – their employees (e.g., Conner, 1993; Bennis, 2000). This "commitment paradox" (Meyer, 2009) led to more attention being given to other targets of employee commitment, including commitment to organizational change.

There are many factors that contribute to employees' commitment to organizational change (Meyer & Hamilton, 2013), but organizational leaders have the potential to play a particularly key role (Oreg & Berson, 2019). Although commitment and leadership have both been studied extensively over the last several decades, research linking them under conditions of organizational change is relatively recent. Our objectives in this chapter are to review this nascent body of research, discuss its implications for practice, and suggest directions for future research. Because the terms "commitment" and "leadership" tend to be used quite loosely in the common vernacular and popular press, and have been defined and operationalized in various ways in the academic literature, we begin with a brief overview and explanation of how they will be treated in this chapter.

11.1   The Meaning of Commitment

The study of commitment dates to the 1960s (e.g., Becker, 1960; Etzioni, 1961; Kanter, 1968), but investigation of its relevance in a work context started in earnest in the 1970s and 1980s (Mowday et al., 1982; Mathieu & Zajac, 1990) and continues today (see Meyer, 2016, 2021). From the outset, commitment has been defined and measured in different ways, making it difficult to interpret and integrate research findings. In an effort to address this confusion as it pertained to organizational commitment, Allen and Meyer (1990; Meyer & Allen, 1991) argued that the varying definitions reflected three distinct themes: commitment as a *desire, obligation*, or *need* to continue a course of action (e.g., remain with an organization). They referred to these as affective, normative, and continuance commitment, respectively, and together these three forms (components) of commitment served as the basis for their three-component model (TCM) of organizational commitment.

A decade later, Meyer and Herscovitch (2001) extended the TCM to apply to commitments more generally and, in so doing, defined commitment as *a force that binds an individual to an entity and/or course of action*. They retained the notion that the binding force could be characterized by different psychological states, or mindsets, reflecting a desire, obligation, and/or need to maintain a relationship or continue a course of action. Moreover, they argued that affective, normative, and continuance commitment would all increase the likelihood that an individual will comply with the "terms" of the commitment (e.g., remain with the organization; complete a project on time). The differences among the different forms of commitment will be observed when one considers the "quality" of the relevant behavior and/or the individual's willingness to exert discretionary effort not required by the terms of the commitment (e.g., provide assistance to co-workers). Affective commitment was considered to be most likely to lead to such discretionary effort, followed by normative and continuance commitment, respectively.

Following in this tradition, Herscovitch and Meyer (2002) defined commitment to an organization change as "a force (mind-set) that binds an individual to a course of action deemed necessary for the successful implementation of a change initiative" (p. 475). They also developed measures of affective, normative, and continuance commitment to organizational change paralleling those developed by Allen and Meyer (1990; Meyer et al., 1993) for organizational commitment. These measures, particularly affective commitment, have been widely used in research on commitment to change (see Bouckenooghe et al., 2015), including much of the research included in this review. Therefore, throughout our review we adopt the three-component conceptualization of commitment to change and make the distinction between affective, normative, and continuance commitment as required.

11.2 The Meaning of Leadership

Regarding the role of leadership in fostering commitment to organizational change, there are two important issues to consider. The first has to do with the different ways that "leadership" has been conceptualized and measured within the organizational sciences in general, and in the study of commitment to change specifically. The second has to do with what is meant by "change leadership" and how it is applied in the context of our review.

11.2.1 Leadership

At the risk of oversimplification, the long-standing interest in leadership within the organizational sciences stems from the desire to answer two key questions: how are leaders different from non-leaders? and what makes a leader effective? Over the years, leadership theory evolved from an emphasis on traits and other individual differences in the 1930s and 1940s (Stogdill, 1948), to behavior in the 1950s and 1960s (Fleishman & Harris, 1962), to situational contingencies in the 1970s and 1980s (House & Mitchell, 1974; Fiedler, 1976). The 1990s saw a shift back to a more "universalist" approach with an emphasis on inspirational forms of leadership, including charismatic (e.g., Conger & Kanungo, 1987; House & Howell, 1992) and transformational (Bass & Riggio, 2006), leadership (Bass, 1985), and these theories have remained popular in the new millennium. The last two decades have also witnessed the introduction of several new genre theories including authentic (Gardner et al., 2011), ethical (Brown & Treviño, 2006), and empowering (Amundsen & Martinsen, 2014) leadership. Common to these theories is a strong emphasis on ethical and moral leadership behavior (Hannah et al., 2014; Mumford & Fried, 2014). Two additional theories that have been influential over the last few decades are leader member exchange (LMX: Liden et al., 1997) and implicit leadership theory (Epitropaki & Martin, 2005). Rather than addressing a particular style of leadership, LMX theory introduced the notion that leaders can vary their leadership style for different followers, forming higher quality exchange relationships with some employees than others, and implicit leadership theory suggests that followers evaluate their leaders based on how well they fit with their implicit theories of the ideal leader. For a comprehensive review of leadership theory, see Yukl and Gardner (2020).

To date, most research on leadership and commitment to change has focused on transformational leadership, no doubt because it was the dominant theory at the time that commitment to change emerged as a construct of interest. As the new genre theories emerged over the last decade, they too started to receive some attention in the change commitment literature. Leadership involves broadening and elevating goals and increasing followers' confidence in their ability to go beyond expectations (Bass, 1985). The most used measure of transformational leadership is the Multidimensional Leadership Questionnaire (MLQ: Avolio & Bass, 2004), which comprises four subscales – idealized influence (serving as a confident role model), inspirational motivation (articulating a compelling vision), intellectual stimulation (encouraging critical evaluation and creativity), and individualized consideration (showing genuine caring and concern for followers) – often combined to yield an overall score. Other measures have been developed with slightly different multidimensional structures (e.g., Podsakoff et al., 1990). Most measures of the new genre leadership styles also include multiple subscales but are often treated as unidimensional for research purposes. We provide more detail about the various theories and measures of leadership, as needed.

11.2.2   Change Leadership

In their recent review of theory and research pertaining to leadership and organizational change, Oreg and Berson (2019) noted that leaders play two key roles in the organizational change process. First, they make strategic decisions about the need for organizational change, the nature of the change, and how it should be implemented. Second, they are instrumental in communicating the decision to those who will be affected by it and whose efforts are required to make the change successful. Theory and research regarding the first role typically focus on attributes of the top management team and how these contribute to their strategic choices and, ultimately, the effectiveness of the change. The second role is addressed by focusing on the leader's behavior and/or leadership style and its implications for employees' reactions to (e.g., resistance, readiness, openness, commitment) and behavioral support for a change.

Our review of leadership and commitment to change addresses the second of the two roles identified by Oreg and Berson (2019). Unlike the research on strategic leadership where the focus is on the top management team, much of the research on employee reactions to change focuses on the leadership of direct managers or supervisors. This includes research addressing the implications of the general styles of leadership discussed in section 11.2.1 (e.g., transformational leadership; empowering leadership). However, we also review research focusing more directly on leaders' change-relevant behavior. Several models of change leadership have been proposed with the expressed purpose of providing direction for the effective implementation of change (e.g., Beer, 1980; Kotter, 1996: see Stouten et al., 2018, for a review and critique). Some of the studies we review in this chapter include measures of the change-relevant behaviors advocated in these models (e.g., Herold et al., 2008; Ling et al., 2018). Still others focus on select change-relevant behaviors such as communication (Sonenshein & Dholakia, 2012), support (Zappalà et al., 2019), and enforcement strategies (Weske et al., 2019) believed to have implications for the development or maintenance of employee commitment to organizational change.

In sum, our objective in this chapter is to address the question of how leadership style and leaders' change-relevant behaviors relate to the development and maintenance of followers' commitment to organizational change. We also consider the mechanisms underlying this relationship and the conditions under which they operate.

11.3 Leadership and Commitment to Organizational Change

The last decade has seen a steady increase in research linking leadership to follower commitment to change (Oreg & Berson, 2019; Peng et al., 2021), with the bulk of the research focusing on affective commitment. We organize the following review around the focal leadership constructs, beginning with transformational leadership, new genre leadership, and then change leadership and change-specific behavior. In each case, we examine the link between leadership style/behavior and followers' affective commitment to change, the mediating mechanisms that help to explain the link, and the moderating conditions that can influence the strength or direction of the relationships. We review the smaller literature involving normative and continuance commitment in Section 11.6.

11.3.1   Transformational Leadership

11.3.1.1   Cross-sectional Studies

The modal study of transformational leadership and change commitment uses a cross-sectional survey design conducted within or across organizations undergoing various forms of change (e.g., merger, mission change, restructuring). These studies quite consistently report that employees who view their managers as more transformational also report stronger affective commitment to the change (Svendsen & Joensson, 2016; Van der Voet et al., 2016; Weiherl & Masal, 2016; Bayraktar & Jiménez, 2020; Dung & Van Hai, 2020; Kim et al., 2021). Mangundjaya and Amir (2021) found a similar positive relationship for charismatic leadership, a style closely aligned with transformational leadership. Among the variables found to mediate the relationship between transformational leadership and commitment are degree of employee participation in the development and implementation of the change (Van der Voet et al., 2016), job satisfaction (Dung & Van Hai, 2020), perceived organizational support (Weiherl & Masal, 2016), quality of change communication (Van der Voet et al., 2016), self-efficacy (Bayraktar & Jiménez, 2020), and pro-change employee behavior (Weiherl & Masal, 2016). Svendsen and Joensson (2016) investigated and found a moderating effect of the personal impact of the change for the employees. That is, although the link between transformational leadership and followers' affective commitment was positive overall, it was stronger among those who were personally affected by the change. In a related vein, Bayraktar and Jiménez (2020) found that the mediating effect of self-efficacy was moderated by the extent of the change. Thus, transformational leadership may be particularly important in building commitment when the change is extensive and/or personally relevant to employees.

Although the foregoing studies provide quite consistent evidence for a link between the direct managers' transformational style and followers' affective commitment to the change, they have some notable limitations.

In most cases (e.g., Bayraktar & Jiménez, 2020; Dung & Van Hai, 2020), all measures are obtained from a single source, which can result in biased estimates of the correlation (Podsakoff et al., 2003). In other cases (e.g., Van der Voet et al., 2016; Weiheri & Masal, 2016), respondents are nested within units (e.g., teams, departments) with a common leader, and this too could bias the observed relationships among variables, if the analyses conducted do not account for the nested nature of the data (Bliese et al., 2018). Finally, the correlation between leadership and commitment observed on a single occasion does not reflect the dynamic nature of the relationship as it unfolds over time. These limitations can be addressed to varying degrees using multi-level and multi-wave longitudinal designs.

11.3.1.2   *Multi-level Cross-sectional Studies*

Multi-level studies help to control for the nesting effects described, and in some cases allow for investigation of higher-level (e.g., organization, unit) effects of leadership on commitment to change (e.g., Ling et al., 2018). In this section, we address studies involving cross-sectional data (Herold et al., 2008; Abrell-Vogel & Rowold, 2014). We discuss those multi-level studies involving longitudinal data in Section 11.3.1.3.

Herold et al. (2008) investigated the implications of both transformational leadership as a general style as well as change-specific leadership behavior on followers' affective commitment to a change. Participants were 342 employees from 30 US organizations in a wide range of industries undergoing varying changes (e.g., work process changes; new technology implementation). To mitigate potential same source bias, some employees reported on the manager's transformational leadership and others described their change-relevant behavior. These ratings were also aggregated to the work unit level to address nesting effects. The measure of change-relevant behavior was developed to reflect those recommended in popular models of change management (e.g., Kotter, 1996). Somewhat surprisingly, they found that the ratings of transformational leadership and leaders' change-relevant behavior were unrelated. Thus, being transformational does not appear to predispose leaders to adopt recommended change leadership behaviors. Across all employees, only transformational leadership correlated positively with followers' affective commitment to the change; ratings of the leaders' change-relevant behavior did not. However, these relationships were moderated by the perceived impact of the change (e.g., increased workload; altered responsibilities). Transformational leadership correlated positively with followers' affective commitment to the change under all conditions except when the impact of the change was low *and* the change-relevant behaviors were used. The relationship between transformational leadership and affective commitment was strongest when perceived impact was strong and the leader *did not* engage in the recommended change-relevant behaviors. Herold et al. (2008) suggested that the benefit of a general transformational style, even when not accompanied by change-relevant "best practices," might be that it contributes to the establishment of a basic level of trust in the leader prior to the change that carries over to trust in the leader during the change process.

Abrell-Vogel and Rowold (2014) also used a cross-sectional multi-level design in an investigation involving twelve German organizations from different sectors undergoing structural changes. Participants were 177 employees from 38 teams and their managers. Rather than treating transformational leadership as a unidimensional construct, Abrell-Vogel and Rowold measured six behavioral components using Podsakoff et al.'s (1990) Transformational Leadership Inventory and examined their combined and unique contributions to the prediction of followers' affective commitment to the change. They also measured the leaders' affective commitment to the change and included it as a group-level variable in a hierarchical linear modeling analysis. Of the six leadership behaviors, only "individualized support" and "providing an appropriate role model" correlated significantly with employees' affective commitment to the change and contributed uniquely to the prediction of commitment when all six components were included in a hierarchical regression analysis. However, the relationship for role modeling was significant only when the leaders themselves were committed to the change. Thus, whereas support from a leader during change seems to be instrumental in fostering affective commitment among followers, serving as a role model does so only when the leaders themselves have a genuine belief in the value of the change.

11.3.1.3   *Longitudinal Studies*

Hill et al. (2012) used a multi-level longitudinal design to investigate the implications of the direct manager's transformational leadership on followers' change commitment. Participants were 1,215 employees of a US government transportation agency undergoing a large-scale restructuring, and commitment was measured on two occasions, twelve months apart. Ratings of the direct managers' transformational leadership measured at Time 1 were aggregated to the group level. Hill et al. found that transformational leadership related positively to affective change commitment at Time 1; the relationship with Time 2 commitment was not significant after controlling for Time 1 commitment. Importantly, this relationship was mediated by perceptions of top-management's change-relevant communication. Overall, employees' perceptions of the quality of top-down and bottom-up communication declined with increasing hierarchical distance (i.e., number of intermediate levels of management), and quality of communication related positively with commitment to the change. Employees' perceptions of their own manager's transformational leadership correlated positively with the perceived quality of communication and indirectly with their affective commitment. Thus, it appears that transformational managers can play an important role in shaping how the top management communication is perceived and evaluated, particularly in the early stages of the change. Hill et al. noted that, in their responses to open-ended questions, employees reported that having a transformational manager helped in fostering a climate of trust and mitigating their cynicism about the change and whether it could be implemented successfully.

Seo et al. (2012) also conducted a multi-level longitudinal study to investigate the short- and longer-term implications of direct managers' transformational leadership. Again, the change involved a major restructuring initiative within a US government transportation agency. Data were collected at two time points near the beginning and middle of the restructuring (approximately one year apart) from 420 employees reporting to 217 managers. Seo et al. found that, when aggregated to the group level, perceptions of the managers' transformational leadership related positively with employees' affective commitment at Time 1, and that this relationship was mediated in part by employees' positive change-relevant affect (e.g., energetic, enthusiastic). Affective commitment at Time 1 was found to predict Time 2 commitment, as well as self-reported behavioral support for the change. Although employees' negative change-relevant affect (e.g., resentful, threatened) did not mediate the relationship between transformational leadership and affective commitment at Time 1, they did mediate the relationship with Time 2 commitment and support behaviors.

A third longitudinal field study involving a government agency undergoing a "full-scale restructuring" was conducted by Shin et al. (2015). In this case, the investigation focused on the moderating effect of the transformational leadership of direct managers, as well as the informational justice climate (a norm for information sharing), on the stability of affective commitment to the change over time. Data were collected from 316 employees from 67 work units near the beginning of the change and again twelve months later. Using hierarchical linear modeling to control for nesting effects, Shin et al. found that employees' affective commitment to the changes was generally quite stable over time, but that employees' initial level of commitment was more likely to be maintained when their manager was perceived as transformational and there was a strong informational justice climate. Affective change commitment at Time 2 related positively to self-reported behavioral support for the change and negatively with turnover intentions.

Finally, Zhao et al. (2016) investigated the joint influence of former and new leaders on the affective commitment of employees to a large Chinese hospitality company undergoing a major strategic change. Participants were 203 employees from 22 teams who experienced change in leadership due to reassignments resulting from the change. The commitment measured in this study was to the "changed organization" rather than a specific change. The transformational leadership of the former leader was measured a week prior to measurement of the new leader's transformational leadership. Zhao et al. found that both the old and new leaders' transformational leadership correlated positively with employees' affective commitment to the new organization. However, the more transformational the old leader was seen to be, the weaker the relationship found for the new leader. Importantly, the employees' affective commitment to the changed organization was found to mediate the negative relationship between employees' perceptions for the new manager's transformational leadership and that manager's ratings of employees' resistance to the change.

11.3.1.4   Summary

Together, studies using a variety of research designs are quite consistent in demonstrating a link between the transformational leadership of direct managers and employees' affective commitment to organizational change. Results of mediation analyses suggest that transformational leaders may be particularly effective in establishing a climate of trust and support, fostering more positive affective reactions to the change, and bolstering employees' self-efficacy in dealing with the change. The implications of transformational leadership for employee's affective commitment appear to be greatest when the change is extensive and/or has a strong personal impact for employees.

11.4   New Genre and Other Leadership Theories

Although still relatively rare, researchers have recently begun to expand their investigation of employee commitment to change to include the new genre leadership theories including authentic leadership (Bakari et al., 2017, 2019), empowering leadership (Jung et al., 2020), and ethical leadership (Rahaman et al., 2021). In many respects, the findings of these studies parallel those for transformational leadership. For example, Jung et al. found that empowering leadership related positively with affective commitment and that this relationship was mediated by risk-taking behavior, particularly under conditions of task complexity. Rahaman et al. found a positive relationship between ethical leadership and employee commitment to change, and that commitment mediated the relationship between ethical leadership and dysfunctional resistance to change. The studies by Bakari and colleagues involving authentic leadership are more difficult to interpret. Although they found a positive relationship with commitment to change, commitment was measured using a combination of affective, continuance, and normative commitment. This practice is contrary to recommendations for the TCM in general (Meyer & Allen, 1991) and its application to change commitment in particular (Herscovitch & Meyer, 2002).

Finally, although not new, LMX theory has also been used to guide the investigation of leadership and commitment to change. In an investigation involving US and Korean employees, Lee et al. (2014) found both direct and indirect links between the quality of employees' exchange relationship with their managers and their affective commitment to change. The indirect relationship was explained by a positive relationship between LMX quality and the amount of downward consultation regarding the change. Although the mediating effect of downward consultation was observed for both US and Korean employees, it was stronger in the US sample, perhaps due to lower levels of power distance (i.e., acceptance of power differential).

Summary: Research stimulated by the new genre theories shows some promise. However, research to date has used a cross-sectional survey design, the limitations of which were discussed in Section 11.3.1. More research using a variety of designs like those for transformational leadership are required before any firm conclusions can be drawn. It will also be important to investigate the incremental contribution of the new genre theories beyond transformational leadership.

11.5 Leader Change-Relevant Behavior

Studies reviewed in this section include those that investigated leader behaviors recommended as part of comprehensive change-management strategies (e.g., Kotter, 1996), as well as those focusing on a more selective set of behaviors (e.g., communication, enforcement strategy, support). Among the former, we noted previously that Herold et al. (2008)

developed a measure of leader change behavior, based on Kotter's model, and investigated how it, together with transformational leadership, related to employees' affective change commitment. They found that the model-based behaviors correlated positively with employees' affective commitment, but only when the leader was not seen as transformational *and* the perceived impact of the change for employees was minimal. Thus, in some contexts, it appears that the model-based behaviors might serve as a substitute for transformational leadership. However, this did not appear to be the case for high-impact changes.

Ling et al. (2018) used a similar measure of change-relevant leader behavior with a sample of 647 employees in 110 teams from 45 Chinese organizations undergoing strategic changes. They found that, when aggregated to a group level, the measure of leader behavior related positively with employees' affective change commitment. Moreover, they found that this relationship could be explained in part by a greater shared sense of collective identity among team members and a stronger sense of personal self-efficacy in dealing with the change. Ling et al. did not measure perceptions of transformational leadership, so comparison of their findings with those of Herold et al. are incomplete. Moreover, although culture differences may help to explain the difference in findings across the two studies, in the absence of a true comparative investigation, such an explanation is speculative.

Nohe et al. (2013) used the measure developed by Herold et al. (2008) in a multi-level study to investigate the relationship between leader change behaviors and team performance, with employees' perceptions of the leaders' charisma and affective commitment to the change as potential mediators. Participants were 142 employees and 33 team leaders in a large German company undergoing an extensive restructuring affecting all employees within the organization. Of particular interest here was the finding that leaders who engaged in more change-relevant behavior were seen as more charismatic, and that perceived charisma correlated positively with employees' affective commitment to the change.

Among the more specific change-relevant behaviors that have been investigated as predictors of employees' affective change commitment are communication (Sonenshein & Dholakia, 2012), enforcement strategy (persuasion and punishment; Weske et al., 2019), and supervisor support (Zappalà et al., 2019). Together, the results of these cross-sectional survey studies suggest that employees have greater affective commitment to a change when leaders communicate in a manner that helps them make sense of the change, when leaders use persuasive (e.g., dialog and suggestion) rather than punitive tactics (e.g., threat of sanctions) to elicit compliance, and when leaders are perceived to be supportive within the change context.

A few studies have taken an implicit leadership theory perspective to the investigation of the relationship between leader behavior and employee commitment (e.g., Magsaysay & Hechanova, 2017; Guerrero et al., 2018; Hechanova et al., 2018). Recall that, according to implicit leadership theory (Epitropaki & Martin, 2005), followers evaluate their leaders against their implicit theories of effective leadership. Accordingly, these studies revealed that employees rated their manager's change-management strategy as more effective when it matched with their ideal, and that the perceived effectiveness of the strategy being used correlated positively with their commitment to the change.

As a complement to these field survey studies, several experimental vignette studies have been conducted in an effort to establish the causal links between leader behavior and followers' commitment to a change (Helpap, 2016; Faupel & Helpap, 2021; Bayraktar & Kabasakal, 2022). Helpap (2016) presented employees from various organizations with case studies of a hypothetical organization undergoing a prototypical structural change. The primary manipulation was whether the direct supervisor used a "programmatic" (cascading top-down) or "participative" (two-way) style in communication about the change. Helpap found that, overall, the participative approach was associated with greater anticipated affective commitment to the change. This effect was moderated by the participants' power distance values (i.e., acceptance of a power differential). The comparative advantage of the participative style was greater for those individuals with low power distance values. Helpap acknowledged that both programmatic and participative communication might be useful in facilitating sense-making in the context of organizational change, but that it was not possible to assess the potential complementary effects of the two styles in the absence of an independent no-communication control group and a fully-crossed design. Importantly, Helpap also found that affective commitment to the change mediated the effect of communication style on participants' intentions to resist the change. In a follow-up study using a similar design, Faupel and Helpap (2021) replicated the main effect of communication style and found that perceptions of procedural fairness mediated the effect.

Bayraktar and Kabasakal (2022) conducted a similar experimental vignette study to investigate the effects of communication content and style on commitment to a change. Participants were 200 individuals with previous experience with organizational change. In a 2 × 2 × 2 design, the investigators manipulated the content (rational versus emotional appeal) and style (strong versus weak) of a leader's voice-recorded communication about a forthcoming merger, along with contextual information (job security versus insecurity). They found main effects of both delivery style and context. Participants reported that they would be more committed to the change when the leader used a strong delivery style (i.e., changes in tone and pace; energetic and enthusiastic) and when they did not perceive a threat of job loss. Moreover, context also had moderating effects on communication effectiveness. When jobs were perceived to be secure, the use of an emotional appeal led to higher commitment. However, when there was a threat of job loss, the rational appeal led to higher commitment. These findings were interpreted in terms of dual process theory (Witte, 1992). Under conditions of threat, individuals focus more on factual and rational information (cognitive processing) to deal with uncertainty, whereas in the absence of threat they are influenced more by the emotional tone of the message (heuristic processing).

Summary: Together, the studies reviewed in this section provide evidence that leaders' change-relevant behavior is important for the establishment of employee commitment to the change. Leaders who want to foster commitment should provide a clear and appealing message, solicit input from employees (where culturally appropriate), and provide the necessary supports. One contradictory finding worth noting is Herold et al.'s (2008) observation that the use of model-based change behaviors was only related to greater affective change commitment when the leader was not seen as transformational, and the change had minimal impact for employees. We discuss this finding in more detail in Section 11.8.

11.6   Beyond Affective Commitment

Although limited, continuance and normative change commitment have received some attention from leadership scholars. Continuance commitment is generally considered to be the least desirable form of commitment in that it contributes only to compliance with the minimal requirements for change (mere compliance: Meyer et al., 2007). It correlates negatively with discretionary behavioral support (Bouckenooghe et al., 2015). It is perhaps not surprising, therefore, that continuance commitment has been found to correlate negatively with those leadership qualities and behaviors found to be positively associated with affective commitment (e.g., Guerrero et al., 2018; Zappalà et al., 2019;

Ouedraogo et al., 2023). In contrast, normative commitment reflects a sense of obligation to support the change and correlates positively with discretionary support for change. Consequently, it is generally found to correlate positively with many of the same leadership measures as affective commitment, including transformational leadership (Dung & Van Hai, 2020; Kim et al., 2021), leadership credibility (Ouedraogo et al., 2023), and perceived supervisor support (Zappalà et al., 2019).

Normative commitment is generally found to correlate positively with affective commitment and, as noted, correlates similarly with other variables. This has raised questions about the meaningfulness and/or uniqueness of the construct (see Bouckenooghe et al., 2015). Despite their positive correlation, however, affective and normative change commitment are generally found to reflect distinct constructs in confirmatory factor analyses (e.g., Hill et al., 2012; Dung & Van Hai, 2020; Kim et al., 2021). Moreover, although the patterns of relationships observed are often quite similar, some differences have also been observed. For example, Seo et al. (2012) found that affective and normative commitment measured early in the change contributed uniquely to the prediction of positive support behaviors twelve months later, but only normative commitment predicted creative behavior in support of the change (positive) and behavioral resistance to the change (negative). Shin et al. (2015) found that affective and normative commitment were both relatively stable over time as the change unfolded but that, unlike affective commitment, the stability of normative commitment was not influenced by the direct managers' transformational leadership.

Finally, it is also important to note that affective, normative, and continuance commitment to change have largely been considered in isolation to this point. Recent research investigating the three components of organizational commitment from a person-centered (profile) perspective has revealed that the individual components of commitment can be experienced differently and relate differently with other variables, depending on how they combine with the other components within a "commitment profile" (see Meyer & Morin, 2016). We discuss how this might also be a viable approach to the investigation of commitment to organizational change in Section 11.7.

11.7 Future Directions

Before considering the practical implications of research on leadership and commitment to change, it is important to acknowledge some of the limits to what we know and to consider how the gaps in our understanding might be addressed in future research. For example, we noted earlier that, despite quite consistent evidence for a positive relationship between transformational leadership and employees' affective commitment to change, much of this evidence comes from studies using a cross-sectional survey methodology with its inherent limitations for drawing causal inference and for understanding dynamic processes as they unfold over time. Fortunately, the multi-level, longitudinal and experimental studies we reviewed provide some corroborating evidence, although they also make it clear that the role(s) played by transformational leaders are more complex than is implied by the positive correlation between leadership and commitment. We need more research of this type.

Like transformational leadership, the new genre leadership styles (e.g., empowering, ethical) have been found to correlate positively with affective commitment to change, as has high quality LMX. Indeed, the relationships are sufficiently similar across the leadership constructs to raise questions about whether any or all can be expected to contribute uniquely to the prediction of commitment. It is also interesting to note that, with few exceptions (e.g., Abrell-Vogel & Rowold, 2014), these leadership constructs have been treated as unidimensional for research purposes despite being multidimensional in theory. Therefore, it is difficult to know whether any specific facet of the broader styles might be more relevant than others for building commitment. One possibility is that these leadership styles are simply consistent with employees' implicit theories of effective leadership, and it is this congruence that explains their commitment (see Magsaysay & Hechanova, 2017; Guerrero et al., 2018; Hechanova et al., 2018). More research is needed to assess the incremental contribution of any particular leadership style over others to the prediction of commitment to change. The same applies to the specific facets of leadership presumed to be reflected within the broader styles. In this regard, it will also be important to consider context. For example, some facets of transformational leadership might be more relevant than others depending on the leadership level (top, middle, immediate), the nature of the change (e.g., radical, incremental, continuous), and the potential impact for employees (e.g., required behavior change, job security). Creating a compelling vision (inspirational motivation) might be most important for a CEO promoting a radical change with a large impact for employees, whereas individualized consideration and intellectual stimulation might be more effective when applied by direct managers. Another important consideration will be the relevant mediating mechanisms (e.g., trust, justice, security, identity) that apply in each context.

Our review also reveals that much of the research on leadership and commitment to change focuses on affective commitment. This is not unique to change commitment but applies more broadly to other workplace commitments, most notably organizational commitment (Meyer et al., 2002). The argument for this focus is often that affective commitment is associated with the most desirable outcomes. Indeed, this argument was inherent in the initial TCM of organizational commitment (Meyer & Allen, 1991) and its more general form (Meyer & Herscovitch, 2001). However, a relatively new and growing body of person-centered (profile) research challenges this assumption (see Meyer & Morin, 2016, for a review). A combination of affective and normative commitment can have even more desirable outcomes than affective commitment alone, perhaps because a feeling of obligation to pursue a course of action (e.g., stay with an organization; support a change initiative) can sustain the activity under conditions that challenge the desire to do so (see Meyer & Parfyonova, 2010).

The consequences of continuance commitment are generally considered to be the least desirable, perhaps only second to a complete lack of commitment. Indeed, research on continuance commitment to the organization reveals a negative relationship with turnover intention, but also very weak or even negative correlations with employee performance and well-being (Meyer et al., 2002; Meyer & Maltin, 2010). Moreover, as noted in Section 11.6, continuance commitment to a change has been found to correlate negatively with cooperation and championing behavior (Bouckenooghe et al., 2015). However, these findings can be deceiving. Person-centered research reveals that strong continuance commitment to the organization can be associated with positive organization- and employee-relevant outcomes when it is combined with strong affective and normative commitment to form a "fully committed" profile (Meyer & Morin, 2016). Under these conditions, the costs associated with the discontinuation of a relationship or activity may be those positive conditions that created the strong desire to continue (affective commitment). It is only when continuance commitment is the dominant or sole basis for commitment that its negative consequences emerge.

To date, only a few studies have taken a person-centered approach to the study of commitment to change, and these applied a simple mid-point split approach to creating profiles (e.g., Herscovitch & Meyer, 2002; Meyer et al., 2007). Nevertheless, they provide some evidence that levels of behavioral support vary across profiles such that relations involving the individual components differ depending on the strength of the other components. In particular, continuance commitment appears to be associated with higher levels of behavioral support when it combines with strong affective and normative commitment than when it is the dominant form of commitment. Therefore, as has been the case for organizational commitment, there may be benefits to applying more advances person-centered analytic techniques to the investigation of commitment to change. For example, research might be conducted to identify the managerial strategies most likely to contribute to the formation of a continuance-dominant profile (e.g., coercive enforcement: Weske et al., 2019), as well as those that might be effective in achieving the synergy of strong affective and normative commitment (Meyer & Parfyonova, 2010).

Most of the research on leadership and commitment to change has been conducted in the context of a specific change initiative. Indeed, the measures of commitment developed by Herscovitch and Meyer (2002) were worded to reflect such a focus. However, the pace of change in the world of work has arguably quickened such that organizations are often in a constant state of change and therefore require employees to be consistently open to, and ready for, change. Speaking specifically in the context of such continuous change in healthcare organizations, Harrison et al. (2022) argue that affective commitment to change might be the key to fostering this readiness, but that the focus needs to shift from commitment to *specific* changes to commitment to change more generally. Leadership will undoubtedly play an important role in fostering this broader commitment, but we need to learn more about how leaders can instill and maintain this commitment under conditions of continuous change.

Finally, research concerning leadership and commitment to change has been conducted in many different countries, and there appears to be considerable similarity in the findings (e.g., positive relationships with transformational leadership). However, there is some evidence the strength for relations can differ across countries (e.g., Lee et al., 2014) or be moderated by differences in cultural values, particularly power distance (e.g., Helpap, 2016). Thus, it might be premature to draw conclusions about the generalizability of existing findings linking leadership and commitment to change across cultures. A more systematic investigation involving multinational comparisons like that conducted by Lee et al. would help in this regard.

11.8   Implications for Practice

The most obvious implication of the research reviewed here is that leadership matters in establishing employee commitment to organizational changes. More specifically, the leadership style of direct managers matters. Employees who perceived their managers as transformational reported being more committed and willing to support an organizational change than those who did not. The same was true for those who viewed their managers as authentic, empowering, and ethical, or who considered themselves to be in a high-quality relationship (LMX) with their managers. These are leadership qualities that can be assessed and used for selection and/or promotion decisions. There is also some evidence that they can be enhanced through training (e.g., Barling et al., 1996).

What leaders *do* in the context of change is also important, and the research reviewed here points to the importance of communicating clearly, providing needed support, fostering a collective identity, seeking employee input (where culturally appropriate), managing emotions, and building confidence (self-efficacy) in employees' ability to cope with the change. Although leaders at the top of the organization obviously play a crucial role in the design and implementation of organizational change (Oreg & Berson, 2019), their ability to communicate with those on the front lines who will be affected by the change, and perhaps critical to its success, may be limited. Direct managers may be seen by employees as the "embodiment" of the organization (Eisenberger et al., 2010) and their primary source of information in forming judgments of organizational support and fairness. Direct managers can also play an important role in enhancing the quality of top-down and bottom-up communications (Hill et al., 2012). Of course, the managers themselves should be committed to the change (Abrell-Vogel & Rowold, 2014) to be effective in this capacity.

Numerous models have been developed over the years to serve as guides to leading change (see Stouten et al., 2018). It is interesting therefore, that the findings regarding the effectiveness of behaviors recommended in these models have provided mixed support (Herold et al., 2008; Nohe et al., 2013; Ling et al., 2018). Most intriguing was Herold et al.'s finding that change-leadership behavior was only related to employees' affective commitment to the change when the leader was not transformational and the change had little impact for employees. In contrast, transformational leadership related most strongly with commitment under high impact conditions. Herold et al. proposed that this may be due in part to the ability of transformational leaders to establish a climate of trust. The fact that transformational leaders did not always behave in accord with the prescriptive models might suggest that such leaders also have the ability to adapt their behavior to the demands of the situation. They can create an appealing vision of the future (inspirational motivation), serve as role models (idealized influence), challenge followers to think critically and creatively (intellectual stimulation), and show genuine concern for the well-being of the followers (individualized consideration). This adaptability and broad behavioral repertoire might be a key strength of the transformational leader. Nevertheless, all things considered, it appears the both leadership style and behavior matter for establishing commitment to change, and that organizations should consider both in their efforts to select, place, and train leaders who will be responsible for managing change.

In sum, although it might be natural to focus on top management and designated change leaders as the key players in implementing change, the results of this review suggest that direct managers can also play an important role in fostering strong commitment and behavioral support for the change within their units. Organizations would be well advised to play attention to this role in the planning and implementation of change, particularly when the impact of the change is likely to be wide-ranging and require the commitment of employees at all levels.

REFERENCES

Abrell-Vogel, C., & Rowold, J. (2014). Leaders' commitment to change and their effectiveness in change: A multilevel investigation. *Journal of Organizational Change Management, 27*(6), 900–921.

Allen, N. J., & Meyer, J. P. (1990). The measurement and antecedents of affective, continuance and normative commitment to the organization. *Journal of Occupational Psychology, 63*(1), 1–18.

Amundsen, S., & Martinsen, Ø. L. (2014). Empowering leadership: Construct clarification, conceptualization, and validation of a new scale. *The Leadership Quarterly, 25*(3), 487–511.

Armenakis, A. & Harris, S. (2009) Reflections: Our journey in organizational change research and practice. *Journal of Change Management, 9*(2), 127–142.

Avolio, B. J., & Bass, B. M. (2004). *Multifactor leadership questionnaire (MLQ),* vol. 29. Palo Alto, CA: Mind Garden.

Axtell, C., Wall, T., Stride, C., Pepper, K., Clegg, C., Gardner, P., & Bolden, R. (2002). Familiarity breeds content: The impact of exposure to change on employee openness and well-being. *Journal of Occupational and Organizational Psychology, 75,* 217–231.

Bakari, H., Hunjra, A. I., Jaros, S., & Khoso, I. (2019). Moderating role of cynicism about organizational change between authentic leadership and commitment to change in Pakistani public sector hospitals. *Leadership in Health Services, 32*(3), 387–404.

Bakari, H., Hunjra, A. I., & Niazi, G. S. K. (2017). How does authentic leadership influence planned organizational change? The role of employees' perceptions: Integration of theory of planned behavior and Lewin's three step model. *Journal of Change Management, 17*(2), 155–187.

Barling, J., Weber, T., & Kelloway, E. K. (1996). Effects of transformational leadership training on attitudinal and financial outcomes: A field experiment. *Journal of Applied Psychology, 81*(6), 827–832.

Baruch, Y. (1998). The rise and fall of organizational commitment. *Human Systems Management, 17*, 135–143.

Bass, B. M. (1985). Leadership: Good, better, best. *Organizational Dynamics, 13* (3), 26–40.

Bass, B. M., & Riggio, R. E. (2006). *Transformational leadership.* Mahwah, NJ: Lawrence Erlbaum Associates.

Bayraktar, S., & Jiménez, A. (2020), Self-efficacy as a resource: A moderated mediation model of transformational leadership, extent of change and reactions to change. *Journal of Organizational Change Management, 33*(2), 301–317.

Bayraktar, S., & Kabasakal, H. (2022). Crafting a change message and delivering it with success: An experimental study. *The Journal of Applied Behavioral Science, 58*(7), 97–119.

Becker, H. S. (1960). Notes on the concept of commitment. *American Journal of Sociology, 66*(1), 32–42.

Beer, M. (1980). *Organization change and development: A systems view.* Santa Monica, CA: Goodyear.

Bennis, W. (2000). Leadership of change. In M. Beer & N. Nohria (eds.), *Breaking the code of change* (pp. 113–121). Boston: Harvard Business School Press.

Bliese, P. D., Maltarich, M. A., & Hendricks, J. L. (2018). Back to basics with mixed-effects models: Nine take-away points. *Journal of Business and Psychology, 33*(1), 1–23.

Bouckenooghe, D., Schwarz, G. M., & Minbashian, A. (2015). Herscovitch and Meyer's three-component model of commitment to change: Meta-analytic findings. *European Journal of Work and Organizational Psychology, 24*(4), 578–595.

Brown, M. E., & Treviño, L. K. (2006). Ethical leadership: A review and future directions. *The Leadership Quarterly, 17*(6), 595–616.

Conger, J. A., & Kanungo, R. N. (1987). Toward a behavioral theory of charismatic leadership in organizational settings. *The Academy of Management Review, 12*(4), 637–647.

Conner, D. R. (1993). *Managing at the speed of change: How resilient managers succeed and prosper where others fail.* New York: Villard Books.

Conner, D. R., & Patterson, R. W. (1982). Building commitment to organizational change. *Training and Development Journal, 36*(1), 18–30.

Dung, L. T., & Van Hai, P. (2020). The effects of transformational leadership and job satisfaction on commitment to organizational change: A three-component model extension approach. *The South Asian Journal of Management, 14*(1), 106–123.

Eby, L. T., Adams, D. M., Russell, J. E. A., & Gaby, S. H. (2000). Perceptions of organizational readiness for change: Factors related to employees' reactions to the implementation of team-based selling. *Human Relations, 53*, 419–442.

Eisenberger, R., Karagonlar, G., Stinglhamber, F., Neves, P., Becker, T. E., Gonzalez-Morales, M. G., & Steiger-Mueller, M. (2010). Leader–member exchange and affective organizational commitment: The contribution of supervisor's organizational embodiment. *Journal of Applied Psychology, 95* (6), 1085–1103.

Epitropaki, O., & Martin, R. (2005). From Ideal to Real: A Longitudinal Study of the Role of Implicit Leadership Theories on Leader-Member Exchanges and Employee Outcomes. *Journal of Applied Psychology, 90*(4), 659–676.

Etzioni, A. (1961). *A comparative analysis of complex organizations*, New York: Free Press.

Faupel, S., & Helpap, S. (2021). Top management's communication and employees' commitment to change: The role of perceived procedural fairness and past change experience. *The Journal of Applied Behavioral Science, 57*(2), 204–232.

Fiedler, F. E. (1976). The leadership game: Matching the man to the situation. *Organizational Dynamics, 4*(3), 6–16.

Fleishman, E. A., & Harris, E. F. (1962). Patterns of leadership behavior related to employee grievances and turnover. *Personnel Psychology, 15*, 43–56.

Gardner, W. L., Cogliser, C. C., Davis, K. M., & Dickens, M. P. (2011). Authentic leadership: A review of the literature and research agenda. *The Leadership Quarterly, 22*(6), 1120–1145.

Guerrero, J. M., Teng-Calleja, M., & Hechanova, M. R. M. (2018). Implicit change leadership schemas, perceived effective change management, and teachers' commitment to change in secondary schools in the Philippines. *Asia Pacific Education Review, 19*(3), 375–387.

Hannah, S. T., Sumanth, J. J., Lester, P., & Cavarretta, F. (2014). Debunking the false dichotomy of leadership idealism and pragmatism: Critical evaluation and support of the newer genre leadership theories. *Journal of Organizational Behavior, 35*, 598–621.

Harrison, R., Chaun, A., Mingashian, A., McMullan, R., & Schwarz, G. (2022). Is gaining affective commitment the missing strategy for successful management in healthcare? *Journal of Healthcare Leadership, 14*, 1–4.

Hechanova, M. R. M., Caringal-Go, J. F., & Magsaysay, J. F. (2018). Implicit change leadership, change management, and affective commitment to change: Comparing academic institutions vs business enterprises. *Leadership & Organization Development Journal, 39*(7), 914–925.

Helpap, S. (2016). The impact of power distance orientation on recipients' reactions to participatory versus programmatic change communication. *The Journal of Applied Behavioral Science, 52*(1), 5–34.

Herold, D. M., Fedor, D. B., Caldwell, S. D., & Liu, Y. (2008). The effects of transformational and change leadership on employees commitment to a change: A multilevel study. *Journal of Applied Psychology, 93*(2), 346–357.

Herscovitch, L., & Meyer, J. P. (2002). Commitment to organizational change: Extension of a three-component model. *Journal of Applied Psychology, 87,* 474–487.

Hill, N. S., Seo, M. G., Kang, J. H., & Taylor, M. S. (2012). Building employee commitment to change across organizational levels: The influence of hierarchical distance and direct managers' transformational leadership. *Organization Science, 23*(3), 758–777.

House, R. J., & Howell, J. M. (1992). Personality and charismatic leadership. *The Leadership Quarterly, 3*(2), 81–108.

House, R. J., & Mitchell, T. R. (1974). Path-goal theory of leadership. *Contemporary Business, 3,* 81–98.

Jaros, S. (2010). Commitment to organizational change: A critical review. *Journal of Change Management, 10*(1), 79–108.

Jung, K. B., Kang, S. W., & Choi, S. B. (2020). Empowering leadership, risk-taking behavior, and employees' commitment to organizational change: The mediated moderating role of task complexity. *Sustainability, 12,* 2340.

Kanter, R. M. (1968). Commitment and social organization: A study of commitment mechanisms in utopian communities. *American Sociological Review, 33,* 499–517.

Kim, H., Im, J., & Shin, Y. H. (2021). The impact of transformational leadership and commitment to change on restaurant employees' quality of work life during a crisis. *Journal of Hospitality and Tourism Management, 48,* 322–330.

Kotter, J. P. (1996). *Leading change.* Boston, MA: Harvard Business Press.

Lee, K., Scandura, T. A., & Sharif, M. M. (2014). Cultures have consequences: A configural approach to leadership across two cultures. *The Leadership Quarterly, 25*(4), 692–710.

Liden, R. C., Sparrowe, R. T., & Wayne, S. J. (1997). Leader–member exchange theory: The past and potential for the future. In G. R. Ferris (ed.), *Research in personnel and human resources management,* vol. 15 (pp. 47–119). Stanford, CT: JAI Press.

Ling, B., Guo, Y., & Chen, D. (2018). Change leadership and employees' commitment to change. *Journal of Personnel Psychology, 17,* 83–93.

Madsen, S. R., Miller, D., & John, C. R. (2005). Readiness for organizational change: Do organizational commitment and social relationships in the workplace make a difference? *Human Resource Development Quarterly, 16,* 213–233.

Magsaysay, J. F., & Hechanova, M. R. M. (2017). Building an implicit change leadership theory. *Leadership & Organization Development Journal, 38*(6), 834–848.

Mangundjaya, W. L., & Amir, M. T. (2021). Testing resilience and work ethics as mediators between charismatic leadership and affective commitment to change. *The Journal of Asian Finance, Economics, and Business, 8*(2), 401–410.

Mathieu, J. E., & Zajac, D. (1990). A review and meta-analysis of the antecedents, correlates, and consequences of organizational commitment. *Psychological Bulletin, 108,* 171–194.

Meyer, J. P. (2009). Commitment in a changing world of work. In H. J. Klein, T. E. Becker, & J. P. Meyer (eds.), *Commitment in organizations: Accumulated wisdom and new directions* (pp. 37–68). Florence, KY: Routledge.

(2016). *Handbook of employee commitment.* Cheltenham: Edward Elgar Publishing.

(2021). Commitment at work: Past, present, and future. In P. Graf & D. J. A. Dozois (eds.), *Handbook on the state of the art in applied psychology* (pp. 19–49). New York: John Wiley & Sons.

Meyer, J. P., & Allen, N. J. (1991). A three-component conceptualization of organizational commitment. *Human Resource Management Review, 1,* 61–89.

Meyer, J. P., Allen, N. J., & Smith, C. A. (1993). Commitment to organizations and occupations: Extension and test of a three-component model. *Journal of Applied Psychology, 78,* 538–551.

Meyer, J. P., & Hamilton, L. (2013). Commitment to organizational change: Theory, research, principles, and practice. In S. Oreg, M. Alexandra, & B. T. Rune (eds.), *The psychology of organizational change: Viewing change from the employee's perspective* (pp. 43–64). Cambridge: Cambridge University Press.

Meyer, J. P., & Herscovitch, L. (2001). Commitment in the workplace: Toward a general model. *Human Resource Management Review, 11*(3), 299–326.

Meyer, J. P., & Maltin, E. R. (2010). Employee commitment and well-being: A critical review, theoretical framework, and research agenda. *Journal of Vocational Behavior, 77*(2), 323–337.

Meyer, J. P., & Morin, A. J. (2016). A person-centered approach to commitment research: Theory, research, and methodology. *Journal of Organizational Behavior, 37*(4), 584–612.

Meyer, J. P., & Parfyonova, N. M. (2010). Normative commitment in the workplace: A theoretical analysis and re-conceptualization. *Human Resource Management Review, 20,* 283–294.

Meyer, J. P., Srinivas, E. S., Lal, J. B., & Topolnytsky, L. (2007). Employee commitment and support for an organizational change: Test of the three-component model in two cultures. *Journal of Occupational and Organizational Psychology, 80*(2), 185–211.

Meyer, J. P., Stanley, D. J., Herscovitch, L., & Topolnytsky, L. (2002). Affective, continuance, and normative commitment to the organization: A meta-analysis of antecedents, correlates, and consequences. *Journal of Vocational Behavior, 61*(1), 20–52.

Mowday, R. T., Porter, L. W., & Steers, R. (1982). *Organizational linkages: The psychology of commitment, absenteeism, and turnover.* San Diego, CA: Academic Press.

Mumford, M. D., & Fried, Y. (2014). Give them what they want or give them what they need? Ideology in the study of leadership. *Journal of Organizational Behavior, 35,* 622–634.

Nohe, C., Michaelis, B., Menges, J. I., Zhang, Z., & Sonntag, K. (2013). Charisma and organizational change: A multilevel study of perceived charisma, commitment to change, and team performance. *The Leadership Quarterly, 24*(2), 378–389.

Oreg, S. (2006). Personality, context, and resistance to organizational change. *European Journal of Work and Organizational Psychology, 15*, 73–101.

Oreg, S., & Berson, Y. (2019). Leaders' impact on organizational change: Bridging theoretical and methodological chasms. *Academy of Management Annals, 13*(1), 272–307.

Oreg, S., Michel, A., & By, R. T. (eds.) (2013). *The psychology of organizational change: Viewing change from the employee's perspective.* Cambridge: Cambridge University Press.

Ouedraogo, N., Zaitouni, M., & Ouakouak, M. L. (2023). Leadership credibility and change success: mediating role of commitment to change. *International Journal of Productivity and Performance Management, 72*(1), 47–65.

Peng, J., Li, M., Wang, Z., & Lin, Y. (2021). Transformational leadership and employees' reactions to organizational change: Evidence from a meta-analysis. *The Journal of Applied Behavioral Science, 57*(3), 369–397.

Podsakoff, P. M., MacKenzie, S. B., Lee, J. Y., & Podsakoff, N. P. (2003). Common method biases in behavioral research: a critical review of the literature and recommended remedies. *Journal of Applied Psychology, 88*(5), 879–903.

Podsakoff, P. M., MacKenzie, S. B., Moorman, R. H., & Fetter, R. (1990). Transformational leader behaviors and their effects on followers' trust in leader, satisfaction, and organizational citizenship behaviors. *The Leadership Quarterly, 1*(2), 107–142.

Rahaman, H. M. S., Camps, J., Decoster, S., & Stouten, J. (2021). Ethical leadership in times of change: the role of change commitment and change information for employees' dysfunctional resistance. *Personnel Review, 50*(2), 630–647.

Reichers, A. E., Wanous, J. P., & Austin, J. T. (1997). Understanding and managing cynicism about organizational change. *Academy of Management Executive, 11*(1), 48–59.

Seo, M. G., Taylor, M. S., Hill, N. S., Zhang, X., Tesluk, P. E., & Lorinkova, N. M. (2012). The role of affect and leadership during organizational change. *Personnel Psychology, 65*(1), 121–165.

Shapiro, D. L., & Kirkman, B. L. (1999). Employees' reaction to the change to work teams: The influence of "anticipatory" injustice. *Journal of Organizational Change Management, 12*, 51–67.

Shin, J., Seo, M. G., Shapiro, D. L., & Taylor, M. S. (2015). Maintaining employees' commitment to organizational change: The role of leaders' informational justice and transformational leadership. *The Journal of Applied Behavioral Science, 51*(4), 501–528.

Sonenshein, S., & Dholakia, U. (2012). Explaining employee engagement with strategic change implementation: A meaning-making approach. *Organization Science, 23*(1), 1–23.

Stanley, D. J., Meyer, J. P., & Topolnytsky, L. (2005). Employee cynicism and resistance to organizational change. *Journal of Business and Psychology, 19*, 429–459.

Stogdill, R. M. (1948). Personal factors associated with leadership: A survey of the literature. *Journal of Psychology, 25*, 35–71.

Stouten, J., Rousseau, D. M., & De Cremer, D. (2018). Successful organizational change: Integrating the management practice and scholarly literatures. *Academy of Management Annals*, *12*(2), 752–768.

Svendsen, M., & Joensson, T. S. (2016). Transformational leadership and change related voice behavior. *Leadership & Organization Development Journal*, *37*(3), 357–368.

Van der Voet, J., Kuipers, B. S., & Groeneveld, S. (2016). Implementing change in public organizations: The relationship between leadership and affective commitment to change in a public sector context. *Public Management Review*, *18*(6), 842–865.

Wanberg, C. R., & Banas, J. T. (2000). Predictors and outcomes of openness to change in a reorganizing workplace. *Journal of Applied Psychology*, *85*, 132–142.

Weiherl, J., & Masal, D. (2016). Transformational leadership and followers' commitment to mission changes. *International Journal of Public Administration*, *39*(11), 861–871.

Weske, U., Boselie, P., van Rensen, E., & Schneider, M. (2019). Physician compliance with quality and patient safety regulations: The role of perceived enforcement approaches and commitment. *Health Services Management Research*, *32*(2), 103–112.

Witte, K. (1992). Putting the fear back into fear appeals: The extended parallel process model. *Communications Monographs*, *59*(4), 329–349.

Yukl, G. A., & Gardner, W. L. (2020). *Leadership in organizations* (9th ed.). London: Pearson.

Zappalà, S., Toscano, F., & Licciardello, S. A. (2019). Towards sustainable organizations: Supervisor support, commitment to change and the mediating role of organizational identification. *Sustainability*, *11*(3), 805.

Zhao, H. H., Seibert, S. E., Taylor, M. S., Lee, C., & Lam, W. (2016). Not even the past: The joint influence of former leader and new leader during leader succession in the midst of organizational change. *Journal of Applied Psychology*, *101*(12), 1730–1738.

CHAPTER 12

Change Leadership
A Social Identity Perspective

Steffen R. Giessner and Kate E. Horton

12.1 Leadership and Organizational Change

This chapter takes a social identity perspective on leading change, shedding light on the vital role that leaders can play in facilitating positive change outcomes. We begin the chapter by examining and reflecting on the (broad) literature on leadership and organizational change. We then move on to consider how leaders can inspire support for change through identity management processes.

Leadership has been defined as "the nature of the influencing process – and its resultant outcomes – that occurs between a leader and followers and how this influencing process is explained by the leader's dispositional characteristics and behaviors, follower perceptions and attributions of the leader" (Antonakis et al., 2004, p. 5). Leadership research has dramatically increased over the last two decades, resulting in many theoretical perspectives (Dinh et al., 2014). Early research focusing on leadership behaviors primarily differentiated between task-oriented and relationship-oriented types of behaviors (Fleishman, 1953; Fiedler, 1964). However, soon after this, another distinct meta-category of leadership behaviors emerged, namely change-oriented behaviors (Ekvall & Arvonen, 1991; Yukl, 2008). Such behaviors include "monitoring the environment to identify threats and opportunities; interpreting events and explaining why major change is needed; articulating an inspiring vision; taking risks to promote change; building a coalition of supporters for a major change; and determining how to implement a new initiative or major change" (Yukl, 2008, p. 712). One may argue that these change-related behaviors are the essence of what leadership is about. Indeed, many scholars agree that leading change is one of the most challenging and vital responsibilities faced by leaders over the course of their careers (Hollander, 1964; Yukl, 2010).

Yet, at the same time, analysis reveals a relative paucity of studies focusing on this topic (Sitkin & Pablo, 2005; Giessner et al., 2016;

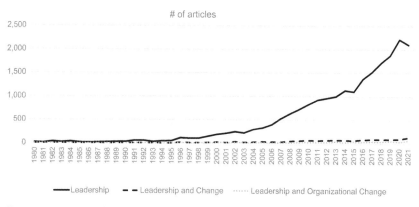

Figure 12.1   Scopus keyword search on published journal articles between 1980 and 2021

Steigenberger, 2017). Indeed, as shown in the results of the literature search depicted in Figure 12.1, while leadership research has grown exponentially in recent decades, organizational change continues to rank low in the priorities of researchers in this area, with limited studies explicitly focusing on the leadership of change. Specifically, a keyword search on Scopus of published journal articles revealed 21,424 publications between 1980 and 2021 with the keyword #leadership.[1] This is in stark contrast to the 1,241 publications that cited the keywords #leadership and #change, and the 557 articles with the keywords #leadership, and #organizational #change. In percentages, articles combining keywords on leadership and change/organizational change thus accounted for only 5.79 and 2.60 percent of leadership studies, respectively. This might be considered surprising given strong evidence that leaders are critical in mobilizing change efforts and in determining the success of change initiatives within their organizations (Kouzes & Posner, 1987; Oreg & Berson, 2019). Yet this analysis also showed that, while research on change leadership is under-represented within the leadership literature, there has been a general increase in studies on this topic in recent decades. Whereas only 72 papers using the keywords #leadership and #change were published between 1980 and 2000, this number increased to 1169 papers between 2001 and 2021.

---

[1] The search was conducted on February 17, 2022. We chose as *Subject Areas*: Psychology, as well as Business, Management and Accounting; *Document Type*: article; *Publication Stage*: final; *Source type*: journal.

This literature has provided a number of valuable contributions to our understanding of leadership and change. An often-cited point of departure on leading change is Lewin's (1947) work. Many authors refer to his work and argue for a three-step approach to leading change reflected in the steps: unfreeze, change, and refreeze. One should note, however, that Lewin never developed such a three-step model to guide change leaders and only theorized about the unfreezing phase (Cummings et al., 2016). The change steps required have been further detailed in subsequent literature. For instance, Beer et al. (1990) suggested that leaders need to take six steps, and Kotter (1996) argued for eight steps in order to successfully lead change efforts. Meanwhile, a recent article by Stouten et al. (2018) integrating management practice and academic literature argued for "ten evidence-based steps" (p. 752). These approaches to leading change have been criticized for their theoretical assumptions and weak empirical evidence (Kanter et al., 1992; Burnes, 1996; By, 2007; Hughes, 2016). A few researchers have, however, argued that the essence of these change models is that leaders should (a) communicate about the change and (b) enable employees to provide inputs for change processes. Moreover, these change leadership aspects have been found to be related to the change commitment (Herold et al., 2008) and change readiness (Lyons et al., 2009) of organizational members.

Research shows that large-scale change initiatives represent major environmental stress factors in the lives of organizations (Giessner et al., 2023), and often result in detrimental consequences for focal workforces, including heightened stress and uncertainty among employees (Elstak et al., 2015; Belschak et al., 2020). Yet, it also finds that leaders can play a pivotal role in managing the change process and in enhancing related outcomes (Oreg & Berson, 2011). Indeed, researchers agree that the success of a change initiative is often contingent on the acceptance and support of the focal workforce (Oreg et al., 2011; Shin et al., 2012), and that leaders bear primary responsibility for building this acceptance among their followers (Shamir, 1999; Venus et al., 2019). Attention has thus turned to the key question of what kinds of leadership behaviors are beneficial in enhancing followers' support and acceptance of change efforts. We consider this question next.

12.2 Leadership Behavior

Researchers have recognized that a range of leadership styles may be valuable in encouraging employee change acceptance and support, including transformational leadership (Oreg & Berson, 2011), charismatic leadership (Waldman & Javidan, 2009), and supportive leadership (Cooke et al., 2021). Crucially, evidence suggests that leaders often act as "sense-givers" during change events, providing visions and meaning around a proposed change, which enhances employees' sensemaking, attitudes, emotions, and behavioral responses to the change (Oreg & Berson, 2019; Venus et al., 2019; Kroon & Reif, 2023). Framework(s) on charismatic-transformational leadership (Bass, 1985; Conger & Kanungo, 1987; Shamir et al., 1993) have been especially highlighted as important within the context of organizational change. This makes intuitive sense as the word "transformational" implies leader characteristics and behaviors that are likely to be well-suited to change management. Maybe the best known model in this field is Bass's (1985) model of transformational leadership which identifies four dimensions: Idealized influence (i.e., being a role model who instills respect and trust; providing a sense of purpose), inspirational motivation (i.e., communicating an inspiring and ambitious vision), intellectual stimulation (i.e., stimulating problem-solving, empowering followers for new challenges), and individualized consideration (i.e., considering the individual needs of followers).

Many studies have shown that transformational leadership is positively related to employees' change reactions and change-related performance (Carter et al., 2013; Faupel & Süß, 2019), change commitment (Bayraktar & Jiménez, 2020), employee health during change (Lundmark et al., 2017), team innovation during change (Paulsen et al., 2013), and perceived company performance (Babić et al., 2014). Furthermore, research finds that transformational leadership is more strongly related to employee change commitment than the above-described change leadership (Herold et al., 2008). Although various mechanisms have been suggested through which transformational leadership impacts employees, all of these are related to the positive relationships these leaders can establish with their followers.

However, transformational leadership might not be effective in the long run of a change. Henricks et al. (2020) found that transformational leadership had only a short-term rather than a long-term influence on employees' attitudes toward change. In addition to the transformational leadership framework of Bass (1985; Avolio & Bass, 1995), a few papers have focused on charisma or visionary leadership in change (Waldman & Javidan, 2009; Venus et al., 2019). In the framework of transformational leadership, this would be reflected in the idealized influence and inspirational motivation dimensions (cf. van Knippenberg & Sitkin, 2013).

Studies on charismatic leadership have focused on ways of communicating (Seyranian & Bligh, 2008), leadership-related social and emotional skills (Groves, 2005), and leaders' commitment and vision pursuit (Waldman & Javidan, 2009). It is interesting to note that charismatic leadership itself might also sometimes be the result of the change process and rather establish itself as a form of resistance to change (Levay, 2010).

While this previous research on charismatic-transformational leadership has shed light on leadership during change, there has been some major criticism aimed at the underlying frameworks. Van Knippenberg and Sitkin (2013) outlined four major problems associated with this perspective. First, while these models provide a multidimensional conceptualization of leadership, they do not offer a theory on how these dimensions interact or relate to each other. Second, as a consequence of this, the frameworks do not provide clear insights into how the dimensions work via distinct processes on different potential outcomes. In other words, most of this research has operationalized transformational leadership as a one-dimensional construct (although it should theoretically be four dimensions) and only provide mediating mechanisms for the overall framework instead of highlighting different mechanisms and consequential outcomes for each subdimension. Third, the charismatic-transformational leadership theories presume that these are effective leadership characteristics. This, however, is problematic as it confounds the independent variable (leadership) with the outcome variable (performance). Illustrating this point, it is noteworthy that this confound is reflected in most of the measures used to operationalize charismatic-transformational leadership. Finally, most of the measures of charismatic-transformational leadership fail to provide convincing evidence of its underlying dimensionality.

These critical points, thus, raise questions about the usefulness of the charismatic-transformational leadership frameworks in the organizational change literature. Furthermore, these criticisms can be applied to other leadership frameworks that provide a multi-dimensional conceptualization of leadership. For instance, research on servant leadership (De Sousa & van Dierendonck, 2014), ethical leadership (Neves et al., 2018; Metwally et al., 2019), authentic leadership (Gill, 2012; Agote et al., 2016), and leadership skills frameworks (e.g., Groves, 2005; Gilley et al., 2009; Aitken & von Treuer, 2021) similarly show that a collection of leadership dimensions may play a positive role in shaping employee change adaptation. However, while these frameworks provide valuable insights, we argue that they might need further clarification, as raised by van Knippenberg and Sitkin (2013). Furthermore, we argue that by purely focusing on leadership characteristics, skills, and competencies this research downplays the social context in which organizational change takes place. Perhaps no one leadership style fits all contexts of change, and the effectiveness of a certain leadership behavior fluctuates over time (Henricks et al., 2020). Indeed, given that so many leadership frameworks have been shown to be effective during organizational change, questions may be raised as to whether these models have something fundamental in common or apply in different situations or at different times.

To address the social dependency of leadership, we focus on the social identity approach (SIA), which has been (a) explicitly developed to explain (social) change processes in society, (b) proven to be applicable in explaining organizational behavior and leadership processes in organizations, and (c) provides a more socially embedded perspective on leadership and organizational change. This theoretical perspective is grounded in Social Identity Theory (Tajfel & Turner, 1986) and the complementary Self-Categorization Theory (Turner et al., 1987), which have been refined and applied to a range of areas, including organizational behavior (Ashforth & Mael, 1989; Hogg & Terry, 2000), leadership (Haslam & Platow, 2001; Hogg, 2001; van Knippenberg & Hogg, 2003), uncertainty management (Hogg, 2000, 2007), life changes and health (Jetten et al., 2012; Haslam et al., 2021), and organizational change contexts (Giessner et al., 2011, 2016; Drzensky & van Dick, 2013; Slater et al., 2016). In the following text, we first outline this framework and explain why it is so relevant for organizational change. We then focus on how this framework can help us to understand leadership during organizational change. After summarizing the literature, we conclude by outlining some future pathways for research in the field.

12.3   Social Identity and Change

While a detailed overview of the social identity approach and research findings in the context of organizational change was provided in the first volume of "The Psychology of Organizational Change" (see Drzensky & van Dick, 2013) and we certainly refer the interested reader to an in-depth read of this excellent chapter, we next briefly summarize the main theoretical assumptions and integrate these with some new insights before we dive into the topic of leadership itself.

The basic premise of Social Identity Theory (SIT, Tajfel & Turner, 1986) is the assumption that our thinking, feelings, and actions are often driven by our self-definitions in terms of group memberships (i.e., our social or group identities). These social identities provide us with psychological meaning and emotional significance. The degree to which we internalize group memberships is referred to as the process or degree of identification. The process by which a group membership becomes salient has been outlined in Self-Categorization Theory (SCT, Turner et al., 1987). Categories and, hence, group memberships become more salient depending on comparative fit (i.e., the differences between members of a group are less than the differences between groups) and normative fit (i.e., there is a match between the expected category and actual behaviors of those category members). Further, some categories or group memberships are more chronically accessible and are, thus, more likely to be used. Given that we spend about a third of our time within organizations, organizational membership is often an important and very accessible group with which we identify (Ashforth & Mael, 1989). Organizational identification represents the degree to which we internalize organizational norms, values, and characteristics (Dutton et al., 1994; Drzensky & van Dick, 2013). Organizational identification has an important impact on individuals' feelings, attitudes, and behaviors. Indeed, meta-analytical evidence has confirmed that organizational identification is positively related to pro-organizational behaviors like higher job involvement and lower turnover, as well as to in-role and extra-role performance (Riketta, 2005; Riketta & van Dick, 2005).

Furthermore, group identification contributes to the enhancement of our self-esteem (Hogg & Abrams, 1990) and provides us with the psychological feeling of social support, which can reduce stress and improve our health (Jetten et al., 2012; Haslam et al., 2021). This aspect of group identities makes them especially relevant for organizational change processes, because organizational changes typically challenge the identity of an organization, creating uncertainty and ambiguity that can weaken employees' levels of identification and cause a divergence between their attitudes and behaviors and the organization's goals and interests. Most large-scale changes create a degree of uncertainty about the future of an organization, while uncertainty reduction is found to be a key motive in shaping individuals' behavior during change events (Elstak et al., 2015).

Uncertainty-identity theory (Hogg, 2007) – a theory that extends the original Social Identity and Self-Categorization theories by elaborating in more depth on how individuals deal with self-uncertainty – argues that individuals are motivated to reduce such uncertainty by identifying with a social group. Especially if the uncertainty is related to something that is of importance to oneself, experiencing uncertainty motivates an individual to find a social group with which they can identify. One important insight of this SIT/SCT extension is that, under uncertainty, we tend to identify with groups that have clear boundaries, structures, and goals – thus with groups that are well defined for us. Researchers have termed this property of a group "entitativity" (Campbell, 1958; Hamilton & Sherman, 1996). In a change context, organizations often undergo a redefinition of who they are and what they do. This is potentially paralleled in new reporting structures, changes in hierarchy and leaders, changes in employees, and changes in goals. This reduction in the entitativity of the organization may be expected to result in lower identification with the current organization and a shift to identify with other social groups like the team, profession, or another organization (cf. Jetten et al., 2000; Hogg et al., 2007).

SIT further predicts that individuals aim to be members of positively evaluated groups and will, therefore, feel threatened if a group to which they belong is negatively evaluated. Thus, in situations of organizational change, if the change itself is seen by employees as resulting in a negative shift in evaluations of the organization's identity, employees will be forced to find ways to cope with this threatening situation. Note, however, that not all organizational changes will be perceived as affecting the organization's identity in a negative way. Indeed, some organizational changes may be relatively minor, while others may be perceived as implying positive effects for employees and their organization's identity. For instance, getting an update of the newest technology in a technology-driven company might be welcomed by employees and may not create any tension between an employee and the organization with which they identify.

In their recent social identity model of organizational change (SIMOC), Mühlemann et al. (2022) propose that employees may either (a) perceive a degree of continuity in their organization's identity following a change or (b) perceive that the change impacts the organization's identity in a positive or a negative way. According to this model, the key to ensuring positive employee adjustment to organizational change rests in either fostering a sense of continuity in pre-existing social identities throughout the change (the so-called identity maintenance pathway) or by ensuring that employees perceive the new organizational identity in a positive light (the so-called identity gain pathway).

Research focusing on identity continuity has long shown that employees who perceive a degree of continuity in their organization's identity from the pre-change to the post-change organization are likely to show more positive reactions to the change (van Knippenberg & van Leeuwen, 2001; Giessner, 2011). For instance, Ullrich et al.'s (2005) case study of a

German industrial company showed that employees' adjustment to a merger and their identification with the post-merger organization was affected by their perceptions of both the current (observable) and the projected continuity of their pre-change organization in the post-merger organization. Similarly, Liang et al. (2022) found that, if an organization embraces an agile organizational identity (where change is a central facet of the organization's identity), then employees may show better post-change adjustment, as the company's changeable/agile nature represents a source of continuity over time.

The SIMOC model adds an additional piece to this picture by suggesting that while post-change adjustment is shaped by employees' perceptions of continuity in the organization's identity, it is also affected by employees' perceptions of gains or losses in the organization's identity following the change. According to this model, organizations can support employee adjustment by fostering a sense of identity gain (i.e., a perception that the organization has gained a positive identity through the change), while, if employees perceive that there is little continuity in the pre-existing identity and that the change represents a loss to the organization, then they will exhibit poor change adjustment.

Beyond this elaboration on how core social identity principles can be applied to the understanding of organizational change, there have also been some specific applications to the context of mergers and acquisitions (M&As; Giessner et al., 2016). What makes this specific change context especially interesting from a social identity perspective is the fact that organizations have to deal with many identities in this situation (i.e., pre-merger identities of the merging organizations and the post-merger identity) as well as with the specific intergroup relationships of the merging organizations prior and during the merger. When we reflect on the leadership aspects, we will base some of our arguments on insights from M&A research.

12.4   A Social Identity Perspective on Leading Change

We next turn to the role leaders can play in facilitating positive change outcomes, drawing on the social identity approach to change leadership. If, as proposed by SIMOC (Mühlemann et al., 2022), leaders can help employees to adjust to organizational change by enhancing a perception of identity continuity (via the identity maintenance pathway) or by emphasizing positive identity developments (via the identity gain pathway), then the next key question concerns the behaviors leaders can enact to facilitate these pathways.

12.4.1   Leaders' Roles in Enhancing Identity Continuity

First turning to the identity maintenance/continuity pathway, van Knippenberg and Hogg (2003) predict in their Social Identity Model of Leadership (SIMOL) that leaders who are prototypical (that is, who embody the collective group identity or in simple terms are seen as "one of us") are likely to be more effective in times of change, because they are better able to project feelings of continuity throughout the change period. In particular, SIMOL proposes that the same change will be more likely to be perceived as consistent with a group's identity when it is championed by a highly prototypical leader, while leaders who are less prototypical (or even worse "outgroup" members) may evoke feelings of identity discontinuity and thus change resistance among their workforces. Empirical research has provided support for this suggestion, for example showing that leader prototypicality is positively related to employees' willingness to change (van Knippenberg & Hogg, 2003; van Knippenberg & van Knippenberg, 2005). Likewise, van Knippenberg et al. (2008) showed that prototypical leaders were more likely to be perceived as "agents of continuity" during a change than their less prototypical counterparts, and that this perception was associated with higher employee change support (see also Rast et al., 2016). The clear implication of such findings is that organizational change projects may benefit from appointing a prototypical leader, who can enhance feelings of continuity during times of change.

Leader prototypicality may be expected to take on particular significance in M&A contexts. Past research suggests that, during M&As, perceived continuity tends to be higher for employees in the dominant or acquirer organization compared to those in the less dominant/acquired organization (van Dick et al., 2006), and choices regarding leadership may be essential to these perceptions. Indeed, in post-merger contexts, leadership positions are perhaps more likely to be filled by representatives of the dominant/acquirer organization than the less dominant/acquired company, meaning leader figures will be prototypical ingroup members for employees from one (dominant) pre-merger organization, while being atypical outgroup members for employees from the other (less dominant) one. As such, the same leader may symbolize continuity for some employees, yet be a source of discontinuity and threat for others (Bobbio et al., 2005; Giessner et al., 2011).

The decision of who becomes a leader after a merger is thus an important one. Yet, research suggests that employees' perceptions of continuity are not only affected by their leaders' characteristics or perceived prototypicality, but also by the visions and actions they take as change leaders. For example, in line with SIMOL theory (van Knippenberg & Hogg, 2003), research suggests that change leaders can go some way to compensate for a lack of prototypicality by adopting a group-oriented attitude that shows fair consideration to all employees. In other words, they can act as champions of the team or organization (Steffens et al., 2014). This assumption is in line with Edwin Hollander's (1964) idea on how leaders are able to manage change. He assumed that leaders need to first earn support from their followers (so-called idiosyncrasy credit), via positive actions toward them, in order to deviate and change the organization subsequently. An experimental study by Jetten et al. (2002) finds support for this suggestion, showing that, in an M&A setting, individuals' evaluations of ingroup versus outgroup leaders (i.e., those from the same group versus those from the other pre-merger group) were not significantly different if outgroup leaders emphasized the importance of equality or demonstrated preferential treatment toward members of the pre-merger outgroup. As such, change leaders' group-oriented behaviors are found to be critical in shaping their followers' attitudes in change contexts and may serve to compensate for a lack of prototypicality where leaders are not regarded as emblematic of their group (see also Duck & Fielding, 2003; van Dick et al., 2007; Giessner et al., 2013).

While SIMOL addresses two aspects of how leaders can enhance a feeling of continuity for their followers (through group prototypicality and group-oriented behaviors), a more recent model of leadership as social identity management put forward by Haslam et al. (2011) as well as Steffens et al. (2014) suggests two more dimensions. Further, a recent measure – the Identity Leadership Inventory (ILI) – provides a valid operationalization of these four leadership dimensions and shows that these aspects can be differentiated across twenty countries (van Dick et al., 2018). The first identity management dimension is called *identity prototypicality* and resembles the above-described group prototypicality. Leaders should be seen as "one of us." The second dimension is called *identity advancement* and resembles group-oriented behavior as described in SIMOL. In simple words, it captures whether the leader is "doing it for us."

The third identity management dimension is labeled *identity entrepreneurship*. The basic idea behind this dimension is that leaders are able to be entrepreneurs of identity by crafting identities or "a shared sense of us" (Reicher & Hopkins, 1996a, 1996b). Leaders can, thus, define values, norms, and ideals. They can achieve this by choosing the "right" competitor that shifts the understanding of "who we are," or by crafting a new possible future identity (Stam et al., 2014). One way to craft such a future identity is shown by Venus et al. (2019), who focused on the role of visionary leadership in determining employee change support. The authors proposed that leaders can promote employee change acceptance by conveying a vision of continuity – that is a sense that while a change may be impactful, the essential identity of an organization will remain unchanged. In other words, leaders can craft a possible future identity that suggests continuity for their organization and its employees. Support for this prediction was found in both a field and a laboratory setting, with evidence showing that, under conditions of uncertainty, leaders could enhance followers' support for change by offering a vision of continuity that afforded a perception of collective continuity in spite of the change. Leaders can thus engage in identity entrepreneurship to enhance change acceptance.

Similarly, another way in which leaders can make use of identity entrepreneurship to facilitate perceptions of collective continuity is by highlighting that an envisioned change is well aligned with the organization's existing (Reicher & Hopkins, 2001) or historical (Lupina-Wegener et al., 2020) identity. By doing so leaders can minimize perceptions of threat and uncertainty by emphasizing that the essence of "who we are" will remain preserved following the change. This observation finds resonance in Liang et al.'s (2022) study of a cross-border M&A, which showed that, if employees regard agility as a defining feature of their organization, then a large-scale change is likely to be viewed as less threatening as it aligns with their existing expectations about who their organization is at its core. Similarly, research has shown that if a change is perceived as a means to restore a valued historical identity or a return to the organization's "past glories" then it is likely to be more positively received (Lupina-Wegener et al., 2020). Here again, employees are able to view the change as compatible with the core legacy features of the organization's past, giving a sense of historical continuity in the organization's identity over time and minimizing perceptions of uncertainty and threat. Research further finds that managers can help to legitimize and support structural change efforts by providing narratives that link the organization's past with its emerging future (Shamir, 1999; Demers et al., 2003). Managers' visionary communication and construction of change-related narratives are thus shown to be critical in facilitating feelings of identity maintenance/continuity that typically enhance employees' acceptance and support for organizational change.

A final identity management dimension suggested by Steffens et al. (2014) is named *identity impresarioship*. This can be defined as "developing structures, events, and activities that give weight to the group's existence and allow group members to live their membership" (Steffens et al., 2014,

p. 1005). Leaders can aim to "make us matter" and thus boost the collective esteem and collective efficacy of employees. While there is currently less research on this dimension, a good example of how this can be achieved is offered in a recent study by Rosa et al. (2020). In a series of experiments, they focused on the role of functional indispensability (i.e., organizational members' strong perceptions of instrumentality in the future organization's goals) during a perceived organizational merger for the commitment of these employees toward the change. In five studies, the researchers demonstrated that participants who experienced functional indispensability (versus none) showed more commitment to the intended organizational merger. Importantly, this effect was explained by the perception of being more representative in this new organization – reflecting a stronger sense of continuity. Thus, identity impresarioship might be another effective way to foster a sense of continuity for employees.

12.4.2 *Leaders' Roles in Enhancing Identity Gain*

We next turn to the second pathway through which leaders can facilitate employee change support, that is their roles in enhancing employees' perceptions of positive identity gain. Research focusing on visionary leadership has long recognized that leaders may encourage support for change events by contrasting the organization's current (suboptimal) circumstances with a positive vision of how things would improve in a future (changed) organization (Conger & Kanungo, 1987; Shamir, 1999). Such visionary leadership is successful in mobilizing change support, because employees are able to understand the need for change and the ways in which the change may confer positive identity gains, thus paving the way for a better future (Stam et al., 2014). Research has more recently turned to the strategies that leaders can use to make their visionary communication more effective.

The research and theorizing on visionary leadership correspond well with the above-mentioned identity management dimensions. We therefore argue that these dimensions may be similarly applied to convey prospective identity gains. Identity impresarioship and identity entrepreneurship behaviors (Haslam et al., 2011; Steffens et al., 2014) seem to be especially valuable in portraying the future identity as one in which the employees matter more and in crafting an even stronger sense of who we are and what we stand for. In this vein, Petrou et al. (2015) showed that employees' responses to visionary communication during times of change may depend on their regulatory focus (Higgins, 1997). More particularly, they found that prevention-focused employees are likely to respond more positively to communication that aligns with their (prevention-focused) orientation, suggesting that leaders may want to target or frame change communication according to the needs and orientations of their followers. In this way, leaders can use a form of identity impresarioship to better address the potential gains of the change for their followers.

Further, Seyranian (2014) examined how leaders can use a set of social identity framing strategies to enrich their change communication and foster follower support for change. Seyranian's analysis showed that the use of inclusive language in change communication was especially valuable in enhancing followers' willingness to support collective action, while leaders could facilitate self-esteem within the group by using positive social identity language connected with the vision of the change. As this empirical study reveals, targeted communication strategies may thus be critical leadership tools in enhancing employees' perceptions of positive identity gain and in mobilizing follower action and support for organizational change.

Another example of this pathway is provided in a field study conducted during a merger between water control boards in the Netherlands in 2005 (Giessner, 2011). The research predicted and found that those employees who experienced a low sense of continuity would still identify with the post-merger organization if they perceived a necessity to merge. The main explanation as to why this is the case is that perceived necessity increases feelings of uncertainty in the current situation and provides a justification for a better future organizational situation. In other words, it enhances perceptions of identity gain. Thus, through identity entrepreneurship, leaders can craft a positive future by portraying the current situation as unfavorable, and the change as a way to advance future gains.

While research into the other two dimensions (i.e., identity prototypicality and identity advancement) has been less common, there is reason to believe that these behaviors may also enhance perceptions of identity gain. For instance, if leaders act as role models for the new organization and champion the rights of group members in the (changed) organization, then followers may develop a greater appreciation of the identity gains that may be accrued from the proposed change.

12.4.3   A Multi-identity Pathway Perspective on Leading Change

While we have so far focused on organizational identity and identification as central to leading change from a social identity approach, research attention has recently turned to understanding how employees' identification with other workplace foci – such as the team or occupation – may shape their reactions to major change. Crucially, while the organization's identity may be fundamentally altered by a large-scale structural change, the occupational identity may represent a source of continuity during a change event. Accordingly, Kroon and Noorderhaven (2018) showed that employees' occupational identification was positively associated with their willingness to cooperate with others in a post-merger organization. Moreover, this relationship was even stronger when individuals wore the same uniform throughout the integration process, conferring a sense of identity continuity over the course of the change.

While occupational identity was shown to act as a source of continuity in the focal case, it may be expected that other (higher/lower order) identities could play a similar role in other circumstances. For example, if an individual strongly identifies with his or her team then this could provide an alternative source of identity continuity or gain throughout the change period. In fact, previous research suggests that these lower-order identities like the team or work group may be even stronger predictors of organizational attitudes and behavior than higher-order identities such as the organization or occupation (van Knippenberg & van Schie, 2000). One way in which leaders can reduce feelings of uncertainty and threat is, thus, to evoke other workplace identities that represent sources of stability and certainty in times of change or that provide a road to identity gain. Consequently, we suggest that, as well as focusing on the organization, leaders can enact the identity management behaviors highlighted above to manage different (team, occupational) identity foci and, in doing so, increase feelings of stability and/or identity gain during the change process. This multi-dimensional, multi-identity perspective therefore provides a socially embedded and evidence-based view on how to manage organizational change.

In Figure 12.2, we provide a visual summary of the pathways a social identity approach might offer for leading change. Here we consider that leaders can focus on different behaviors and foci of identity to establish continuity or identity gains, thus facilitating employee adjustment during change processes.

12.5   Are Many Heads Better than One? Considering Leadership in the Plural and Identity Management

So far, our perspective – as most perspectives on leadership – has offered a classical, hierarchical view on leadership within organizations: One leader

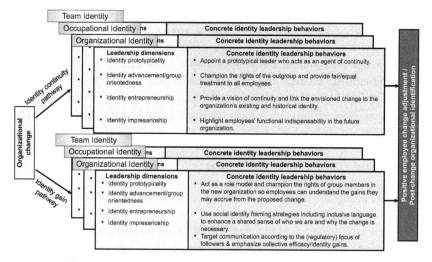

Figure 12.2   A multi-identity pathway model on leading change

is leading a group of employees and there are sublayers of leaders within this pyramid. The effectiveness of such a leadership approach depends, therefore, very much on the qualities of the formal leader (Hogan & Kaiser, 2005). However, the increasing complexity of the decisions to be taken, the tasks to be solved, and the diversity of the workforces to be represented by the leader may imply some shortcomings of solely representing leadership as a vertical, one leader model (Yukl, 2010; Denis et al., 2012; Clegg et al., 2021). As a consequence, there has increasingly been a focus on horizontal forms of leadership involving more than one individual in the leader role. The scientific literature has used different terminologies to refer to this, like shared leadership (Pearce & Conger, 2003), distributed leadership (Gronn, 2002), and complexity leadership (Uhl-Bien & Marion, 2009). A general term to summarize all of these approaches might be "leadership in the plural," as all of these approaches focus on the "combined influence of multiple leaders in specific organizational situations" (Denis et al., 2012, p. 211).

Such plural forms of leadership have also started to be considered in the context of organizational change (Heck & Hallinger, 2010; Canterino et al., 2020; By, 2021). In a way, a focus on leadership in the plural might provide a more realistic perspective on how complex organizations and complex change processes are actually led and implemented (Mulder et al., 2020). Indeed, even at the CEO-level of organizations, there are numerous examples of companies having more than one leader – like Netflix and DSM currently or Salesforce.com, SAP, and Oracle previously. We do not argue here that having multiple leaders has only advantages. It also involves risk and implies a lot of work (Denis et al., 2012; Mulder et al., 2020). But we want to suggest that a consideration of leadership in the plural offers a valuable perspective on understanding leadership in complex situations (Fransen et al., 2020) and it is, therefore, also important to consider this for organizational change.

Social identity researchers have begun to consider the value of such a leadership model. For instance, Fransen et al. (2020) developed a 5R Shared Leadership Program for sport leaders. The main focus here is on applying principles of the social identity approach to a team of leaders. The program focuses on establishing a consensual support for leaders and on the sharing (or distribution) of leadership roles within sport teams. Given that this can be considered as the first step of a social identity approach on multiple leadership, we will only provide some issues to be considered for future research on identity management for organizational change in the context of multiple leadership.

We discussed the importance of a leader being group prototypical (i.e., identity prototypicality) in Section 12.4. While the principle of prototypicality has so far been primarily applied to one leader, it may also be applied to a group of leaders. The advantage here is that multiple leaders might be better able to represent a diverse organization. Further, a multiple leadership team might actually be of value in establishing continuity by ensuring that one leader represents a connection between the past and the present while, at the same time, other leaders personify the change. Multiple leaders might also be better positioned to engage in various identity advancement actions, showing that they are doing it for the employees and the organization. In addition, it seems possible to apply identity impresarioship and identity entrepreneurship behaviors to a team of leaders.

However, it should be noted that there may be challenges in ensuring that a multiple leadership group is capable of providing coherent identity management (cf. Fransen et al., 2020) and in quickly adjusting to circumstances and demands over time (cf. Mulder et al., 2020). Leadership in the plural would certainly require initial identity development within the leadership team before it has the chance to function well. We recommend that future research on the social identity approach to leadership thus pays greater attention to leadership in the plural and to the opportunities and challenges that this may offer for employee adjustment to change.

12.6   To Conclude

A social identity perspective on leadership offers a valuable approach to managing change. In this vein, we present a multi-identity pathway model, which outlines how through identity prototypicality, advancement, entrepreneurship, and impresarioship, leaders can facilitate identity continuity and gain pathways and, in doing so, enhance employees' acceptance and support for change. These pathways may be applied to multiple identities within the organizational context. Furthermore, we suggest that, as organizational change is often a complex process, having more than one leader involved in leading change might be a valuable alternative to the classic "one-leader" approach that has dominated past research on change. While the principles of our social identity perspective can certainly be applied to such a scenario, more theorizing and research is needed to develop concrete suggestions on how such an approach could be applied in practice.

REFERENCES

Agote, L., Aramburu, N., & Lines, R. (2016). Authentic leadership perception, trust in the leader, and followers' emotions in organizational change processes. *The Journal of Applied Behavioral Science, 52*(1), 35–63.

Aitken, K., & von Treuer, K. (2021). Leadership behaviours that foster organisational identification during change. *Journal of Organizational Change Management, 34*(2) 311–326.

Antonakis, J., Cianciolo, A. T., & Sternberg R. J (2004). Leadership: Past, present, and future. In J. Antonakis, A. T. Cianciolo, and R. J. Sternberg (eds.), *The nature of leadership* (pp. 3–15). Thousand Oaks, CA: Sage Publications, Inc.

Ashforth, B. E., & Mael, F. (1989). Social identity theory and the organization. *Academy of Management Review, 14*(1), 20–39.

Avolio, B. J., & Bass, B. M. (1995). Individual consideration viewed at multiple levels of analysis: A multi-level framework for examining the diffusion of transformational leadership. *The Leadership Quarterly, 6*(2), 199–218.

Babić, V. M., Savović, S. D., & Domanović, V. M. (2014). Transformational leadership and post-acquisition performance in transitional economies. *Journal of Organizational Change Management, 27*(6), 856–876.

Bass, B. M. (1985). *Leadership and performance beyond expectations.* New York: Free Press.

Bayraktar, S., & Jiménez, A. (2020). Self-efficacy as a resource: A moderated mediation model of transformational leadership, extent of change and reactions to change. *Journal of Organizational Change Management, 33*(2), 301–317.

Beer, M., Eisenstat, R. A., & Spector, B. (1990). Why change programs don't produce change. *Harvard Business Review, 68*(6), 158–166.

Belschak, F. D., Jacobs, G., Giessner, S. R., Horton, K. E., & Bayerl, P. S. (2020). When the going gets tough: Employee reactions to large-scale organizational change and the role of employee Machiavellianism. *Journal of Organizational Behavior, 41*(9), 830–850

Bobbio, A., van Knippenberg, D., & van Knippenberg, B. (2005). Leading change: Two empirical studies from a social identity theory of leadership perspective. *Poster presented at the EAESP medium sized meeting "Academy colloquium on social identity in organizations".* Amsterdam, The Netherlands, June.

Burnes, B. (1996). No such thing as . . . a "one best way" to manage organizational change. *Management Decision, 34*(10), 11–18.

By, R. T. (2007). Ready or not . . . *Journal of Change Management, 7*(1), 3–11.

(2021). Leadership: In pursuit of purpose. *Journal of Change Management, 21* (1), 30–44.

Campbell, D. T. (1958). Common fate, similarity, and other indices of the status of aggregates of persons as social entities. *Behavioral Science, 3*(1), 14–25.

Canterino, F., Cirella, S., Piccoli, B., & Shani, A. B. R. (2020). Leadership and change mobilization: The mediating role of distributed leadership. *Journal of Business Research, 108*, 42–51.

Carter, M. Z., Armenakis, A. A., Feild, H. S., & Mossholder, K. W. (2013). Transformational leadership, relationship quality, and employee performance during continuous incremental organizational change. *Journal of Organizational Behavior, 34*(7), 942–958.

Clegg, S., Crevani, L., Uhl-Bien, M., & By, R. T. (2021). Changing leadership in changing times. *Journal of Change Management, 21*(1), 1–13.

Conger, J. A., & Kanungo, R. N. (1987). Towards a behavioral theory of charismatic leadership in organizational settings. *Academy of Management Review, 12*(4), 637–647.

Cooke, F. L., Wood, G., Wang, M., & Li, A. S. (2021). Riding the tides of mergers and acquisitions by building a resilient workforce: A framework for studying the role of human resource management. *Human Resource Management Review, 31*(3), 100747.

Cummings, S., Bridgman, T., & Brown, K. G. (2016). Unfreezing change as three steps: Rethinking Kurt Lewin's legacy for change management. *Human Relations, 69*(1), 33–60.

De Sousa, M. J. C., & van Dierendonck, D. (2014). Servant leadership and engagement in a merge process under high uncertainty. *Journal of Organizational Change Management, 27*(6), 877–899.

Demers, C., Giroux, N., & Chreim, S. (2003). Merger and acquisition announcements as corporate wedding narratives. *Journal of Organizational Change Management, 16*(2), 223–242.

Denis, J. L., Langley, A., & Sergi, V. (2012). Leadership in the plural. *Academy of Management Annals, 6*(1), 211–283.

van Dick, R., Hirst, G., Grojean, M. W., & Wieseke, J. (2007). Relationships between leader and follower organizational identification and implications for follower attitudes and behaviour. *Journal of Occupational and Organizational Psychology*, *80*(1), 133–150.

van Dick, R., Lemoine, J. E., Steffens, N. K., Kerschreiter, R., Akfirat, S. A., Avanzi, L., et al. (2018). Identity leadership going global: Validation of the Identity Leadership Inventory across 20 countries. *Journal of Occupational and Organizational Psychology*, *91*(4), 697–728.

van Dick, R., Ullrich, J., & Tissington, P. A. (2006). Working under a black cloud: How to sustain organizational identification after a merger. *British Journal of Management*, *17*(S1), S69–S79.

Dinh, J. E., Lord, R. G., Gardner, W. L., Meuser, J. D., Liden, R. C., & Hu, J. (2014). Leadership theory and research in the new millennium: Current theoretical trends and changing perspectives. *The Leadership Quarterly*, *25*(1), 36–62.

Drzensky, F., & van Dick, R. (2013). Organizational identification and organizational change. In S. Oreg, A. Michel, & R. T. By (eds.), *The psychology of organizational change: Viewing change from the employee's perspective* (pp. 275–297). Cambridge: Cambridge University Press.

Duck, J. M., & Fielding, K. S. (2003). Leaders and their treatment of subgroups: Implications for evaluations of the leader and the superordinate group. *European Journal of Social Psychology*, *33*(3), 387–401.

Dutton, J. E., Dukerich, J. M., & Harquail, C. V. (1994). Organizational images and member identification. *Administrative Science Quarterly*, *39*(2), 239–263.

Ekvall, G., & Arvonen, J. (1991). Change-centered leadership: An extension of the two-dimensional model. *Scandinavian Journal of Management*, *7*(1), 17–26.

Elstak, M. N., Bhatt, M., van Riel, C. B. M., Pratt, M. G., & Berens, G. A. J. M. (2015). Organizational identification during a merger: The role of self-enhancement and uncertainty reduction motives during a major organizational change. *Journal of Management Studies*, *52*(1), 32–62.

Faupel, S., & Süß, S. (2019). The effect of transformational leadership on employees during organizational change: An empirical analysis. *Journal of Change Management*, *19*(3), 145–166.

Fiedler, F. E. (1964). Contingency model of leadership effectiveness. *Advances in Experimental Social Psychology*, *1*, 149–190.

Fleishman, E. A. (1953). The description of supervisory behavior. *Journal of Applied Psychology*, *37*(1), 1–6.

Fransen, K., Haslam, S. A., Steffens, N. K., Peters, K., Mallett, C. J., Mertens, N., & Boen, F. (2020). All for us and us for all: Introducing the 5R shared leadership program. *Psychology of Sport and Exercise*, *51*, 101762.

Giessner, S. R. (2011). Is the merger necessary? The interactive effect of perceived necessity and sense of continuity on post-merger identification. *Human Relations*, *64*(8), 1079–1098.

Giessner, S. R., Dawson, J., Horton, K. E., & West, M. (2023). The impact of supportive leadership on employee outcomes during organizational mergers: An organizational-level field study. *Journal of Applied Psychology*, *108*(4), 686–697.

Giessner, S. R., Horton, K. E., & Humborstad, S. I. W. (2016). Identity management during organizational mergers: Empirical insights and practical advice. *Social Issues and Policy Review*, *10*(1), 47–81.

Giessner, S. R., van Knippenberg, D., van Ginkel, W., & Sleebos, E. (2013). Team-oriented leadership: The interactive effects of leader group prototypicality, accountability, and team identification. *Journal of Applied Psychology*, *98*(4), 658.

Giessner, S. R., Ullrich, J., & van Dick, R. (2011). Social identity and corporate mergers. *Social and Personality Psychology Compass*, *5*(6), 333–345.

Gill, C. (2012). The role of leadership in successful international mergers and acquisitions: Why Renault–Nissan succeeded and DaimlerChrysler–Mitsubishi failed. *Human Resource Management*, *51*(3), 433–456.

Gilley, A., McMillan, H. S., & Gilley, J. W. (2009). Organizational change and characteristics of leadership effectiveness. *Journal of Leadership & Organizational Studies*, *16*(1), 38–47.

Gronn, P. (2002). Distributed leadership as a unit of analysis. *Leadership Quarterly*, *13*(4), 423–451.

Groves, K. S. (2005). Linking leader skills, follower attitudes, and contextual variables via an integrated model of charismatic leadership. *Journal of Management*, *31*(2), 255–277.

Hamilton, D. L., & Sherman, S. J. (1996). Perceiving persons and groups. *Psychological Review*, *103*(2), 336–355.

Haslam, C., Haslam, S. A., Jetten, J., Cruwys, T., & Steffens, N. K. (2021). Life change, social identity, and health. *Annual Review of Psychology*, *72*, 635–661.

Haslam, S. A., & Platow, M. J. (2001). The link between leadership and followership: How affirming social identity translates vision into action. *Personality and Social Psychology Bulletin*, *27*(11), 1469–1479.

Haslam, S. A., Reicher, S. D., & Platow, M. J. (2011). *The new psychology of leadership: Identity, influence and power*. Oxon: Psychology Press.

Heck, R. H., & Hallinger, P. (2010). Testing a longitudinal model of distributed leadership effects on school improvement. *The Leadership Quarterly*, *21*(5), 867–885.

Henricks, M. D., Young, M., & Kehoe, E. J. (2020). Attitudes toward change and transformational leadership: A longitudinal study. *Journal of Change Management*, *20*(3), 202–219.

Herold, D. M., Fedor, D. B., Caldwell, S., & Liu, Y. (2008). The effects of transformational and change leadership on employees' commitment to a change: A multilevel study. *Journal of Applied Psychology*, *93*(2), 346.

Higgins, E. T. (1997). Beyond pleasure and pain. *American Psychologist*, *52*(12), 1280–1300.

Hogan, R., & Kaiser, R. B. (2005). What we know about leadership. *Review of General Psychology*, *9*(2), 169–180.

Hogg, M. A. (2000). Subjective uncertainty reduction through self-categorization: A motivational theory of social identity processes. *European Review of Social Psychology*, *11*(1), 223–255.

(2001). A social identity theory of leadership. *Personality and Social Psychology Review*, *5*(3), 184–200.

(2007). Uncertainty-identity theory. In M. P. Zanna (ed.), *Advances in experimental social psychology*, vol. 39 (pp. 69–126). San Diego: Academic Press.

Hogg, M. A., & Abrams, D. (1990). Social motivation, self-esteem and social identity. In D. Abrams & M. A. Hogg (eds.), *Social identity theory: Constructive and critical advances* (pp. 28–47). New York: Harvester Wheatsheaf.

Hogg, M. A., Sherman, D. K., Dierselhuis, J., Maitner, A. T., & Moffitt, G. (2007). Uncertainty, entitativity, and group identification. *Journal of Experimental Social Psychology*, *43*(1), 135–142.

Hogg, M. A., & Terry, D. J. (2000). The dynamic, diverse, and variable faces of organizational identity. *Academy of Management Review*, *25*(1), 150–152.

Hollander, E. P. (1964). *Leaders, groups, and influence*. New York: Oxford University Press.

Hughes, M. (2016). Leading changes: Why transformation explanations fail. *Leadership*, *12*(4), 449–469.

Jetten, J., Duck, J., Terry, D. J., & O'Brien, A. (2002). Being attuned to intergroup differences in mergers: The role of aligned leaders for low-status groups. *Personality and Social Psychology Bulletin*, *28*(9), 1194–1201.

Jetten, J., Haslam, C., & Alexander, S. H. (eds.) (2012). *The social cure: Identity, health and well-being*. New York: Psychology Press.

Jetten, J., Hogg, M. A., & Mullin, B. A. (2000). In-group variability and motivation to reduce subjective uncertainty. *Group Dynamics: Theory, Research, and Practice*, *4*(2), 184–198.

Kanter, R. M., Stein, B. A., & Jick, T. D. (1992). *The challenge of organizational change*. New York: Free Press.

van Knippenberg, D., & Hogg, M. A. (2003). A social identity model of leadership effectiveness in organizations. *Research in Organizational Behavior*, *25*, 243–295.

van Knippenberg, B., & van Knippenberg, D. (2005). Leader self-sacrifice and leadership effectiveness: The moderating rle of leader prototypicality. *Journal of Applied Psychology*, *90*(1), 25–37.

van Knippenberg, D., van Knippenberg, B., & Bobbio, A. (2008). Leaders as agents of continuity: Self continuity and resistance to collective change. In F. Sani (ed.), *Self-continuity: Individual and collective perspectives* (pp. 175–186). New York: Psychology Press.

van Knippenberg, D., & van Leeuwen, E. (2001). Organizational identity after a merger: Sense of continuity as the key to post-merger identification. In M.

A. Hogg & D. J. Terry (eds.), *Social identity processes in organizational contexts* (pp. 249–264). Philadelphia, PA: Psychology Press.

van Knippenberg, D., & van Schie, E. C. (2000). Foci and correlates of organizational identification. *Journal of Occupational and Organizational Psychology*, *73*(2), 137–147.

van Knippenberg, D., & Sitkin, S. B. (2013). A critical assessment of charismatic–transformational leadership research: Back to the drawing board? *Academy of Management Annals*, *7*(1), 1–60.

Kotter, J. P. (1996). *Leading change*. Boston, MA: Harvard Business Review Press.

Kouzes, J. M., & Posner, B. Z. (1987). *The leadership challenge: How to get extraordinary things done in organizations*. San Francisco: Jossey-Bass.

Kroon, D. P., & Noorderhaven, N. G. (2018). The role of occupational identification during post-merger integration. *Group & Organization Management*, *43*(2), 207–244.

Kroon, D. P., & Reif, H. (2023). The role of emotions in middle managers' sensemaking and sensegiving practices during post-merger integration. *Group & Organization Management*, *48*(3), 790–832

Levay, C. (2010). Charismatic leadership in resistance to change. *The Leadership Quarterly*, *21*(1), 127–143.

Lewin, K. (1947). Group decision and social change. In: T. M. Newcomb & E. L. Hartley (eds.), *Readings in social psychology* (pp. 330–344), New York: Henry Holt.

Liang, S., Lupina-Wegener, A., Ullrich, J., & van Dick, R. (2022). "Change is our continuity": Chinese managers' construction of post-merger identification after an acquisition in Europe. *Journal of Change Management*, *22* (1), 59–78.

Lundmark, R., Hasson, H., von Thiele Schwarz, U., Hasson, D., & Tafvelin, S. (2017). Leading for change: Line managers' influence on the outcomes of an occupational health intervention. *Work & Stress*, *31*(3), 276–296.

Lupina-Wegener, A. A., Liang, S., van Dick, R., & Ullrich, J. (2020). Multiple organizational identities and change in ambivalence: The case of a Chinese acquisition in Europe. *Journal of Organizational Change Management*, *33*(7), 1253–1275.

Lyons, J. B., Swindler, S. D., & Offner, A. (2009). The impact of leadership on change readiness in the US military. *Journal of Change Management*, *9*(4), 459–475.

Metwally, D., Ruiz-Palomino, P., Metwally, M., & Gartzia, L. (2019). How ethical leadership shapes employees' readiness to change: the mediating role of an organizational culture of effectiveness. *Frontiers in Psychology*, *10*, 2493.

Mühlemann, N., Steffens, N. K., Ullrich, J., Haslam, S. A., & Jonas, K. (2022). Understanding responses to an organizational takeover: Introducing the social identity model of organizational change. *Journal of Personality and Social Psychology*, *123*(5), 1004–1023.

Mulder, F., Giessner, S. R., & Caldas, M. (2020). Leadership: Why many heads are better than one. *RSM Discovery – Management Knowledge*, *38*, 16–18.

Neves, P., Almeida, P., & Velez, M. J. (2018). Reducing intentions to resist future change: Combined effects of commitment-based HR practices and ethical leadership. *Human Resource Management*, *57*(1), 249–261.

Oreg, S., & Berson, Y. (2011). Leadership and employees' reactions to change: The role of leaders' personal attributes and transformational leadership style. *Personnel Psychology*, *64*(3), 627–659.

(2019). Leaders' impact on organizational change: Bridging theoretical and methodological chasms. *Academy of Management Annals*, *13*(1), 272–307.

Oreg, S., Vakola, M., & Armenakis, A. (2011). Change recipients' reactions to organizational change: A 60-year review of quantitative studies. *The Journal of Applied Behavioral Science*, *47*(4), 461–524.

Paulsen, N., Callan, V. J., Ayoko, O., & Saunders, D. (2013). Transformational leadership and innovation in an R&D organization experiencing major change. *Journal of Organizational Change Management*, *26*(3), 595–610.

Pearce, C. L., & Conger, J. A. (2003). *Shared leadership: Reframing the hows and whys of leadership*. London: Sage publications.

Petrou, P., Demerouti, E., & Häfner, M. (2015). When fit matters more: The effect of regulatory fit on adaptation to change. *European Journal of Work and Organizational Psychology*, *24*(1), 126–142.

Rast III, D. E., Hogg, M. A., & Giessner, S. R. (2016). Who trusts charismatic leaders who champion change? The role of group identification, membership centrality, and self-uncertainty. *Group Dynamics: Theory, Research, and Practice*, *20*(4), 259.

Reicher, S. D., & Hopkins, N. (1996a). Seeking influence through characterizing self-categories: An analysis of anti-abortionist rhetoric. *British Journal of Social Psychology*, *35*, 297–311.

(1996b). Self-category constructions in political rhetoric: An analysis of Thatcher's and Kinnock's speeches concerning the British miners' strike (1984–5). *European Journal of Social Psychology*, *26*, 353–371.

Reicher, S., & Hopkins, N. (2001). *Self and nation*. London: Sage.

Riketta, M. (2005). Organizational identification: A meta-analysis. *Journal of Vocational Behavior*, *66*(2), 358–384.

Riketta, M., & van Dick, R. (2005). Foci of attachment in organizations: A meta-analytic comparison of the strength and correlates of workgroup versus organizational identification and commitment. *Journal of Vocational Behavior*, *67*(3), 490–510.

Rosa, M., Giessner, S., Guerra, R., Waldzus, S., Kersting, A. M., Veličković, K., & Collins, E. C. (2020). They (don't) need us: Functional indispensability impacts perceptions of representativeness and commitment when lower-status groups go through an intergroup merger. *Frontiers in Psychology*, *10*, 2772.

Seyranian, V. (2014). Social identity framing communication strategies for mobilizing social change. *The Leadership Quarterly*, *25*(3), 468–486.

Seyranian, V., & Bligh, M. C. (2008). Presidential charismatic leadership: Exploring the rhetoric of social change. *The Leadership Quarterly, 19*(1), 54–76.

Shamir, B. (1999). Leadership in boundaryless organizations: Disposable or indispensable? *European Journal of Work and Organizational Psychology, 8* (1), 49–71.

Shamir, B., House, R. J., & Arthur, M. B. (1993). The motivational effects of charismatic leadership: A self-concept based theory. *Organization Science, 4* (4), 577–594.

Shin, J., Taylor, M. S., & Seo, M.-G. (2012). Resources for change: The relationships of organizational inducements and psychological resilience to employees' attitudes and behaviors towards organizational change. *Academy of Management Journal, 55*(3), 727–748.

Sitkin, S. B., & Pablo, A. L. (2005). The neglected importance of leadership in mergers and acquisitions. In G. K. Stahl & M. E. Mendenhall (eds.), *Mergers and acquisitions: Managing culture and human resources* (pp. 208–223). Stanford, CA: Stanford University Press.

Slater, M. J., Evans, A. L., & Turner, M. J. (2016). Implementing a social identity approach for effective change management. *Journal of Change Management, 16*(1), 18–37.

Stam, D., Lord, R. G., Knippenberg, D. V., & Wisse, B. (2014). An image of who we might become: Vision communication, possible selves, and vision pursuit. *Organization Science, 25*(4), 1172–1194.

Steffens, N. K., Haslam, S. A., Reicher, S. D., Platow, M. J., Fransen, K., Yang, J., et al. (2014). Leadership as social identity management: Introducing the Identity Leadership Inventory (ILI) to assess and validate a four-dimensional model. *The Leadership Quarterly, 25*(5), 1001–1024.

Steigenberger, N. (2017). The challenge of integration: A review of the M&A integration literature. *International Journal of Management Reviews, 19*(4), 408–431.

Stouten, J., Rousseau, D. M., & De Cremer, D. (2018). Successful organizational change: Integrating the management practice and scholarly literatures. *Academy of Management Annals, 12*(2), 752–788.

Tajfel, H., & Turner, J. C. (1986). The social identity theory of intergroup behaviour. In S. Worchel & W. G. Austin (eds.), *Psychology of intergroup relations* (pp. 7–24). Chicago: Nelson-Hall.

Turner, J. C., Hogg, M. A., Oakes, P. J., Reicher, S. D., & Wetherell, M. S. (1987). *Rediscovering the social group: A self-categorization theory*. Oxford: Blackwell.

Uhl-Bien, M., & Marion, R. (2009). Complexity leadership in bureaucratic forms of organizing: A meso model. *The Leadership Quarterly, 20*(4), 631–650.

Ullrich, J., Wieseke, J., & van Dick, R. (2005). Continuity and change in mergers and acquisitions: A social identity case study of a German industrial merger. *Journal of Management Studies, 42*(8), 1549–1569.

Venus, M., Stam, D., & van Knippenberg, D. (2019). Visions of change as visions of continuity. *Academy of Management Journal*, *62*(3), 667–690.

Waldman, D. A., & Javidan, M. (2009). Alternative forms of charismatic leadership in the integration of mergers and acquisitions. *The Leadership Quarterly*, *20*(2), 130–142.

Yukl, G. (2008). How leaders influence organizational effectiveness. *The Leadership Quarterly*, *19*(6), 708–722.

  (2010). *Leadership in organizations* (7th ed.). New York: Prentice Hall.

PART VI

Conclusions and Commentary

CHAPTER 13

Commentary
Developments in the Recognition of Crucial Roles of Change Dynamics

Jean M. Bartunek

The first edition of *The Psychology of Organizational Change* (Oreg et al., 2013) was quite novel in focusing on change from the perspective of the employee, the recipient of change. As anyone remotely connected with the study – or experience – of organizational change knows, both scholarly and practitioner emphasis regarding organizational change has tended to be much more on change agents, what they do right, as opposed to what change recipients do that is not right (aka resistance) for accomplishing change. Even when the same people, such as senior managers in multinational organizations, play both change agent and change recipient roles (e.g. Balogun et al., 2015), there are differences in how others expect them to act in each role.

Since that volume was published there has been scholarly attention to a variety of dimensions of planned organizational change. In particular, there has been more attention to change processes and dynamics, not just individual or organizational outcomes of prespecified change initiatives. So, I have been looking forward to reading these chapters in order to get some sense of what has evolved in the understanding of how planned change is experienced by those who did not initiate it.

This volume extends the work of the earlier one. It focuses somewhat less attention on outcomes of particular change initiatives and more on their antecedents, including the psychological mechanisms or dynamics that take place during the course of change. Like the prior volume it focuses on planned change, but the types of planned change it includes are considerably varied, and the dynamics it includes have sometimes eluded attention from others. Thus, it makes some valuable new contributions that go beyond the initial volume, in particular in showing the importance of mediators of relationships between initiating factors and outcomes of change, drawing attention to such dynamics more than before.

Each chapter is worth reading on its own, and there are many themes cross-cutting sets of chapters. Further, several of the chapters involve their own data gathering, which is a highlight of this edition.

For this concluding chapter, I have created Table 13.1, which outlines the focus of each chapter, its core dynamics, and the outcomes it addresses. In the following sections, I will address some of the themes that are particularly salient within and across chapters. These are:

1. Types of organizational changes, Chapters 5 and 6.
2. The importance of change leaders, Chapters 11 and 12.
3. The development of change leaders, Chapters 9 and 10.
4. The importance of affective processes in change, Chapters 2 and 4.
5. The importance of sensemaking and cognitive processes in change, Chapter 9.
6. The importance of identity processes in change, Chapters 7, 8, and 12.
7. The importance of temporal processes in change, Chapter 3.

13.1   Themes Addressed in the Chapters

While some of these themes overlap some with themes from the original volume, when this is the case, they expand the discussion. Some of the themes here did not receive much attention at all in the prior volume. In addition, while the prior volume focuses more on outcomes of changes, the chapters in this volume focus more on multiple types of change dynamics. Finally, some processes (such as sensemaking) are alluded to in multiple chapters, although they receive primary attention in a smaller number of chapters. I will discuss each of the themes named by focusing on their discussion in a small number of chapters in which they are particularly salient.

13.1.1   Types of Changes

Certainly, there are many types of changes alluded to in the chapters. However, there are two chapters that categorize different types of changes in particularly valuable ways. My focus will be on the innovative categorization processes used in these chapters.

In Chapter 5, Van Ruysseveldt, van Dam, De Witte, and Nikolova addressed how employee responses to changes in their organizations depend on core characteristics of multiple types of change. The authors did a particularly ingenious job of creating categories of changes. In

Table 13.1 Chapters, their main emphases, dynamics addressed, and outcomes of change

Chapter	Main emphasis	Dynamics addressed	Outcomes of change
2. Neves	Review literature on resistance and its predictors, including intentions to resist change	Change history, individual differences, leadership, organization	Intent to resist future change
3. Belschak & Jacobs	Temporal dimensions of change	Time-related aspects of change, including phase models	Positive and/or negative change outcomes that may evolve over time
4. Rafferty Troth, & Jordan	Review literature on emotional responses to organizational change	The multiple roles of differing types of emotions	Emotional responses that affect change success and failure
5. Van Ruysseveldt, van Dam, De Witte, & Nikolova	How types of change affect employee responses to change	The roles of growth, decline, and low and high innovation during change	Emotional exhaustion and active learning
6. Gonzalez & Kanitz	Impacts of types of technological change on employee responses	The roles of cognitive perspectives, stress and coping perspectives, leader behaviors, and antecedent response relationships	Work-related outcomes (e.g., perception of job characteristics, job satisfaction, job performance, job insecurity); personal outcomes (stress, anxiety)
7. Lupina-Wegener, van Dick, & Liang	Identification processes and identity leader process during M&A	Roles of identity, cultural factors, and political contexts in identification change during M&A	Failed merger
8. Liang, van Dick, Ullrich, & Lupina-Wegener	Social identity processes during Chinese–European M&A	Criticism during acquisitions; Characteristics of (changing) organizational identity of both acquiring and acquired organization	Intergroup Sensitivity effects; attitudes toward an acquisition; coping with acquisition-related change

Table 13.1 (*cont.*)

Chapter	Main emphasis	Dynamics addressed	Outcomes of change
9. Abildgaard, Nielsen, & Olsen	The impact of change management training on managers competencies and sense-making for change	The importance of both individual and shared sensemaking	Learnings about others' change perceptions, about making sense of one's own role in change, and about change management competence
10. Hastings, Bouckenooghe, & Schwarz	The development of mindset activation theory	The development of links between desired leadership behaviors in both top down and bottom up change initiatives	More or less successful change outcomes
11. Meyer & Beletski	Relationships between types of leader behaviors and commitment to change	Employees' change-relevant perceptions and affect mediate relationships between leader behavior and commitment	Commitment to change
12. Giessner & Horton	Social identity perspectives on styles of leading change, especially in M&A	Several dimensions of social identity (e.g., uncertainty identity, identity continuity) play mediating roles	Positive change outcomes

particular, based on extensive quantitative and qualitative literature, the authors identified six types of organizational change, and then further synthesized these using two important and non-mutually exclusive dimensions. This work resulted in a "qualitative" axis representing the degree to which the organization was engaging in process and/or product innovation and a "quantitative" access that distinguished between growth and decline, indicated at least partially by restructuring. These two axes can occur simultaneously. They then focused on how the categories affected two important outcomes of change, employees' emotional exhaustion, and adaptive learning.

Findings of their survey data collection indicated that combinations of characteristics had particularly significant impacts. For example, change that includes decline, restructuring and innovation is most detrimental and leads to high levels of exhaustion and moderate active learning, while combining product innovation and growth leads to relatively low levels of emotional exhaustion and high levels of active learning.

In Chapter 6, Gonzalez and Kanitz synthesized relevant research pertinent to types of technological change. Based on an extensive review, they identified multiple types of technological changes and categorized them based on two dimensions, the scale of change (broad versus narrow), and the degree of change (radical versus incremental). For example, the introduction of organization-wide enterprise planning systems illustrates a broad and radical change, while implementation of an information technology service management system represents a broad and incremental change. Department or division-wide ERP systems represent narrow and radical changes, while new system updates represent narrow and incremental changes. As they say in their chapter, they focused on these dimensions because of their implications for employee psychology, especially because they range in the extent and breadth to which they cause disturbance in the status quo.

These two chapters in particular suggest the value of searching for nonobvious underlying dimensions of types of change, such as levels of effects on the status quo, degree of prevalence of innovation, and degree of growth and/or decline. The types of categorizations may and do vary, but in both cases the categorizations the authors carry out enable deeper understandings of change than does a simple listing of changes. This can have implications for a much more profound understanding of what is going on in organizational change than appears on the surface.

13.1.2   The Importance of Leaders and Change Leaders

As is obvious, change comes about through leaders, whether they be in formal managerial roles, formal change agent roles, and/or in informal change leadership roles (e.g., Farmer, 2017); change cannot occur without some type of initiative. While many chapters discuss change leaders in some capacity, Chapters 11 and 12 emphasize the leadership role.

In Chapter 11, Meyer and Beletski discuss the important role of commitment to change, and emphasize that organizational leaders are likely to play a particularly key part in accomplishing commitment. They note that most scholarship addressing leadership and commitment to change has focused on transformational leadership, although some "new genres" of leadership (such as authentic, ethical, and empowering leadership) have also received attention.

They also note that change leadership includes making strategic decisions about change and communicating them well. These decision-making and communication roles are particularly important with regard to achieving employee commitment to change. For example, change leaders who want to foster commitment need to provide a clear and appealing message, solicit input from employees (where culturally appropriate), and provide the necessary supports for affective and other types of commitment. However, a good deal remains to be learned about the specifics of particular leader behaviors at different times in the change process as well as what is needed to achieve normative and continuance commitment as well as affective commitment.

In Chapter 12, Giessner and Horton (discussed in more detail below) focus on relationships between change leadership and social identity. They raise questions about the value of transformational leadership for some dimensions of change and, instead, focus on social identity, as developed by Tajfel and Turner (1986), which is crucial for leaders to have as a focus.

One of their major emphases is the role of leadership in accomplishing perceptions of identity continuity (van Knippenberg & Hogg, 2003), especially in the midst of change such as mergers and acquisitions. They suggest that leaders who are prototypical, and who embody a group identity, are more likely than others to project perceptions of continuity during change. Indeed, prototypicality is one of four dimensions of identity that leaders should embody during change. Others include identity advancement (group-oriented behavior), identity entrepreneurship (crafting a shared and continuing sense of identity), and, finally, identity impresarioship, which enables finding ways to make a group feel they truly matter, to boost self-esteem. All of these can foster commitment to change.

Finally, they also discuss the importance of visionary leadership by emphasizing a positive vision of how things may improve in the future. Such vision can help employees perceive an identity gain as a result of change.

These chapters focus on some of the crucial roles of leaders in change, roles that are not always the attention of authors like Kotter (2012), who focus much more on tasks. Their work makes clear that there is no one best way for leaders to act and that the approaches leaders take along the paths of change matter considerably.

13.1.3   The Development of Leaders

If managers and other leaders play crucial roles in processes of organizational change, it is important that they lead change skillfully. But this is not always easy to accomplish. Two of the chapters address ways of developing effective change leadership skills in managers and other change leaders.

In Chapter 9, Abildgaard, Nielsen, and Olsen argue that there are multiple tools and approaches that managers must use to initiate and accomplish organizational change well. That is, change managers must develop appropriate change management competencies in areas such as readiness for change, understanding of change, change communication, mobilization of subordinates, and handling resistance. Abildgaard and colleagues present the Change Management Competency Intervention (CMCI), developed by Workz A/S, which makes use of workshops using serious game simulations to develop managers' skill in these competencies.

As the authors summarize, the CMCI includes several days of workshops that foster an understanding and vocabulary for the human side of change management. In particular, the CMCI addresses several change-related topics designed to help deal with resistance to change, understanding different phases of change, and influencing and managing stakeholders.

The authors conducted interviews shortly after a CMCI workshop, and then a longer time after one implementation of the workshop ended to determine its impacts. They found, among other learnings, that the workshop was successful in helping managers learn that change perceptions are situated in particular contexts and are individual, that it was important for them to come to understand their own roles in change, and there was a need for the managers to increase awareness of employee diversity and to improve change communication.

In Chapter 10, Hastings, Bouckenooghe, and Schwarz begin developing a new theory of mindset development for leaders. They introduce mindset activation theory as a means of leader development that can help leaders switch back and forth between fixed and growth mindsets. That is, they link fixed mindsets with top-down approaches to change and growth mindsets with bottom-up approaches to change. They argue that both are necessary, and that the major concern is being able to apply the appropriate mindset based on the type of change that is called for.

Mindsets differ in their assumptions. A fixed mindset assumes that success reflects a level of natural ability, while a growth mindset assumes that success results from the quality of strategies used in a change situation, along with the effort applied, especially efforts to learn. Leaders with a fixed mindset bring a performance orientation with fixed goals to their work. Leaders with a growth mindset emphasizing learning along with openness to ideas. Thus, where they are successful differs.

A fixed mindset is also consistent with episodic temporal framing of change, while a growth mindset is consistent with continuous temporal framing. Those with fixed mindsets manage change as a sequence of activities with fixed goals, while growth mindsets are associated with activities that foster the emergence of new possibilities, including learning from failure. A fixed mindset is also consistent with separation of leaders and followers, while growth mindset leadership fosters ideas arising from everywhere, with leaders acting as facilitators.

Finally, there are several ways a growth mindset can be promoted, including framing a task as a learning outcome, reading materials from a growth mindset perspective, and praising performance through a growth mindset perspective. A fixed mindset can be fostered by framing tasks in terms of performance outcomes, reading materials from a fixed mindset perspective, and praising performance in terms of personal attributes (e.g., "you're so smart").

As these two chapters show, effective change leadership does not just happen. There are ways of developing effective leaders, through training programs and through efforts, however enacted, to foster adaptability. Such programs may often be very important in helping leaders develop skills that would not ordinarily be recognized as crucial in change.

13.1.4 *Affective Processes*

In Chapter 2, Neves develops an updated version of resistance to change and its importance. He discusses predictors of resistance as including change-specific factors, individual-related factors, leadership factors, and organizational factors, and suggests ways that these interact.

Rather than focusing only on resistance to current changes, Neves focuses on intentions to resist future changes, something equivalent (though in the opposite direction) to readiness for change. He notes that individuals learn about the past and present behaviors of other organizational members, and that the history of changes in the organization is particularly important in affecting organizational members' intentions to resist future changes. There are several factors associated with this history, including the perceived value, threat, and information about a possible change (change-specific factors), the degree to which organization members think they can satisfy their needs (individual related factors), ethical and empowering leadership (leadership factors), and psychological safety (organizational factors).

A wide range of emotions is the primary focus of Chapter 4 by Rafferty, Troth, and Jordan, which focuses on developing an integrative framework depicting change recipients' emotional responses to change. Their chapter discusses multiple theories of emotion, including frequently discussed models such as appraisal theory, affective events theory, and the broaden and build theory. They also argue that other theories, such as emotion regulation (Gross, 1998; Gross & John, 2003) and emotional contagion (Kelly, 2001), have not received adequate attention in the change field.

The chapter suggests that structural descriptions of "resistance" to change as simply present or not do not recognize how nuanced change responses actually are. Rather, the authors argue that it is crucial to understand processes and phases of various emotional responses to change. The authors recognize that models of emotional reactions to events have been developed for a large range of events, including an affect infusion model and a transactional model of stress and coping, that affect primary and then secondary appraisals of events, and then have an impact on later emotions.

The authors noted with some concern that most research addressing emotions as mediators between change approaches and responses to change focus almost entirely on the valence of emotions. Only rarely is activation studied, though it is very important (Oreg et al., 2018). Finally, they suggest the importance of emotional intelligence on the part of both change leaders and change recipients. This is an ability that change recipients can develop that is positively associated with workplace wellbeing.

These two chapters carry out important tasks in emphasizing the importance of emotions in change. For many years, resistance was largely the only emotion and related action considered. It is crucial that more emotions and their roles be appreciated even while it is still important to recognize the importance of resistance.

13.1.5   Cognitive Factors, Especially Sensemaking

Although sensemaking and the larger issues of cognitive frames were not the only foci of any of the chapters, related terms were mentioned in almost all of the chapters. Two of the chapters, Chapters 6 and 9, discuss this topic in comparative detail. They do so in relation, respectively, to varieties of technological change and change management training for managers.

In Chapter 6, Gonzalez and Kanitz discuss several cognitive perspectives that explain how and why new technologies are accepted and used. They focus in particular on two models, the Technology Acceptance Model (TAM) and its extensions and the Unified Theory of Acceptance and Use of Technology (UTAUT). TAM focuses on two cognitive factors in the implementation of new technology: perceived ease of use and usefulness. UTAUT focuses on four key factors (performance expectancy, effort expectancy, social influence, and facilitating conditions) that predict behavioral intention and, ultimately, actual technology use.

In Chapter 9, Abildgaard, Nielsen, & Olsen discuss sensemaking as the appropriate theoretical framework for analyzing the development of change competencies in the change management competency intervention (CMCI). The authors note that concepts of sensemaking have regularly been applied to both the creation and understanding of change processes and note several reasons for using it to attend to this intervention. This is because sensemaking emphasizes ongoing interactions between perception and enactment, is both an ongoing and retrospective process, emphasizes the importance of identity and self-perception, and takes into account collective processes of making sense of situations.

The role of cognitive processes in change has been recognized for some time. Chapters such as these and others in the text that speak to these processes remind us of their continuing importance.

13.1.6   Identity Processes

Three of the chapters focus on multiple types of identity processes. Chapter 7, by Lupina-Wegener, van Dick, and Liang, addresses social identity and identification change in cross-border mergers and acquisitions, especially as this is affected by the identity leadership of the chairman of the acquiring company. They present a case study of the acquisition of a European company by a Chinese company and describe several identity-related problems that occurred during the course of the acquisition.

They note that organizational identification involves the perception of the "sharedness" of a particular organizational identity, but such perceptions are very difficult to maintain during acquisitions. This is particularly the case when members of acquired organizations try to determine where they fit in the new organization, and even more likely when the acquiring company is from a particular national culture that differs considerably from the national culture of the company that is acquired. Thus, identity leadership, which comprises identity prototypicality, identity advancement, identity entrepreneurship, and identity impresarioship (these are also recognized in Chapter 12), is particularly important during such acquisitions. Such leadership affects the perceived congruence and continuity of an organization's identity during the course of the changes.

Lupina-Wegener et al.'s case study identified the different pre-merger identities and contexts of the companies, which by definition would make mergers difficult under any circumstances, and, indeed the acquisition failed. However, their focus in explaining the failure was primarily on the poor identity leadership of the chairman of the Chinese company.

Chapter 8, by Liang, van Dick, Ullrich, and Lupina-Wegener, provides companion studies to that of Chapter 7. Building on social identity theory and social categorization theory, it focuses on how, when combining two companies into one, mergers or acquisitions might threaten the continuity of pre-merger identities of both the acquiring and acquired companies.

This chapter describes three small studies. In the first, an experiment, the authors studied "intergroup sensitivity effects" by comparing how people who are categorized as belonging to an acquiring company respond to criticisms from members of the acquired company or their own company. Consistent with expectations, these employees responded more negatively to the criticism given by employees from the acquired organization than their own. In a second study, the authors interviewed members of a European organization to determine how they constructed their multiple identities over time after being acquired by a Chinese organization. They found that, early on, the orientation toward the acquisition was ambivalent, but it became more positive over time. In the third study they interviewed members of the Chinese acquiring organization to determine how they adapted to the changes that followed the acquisition. They found that the managers viewed the acquisition as an opportunity to enhance their inferior pre-merger identity and took several steps to help the merger succeed, including an organizational unit that enabled their collaboration with their European colleagues.

Finally, Chapter 12 also focuses on social identity in terms of the role of leadership. Consistent with Chapter 7, Giessner and Horton emphasize the importance of our social, group, and organizational identities, especially when organization members are threatened with identity uncertainty, something that is often the case in organizational change. In addition, this chapter describes Mühlemann et al.'s (2022) social identity model of organizational change, which emphasizes that change may affect continuity of identity and perceptions of identity as positive or negative. It emphasizes how organizations can support employee adjustment by fostering continuity and even positive gains in identity as a result of change. In addition, it suggests the importance of focusing on identity gain as a way to mobilize support for change.

The multiple roles of identity – individual identity, social identity, organizational identity, and so on – are now getting much more attention than they used to and will likely receive more attention in the future. This set of chapters does a very good job of highlighting their importance and showing some of the ways they are important for every single type of organizational change.

13.1.7 Temporal Processes

Chapter 3, by Belschak and Jacobs, focuses extensively on temporal processes, though such processes are hinted at in several of the chapters. As Belschak and Jacobs note, organizational change is an inherently temporal phenomenon, and has a number of time-based dimensions. For example, individual and situational characteristics affect the experience of time, and the frequency, pace, and duration of a change event affects its outcomes.

The chapter also discusses multiple phase models of organizational change. The first, of course, is Lewin's three phase model, but there are other such models as well. In particular, Stouten et al. (2018) have integrated multiple phase models into a ten-step model that represents appropriate change management actions at different times. The authors also present a change curve developed from the point of view of recipients of change, that suggests that the experience of change for recipients often starts with high expectations, moves into the valley of despair, and (hopefully) concludes with a "good ending." The form the change curve takes is affected by several characteristics of change agents and their reactions to particular change events, as well as characteristics of the change itself and the management of change.

It is important that temporality was formally addressed in this book. Clearly many dimensions of it, on both organization-wide and individual levels, play crucial roles in change processes.

13.2 Developments and Next Steps

13.2.1 Developments from the First Volume to the Present Volume

As is evident here, and as the introduction to the book suggests, in this volume the emphasis is less on discrete outcomes of change (though they are crucial, of course) and more on the management of change and the dynamics of change that, hopefully, help to achieve positive outcomes. In our last chapter in the initial volume, Dick Woodman and I (Woodman & Bartunek, 2013) categorized the chapters in terms of whether their explanatory variables and their outcomes emphasized the organizational level or individual level. That type of categorization would not be appropriate in this volume, where the emphasis is much more on dynamics of change, and both sources of change and outcomes of change vary widely, as is shown in Table 13.1.

There are other important developments from the last volume. Some of the constructs emphasized strike me as new from the prior version. These are, particularly, discussions of roles of emotions, of temporality, and of various aspects of social identity in change. Emotions have been recognized as playing roles in the acceptance of change since the very beginning of the study of planned change. However, their role has often been limited to, basically, positive and negative emotions. In recent years, however, the understanding of roles of emotions in relation to change has expanded considerably (e.g. Oreg et al., 2018). It is good to see in this book an expanded appreciation for emotional experiences and expressions, one that incorporates resistance (including anticipatory resistance), and also goes far beyond it.

It is also useful to find an extended discussion of temporality. This is a topic that has garnered a great deal of attention in organizing in recent years, in a number of organizational venues (e.g. Bartunek & Woodman, 2015; Jansen et al., 2016; Kunisch et al., 2017). Paying attention to temporality, especially its nonlinear dimensions, is particularly important in appreciation of any kind of significant change.

The discussion of various dimensions of identity is fascinating. This is also an area that has literally exploded in popularity in recent years (e.g., Gioia et al., 2013; Conroy & O'Leary-Kelly, 2014; Cloutier & Ravasi, 2020). The chapters discussing this topic raise several important dimensions about the kind of roles identity plays in planned change, whether leaders and other organizational members are aware of it or not.

It was also fascinating to read the chapters that discussed different ways of categorizing what might on the surface seem similar types of change. This categorizing certainly goes well beyond organizational and individual emphases and shows some of what can be "hidden" in the more surface types of changes.

Overall, then, I am grateful to see the progression not only of interest but also in sophistication of the approaches to the psychology of organizational change in these chapters. They bode well for future developments in change and for future insights into what kinds of change are really going on, for multiple types of organizational members, whether this is apparent on the surface or not.

13.2.2   Next Steps

This section of the commentary is definitely not meant to force the editors to compile a next edition of the book. However, it is meant to suggest some possible further directions that can be taken, based on research, especially in management. I will suggest just a few ideas.

One of these is sparked by the fact that there is some disagreement across some of the chapters. For example, should resistance to change be a focus (Neves) or is it out of date (Rafferty et al.)? Is transformational leadership helpful in achieving positive outcomes (Meyer and Beletski) or is a focus on social identity more important (Giessner and Horton)? For me, these disagreements are a healthy sign. One of the major developments associated with organizational change in recent years is the recognition of its dualistic and paradoxical dimensions (e.g., Smith & Lewis, 2011; Bartunek et al., 2021). The more there are differing perspectives on change that co-exist (even as chapters in a book) the more the opportunities for unexpected findings.

A second idea is sparked by the fact that, with the exception of one partial case study (Chapter 7), all of the chapters use variance approaches to studying change, emphasizing predictor variables, outcome variables, and mediators and moderators. But in management, more and more studies of change are process studies in which the progression of change is explored as it naturally develops over time (e.g. Feldman, 2000; Lüscher & Lewis, 2008; Jarzabkowski et al., 2019). This represents a very different research methods skill set but could helpfully complement the approaches described in these chapters.

A third idea is that the chapters all focus on changes that are within organizations or encompass two organizations that are merging. There is no emphasis on the larger society. Thus, intents to change outcome variables are largely internal. Yet there is more and more attention being paid to organizational ecosystems and the need for organizations to make a broader impact in society, not just within themselves (e.g., Jarzabkowski et al., 2021; Williams & Whiteman, 2021; Mohrman & Bartunek, 2023). What does it mean when planned change is aimed beyond the organization?

Finally, by focusing on planned change, the chapters in the book do not really address emergent change as it comes from the nonlinear systems literature (e.g. Plowman et al., 2007; Howard-Grenville et al., 2017). Yet there is more and more recognition of change that does not occur linearly and that is not necessarily led from the top. What happens when the change recipients are the organization leaders, and the people actually leading the change do not see themselves as doing so?

These final comments are not a judgment on this book, which is a very valuable contribution and provides clear developments from prior knowledge. They simply signal that organizational change is alive and well – and continuing to change – and invite us to keep learning from it.

REFERENCES

Balogun, J., Bartunek, J. M., & Do, B. (2015). Senior managers' sensemaking and responses to strategic change. *Organization Science*, 26(4), 960–979.

Bartunek, J. M., Putnam, L. L., & Seo, M. (2021). Dualisms and dualities in the ongoing development of organization development. In M. S. Poole & A. H. Van de Ven (eds.), *Oxford handbook of organizational change and innovation* (2nd ed., pp. 50–76). Oxford: Oxford University Press.

Bartunek, J. M., & Woodman, R. W. (2015). Beyond Lewin: Toward a temporal approximation of organization development and change. *Annual Review of Organizational Psychology and Organizational Behavior*, 2, 157–182.

Cloutier, C., & Ravasi, D. (2020). Identity trajectories: Explaining long-term patterns of continuity and change in organizational identities. *Academy of Management Journal*, 63(4), 1196–1235.

Conroy, S. A., & O'Leary-Kelly, A. M. (2014). Letting go and moving on: Work-related identity loss and recovery. *Academy of Management Review*, 39, 67–87.

Farmer, N. (2017). *The invisible organization: How informal networks can lead organizational change*. London: Routledge.

Feldman, M. S. (2000). Organizational routines as a source of continuous change. *Organization Science, 11*, 611–629.

Gioia, D. A., Patvardhan, S. D., Hamilton, A. L., & Corley, K. G. (2013). Organizational identity formation and change. *Academy of Management Annals, 7*(1), 123–193.

Gross, J. (1998). Antecedent- and response-focused emotion regulation: Divergent consequences for experience, expression, and physiology. *Journal of Personality and Social Psychology, 74*(1), 224–237.

Gross, J., & John, O. P. (2003). Individual differences in two emotion regulation processes: Implications for affect, relationships, and well-being. *Journal of Personality and Social Psychology, 85*(2), 348–362.

Howard-Grenville, J., Nelson, A. J., Earle, A. G., Haack, J. A., & Young, D. M. (2017). "If chemists don't do it, who is going to?" Peer-driven occupational change and the emergence of green chemistry. *Administrative Science Quarterly, 62*(3), 524–560.

Jansen, K. J., Shipp, A. J., & Michael, J. H. (2016). Champions, converts, doubters, and defectors: The impact of shifting perceptions on momentum for change. *Personnel Psychology, 69*, 673–707.

Jarzabkowski, P., Dowell, G. W., & Berchicci, L. (2021). Strategy and organization scholarship through a radical sustainability lens: A call for 5.0. *Strategic Organization, 19*(3), 449–455.

Jarzabkowski, P., Lê, J., & Balogun, J. (2019). The social practice of coevolving strategy and structure to realize mandated radical change. *Academy of Management Journal, 62*(3), 850–882.

Kelly, J. R. (2001). Mood and emotion in groups. *The Blackwell handbook of social psychology, 3*, 164–181.

van Knippenberg, D., & Hogg, M. A. (eds.) (2003). *Leadership and power: Identity processes in groups and organizations.* Los Angeles: Sage.

Kotter, J. P. (2012). *Leading change.* Boston: Harvard Business School Press.

Kunisch, S., Bartunek, J. M., Mueller, J., & Huy, Q. N. (2017). Time in strategic change research. *Academy of Management Annals, 11*(2), 1005–1064.

Lüscher, L. S., & Lewis, M. W. (2008). Organizational change and managerial sensemaking: Working through paradox. *Academy of Management Journal, 51*(2), 221–240.

Mohrman, S. A., & Bartunek, J. M. (2023). How can ODC help accomplish a sustainable future? A joint reflection. *Research in Organizational Change and Development, 30*, 1–26.

Mühlemann, N., Steffens, N. K., Ullrich, J., Haslam, S. A., & Jonas, K. (2022). Understanding responses to an organizational takeover: Introducing the social identity model of organizational change. *Journal of Personality and Social Psychology, 123*(5), 1004–1023.

Oreg, S., Bartunek, J., Lee, G., & Do, B. (2018). An affect-based model of recipients' responses to organizational change events. *Academy of Management Review, 43*, 65–86.

Oreg, S., Michel, A., & By, R. T. (eds.) (2013). *The psychology of organizational change: Viewing change from the employee's perspective.* Cambridge: Cambridge University Press.

Plowman, D. A., Baker, L. T., Beck, T. E., Kulkarni, M., Solansky, S. T., & Travis, D. V. (2007). Radical change accidentally: The emergence and amplification of small change. *Academy of Management Journal, 50*(3), 515–543.

Smith, W. K., & Lewis, M. W. (2011). Toward a theory of paradox: A dynamic equilibrium model of organizing. *Academy of Management Review, 36,* 381–403.

Stouten, J., Rousseau, D. M., & De Cremer, D. (2018). Successful organizational change: Integrating the management practice and scholarly literature. *Academy of Management Annals, 12*(2), 752–788.

Tajfel, H., & Turner, J. C. (1986). The social identity theory of intergroup behaviour. In S. Worchel & W. G. Austin (eds.), *Psychology of intergroup relations* (pp. 7–24). Chicago: Nelson-Hall.

Williams, A., & Whiteman, G. (2021). A call for deep engagement for impact: Addressing the planetary emergency. *Strategic Organization, 19*(3), 526–537.

Woodman, R. W., & Bartunek, J. M. (2013). Commentary: Change processes and action implications. In S. Oreg, A. Michel, & R. By (eds.), *The psychology of organizational change* (pp. 301–323). Cambridge: Cambridge University Press.

Index

Barsade, S.G., 85
Bartel, C.A., 84
Bartram, D., 186
Bartunek, Jean M., 6, 11, 42, 47, 48, 58, 77, 78, 212, 291, 303
Battilana, J., 50, 185, 208, 212
Battistelli, A., 19, 23, 31
Bayerl, P.S., 60
Beard, C., 187, 189, 201
Bedeian, A G, 185
Bedeian, A.G., 6, 122
Begley, T.M., 58
behavioural
    intentions, 27, 29, 127, 128
    reactions, 5, 42, 57
    resistance, 30, 132, 251
    resistance to change, 27
    responses, 75, 76, 122, 133, 215
    responses to change, 77, 266
behavioural engagement with technology, 131
Beletski, Leonid V., 10, 296, 304
Belkin, L.J., 70
Belschak, Frank, 6, 44, 45, 48, 53, 57, 58, 59, 265, 302
Belt Road Initiative, 153, 155, 161
benefits of change, 17, 27, 33
benevolence, 164
benevolent leadership, 165
bereavement, 52
Berger, C.R., 16, 25, 29, 34
Berson, Y., 6, 18, 20, 31, 208, 213, 238, 240, 241, 255, 264, 265, 266
Bickerich, K., 185
Bommer, W.H., 18
Bordia, P., 15, 27, 46, 50, 52, 85
bottom-up change initiatives, 60
bottom-up change processes, 10, 208–209, 210, 211, 212, 218, 221, 222, 223, 224, 225, 227
bottom-up communications, 255
Bouckenooghe, Dave, 9, 10, 46, 60, 237, 239, 250, 253, 298
Bovey, W.H., 18
Boyatzis, R.E., 193
Boyd, J., 47
Branigan, C., 72
Brinkmann, S., 193
broad and incremental, 8, 125
broad and radical, 8, 123
broaden and build theory, 72, 73, 87, 299
broaden and build theory of positive emotions, 67, 68, 69
Brown, M.E., 28, 240
Brown, S.A., 124, 125, 127, 128, 133
Bruckman, J.C., 16, 21
Buchanan, D., 130, 139

Buckley, P.J., 151, 153
Buono, A.F., 54, 57
Burke, C.S., 54
Burnes, B, 49, 201
Burnes, Bernard, 208, 212, 224, 226, 265
By, Rune Todnem, 3, 21, 148, 170, 185, 237, 265, 278, 291

Cable, D.M., 19, 132
Caetano, A., 19
Calabrese, R.J., 16, 25, 29, 34
Callan, V.J., 52, 82
Campbell, D.T., 270
CAPS, 225
CAPS framework, 215, 216
Carey, M., 192
Carucci, R., 21
Cary, J., 71
Casciaro, T., 50
causal relationships, 46
challenge appraisal, 20, 27, 70
challenge-hindrance framework, 102
change
    degree of, 122
    incremental, 122, 295
    radical, 122, 252, 295
    scale of, 122
change commitment, 10, 71, 98, 241, 242, 244, 246, 247, 250, 266
change communication, 33, 185, 198, 242, 276, 297
change curve, 7, 42, 51–58, 59, 61, 302
change history, 24, 27, 32, 45, 46, 47, 50, 60, 71
change implementation process, 24, 71, 77
change leaders, 9, 10, 11, 213, 256, 296, 297, 299
change leadership, 237, 239, 242, 265, 266, 298
    behaviours, 208, 223, 243
    concept, 10
    contributions, 223
    development, 50, 210
    discussion, 210
    models, 241
    processes, 212
    research, 264
    skills, 297
    social identity, 11, 271, 296
change management, 24, 27, 30, 43, 50, 116, 203, 243, 266
    human side, 297
change management actions, 50, 202, 302
change management activities, 55, 58, 60, 61
    communication, 17, 21, 60, 71, 85, 97, 116, 132, 137, 138, 197
    leadership, 60